Matrix Factorization for Multimedia Clustering

Other related titles:

You may also like

- PBPC085 | Kumar | Detecting Misinformation and Toxicity in Social Media: Techniques and Applications | contracted May 2025 (Multimedia Book Series)
- PBPC082 | Dalal | Generative AI in Multimedia Content Processing: Security and Privacy Perspectives | Contracted Sept 2024 (Multimedia Book Series)
- PBSE029 | Rani | Machine Learning and Deep Learning Driven Techniques for Multimodal Data Security in the Internet of Multimedia Things | contracted Sept 2024 (Multimedia book Series)
- PBPC048 | Raj | Demystifying Graph Data Science | Published Oct 2022

We also publish a wide range of books on the following topics:
Computing and Networks
Control, Robotics and Sensors
Electrical Regulations
Electromagnetics and Radar
Energy Engineering
Healthcare Technologies
History and Management of Technology
IET Codes and Guidance
Materials, Circuits and Devices
Model Forms
Nanomaterials and Nanotechnologies
Optics, Photonics and Lasers
Production, Design and Manufacturing
Security
Telecommunications
Transportation

All books are available in print via https://shop.theiet.org or as eBooks via our Digital Library https://digital-library.theiet.org.

IET COMPUTING SERIES 81

Matrix Factorization for Multimedia Clustering

Models, techniques, optimization, and applications

Hangjun Che, Xin Wang, Xing He, Man-Fai Leung, and Baicheng Pan

The Institution of Engineering and Technology

About the IET

This book is published by the Institution of Engineering and Technology (The IET).

We inspire, inform and influence the global engineering community to engineer a better world. As a diverse home across engineering and technology, we share knowledge that helps make better sense of the world, to accelerate innovation and solve the global challenges that matter.

The IET is a not-for-profit organisation. The surplus we make from our books is used to support activities and products for the engineering community and promote the positive role of science, engineering and technology in the world. This includes education resources and outreach, scholarships and awards, events and courses, publications, professional development and mentoring, and advocacy to governments.

To discover more about the IET please visit https://www.theiet.org/

About IET books

The IET publishes books across many engineering and technology disciplines. Our authors and editors offer fresh perspectives from universities and industry. Within our subject areas, we have several book series steered by editorial boards made up of leading subject experts.

We peer review each book at the proposal stage to ensure the quality and relevance of our publications.

Get involved

If you are interested in becoming an author, editor, series advisor, or peer reviewer please visit https://www.theiet.org/publishing/publishing-with-iet-books/ or contact author_support@theiet.org.

Discovering our electronic content

All of our books are available online via the IET's Digital Library. Our Digital Library is the home of technical documents, eBooks, conference publications, real-life case studies and journal articles. To find out more, please visit https://digital-library.theiet.org.

In collaboration with the United Nations and the International Publishers Association, the IET is a Signatory member of the SDG Publishers Compact. The Compact aims to accelerate progress to achieve the Sustainable Development Goals (SDGs) by 2030. Signatories aspire to develop sustainable practices and act as champions of the SDGs during the Decade of Action (2020-30), publishing books and journals that will help inform, develop, and inspire action in that direction.

In line with our sustainable goals, our UK printing partner has FSC accreditation, which is reducing our environmental impact to the planet. We use a print-on-demand model to further reduce our carbon footprint.

Whilst every reasonable effort has been undertaken by the Publisher and its licensors to acknowledge copyright on material reproduced, if there has been an oversight, please contact the Publisher and we will endeavour to correct this upon a reprint.

Trade mark notice: Product or corporate names referred to within this publication may be trade marks or registered trade marks and are used only for identification and explanation without intent to infringe.

Where an author and/or contributor is identified in this publication by name, such author and/or contributor asserts their moral right under the CPDA to be identified as the author and/or contributor of this work.

British Library Cataloguing in Publication Data

A catalogue record for this product is available from the British Library

ISBN 978-1-83724-199-6 (hardback)
ISBN 978-1-83724-200-9 (PDF)

Typeset in India by MPS Limited

Cover image: Ekaterina Goncharova/Moment/via Getty Images

Contents

Foreword

Multimedia (and more generally multimodal data) stands as one of the most demanding and exciting aspects of the information era. The processing of multimedia has been an active research area with applications in secure multimedia contents on social networks, digital forensic, digital cinema, education, secured e-voting systems, smart healthcare, automotive applications, the military, finance, insurance, and more. The advent of the Internet of Things (IoT), cyber-physical systems (CPSs), robotics as well as personal and wearable devices now provide many opportunities for the multimedia community to reach out and develop synergies.

Our book series comprehensively defines the current trends and technological aspects of multimedia research with a particular emphasis on interdisciplinary approaches. The authors will review a broad scope to identify challenges, solutions and new directions The published books can be used as references by practicing engineers, scientists, researchers, practitioners, and technology professionals from academia, government and Industry working on state-of-the-art multimedia processing and security in Industry 5.0 applications. It will also be useful to senior undergraduate and graduate students as well as PhD students and Postdoc researchers.

This book entitled "Matrix Factorization for Multimedia Clustering: Models, techniques, optimization and applications" provides a detailed study of matrix and tensor factorization techniques applied to multimedia clustering. It explores a range of models and their enhancements through graph structures, regularization methods, and optimization strategies. The content addresses practical challenges in managing high-dimensional, multi-view, and multi-modal multimedia data. Core topics such as graph theory and optimization algorithms are introduced, along with applications in areas including fake news detection, community detection, image clustering, and biomedical data analysis. Further, the book balances theoretical explanation with practical application, offering clear mathematical derivations and experimental analysis. It is intended for researchers, engineers, and graduate students working in multimedia processing, machine learning, and data clustering.

We hope the readers will find this book of great value in its visionary words.

Dr. Amit Kumar Singh, Book Series Editor
Department of Computer Science and Engineering
National Institute of Technology, Patna 800005, India

Prof. Stefano Berretti, Book Series Editor
Department of Information Engineering
University of Florence, Florence 50139, Italy

About the authors

Hangjun Che is an associate professor with the College of Electronic and Information Engineering at Southwest University, China. His research focuses on neurodynamic optimization, sparse coding, and nonnegative matrix factorization. He has published 50+ papers and obtained 6 software copyrights and several pending patents. He serves as a regular journal reviewer and is an advisory editorial board member of *Data Technologies and Applications*, an associate editor of *Intelligent Systems with Applications*, an editorial board member of *Artificial Intelligence and Applications*, and *Journal of Social Computing*. He is a member of IEEE and CCF. He received his Ph.D. degree in computer science from the City University of Hong Kong, China.

Xin Wang is a professor at the School of Electronic and Information Engineering, Southwest University, China. His current research interests include complex networks, impulsive control, multi-agent systems, and adaptive control. He has published over 60 papers in authoritative journals and conference papers and is a regular journal reviewer. He is a member of IEEE and CAA. He obtained his PhD degree in computer science and technology from Chongqing University, China.

Xing He is a professor with the College of Electronic and Information Engineering, Southwest University, China. He focuses his research on neural networks and bifurcation theory. He has published over 100 papers and is a regular journal reviewer. He is a senior member of IEEE. He obtained his PhD degree in computer science and technology from Chongqing University, China.

Man-Fai Leung is a lecturer with the School of Computing and Information Science in the Faculty of Science and Engineering at Anglia Ruskin University, Cambridge, UK. His research interests include intelligent systems, optimization, computational intelligence, and their applications. He serves as an associate editor for *Complex & Intelligent Systems*, and *Intelligent Systems with Applications*. He has served as the publications chair for the 10th, 11th, and 13th International Conference on Information Science and Technology. He is a member of IEEE. He received his PhD degree in computer science from the City University of Hong Kong, China.

Baicheng Pan is pursuing his MS degree in information and communication engineering with the College of Electronic and Information Engineering at Southwest University, China. His research interests include optimization theory and applications, machine learning, multi-view clustering, nonnegative matrix factorization, tensor factorization, and deep matrix factorization. He received his BS degree from Huazhong University of Science and Technology, Wuhan, China.

Chapter 1
Introduction to matrix factorization

Matrix factorization, particularly non-negative matrix factorization (NMF) and its extensions, serves as a cornerstone for uncovering latent structures in high-dimensional data. This chapter begins with the fundamentals of NMF, a technique inspired by psychological and physiological evidence to decompose data into non-negative basis and coefficient matrices. Then, the advanced variants of NMF, such as non-negative matrix tri-factorization (NMTF), which enables co-clustering through three-factor decomposition, and deep matrix factorization (DMF), which employs hierarchical layers to capture complex data patterns, are introduced briefly. Further, the applications of NMF and its extensions in multi-view clustering are discussed, highlighting their effectiveness in multimedia clustering tasks. By synthesizing theoretical formulations and optimization objectives, a brief overview of matrix factorization techniques and their pivotal role in multimedia clustering is exhibited.

1.1 Non-negative matrix factorization

Motivated by the evidence in Psychology [1] and Physiology [2], NMF was first proposed in Nature [3] to learn the parts of an object. It can be expressed as follows:

$$X \approx AB^\top$$
$$\text{s.t. } A \geq 0, B \geq 0,$$

$$(1.1)$$

$X \in R_+^{m \times n}$ is the data matrix, $A \in R_+^{m \times k}$ is the basis matrix, and $B \in R_+^{n \times k}$ is the coefficient matrix, where exists $k \ll m$ generally. NMF gets a feature whose basis is the column vector of A, so the row vector of B can replace the original data and be seen as the extracted feature. k is the number of components defined according to demands. For clustering, it can be set to the number of clusters. For data reconstruction, the bigger k is, the better the data matrix X is reconstructed. It is one of the most popular algorithms for data processing, which is widely used in hyperspectral unmixing [4], text mining [5], medical data [6], gene selection, and tumor classification [7].

NMF is designed to uncover the inherent structure within data and to yield comprehensible, reduced representations of the input data. The Frobenius norm is always adopted to represent the reconstructive error, and the mathematical expression for NMF can be written as follows [8]:

$$\min_{A,B} \|X - AB^\top\|_F^2$$
$$\text{s.t. } A \geq 0, B \geq 0. \tag{1.2}$$

1.2 Non-negative matrix tri-factorization

NMTF is an extension of NMF:

$$X \approx ABC^\top$$
$$\text{s.t. } A \geq 0, B \geq 0, C \geq 0, \tag{1.3}$$

where the NMTF captures the geometric structure of both the sample space and feature sample space in a lower-dimensional space. $X \in R_+^{m \times n}$ is the data matrix, $A \in R_+^{m \times k_1}$ is the feature indicator matrix, $B \in R_+^{k_1 \times k_2}$ is the coefficient matrix, and $C \in R_+^{n \times k_1}$ is the sample indicator matrix.

NMTF allows for the simultaneous clustering of both feature and sample spaces, making it a valuable method for co-clustering tasks (e.g. text mining [9] and gene expression [10]). Graph dual regularized NMTF (DNMTF) combines manifold learning with the standard NMTF method [11]. Deng *et al.* [12] developed tri-regularized NMTF, which adds graph regularization, the l_1-norm, and NMTF to the objective function. Ding *et al.* [13] were the first to express the opinion that unconstrained NMTF is equal to NMF, whereas constrained NMTF introduces new features to NMF. Additionally, Ding introduced orthogonal NMTF (ONMTF). Orthogonality constraints in ONMTF are able to enforce the parts-based representation and lead to a rigorous clustering interpretation. After that, Wang and Huang [14] proposed penalized NMF (PNMTF), in which three penalty terms are integrated to ensure the near orthogonality of the matrix. Peng *et al.* [15] proposed the correntropy-based orthogonal NMTF (CNMTF) algorithm. The main features of CNMTF are the application of orthogonality constraints and the use of correntropy to measure similarity.

The basic model of NMTF with the Frobenius norm can be formulated as:

$$\min_{A,B,C} \|X - ABC^\top\|_F^2$$
$$\text{s.t. } A \geq 0, B \geq 0, C \geq 0 \tag{1.4}$$

1.3 Deep matrix factorization

Traditional NMF models yield a single-layer outcome, a simplistic decomposition approach that constrains their capability to encapsulate complex patterns and to delve into intricate relationships within data. To address this limitation, a multilayer decomposition model is proposed [16]:

$$X \approx A_1 B_1,$$
$$X \approx A_1 A_2 B_2,$$
$$\vdots$$
$$X \approx A_1 A_2 \ldots A_{r-1} A_r A_{r+1} \ldots A_R B_R,$$

(1.5)

Where $A_1 \in \mathbb{R}^{m \times l_1}, A_2 \in \mathbb{R}^{l_1 \times l_2}, A_r \in \mathbb{R}^{l_{r-1} \times l_r}, A_R \in \mathbb{R}^{l_{R-1} \times l_R}$, and $B_R \in \mathbb{R}^{l_R \times n}$. The variable l_r denotes the size of the r-th layer. This decomposition technique is termed DMF. It accomplishes dimensionality reduction and feature extraction by decomposing the original data matrix into a product of multiple non-negative matrices. Compared to traditional NMF methods, DMF incorporates principles from deep neural networks in its learning process, facilitating the acquisition of more complex and abstract feature representations. This enhancement renders it more adept at handling intricate multi-view data.

The basic deep matrix factorization with the Frobenius norm is formulated as:

$$\min_{A_r, B_r} \|X - A_1 A_2 \cdots A_r \cdots A_R B_R\|_F^2$$

(1.6)

$$\text{s.t. } A_r \geq 0, \ B_r \geq 0.$$

1.4   The application of matrix factorization in multimedia clustering

NMF is known to generate improved clustering results when combined with manifold learning, which preserves the geometrical structure of data distribution [17]. Thus, many multi-view NMF methods with graph regularization have been proposed in [18–20]. Specifically, an extension of MultiNMF is proposed in [18], which constrains the coefficient matrix in each view with a graph regularization. In [19], sparse feature and data graph of each view are constructed based on the self-expressiveness principle, which more effectively exploits the graph structure than previous multi-view methods. In [20], a multi-manifold multi-view NMF method is proposed, which utilizes manifold regularization to constrain the coefficient matrix and the consensus matrix. Furthermore, the general objective function can be summarized as:

$$\min_{A^{(v)}, B^{(v)}} R(\Phi(X^{(v)}, (A^{(v)}, B^{(v)}, \cdots, Z^{(v)}))) + L(Z^{(v)})$$

(1.7)

$$\text{s.t. } A^{(v)} \geq 0, \ B^{(v)} \geq 0, \cdots, Z \geq 0, \quad v = 1, 2, \cdots, V$$

where $X^{(v)} \in \mathbb{R}^{m_v \times n}$ denotes the data matrix in vth view, $A^{(v)}$ and $B^{(v)}$ denote the basic matrix or layer matrix in vth view, and $Z^{(v)}$ denotes the coefficient matrix in vth view. $\Phi(\cdot)$ denotes a kind of matrix factorization, $R(\cdot)$ denotes a kind of matrix norm, and $L(\cdots)$ denotes the regularization in coefficient matrix $Z^{(v)}$.

1.5   Chapter summary

This chapter systematically introduces the theory and applications of matrix factorization, with a focus on NMF and its extensions (NMTF and DMF). Then, the general forms of matrix factorization in multimedia clustering are introduced and analyzed.

References

[1]   Palmer S.E.: "Hierarchical structure in perceptual representation." *Cogn. Psychol.* 1977;9(4):441–74.

[2]   Wachsmuth E., Oram M., Perrett D.: "Recognition of objects and their component parts: responses of single units in the temporal cortex of the macaque." *Cereb. Cortex.* 1994;4(5):509–22.

[3]   Lee D.D., Seung H.S.: "Learning the parts of objects by non-negative matrix factorization." *Nature.* 1999;401(6755):788–91.

[4]   Lu X., Dong L., Yuan Y.: "Subspace clustering constrained sparse NMF for hyperspectral unmixing." *IEEE Trans. Geosci. Remote Sens.* 2019; 58(5):3007–19.

[5]   Hassani A., Iranmanesh A., Mansouri N.: "Text mining using nonnegative matrix factorization and latent semantic analysis." *Neural Comput. Appl.* 2021;33(20):13745–66.

[6]   Yu N., Wu M.J., Liu J.X., Zheng, C.H., Xu Y.: "Correntropy-based hypergraph regularized NMF for clustering and feature selection on multi-cancer integrated data." *IEEE Trans. Cybern.* 2021;51(8):3952–63.

[7]   Jiao C.N., Gao Y.L., Yu N., Liu, J.-X., Qi, L.Y.: "Hyper-graph regularized constrained NMF for selecting differentially expressed genes and tumor classification." *IEEE J. Biomed. Health Inform.* 2020;24(10):3002–11.

[8]   Lee D., Seung H.S.: "Algorithms for non-negative matrix factorization." In *Proceedings of the 14th International Conference on Neural Information Processing Systems*. Cambridge, MA, USA: MIT Press; 2000. pp. 535–541.

[9]   Salah A., Ailem M., Nadif M.: "Word co-occurrence regularized non-negative matrix tri-factorization for text data co-clustering." in *Proceedings of AAAI Conference on Artificial Intelligence*; 2018. Vol. 32. pp. 3992–9.

[10]   Hwang T., Atluri G., Xie M., *et al.*: "Co-clustering phenome–genome for phenotype classification and disease gene discovery." *Nucl. Acids Res.* 2012;40(19):e146.

[11]   Shang F., Jiao L., Wang F.: "Graph dual regularization non-negative matrix factorization for co-clustering." *Pattern Recognit.* 2012;45(6):2237–50.

[12]   Deng P., Li T., Wang H., *et al.*: "Tri-regularized nonnegative matrix tri-factorization for co-clustering." *Knowl. Based Syst.* 2021;226:107101.

[13]   Ding C., Li T., Peng W., Park, H.: "Orthogonal nonnegative matrix t-factorizations for clustering." in *Proceedings of the 12th ACM SIGKDD International Conference on Knowledge Discovery and Data Mining*; 2006. pp. 126–35.

[14] Wang S., Huang A.: "Penalized nonnegative matrix tri-factorization for co-clustering." *Expert Syst. Appl.* 2017;78:64–73.

[15] Peng S., Ser W., Chen B., Lin Z.: "Robust orthogonal nonnegative matrix tri-factorization for data representation." *Knowl. Based Syst.* 2020;201:106054.

[16] Trigeorgis G., Bousmalis K., Zafeiriou S., Schuller, B.W.: "A deep matrix factorization method for learning attribute representations." *IEEE Trans. Pattern Anal. Mach. Intell.* 2016;39(3):417–29.

[17] Cai D., He X., Han J., Huang, T.S.: "Graph regularized nonnegative matrix factorization for data representation." *IEEE Trans. Pattern Anal. Mach. Intell.* 2011;33(8):1548–60.

[18] Wang Z., Kong X., Fu H., Li M., Zhang Y.: "Feature extraction via multi-view non-negative matrix factorization with local graph regularization." in *2015 IEEE International Conference on Image Processing (ICIP)*. Canada: IEEE; 2015. pp. 3500–4.

[19] Luo P., Peng J., Guan Z., Fan J.: "Dual regularized multi-view non-negative matrix factorization for clustering." *Neurocomputing*. 2018;294:1–11.

[20] Zong L., Zhang X., Zhao L., Yu, H., Zhao, Q.: "Multi-view clustering via multi-manifold regularized non-negative matrix factorization." *Neural Netw.* 2017;88:74–89.

Chapter 2

Preliminary of tensor factorization

This section introduces three essential techniques for decomposing tensors, vital for interpreting multidimensional datasets. It first delves into CANDECOMP/PARAFAC (CP) decomposition, which represents a tensor as a sum of rank-one components. This method delivers a clear and interpretable format, proving especially effective for classification tasks, particularly when sparsity in the factor matrix sharpens feature distinction. The discussion then shifts to Tucker decomposition, a higher-dimensional adaptation of matrix singular value decomposition (SVD). Known for its versatility, this approach supports varying ranks across modes and uses a core tensor to reflect interactions among factor matrices, making it ideal for applications like dimensionality reduction and pattern detection. Next, the text examines tensor singular value decomposition (t-SVD), an extension of matrix SVD tailored to third-order tensors. By breaking the tensor into orthogonal elements and an f-diagonal tensor, t-SVD simplifies tasks such as data compression. Together, these approaches provide a comprehensive set of tools for tackling complex, high-dimensional data, each offering distinct strengths suited to specific analytical demands.

2.1   CP decomposition

CP decomposition, also known as CANDECOMP/PARAFAC, is a tensor factorization technique designed to reduce dimensionality while preserving the inherent structure of the data [1]. This method decomposes a tensor into a sum of rank-one tensors, as expressed by the formula $\mathscr{X} \approx \sum_{r=1}^{R} \mathbf{a}_r \circ \mathbf{b}_r \circ \mathbf{c}_r = [[A, B, C]]$. In this context, R represents the rank of the decomposition, while $\mathbf{a}_r \in \mathbb{R}^I$, $\mathbf{b}_r \in \mathbb{R}^J$, and $\mathbf{c}_r \in \mathbb{R}^K$ are the factor vectors corresponding to the first, second, and third modes, respectively. The symbol $\circ$ denotes the outer product, and $[[A, B, C]]$ signifies the CP decomposition structure. The properties of the matrix A are particularly important for classification tasks; specifically, a sparse A matrix enhances feature interpretability and distinctiveness, thereby improving classifier performance. Consequently, sparsity is a critical factor in optimizing classification outcomes.

2.2   Tucker decomposition

Tucker decomposition is a higher-order extension of matrix SVD, which factorizes a tensor into a core tensor and a set of factor matrices for each mode [1]. For a

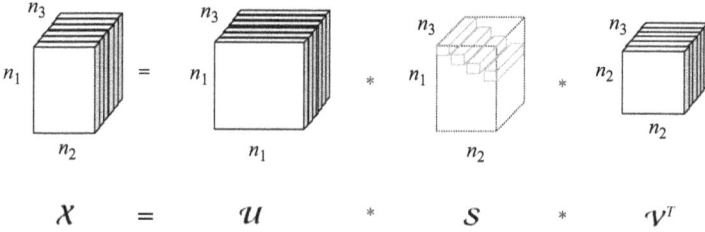

Figure 2.1   The visualization of tensor singular value decomposition

third-order tensor $\mathscr{X} \in \mathbb{R}^{I \times J \times K}$, the decomposition is given by $\mathscr{X} \approx \mathscr{G} \times_1 \mathbf{A} \times_2 \mathbf{B} \times_3 \mathbf{C} = \sum_{p=1}^{P} \sum_{q=1}^{Q} \sum_{r=1}^{R} g_{pqr} \mathbf{a}_p \circ \mathbf{b}_q \circ \mathbf{c}_r$. Here, $\mathbf{A} \in \mathbb{R}^{I \times P}$, $\mathbf{B} \in \mathbb{R}^{J \times Q}$, and $\mathbf{C} \in \mathbb{R}^{K \times R}$ are factor matrices, typically orthogonal, that can be interpreted as principal components for each mode. The core tensor $\mathscr{G} \in \mathbb{R}^{P \times Q \times R}$ captures the interactions among the components of the factor matrices. The symbols $\mathbf{a}_p$, $\mathbf{b}_q$, and $\mathbf{c}_r$ represent the columns of the factor matrices $\mathbf{A}$, $\mathbf{B}$, and $\mathbf{C}$, respectively, while $\circ$ denotes the outer product. The parameters P, Q, and R specify the ranks for each mode. Tucker decomposition is widely applied in fields, such as dimensionality reduction, feature extraction, data compression, and pattern recognition. Its flexibility, allowing different ranks across modes, sets it apart from CP decomposition and makes it highly adaptable to various data structures. Additionally, the core tensor enhances interpretability by revealing relationships within the data.

2.3   Tensor singular value decomposition

For the third-order tensor $\mathscr{X} \in \mathbb{R}^{n_1 \times n_2 \times n_3}$, t-SVD [2,3] yields the factorization: $\mathscr{X} = \mathscr{U} * \mathscr{S} * \mathscr{V}^{\top}$, where $\mathscr{U} \in \mathbb{R}^{n_1 \times n_1 \times n_3}$ and $\mathscr{V} \in \mathbb{R}^{n_2 \times n_2 \times n_3}$ are orthogonal tensors, and $\mathscr{S} \in \mathbb{R}^{n_1 \times n_2 \times n_3}$ is an f-diagonal tensor (i.e., each frontal slice is a diagonal matrix). We also present the diagram of t-SVD in Figure 2.1. From the figure, the tensor $\mathscr{X}$ is decomposed as the product of three tensors.

2.4   Chapter summary

This chapter has introduced core tensor factorization techniques essential for multidimensional data analysis. Beginning with CP decomposition, we examined its representation of tensors as linear combinations of rank-one components, highlighting its unique interpretability for classification tasks. Subsequent discussion centered on Tucker decomposition, which extends matrix SVD to higher orders. This approach offers enhanced versatility through mode-specific rank constraints and interaction modeling via a core tensor. Finally, t-SVD was analyzed as a third-order extension of matrix SVD. Its orthogonal factor tensors and f-diagonal core enable effective dimensionality reduction and feature extraction. Collectively, these methodologies establish a robust framework for interpreting and manipulating complex high-dimensional data structures.

References

[1] Kolda T.G., Bader B.W.: "Tensor decompositions and applications." *SIAM Rev.* 2009;51(3):455–500.

[2] Gao Q., Xia W., Wan Z., Xie D., Zhang P.: "Tensor-SVD based graph learning for multi-view subspace clustering." in *Proceedings of the AAAI Conference on Artificial Intelligence*; 2022. Vol. 34. pp. 3930–7.

[3] Kilmer M.E., Martin C.D.: "Factorization strategies for third-order tensors." *Linear Algebra Appl.* 2011;435(3):641–58.

Chapter 3
Graph theory

Graph theory is a branch of mathematics that studies graph structures composed of vertices (nodes) and edges (lines connecting nodes). Vertices represent entities, while edges show relationships or connections between entities. Graph theory is widely used in computer science, network analysis, biology, sociology, and other fields. Basic concepts include paths (sequences of vertices), cycles (paths where the start and end are the same), and connectivity (whether a path exists between any two vertices in the graph). Graphs can be classified as directed graphs (edges have direction) and undirected graphs (edges have no direction), as well as weighted graphs (edges have weights) and unweighted graphs.

3.1 Graph Laplacian regularization

Graph regularization is a machine learning technique applied to graph-structured data, aimed at improving the generalization ability of models by utilizing graph structural information between data points. In graph regularization, graphs typically represent the relationships or similarities between data points, where nodes represent data points and edges represent connections or similarities between data points. For a graph $G = (V, E, A)$, where $V = \{v_1, v_2, \cdots, v_n\}$ represents the nodes of the graph, $E = \{e_{ij} | v_i \in V \wedge v_j \in V\}$ represents the edges of the graph, and $A = [A_{ij}]^{n \times n}$ represents the adjacency matrix of the graph, where A_{ij} represents the relationship between nodes V_i and V_j. For an unweighted graph G, if e_{ij} belongs to E, then $A_{ij} = 1$; otherwise, $A_{ij} = 0$. The expression of the graph Laplacian regularization is:

$$\min_V \frac{1}{2} \sum_{i=1}^{n} \sum_{j=1}^{n} ||v_i - v_j||_2^2 a_{ij} = \min_V \text{tr}(VL(V)^T), \tag{3.1}$$

where A describes the degree of similarity between data points, $L = \hat{W} - W$ denotes the graph Laplacian matrix, and $\hat{W}$ is a diagonal matrix with $\hat{w}_{jj} = \sum_{i=1}^{n} w_{ij}$, $W = \frac{A + (A)^T}{2}$.

3.2   Propagation regularization based on graph Laplacian regularization

The graph Laplace regularization is widely used for its ability to effectively discover the nonlinear structural information of the data [1]. Moreover, to provide new supervisory signals to the nodes in the graph and supply additional information to improve model reliability, a propagation regularization is proposed based on the graph Laplacian regularization [2]. The propagation regularization is expressed as:

$$L_{\text{p-reg}} = \frac{1}{q}\phi(V, \hat{A}V) \tag{3.2}$$

where $A = [a_{ij}] \in R^{q \times q}$ is a similarity matrix that describes the degree of similarity between data points, and $\hat{A} = D^{-1}A$ is a normalized similarity matrix, where $D = [d_{ij}] \in R^{q \times q}$ is a diagonal degree matrix with $d_{ij} = \sum_{j=1}^{q} a_{ij}$. $\hat{A}V$ is the further propagated output, and $\phi(V, \hat{A}V)$ is a function to measure the difference between V and $\hat{A}V$ directly. When using squared error as ϕ and denoting it as ϕ_{SE}, we have

$$\phi_{\text{SE}}(V, \hat{A}V) = \frac{1}{2}\sum_{i=1}^{q} ||(\hat{A}V)_i^T - (V)_i^T||_2^2 = \frac{1}{2}||\hat{A}V - V||_F^2 \tag{3.3}$$

where $(\cdot)_i^T$ denotes the vector of the ith row in a matrix. $\phi_{\text{SE}}(V, \hat{A}V)$ is node-centric, which involves aggregating the information from a node's neighbors to serve as supervision targets [2]. This allows each node to acquire additional categorical information from its neighbors, aiding in better determining their positions and roles within the data, particularly in capturing complex nonlinear structures.

3.3   Hyper-graph regularization

A hyper-graph is an extension of a graph, where an edge can connect any number of nodes, not just two, allowing for a more flexible description of complex relationships.

As shown in Figure 3.1, the key difference between a simple graph and a hyper-graph is that a graph's edge only connects two nodes, whereas a hyper-graph's edge connects multiple nodes, preserving multivariate relationships without reducing them to binary ones.

Hyper-graph $G = (V, E, W)$ comprises a vertex set V, a hyper-edge set E, and a diagonal hyper-edge weight matrix W. The incidence matrix $H \in R^{|V| \times |E|}$ is defined as follows:

$$H(v, e) = \begin{cases} 1, & \text{if } v \in e. \\ 0, & \text{if } v \notin e. \end{cases} \tag{3.4}$$

where W_i denotes the weight of hyper-edge e_i. Specifically, W_i is defined as:

$$W_i = \sum_{v_x, v_y \in e_i} \exp\left(-\frac{||v_x - v_y||_2^2}{\sigma^2}\right) \tag{3.5}$$

Graph

Hyper-graph of sample space and its incidence matrix

	e_1	e_2	e_3
v_1^1	0	1	0
v_2^1	1	0	0
v_3^1	1	0	1
v_4^1	1	0	0
v_5^1	0	1	0
v_6^1	0	1	0
v_7^1	0	0	1
v_8^1	0	1	1

Adjacency matrix of graph

	v_1	v_2	v_3	v_4	v_5	v_6	v_7	v_8
v_1	0	0	0	1	0	1	0	0
v_2	0	0	0	0	1	0	0	0
v_3	0	0	0	0	0	1	1	1
v_4	1	0	0	0	0	0	0	0
v_5	0	1	0	0	0	0	0	0
v_6	1	0	1	0	0	0	0	0
v_7	0	0	1	0	0	0	0	0
v_8	0	0	1	0	0	0	0	0

Hyper-graph of feature space and its incidence matrix

	e_1	e_2	e_3
v_1^2	1	0	0
v_2^2	1	0	0
v_3^2	1	1	0
v_4^2	0	0	1
v_5^2	0	0	1
v_6^2	0	1	1
v_7^2	0	1	0
v_8^2	0	1	0

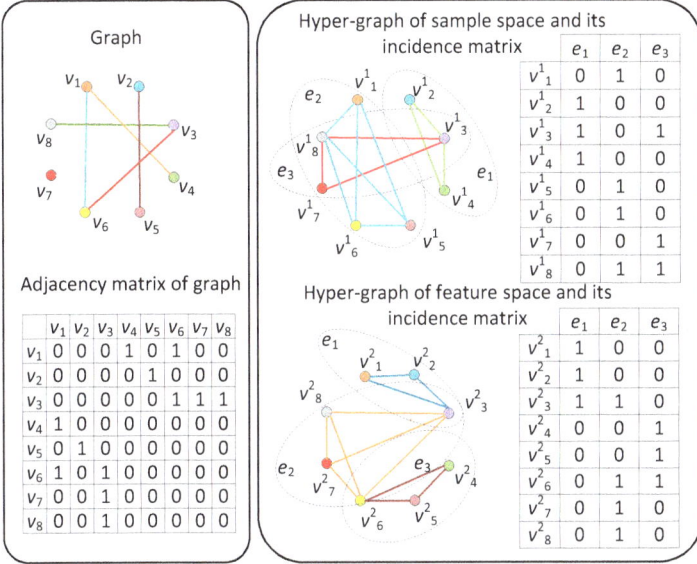

Figure 3.1 *The comparison between the graph and the hyper-graph. v_n represents the nth vertex in graph. v_n^1 represents the nth vertex in the hyper-graph of the sample space and v_n^2 represents the nth vertex in the hyper-graph of feature space, respectively. e_n denotes the nth hyper-edge of the hyper-graph*

The σ^2 is defined as follows:

$$\sigma^2 = \sum_{v_x, v_y \in e_i} \frac{\|v_x - v_y\|_2^2}{k} \tag{3.6}$$

where k denotes the number of k-nearest neighbors for each vertex.

$d(v)$ denotes the degree of a vertex v, which is defined as:

$$d(v) = \sum_{e \in E} w(e)\boldsymbol{H}(v, e) \tag{3.7}$$

$f(e)$ denotes the degree of an edge e, which is defined as:

$$f(v) = \sum_{v \in V} \boldsymbol{H}(v, e) \tag{3.8}$$

V_x and V_y represent the sample points $\boldsymbol{X}_x$ and $\boldsymbol{X}_y$, respectively.

Assuming that the diagonal matrix $\boldsymbol{D}_v$ comprises $d(v)$ and the diagonal matrix $\boldsymbol{D}_e$ comprises $f(e)$, the unnormalized hyper-graph Laplacian matrix $\boldsymbol{L}_{\text{hyper}}$ is calculated as $\boldsymbol{L}_{\text{hyper}} = \boldsymbol{D}_v - \boldsymbol{S}$, where $\boldsymbol{S} = \boldsymbol{HWD}_e^{-1}\boldsymbol{H}^{-1}$.

3.4   Optimal consensus graph learning

An optimal graph is an extension of a simple graph, referring to a graph structure that meets a specific optimization goal under given constraints. The expression is as follows:

The similarity matrix W is obtained using the following method:

$$(W)_{ij} = \begin{cases} 1, & \text{if } x_i \in N_k(x_j) \text{ or } x_j \in N_k(x_i), \\ 0, & \text{otherwise,} \end{cases} \tag{3.9}$$

in which $N_k(x_i)$ represents the set of kNN of sample x_i. Then, the optimal consensus similarity matrix W^* construction method is

$$(W^*)_{ij} = \min\{(W^1)_{ij}, (W^2)_{ij}, \dots, (W^P)_{ij}\}. \tag{3.10}$$

If there is an incorrect neighbor assignment in the similarity matrix of one view and not in another, there will be no misclassification of neighboring samples in the similarity matrix of the ultimate consensus optimal graph.

Let $\hat{W}^* = diag\{\sum_{i=1}^n (W^*)_{i1}, \sum_{i=1}^n (W^*)_{i2}, \dots, \sum_{i=1}^n (W^*)_{in}\}$ denote the consensus degree matrix and $L^* = \hat{W}^* - W^*$ denote the consensus Laplacian matrix. The optimal graph learning is

$$\min_V \sum_{i=1}^n \sum_{j=1}^n ||(v)_i - (v)_j||_2^2 (W^*)_{ij} \Rightarrow \min_V \text{tr}[VL^*(V)^T], \tag{3.11}$$

s.t. $V \geq 0$.

3.5   Chapter summary

Graph theory, an important branch of mathematics, studies graph structures composed of nodes and edges and is widely applied in computer science, network analysis, biology, and sociology. Graph Laplacian regularization introduces the Laplacian matrix as a regularization term, leveraging graph structural information to constrain model outputs, ensuring that predictions of adjacent nodes tend to be consistent, thereby enhancing the model's generalization ability. Building on this, propagation regularization further utilizes information from neighboring nodes to provide additional supervisory signals, improving the model's robustness and reliability. Hypergraphs, as an extension of graphs, allow an edge to connect multiple nodes, enabling more flexible capture of complex high-order relationships, making them suitable for describing multivariable associations. Optimal graph learning constructs a consensus similarity matrix from multi-view data, optimizing the graph structure under specific constraints to minimize the objective function, thereby enhancing the discriminative ability of the graph structure. These methods demonstrate significant theoretical value and practical potential in fields such as data mining, network design, and recommendation systems.

References

[1] Chen K., Che H., Li X., Leung M.-F.: "Graph non-negative matrix factorization with alternative smoothed L_0 regularizations." *Neural Comput. Appl.* 2022;35(14):9995–10009.

[2] Yang H., Ma K., Cheng J.: "Rethinking graph regularization for graph neural networks." in *Proceedings of the AAAI Conference on Artificial Intelligence*; 2021. Vol. 35. pp. 4573–81.

Chapter 4
Optimization theory

Multiplicative update (MU) and the alternating direction method of multipliers (ADMM) are integral techniques in optimization theory. MU is an iterative algorithm that is particularly effective for optimization problems, especially those with constraints. It adjusts variable values incrementally to approximate the optimal solution. Unlike traditional additive update methods, MU updates variables by multiplying them by a factor, which helps maintain the proportional relationships among variables. This is particularly useful when dealing with problems that have proportional constraints. One of the key advantages of the MU method is its strong convergence properties, enabling it to quickly find optimal solutions under certain conditions. In contrast, ADMM is an algorithm designed to solve constrained optimization problems by breaking down the original problem into smaller subproblems to simplify the solution process. ADMM introduces Lagrange multipliers, also known as dual variables, to handle constraints and alternately optimizes the primal variables and dual variables. A notable feature of this method is its modular structure, which makes it easily applicable to large-scale problems and distributed computing environments. ADMM has wide-ranging applications in fields, such as signal processing, image processing, and machine learning, especially when dealing with sparse optimization problems. Both algorithms are important tools in optimization theory, each with its own strengths and applicability in different scenarios.

4.1 Multiplicative update

4.1.1 Optimization algorithm

The generalized multiplicative update is an iterative optimization method suitable for optimization problems involving non-negative variables. Its core idea is to adjust the values of variables by multiplying them by an update factor, thereby gradually approaching the optimal solution while maintaining non-negativity. This algorithm can be applied to a variety of optimization problems, including, but not limited to, non-negative matrix factorization (NMF) and non-negative tensor factorization (NTF).

Generalized multiplicative update framework

The generalized multiplicative update framework involves several key steps:

Initialization: Select initial values for the variables, ensuring they are non-negative. Set the learning rate or step size to control the magnitude of each update. Define the maximum number of iterations and the convergence threshold.

Objective Function: Define the objective function $f(x)$, where x is a vector or matrix of non-negative variables. The objective function is typically convex but can also be non-convex, depending on the nature of the problem.

Update Rule: In each iteration, update the variables x. The update rule is usually based on the gradient information of the objective function and takes the form:

$$x_{ij} \leftarrow x_{ij} \cdot \frac{\partial f(x)}{\partial x_{ij}}^{-1}$$

or more generally:

$$x_{ij} \leftarrow x_{ij} \cdot \frac{N_{ij}}{D_{ij}}$$

where N_{ij} and D_{ij} are the numerator and denominator terms, respectively, calculated based on the objective function and constraints.

Iterative Steps: In each iteration, update each variable x_{ij} until convergence criteria are met.

Convergence Check: Check if the change in the objective function value or the variables is smaller than the predefined threshold.

4.1.2   *Optimization problem example on multiplicative update*

In the given data matrix $X \in R^{p \times q}$, p and q represent the data dimension and sample size, respectively. The objective of the NMF model is to discover the non-negative matrices $U = [u_{ij}] \in R^{p \times r}$ and $V = [v_{ij}] \in R^{q \times r}$. Here, u_{ij} and v_{ij} represent the ijth element in the matrices U and V, respectively, and r represents the desired reduced dimension. Using the basis matrix U and the coefficient matrix V, the relationship between the matrices is approximated as $X \approx UV^T$. The measure of similarity is accomplished by computing the distance. The commonly employed distance metric is the Frobenius norm, which represents the squared Euclidean distance between two matrices. Thus, the NMF model is expressed as an optimization problem:

$$\min_{U,V} ||X - UV^T||_F^2, \quad \text{s.t.} \quad U, V \geq 0 \tag{4.1}$$

where $|| \cdot ||_F$ represents the Frobenius norm. The constraints $U \geq 0$ and $V \geq 0$ indicate that all elements of matrices U and V are non-negative. The objective function of problem (4.1) is known to be convex only in either U or V, which makes it impossible to find the global minimum. Therefore, the following multiplicative update rules are proposed to achieve the optimal solutions [1]:

$$u_{ij} \leftarrow u_{ij} \frac{(XV)_{ij}}{(UV^TV)_{ij}}, \quad v_{ij} \leftarrow v_{ij} \frac{(X^TU)_{ij}}{(VU^TU)_{ij}}. \tag{4.2}$$

4.2   Alternating direction method of multipliers

4.2.1   *Optimization algorithm*

The ADMM is an effective algorithm in optimization problems, particularly suited for large-scale problems. Its core idea is to decompose a challenging optimization problem into several simpler subproblems and coordinate the solutions of these subproblems using multiplier methods (Lagrange multipliers) [4]. ADMM achieves global optimization by alternately updating each variable. Consider the following optimization problem:

$$\min_{\mathbf{x},\mathbf{z}} f(\mathbf{x}) + g(\mathbf{z})$$
$$\text{s.t. } A\mathbf{x} + B\mathbf{z} = \mathbf{c} \tag{4.3}$$

where $f(x)$ and $g(z)$ are the objective functions involving variables x and z, respectively, A and B are given matrices, and c is a constant vector. ADMM introduces auxiliary variables y and Lagrange multipliers to transform the constrained problem into a form that is easier to solve. By alternately optimizing x and z and using multipliers to handle the constraints, ADMM efficiently solves the optimization problem.

General ADMM algorithm framework

The ADMM algorithm is structured as follows:

Initialization:

* Choose initial values for $\mathbf{x}^{(0)}, \mathbf{z}^{(0)}, \mathbf{y}^{(0)}$.
* Set the penalty factor ρ (often referred to as the regularization parameter) and the number of iterations.

Iterative Steps: In the kth iteration, alternately perform the following steps:

Step 1: Update x (while keeping z and y fixed):

$$\mathbf{x}^{(k+1)} = \arg\min_{\mathbf{x}} \left[f(\mathbf{x}) + \frac{\rho}{2}\|A\mathbf{x} + B\mathbf{z}^{(k)} - \mathbf{c} + \mathbf{y}^{(k)}\|_2^2 \right]$$

Step 2: Update z (while keeping x and y fixed):

$$\mathbf{z}^{(k+1)} = \arg\min_{\mathbf{z}} \left[g(\mathbf{z}) + \frac{\rho}{2}\|A\mathbf{x}^{(k+1)} + B\mathbf{z} - \mathbf{c} + \mathbf{y}^{(k)}\|_2^2 \right]$$

Step 3: Update the multiplier y:

$$\mathbf{y}^{(k+1)} = \mathbf{y}^{(k)} + A\mathbf{x}^{(k+1)} + B\mathbf{z}^{(k+1)} - \mathbf{c}$$

Convergence Check: The iteration stops when $\mathbf{x}$, $\mathbf{z}$, and $\mathbf{y}$ converge. Common convergence criteria include:

- Small changes between successive values of $\mathbf{x}$ and $\mathbf{z}$ (e.g., $\|\mathbf{x}^{(k+1)} - \mathbf{x}^{(k)}\|$ is smaller than a threshold).
- Small changes in the Lagrange multiplier $\mathbf{y}$ (e.g., $\|\mathbf{y}^{(k+1)} - \mathbf{y}^{(k)}\|$ is smaller than a threshold).

Updating $\mathbf{x}$ and $\mathbf{z}$: In each step, ADMM alternately minimizes the subproblems for $\mathbf{x}$ and $\mathbf{z}$. This process simplifies the optimization by fixing other variables during each update.

Multiplier Update: ADMM updates the multiplier $\mathbf{y}$ to adjust the satisfaction of the constraints, ensuring that the constraints are strictly considered in the optimization process.

Penalty Factor ρ: The factor ρ controls the penalty for constraint violations and affects the convergence speed. Typically, a suitable value for ρ needs to be chosen before starting the algorithm.

4.2.2 *Optimization problem example on ADMM*

The model obtained from article [2] is as follows:

$$
\begin{aligned}
&\min_{\mathbf{Z}^{(v)}, \mathbf{P}^{(v)}, \mathbf{H}^{(v)}, \mathbf{F}, \mathbf{A}, \theta^{(v)}} \quad \|\mathscr{Z}\|_{\omega,\circledast} + \alpha \sum_{v=1}^{V} \|\mathbf{X}^{(v)} - \mathbf{P}^{(v)}\mathbf{H}^{(v)}\|_F^2 \\
&+ \beta \sum_{v=1}^{V} \|\mathbf{H}^{(v)} - \mathbf{H}^{(v)}\mathbf{Z}^{(v)}\|_F^2 + 2\gamma tr(\mathbf{F}^T \mathbf{L}_\mathbf{A}\mathbf{F}) \\
&+ \sum_{v=1}^{V} \theta^{(v)} \|\mathbf{Z}^{(v)} - \mathbf{A}\|_F^2, \\
&\text{s.t. } \mathscr{Z} = \Phi(\mathbf{Z}^{(1)}, \mathbf{Z}^{(2)}, \cdots, \mathbf{Z}^{(V)}), \\
&a_i \geq 0, \ a_i^T \mathbf{1} = 1, \ \mathbf{F}^T\mathbf{F} = \mathbf{I}, \ \mathbf{P}^{(v)^T}\mathbf{P}^{(v)} = \mathbf{I},
\end{aligned}
\tag{4.4}
$$

where $\theta^{(v)} = 1/(2\|\mathbf{Z}^{(v)} - \mathbf{A}\|_F)$ is an adaptive weight parameter, α, β, and γ are trade-off parameters. Model (4.4) is an optimization problem with multiple variables, and an algorithm based on ADMM is designed to solve it. We introduce the auxiliary variable $\mathscr{G}$, and let $\mathscr{Z} = \mathscr{G}$. The augmented Lagrangian function of model (4.4) can be represented as follows:

$$
\begin{aligned}
&\min_{\mathbf{Z}^{(v)}, \mathbf{P}^{(v)}, \mathbf{H}^{(v)}, \mathbf{F}, \mathbf{A}, \theta^{(v)}} \quad \|\mathscr{G}\|_{\omega,\circledast} + \alpha \sum_{v=1}^{V} \|\mathbf{X}^{(v)} - \mathbf{P}^{(v)}\mathbf{H}^{(v)}\|_F^2 \\
&+ \beta \sum_{v=1}^{V} \|\mathbf{H}^{(v)} - \mathbf{H}^{(v)}\mathbf{Z}^{(v)}\|_F^2 + 2\gamma tr(\mathbf{F}^T \mathbf{L}_\mathbf{A}\mathbf{F}) \\
&+ \sum_{v=1}^{V} \theta^{(v)} \|\mathbf{Z}^{(v)} - \mathbf{A}\|_F^2 + \Psi(\mathscr{W}, \mathscr{Z} - \mathscr{G}), \\
&\text{s.t. } a_i \geq 0, \ a_i^T \mathbf{1} = 1, \ \mathbf{F}^T\mathbf{F} = \mathbf{I}, \mathbf{P}^{(v)^T}\mathbf{P}^{(v)} = \mathbf{I},
\end{aligned}
\tag{4.5}
$$

where

$$
\Psi(\mathscr{W}, \mathscr{Z} - \mathscr{G}) = \langle \mathscr{W}, \mathscr{Z} - \mathscr{G} \rangle + \frac{\rho}{2}\|\mathscr{Z} - \mathscr{G}\|_F^2,
\tag{4.6}
$$

Update F: With all other variables fixed, the solution of the subproblem for F can be derived from problem (4.5) as follows:

$$\min_{F^TF=I} \ \mathrm{tr}(F^TL_AF). \tag{4.7}$$

Problem (4.7) can be solved by calculating the c smallest eigenvalues of L_A.

Update A: With all other variables fixed, the solution of subproblem for A can be derived from problem (4.5) as follows:

$$\min_A \ 2\gamma \ \mathrm{tr}(F^TL_AF) + \sum_{v=1}^V \theta^{(v)}||A - Z^{(v)}||_F^2,$$
$$\text{s.t. } a_{i,j} \geq 0, \ a_i\mathbf{1} = 1, \ F^TF = I. \tag{4.8}$$

Problem (4.8) can be transformed into the following:

$$\min_A \gamma \sum_{i,j=1}^n ||f_i - f_j||_2^2 a_{ij} + \sum_{v=1}^V \theta^{(v)} \sum_{i,j=1}^n (a_{ij} - z_{i,j}^{(v)})^2,$$
$$s.t. \ a_{i,j} \geq 0, a_i\mathbf{1} = 1, \ F^TF = I. \tag{4.9}$$

problem (4.9) is equivalent to the following form:

$$\min_{a_i \geq 0, a_i\mathbf{1}=1} ||a_i - (\sum_{v=1}^V \theta^{(v)} z_i^{(v)} - \gamma e_i/2)/\sum_{v=1}^V \theta^{(v)}||_2^2. \tag{4.10}$$

Problem (4.10) can be solved by an efficient iterative algorithm [3]. To speed up the computation, γ is initialized as a constant; at each iteration, if the number of connected components is greater than or less than c, we divide or multiply γ by 2. Therefore, γ is a self-tuned parameter.

Update $Z^{(v)}$: With all other variables fixed, the solution of subproblem for $Z^{(v)}$ can be derived from problem (4.5) as follows:

$$\begin{aligned} Z^{(v)*} &= \underset{Z^{(v)}}{\mathrm{argmin}} \ \sum_{v=1}^V \beta ||H^{(v)} - H^{(v)}Z^{(v)}||_F^2 \\ &\quad + \sum_{v=1}^V \theta^{(v)}||A - Z^{(v)}||_F^2 + \Psi(\mathscr{W}, \mathscr{Z} - \mathscr{G}), \\ &= \underset{Z^{(v)}}{\mathrm{argmin}} \ \sum_{v=1}^V \beta ||H^{(v)} - H^{(v)}Z^{(v)}||_F^2 \\ &\quad + \sum_{v=1}^V \theta^{(v)}||A - Z^{(v)}||_F^2 + \langle \mathscr{W}, \mathscr{Z} - \mathscr{G} \rangle \\ &\quad + \frac{\rho}{2}||\mathscr{Z} - \mathscr{G}||_F^2. \end{aligned} \tag{4.11}$$

Since all $Z^{(v)}$ are stacked into a tensor to form $\mathscr{Z}$, for each $Z^{(v)}$, we have

$$\begin{aligned} Z^{(v)*} &= \underset{Z^{(v)}}{\mathrm{argmin}} \ \theta^{(v)}||A - Z^{(v)}||_F^2 \\ &\quad + \beta ||H^{(v)} - H^{(v)}Z^{(v)}||_F^2 \\ &\quad + \frac{\rho}{2}||Z^{(v)} - G^{(v)} + W^{(v)}/\rho||_F^2. \end{aligned} \tag{4.12}$$

Taking the derivative with respect to $\mathbf{Z}^{(v)}$ and setting it to zero, $\mathbf{Z}^{(v)^*}$ is obtained as follows:

$$\mathbf{Z}^{(v)^*} = \mathbf{B}^{(v)^{-1}}\mathbf{C}^{(v)}, \tag{4.13}$$

where $\mathbf{B}^{(v)} = 2\beta\mathbf{H}^{(v)^T}\mathbf{H}^{(v)} + 2\theta^{(v)}\mathbf{I} + \rho\mathbf{I}, \mathbf{C}^{(v)} = 2\beta\mathbf{H}^{(v)^T}\mathbf{H}^{(v)} + 2\theta^{(v)}\mathbf{A} + \rho(\mathbf{G}^{(v)} - \mathbf{W}^{(v)}/\rho)$.

Update $\mathscr{G}$: With all other variables fixed, the solution of subproblem for $\mathscr{G}$ can be derived from problem (4.5) as follows:

$$\begin{aligned}
\mathscr{G}^* &= \underset{\mathscr{G}}{\operatorname{argmin}}\ \alpha||\mathscr{G}||_{\omega,\circledast} + \Psi(\mathscr{W}, \mathscr{Z} - \mathscr{G}) \\
&= \underset{\mathscr{G}}{\operatorname{argmin}}\ \alpha||\mathscr{G}||_{\omega,\circledast} + \rho/2||\mathscr{G} - (\mathscr{Z} + \mathscr{W}/\rho)||_F^2.
\end{aligned} \tag{4.14}$$

According to Theorem 3, the solution of problem (4.14) can be obtained as follows:

$$\mathscr{G}^* = \Gamma_{\tau*\omega}(\mathscr{Z} + \mathscr{W}/\rho). \tag{4.15}$$

Update $\mathbf{P}^{(v)}$: With all other variables fixed, the solution of subproblem for $\mathbf{P}^{(v)}$ can be derived from problem (4.5) as follows:

$$\begin{aligned}
\mathbf{P}^{(v)^*} &= \underset{\mathbf{P}^{(v)}}{\operatorname{argmin}}\ ||\mathbf{X}^{(v)} - \mathbf{P}^{(v)}\mathbf{H}^{(v)}||_F^2 \\
&= \underset{\mathbf{P}^{(v)}}{\operatorname{argmin}}\ ||\mathbf{X}^{(v)^T} - \mathbf{H}^{(v)^T}\mathbf{P}^{(v)^T}||_F^2.
\end{aligned} \tag{4.16}$$

According to Theorem 4, the solution of problem (4.16) is:

$$\mathbf{P}^{(v)^*} = \mathbf{U}^{(v)}\mathbf{V}^{(v)^T}, \tag{4.17}$$

where $\mathbf{U}^{(v)}$ and $\mathbf{V}^{(v)^T}$ are the left and right singular values of singular value decomposition (SVD) of $\mathbf{X}^{(v)}\mathbf{H}^{(v)^T}$.

Update $\mathbf{H}^{(v)}$: With all other variables fixed, the solution of subproblem for $\mathbf{H}^{(v)}$ can be derived from problem (4.5) as follows:

$$\underset{\mathbf{H}^{(v)}}{\min}\ \alpha||\mathbf{X}^{(v)} - \mathbf{P}^{(v)}\mathbf{H}^{(v)}||_F^2 + \beta||\mathbf{H}^{(v)} - \mathbf{H}^{(v)}\mathbf{Z}^{(v)}||_F^2. \tag{4.18}$$

Taking the derivative with respect to $\mathbf{H}^{(v)}$ and setting it to zero, we can obtain the following:

$$\mathbf{M}^{(v)}\mathbf{H}^{(v)} + \mathbf{H}^{(v)}\mathbf{Q}^{(v)} = \mathbf{K}^{(v)}, \tag{4.19}$$

where $\mathbf{M}^{(v)} = \alpha\mathbf{P}^{(v)^T}\mathbf{P}^{(v)}, \mathbf{Q}^{(v)} = \beta(\mathbf{I} + \mathbf{Z}\mathbf{Z}^{(v)^T} - \mathbf{Z}^{(v)} - \mathbf{Z}^{(v)^T}), \mathbf{K}^{(v)} = \alpha\mathbf{P}^{(v)^T}\mathbf{X}^{(v)}$, Equation (4.19) is a Sylvester equation, which can be efficiently solved via lyap function in MATLAB®.

Adaptive weight $\theta^{(v)}$ can be updated as follows:

$$\theta^{(v)^*} = \frac{1}{2||\mathbf{Z}^{(v)} - \mathbf{A}||_F}. \tag{4.20}$$

Lagrange multiplier can be updated as follows:

$$\mathscr{W}^* = \mathscr{W} + \rho(\mathscr{Z} - \mathscr{G}). \tag{4.21}$$

Algorithm 1: AMSLDO for multi-view clustering.

Input: Multi-view data: $\{X^{(1)}, \ldots, X^{(V)}\}$, number of clusters c, trade-off parameters α, and β, weight vector w.
Initialize: $\theta^{(v)} = 1/V$, $\rho = 0.1$, number of neighbors $g = 10$, $\rho_{max} = 10^{10}$, $\eta = 2$, $\gamma = 0.1$, $k = 80$, $Iter_{max} = 50$, $\varepsilon = 10^{-7}$.
while not convergence **do**
    1. Update F by Eq. (4.7);
    2. Update A by Eq. (4.10);
    3. Update Z by Eq. (4.13);
    4. Update $\mathcal{G}$ by Eq. (4.15);
    5. Update $P^{(v)}$ by Eq. (4.17);
    6. Update $H^{(v)}$ by Eq. (4.19);
    7. Update $\theta^{(v)}$ by Eq. (4.20);
    8. Update Lagrange multipliers by Eq. (4.21);
    9. Update penalty parameters by Eq. (4.22);
    10. Check the convergence condition by Eq. (4.23).
end
Output consensus matrix A with exact c connected components.

Penalty parameter ρ can be updated as follows:

$$\rho^* = \min(\eta\rho, \rho_{max}), \qquad (4.22)$$

where ρ_{max} is the maximum value of the penalty parameter, and η is a parameter designed to speed up convergence.

The convergence condition of the model is set as follows:

$$||Z^{(v)} - G^{(v)}||_\infty < \varepsilon, \qquad (4.23)$$

where ε denotes the convergence threshold, the solution procedure of the proposed model is summarized in Algorithm 1.

4.3   Chapter summary

This chapter has underscored the significance of MU and ADMM in optimization theory. MU's iterative approach, particularly suited for problems with constraints, ensures proportionality and non-negativity, offering strong convergence properties. ADMM, conversely, excels in large-scale and constrained optimization by decomposing complex problems and utilizing Lagrange multipliers, thus demonstrating its efficacy in various fields such as signal and image processing. Both methods have been illustrated through practical examples, emphasizing their adaptability and effectiveness in solving real-world optimization challenges. As the complexity of optimization problems continues to escalate, the utility of MU and ADMM in providing efficient solutions remains pivotal. Future work may delve into their integration with new technologies and applications in emerging domains, further expanding their impact on optimization theory and practice.

References

[1]   Dong Y., Che H., Leung M.F., Liu C, Yan Z.: "Centric graph regularized log-norm sparse non-negative matrix factorization for multi-view clustering." *Signal Process.* 2024;217:109341.

[2]   Guo W., Che H., Leung M.F. Yan Z.: "Adaptive multi-view subspace learning based on distributed optimization." *Internet of Things.* 2024;26:101203.

[3]   Duchi J., Shalev-Shwartz S., Singer Y., Chandra T.D.: "Efficient projections onto the l 1-ball for learning in high dimensions." in *Proceedings of the 25th International Conference on Machine learning.* New York: ACM; 2008. pp. 272–9.

[4]   Boyd S., Parikh N., Chu E., Peleato B., Eckstein J.: "Distributed optimization and statistical learning via the alternating direction method of multipliers." *Foundations and Trends® in Machine learning.* Now Publishers: Inc: 2011;3(1):1–122.

Chapter 5

Graph and smoothed l_0 regularized non-negative matrix factorization for clustering

Graph non-negative matrix factorization (GNMF) can discover the data's intrinsic low-dimensional structure embedded in the high dimensional space. Therefore, it has superior performance for data representation and clustering. Unfortunately, it is sensitive to noise and outliers. In this chapter, to improve the robustness of GNMF, an l_0 norm is introduced to enhance the sparsity of factorized matrices. As the l_0 norm is discontinuous and minimizing it is an NP-hard problem, five functions approximating the l_0 norm are used to transform the problem of the sparse graph non-negative matrix factorization (SGNMF) to a global optimization problem. Finally, the multiplicative updating rules (MUR) are designed to solve the problem, and the convergence of the algorithm is proven. In the experiment, the accuracy and normalized mutual information of clustering results show the superior performance of SGNMF on five public datasets.

5.1 Sparsity-constrained graph non-negative matrix factorization

5.1.1 Alternative smoothed l_0 approximate functions

The l_0 norm computes the number of nonzero elements of a vector, which is used to enforce the required sparsity. Sparsity is always required to eliminate useless information and enhance interpretability.

The l_0 norm is described as follows:

$$\|(\boldsymbol{x})\|_0 = \sum_{i=1}^{n} 1 - \sigma(x_{ij}). \tag{5.1}$$

$\sigma(x)$ is the unit impulse function, it is discontinuous and minimizing it is an NP-hard problem. To solve it, each situation needs to be enumerated.

However, several functions are used to approximate the l_0 norm, and they all have the following form:

$$\lim_{\sigma \to \infty} f(x, \sigma) = \begin{cases} 1 \ (x = 0) \\ 0 \ (\text{others}) \end{cases}. \tag{5.2}$$

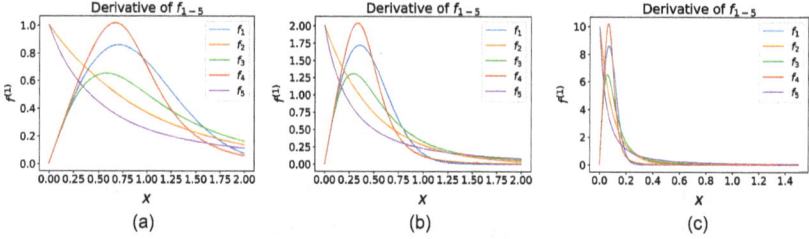

Figure 5.1   *Derivatives of five alternative approximation functions (a) $\sigma = 1$, (b) $\sigma = 0.5$, (c) $\sigma = 0.1$*

σ is used to control the degree of approaching the l_0 norm. In this paper, four previously proposed functions are used to approximate the l_0 norm to measure the sparsity of the matrices factorized by GNMF:

- Inv. Gaussian [1]: $f_1(x) = 1 - e^{-\frac{x^2}{\sigma^2}}$.
- Inv. Laplacian [2]: $f_2(x) = 1 - e^{-\frac{|x|}{|\sigma|}}$.
- Comp. inv. func [3]: $f_3(x) = \frac{x^2}{x^2 + \sigma^2}$.
- Symmetric. CT [4]: $f_4(x) = \sin\left(\arctan\left(\frac{x^2}{\sigma^2}\right)\right)$.

The functions f_1, f_3, and f_4 have the following properties:

$$\lim_{x \to 0} \nabla f(x, \sigma) = 0. \tag{5.3}$$

As the updating rules of NMF and GNMF are equivalent to those of the gradient descent method [5], they may just lead values to be very small but not zero, and thus sparsity is not achieved.

Before presenting our algorithm, we introduce a function f_5, which is easy to calculate and concave for R_+:

$$f_5(x) = \frac{|x|}{|x| + \sigma}. \tag{5.4}$$

The second derivative of f_5 is less than 0:

$$f_5^{(2)} = -\frac{2\sigma}{(\sigma + x)^3} < 0. \tag{5.5}$$

It is obvious that f_5 satisfies (5.2). As shown in Figure 5.1, the derivation becomes much larger as x approaches zero. This makes f_5 more efficient in leading to sparsity. As shown in Figure 5.2, the smaller σ is, f_{1-5} is closer to the l_0 norm.

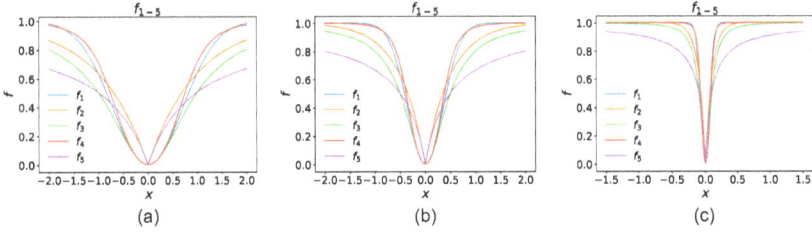

Figure 5.2   Comparisons of the five functions with different σ (a) $\sigma = 1$, (b) $\sigma = 0.5$, (c) $\sigma = 0.1$

5.1.2   Sparsity-constrained GNMF

The sparsity of the features extracted by GNMF can be expressed by the l_0 norm, as shown in the following equation:

$$\sum_{j=0}^{n} \|(b_j)\|_0. \tag{5.6}$$

In addition, the optimization problem is described as follows:

$$\min_{B \geqslant 0} \sum_{j=0}^{n} \|(b_j)\|_0. \tag{5.7}$$

As the l_0 norm is discontinuous and the problem is NP-hard, we use $f(x, \sigma)$ to replace the l_0 norm, making the problem solvable and leading to the following problem:

$$\min_{B \geqslant 0} \sum_{j=0}^{n} \sum_{k=0}^{c} f(b_{jk}, \sigma). \tag{5.8}$$

By adding this term as a regularization, the sparsity-constrained GNMF (SGNMF) is obtained as follows:

$$\min_{A, B \geqslant 0} \|X - AB^T\|_F + \lambda \operatorname{tr}\left(B^T L B\right) + \beta \sum_{j=0}^{n} \sum_{k=0}^{c} f(b_{jk}, \sigma). \tag{5.9}$$

By solving problem (5.9), the extracted features can get a deeper structure of the original data by the regularizer of GNMF, some noise can be eliminated, and it can be ensured that NMF learns parts of the object. In addition, the interpretability of the data led by sparsity is obtained.

5.2   Optimization algorithm

5.2.1   Updating rules

The problem of NMF and GNMF is non-convex, and an optimal solution is not guaranteed. Therefore, a solution can find local optima of SGNMF.

Denote $\Omega \in R_{+}^{m \times c}$ and $\Theta \in R_{+}^{n \times c}$, respectively, as the Lagrangian multipliers for the constraints $a_{ik} \geqslant 0$, $b_{jk} \geqslant 0$. ω_{ik} is the element in the ith row and kth column of

Ω. θ_{jk} is the element in the jth row and kth column of Θ. The objective function can be transformed as follows:

$$\mathrm{tr}\left((X - AB^T)(X - AB^T)^T\right) + \lambda\,\mathrm{tr}\left(B^T LB\right) + \beta \sum_{j=0}^{n}\sum_{k=0}^{c} f(b_{jk}, \sigma)$$

$$= \mathrm{tr}\left(XX^T\right) - 2\,\mathrm{tr}\left(XBA^T\right) + \mathrm{tr}\left(AB^T BA^T\right) + \lambda\,\mathrm{tr}\left(B^T LB\right) + \beta \sum_{j=0}^{n}\sum_{k=0}^{c} f(b_{jk}, \sigma). \tag{5.10}$$

The Lagrangian function is formulated as:

$$\mathcal{L} = \mathrm{tr}\left(XX^T\right) - 2\,\mathrm{tr}\left(X\,BA^T\right) + \mathrm{tr}\left(AB^T BA^T\right) + \lambda\,\mathrm{tr}\left(B^T LB\right)$$
$$+ \beta \sum_{j=0}^{n}\sum_{k=0}^{c} f(b_{jk}, \sigma) + \mathrm{tr}\left(\Omega A^T\right) + \mathrm{tr}\left(\Theta B^T\right). \tag{5.11}$$

Denote $f^{(d)}$ as the dth derivative. The partial derivatives of $\mathcal{L}$ with respect to A and B are

$$\frac{\partial \mathcal{L}}{\partial A} = -2XB + 2AB^T B + \Omega, \tag{5.12}$$

$$\frac{\partial \mathcal{L}}{\partial B} = -2X^T A + 2BA^T A + 2\lambda LB + \beta f^{(1)}(b_{jk,\sigma}) + \Theta. \tag{5.13}$$

Using the Karush–Kuhn–Tucker (KKT) conditions $a_{ik}\omega_{ik} = 0$ and $\theta_{jk}b_{jk} = 0$, the following equations for a_{ik} and b_{jk} are obtained:

$$-(X\,B)_{ik}a_{ik} + \left(AB^T B\right)_{ik} a_{ik} = 0, \tag{5.14}$$

$$-\left(X^T A\right)_{jk} b_{jk} + \left(BA^T A\right)_{jk} b_{jk} + \lambda(LB)_{jk}b_{jk} + \beta f^{(1)}(b_{jk}, \sigma)b_{jk} = 0. \tag{5.15}$$

Based on (5.14) and (5.15), the following updating rules are proposed:

$$a_{ik} \leftarrow a_{ik}\frac{(XB)_{ik}}{\left(AB^T B\right)_{ik}}. \tag{5.16}$$

$$b_{jk} \leftarrow b_{jk}\frac{\left(X^T A + \lambda WB\right)_{jk}}{\left(BA^T A + \lambda DB\right)_{jk} + 0.5\beta f^{(1)}(b_{jk}, \sigma)}. \tag{5.17}$$

It is obvious that the updating rules are equal to those of NMF when $\lambda = 0$ and $\beta = 0$. They are equal to those of GNMF when $\beta = 0$. The whole algorithm of SGNMF is described in Algorithm 1.

5.2.2 Convergence study

The proof of convergence for the updating rules (5.16) is the same as that for NMF. Therefore, convergence is needed to prove under the updating rule (5.17). To prove the convergence, following definition and lemmas are given.

Algorithm 1 Algorithm of SGNMF.

Require: X: data matrix($X \in \mathscr{R}_+^{m \times n}$, each column vector is a sample); r: max
    iteration; k: number of components; e: max error tolerance; λ, β, σ_1: parameters
    in SGNMF; σ_2: parameter in f_{1-5}; p: number of neighborhoods.
Ensure: A: basis matrix; B: coefficient matrix.

  1: **if** X is from images **then**
  2:     **for** element x in X **do**
  3:         normalize x
  4:     **end for**
  5: **end if**
  6: *counter* $= 0$
  7: initialize the basis matrix $A(A \in R_+^{m \times c})$ and the coefficient matrix $B(B \in R_+^{n \times c})$
     with NNDSVD [6].
  8: $W \leftarrow$ Adjacency matrix
  9: $D \leftarrow$ Degree matrix
10: Laplacian matrix: $L = D - W$
11: *error* $\leftarrow$ objective function value of SGNMF
12: **while** *error* $> e$ and *counter* $< r$ **do**
13:     **for** element a in A **do**
14:         $Den_1 \leftarrow$ denominator of updating rule (5.16) for a
15:         **if** $Den_1 \neq 0$ **then**
16:            $a \leftarrow$ the new a (computed by updating rule (5.16))
17:         **end if**
18:     **end for**
19:     **for** element b in B **do**
20:         $Den_2 \leftarrow$ denominator of updating rule (5.17) for b
21:         **if** $Den_2 \neq 0$ **then**
22:            $b \leftarrow$ the new b (computed by updating rule (5.17))
23:         **end if**
24:     **end for**
25:     *error* $\leftarrow$ value of (5.9)
26:     *counter* $=$ *counter* $+ 1$
27: **end while**
28: **return** A, B

Definition 1. *$\varphi(b, b')$ is an auxiliary function for a function $F(b)$ if*

$$\varphi(b, b') \geqslant F(b), \quad \varphi(b', b') = F(b').$$

The property of the auxiliary function is shown in the following lemma.

Lemma 1. *1. Let φ be an auxiliary function of F. Under the following updating rule,
F is non-increasing:*

$$b^{t+1} = \arg\min_{b} \ \varphi(b, b'). \tag{5.18}$$

Proof. $F\left(b^{t+1}\right) \leq \varphi\left(b^{t+1}, b^t\right) \leq \varphi\left(b^t, b^t\right) = F\left(b^t\right)$.

Theorem 1. *If $\alpha(x)$ is concave, the objective function*

$$\mathscr{F} = \|X - AB^T\|_F + \lambda \operatorname{Tr}(BLB^T) + \sum_{k=1, j=1}^{c,n} \beta \alpha(b_{jk}) \tag{5.19}$$

will be non-increasing under the following updating rules:

$$b_{jk}^{t+1} = b_{jk}^t \frac{(X^T A + \lambda WB)_{jk}}{(BA^T A + \lambda DB)_{jk} + 0.5\beta \alpha^{(1)}(b_{jk}^t)}. \tag{5.20}$$

Denote $\mathscr{F}$ as an objective function of SGNMF with respect to B,

$$\mathscr{F}_{jk}^{(1)} = \left(-2X^T A + 2BA^T A + 2\lambda LB\right)_{jk} + \beta \alpha^{(1)}(b_{jk}), \tag{5.21}$$

$$\mathscr{F}_{jk}^{(2)} = 2\left(A^T A\right)_{kk} + 2\lambda L_{jj} + \beta \alpha^{(2)}(b_{jk}). \tag{5.22}$$

Denote φ as an auxiliary function of $\mathscr{F}_{jk}$ as follows:

$$\begin{aligned}
\varphi(b, b') = &\mathscr{F}_{jk}(b') + \mathscr{F}_{jk}^{(1)}(b)(b - b') \\
&+ \frac{\left(BA^T A\right)_{jk} + \lambda(DB)_{jk} + 0.5\beta \alpha^{(1)}(b_{jk}^t)}{b_{jk}^t}\left(b - b_{jk}^t\right)^2.
\end{aligned} \tag{5.23}$$

By finding the extreme point of (5.23), it is easy to derive updating rules (5.17), and if φ is the auxiliary function of $\mathscr{F}$, convergence is proven by Lemma 1. As $\alpha(x)$ is concave, the first-order Taylor approximation of $\alpha(b)$ is greater than or equal to $\alpha(b)$.

$$\alpha(b_{jk}^t) + \alpha^{(1)}(b_{jk}^t)(b - b_{jk}^t) \geqslant \alpha(b_{jk})$$

From this, we obtain the following:

$$\sum_{i=2}^{\infty} \frac{\alpha^{(i)}(b_{jk}^t)}{i!}(b - b_{jk}^t)^i \leqslant 0. \tag{5.24}$$

By adding (5.19) to both sides of (5.24), we obtain the following: φ_1 is greater than $\mathscr{F}$:

$$\begin{aligned}
\varphi_1(b, b_{jk}^t) = &\mathscr{F}_{jk}(b') + \mathscr{F}_{jk}^{(1)}(b_{jk}^t)(h - h_{jk}^t) \\
&+ \left((A^T A)_{kk} + \lambda L_{jj}\right)(b - b_{jk}^t)^2.
\end{aligned} \tag{5.25}$$

Then, to prove that $\varphi(b, b_{jk}^t)$ is greater than $\varphi_1(b, b_{jk}^t)$, the following is given:

$$\left(BA^T A\right)_{jk} = \sum_{l=1}^{c} h_{jl}^t \left(A^T A\right)_{lk} \geq b_{jk}^t \left(A^T A\right)_{kk}, \tag{5.26}$$

$$\lambda(DB)_{jk} = \lambda \sum_{l=1}^{m} D_{jl} b_{lk}^t \geq \lambda D_{jj} b_{jk}^t \geq \lambda(D - W)_{jj} b_{jk}^t = \lambda L_{jj} b_{jk}^t. \tag{5.27}$$

With the above inequality, it is easy to verify that the third term of $\varphi_2(h, h_{ab}^{(t)})$ is greater than the third term of $\varphi_1(h, h_{ab}^{(t)})$. Therefore, $\varphi(h, h_{ab}^{(t)}) \geq \varphi_1(h, h_{ab}^{(t)})$ holds. Besides,

$$\varphi(h_{ab}^t, h_{ab}^t) = F_{ab}(h_{ab}^t).$$

As $\varphi(h, h_{ab}^t)$ is an auxiliary function of $\mathcal{F}$, the proof completes. The proof mainly follows the approach in [5]. □

Lemma 2. *The updating rules (5.17) are equivalent to the gradient descent method.*

Proof.   The gradient descent method can be expressed as follows:

$$b_{jk} \leftarrow b_{jk} - \eta_{jk} \frac{\partial \mathcal{F}}{\partial b_{jk}}. \tag{5.28}$$

where η is the learning rate. Following Deng Cai's [5] paper, η can be set as:

$$\frac{b_{jk}}{2(\boldsymbol{BG}^T\boldsymbol{G} + \lambda \boldsymbol{DB})_{jk} + \beta \alpha^{(1)}(b_{jk})}.$$

Then, we obtain the following:

$$
\begin{aligned}
b_{jk} - \eta_{jk} \frac{\partial \mathcal{F}}{\partial b_{jk}} &= b_{jk} - \frac{b_{jk}}{\left(2\boldsymbol{BA}^T\boldsymbol{A} + 2\lambda \boldsymbol{DB}\right)_{jk} + \beta \alpha^{(1)}(b_{jk})} \frac{\partial \mathcal{F}}{\partial b_{jk}} \\
&= b_{jk} - \frac{b_{jk}}{2\left(\boldsymbol{BA}^T\boldsymbol{A} + \lambda \boldsymbol{D}\,\boldsymbol{B}\right)_{jk} + \beta \alpha^{(1)}(b_{jk})} \\
&\qquad \left(\left(-2\boldsymbol{X}^T\boldsymbol{A} + 2\boldsymbol{BA}^T\boldsymbol{A} + 2\lambda \boldsymbol{LB}\right)_{jk} + \beta \alpha^{(1)}(b_{jk})\right) \\
&= b_{jk} \frac{\left(\boldsymbol{X}^T\boldsymbol{A} + \lambda \boldsymbol{WB}\right)_{jk}}{\left(\boldsymbol{BA}^T\boldsymbol{A} + \lambda \boldsymbol{DB}\right)_{jk} + 0.5\beta \alpha^{(1)}(b_{jk})}.
\end{aligned}
\tag{5.29}
$$

It is obvious that (5.29) is equivalent to (5.17). The proof is complete.

□

Lemma 2 indicates that the objective function is updated along with the negative gradient direction in the feasible region.

5.3   Experimental results

In this section, SGNMF is used to cluster five public dataset. The clustering results, convergence performance, and the effect of the parameters are discussed.

5.3.1   Description of datasets

The information of the datasets is listed as follows, and the summary of the datasets is provided in Table 5.1.

Table 5.1   Dataset description

Dataset	Feature number	Sample number	Clustering number
YALE	77 760	165	15
USPS	256	400	10
UMIST	2576	564	20
LIBRAS	90	360	15
JAFFE	65 536	213	10

- **YALE:** It contains 165 grayscale images of 15 persons, each with different facial expressions or configurations.
- **USPS:** A dataset consists of consists of 9298 images, which are 16×16 grayscale pixels. In our experiment, 400 images are used for clustering to show the performance of the algorithm.
- **UMIST:** It consists of 564 images of 20 persons, each shown in a range of poses from profile to frontal views. Each image is resized to 46×56 pixels.
- **LIBRAS**: It is a dataset from the UCI dataset [7], consisting of 15 classes with 24 instances. Each class references to a hand movement type in LIBRAS.
- **JAFFE:** It consists of 213 images from 10 Japanese female expressers, each with different facial expressions, which are all 256×256 pixels.

5.3.2   Compared algorithms

To compare the performance of the proposed approach, accuracy(ACC) and normalized mutual information (NMI) are used. The detailed information of comparison algorithms is listed as follows:

- K-means: It is the most classic clustering algorithm. Through several iterations, it can cluster very quickly and efficiently.
- K-means++: It is an algorithm based on K-means. But it avoids uncertain performance caused by random initialization of K-means.
- Spectral clustering (SP-clustering): It is a clustering method based on the graph theory, which transforms the partition of data into the segmentation of the graph. In the experiment, K-means++ is used to get the label of each sample. Ncut is used to cut the graph, and K-neighbors is used to construct the graph. The weight on the edge is computed by a Gaussian kernel function.
- NMF-based clustering: NMF is used to extract the features of each sample. Then, K-means++ is used to get the tag of the sample. When extracting the feature, the number of columns of the basis matrix in NMF is set to the number of items, and the number of iterations of the algorithm is 200. SVD initialization and

* http://vision.ucsd.edu/content/yale-face-database.
† https://www.kaggle.com/bistaumanga/usps-dataset.
‡ https://www.visioneng.org.uk/datasets/.
§ https://zenodo.org/record/3451524#.YZVNGsWHqUk.

normalization of the basis matrix is used to increase the stability and speed up convergence.

- KKM (kernel K-means): The algorithm is almost similar to K-means, but it pays more attention on the kernel space rather than the Euclidean space.
- RKKM (robust kernel K-means): By introducing a sparsity-induced norm, the effect of outliers, which is sensitive for K-means, can decrease, and a more stable result is obtained.
- AASC (affinity aggregation for spectral clustering): AASC is an algorithm proposed in [8] that extends spectral clustering to a setting with multiple affinities available.
- RMKKM (robust multi-kernel K-means): Based on RKKM, it introduces multiple kernel functions to explore a better Hilbert space, which was proposed in [9].
- CFSFDP (clustering by fast search and find of density peaks): It is a clustering algorithm based on the density of data samples, which was proposed in [10].

For KKM, RKKM, RMKKM and AASC, they can be executed by the following codes.[|] The remaining algorithms can be executed in our repository.[¶]

5.3.3   Basis normalization and NNDSVD initialization

The basis of data matrix X/ space is the basic unit vector group. SGNMF learns a space whose basis consists of the column vector of matrix A. To maintain the length of the basis the same, we can achieve it as follows:

$$a_{ik} = \frac{a_{ik}}{\sqrt{\sum_{i=0}^{m} a_{ik}^2}} \tag{5.30}$$

$$b_{jk} = b_{jk} \times \sqrt{\sum_{i=0}^{m} a_{ik}^2} \tag{5.31}$$

Besides, NNDSVD [6] is used to accelerate convergence and enhance stability in the experiment.

5.3.4   Clustering results

In the comparison experiments, the component number is set equal to the number of clusters for each dataset. Each algorithm clusters the dataset for 20 times, and the mean and standard error of the ACC and NMI are given. For image datasets, the data is normalized before clustering. The clustering results are presented in Tables 5.2 and 5.3, where the top three NMI and ACC's means are highlighted in bold. The results are summarized as follows:

- SGNMF outperforms the other methods. For the proposed algorithms using five smooth functions, at least one ranks in the top three each time. For ACC, SGNMF

[|] https://github.com/csliangdu/RMKKM.
[¶] https://github.com/chen12304/SGNMF.

Table 5.2   AccSGNMF has a more stable result. These five functions used in SGNMF have at least three which have a standard error less than 1, for comparison algorithms, the standard errors are almost higher than 1uracy of the algorithms' results

Dataset		YALE (%)	USPS (%)	UMIST (%)	LIBRAS (%)	JAFFE (%)
K-means		58.24 ± 3.11	64.24 ± 1.37	42.28 ± 2.04	44.69 ± 2.26	82.16 ± 6.18
K-means++		60.82 ± 2.47	65.05 ± 2.12	42.29 ± 1.66	45.42 ± 2.27	88.57 ± 4.15
SP-cluster		$\mathbf{66.55 \pm 1.22}$	59.2 ± 0.56	59.2 ± 2.32	50.38 ± 1.23	79.84 ± 7.1
NMF		59.09 ± 1.85	57.25 ± 1.58	58.09 ± 1.53	46.73 ± 3.36	85.8 ± 5.303
KKM		41 ± 2.71	45.12 ± 5.49	43.82 ± 5.34	47.55 ± 6.83	62.54 ± 7.25
RKKM		41.06 ± 2.7	45.3 ± 5.47	43.84 ± 5.36	47.85 ± 6.87	62.77 ± 7.52
AASC		40.64 ± 2.63	52.54 ± 2.27	47.15 ± 2.72	47.34 ± 1.1	30.35 ± 1.05
RMKKM		52.18 ± 3.92	63.88 ± 7.41	57.45 ± 6.46	$\mathbf{62.85 \pm 8.15}$	87.07 ± 5.69
CFSFDP		$\mathbf{64.85}$	58.75	51.13	46.94	84.04
SGNMF	f_1	62.3 ± 0.62	$\mathbf{65.18 \pm 2.7}$	61.53 ± 2.96	51.46 ± 1.3	$\mathbf{92.32 \pm 0.27}$
	f_2	62.21 ± 1.45	$\mathbf{65.6 \pm 1.84}$	61.69 ± 1.23	$\mathbf{52.43 \pm 0.56}$	92.3 ± 0.29
	f_3	62 ± 0.47	61.5 ± 0.35	$\mathbf{62.3 \pm 0.48}$	51.32 ± 0.61	$\mathbf{92.44 \pm 0.53}$
	f_4	62.27 ± 0.79	64.16 ± 2.98	$\mathbf{62.2 \pm 0.72}$	51.08 ± 0.62	92.02 ± 1.05
	f_5	$\mathbf{62.45 \pm 1.11}$	64.53 ± 1.11	$\mathbf{62.23 \pm 0.7}$	$\mathbf{52.47 \pm 0.41}$	92.42 ± 0.22

Table 5.3   NMI of algorithms' results

Dataset		YALE (%)	USPS (%)	UMIST (%)	LIBRAS (%)	JAFFE (%)
K-means		65.65 ± 1.52	62.72 ± 1.69	64.93 ± 1.22	59.45 ± 1.3	86.75 ± 3.83
K-means++		66.54 ± 1.09	62.48 ± 1.25	65.32 ± 1.39	59.51 ± 1.18	89.86 ± 2.39
SP-cluster		$\mathbf{69.16 \pm 0.98}$	64.71 ± 0.32	81.71 ± 1.7	64.07 ± 0.27	87.82 ± 3.65
NMF		64.63 ± 0.8	57.22 ± 1.08	57.8 ± 1.14	59.55 ± 1.06	$\mathbf{90.19 \pm 0.79}$
KKM		45.71 ± 2.45	40.22 ± 5.6	35.04 ± 3.44	42.45 ± 6.05	69.62 ± 5.5
RKKM		46.01 ± 2.58	40.57 ± 5.43	35.06 ± 3.46	42.82 ± 5.94	70.17 ± 5.65
AASC		46.83 ± 2.68	41.94 ± 1.01	39.39 ± 1.61	43.97 ± 1.45	27.22 ± 0.77
RMKKM		55.58 ± 2.6	62.57 ± 5.64	56.33 ± 4.14	63.52 ± 5.91	89.37 ± 2.9
CFSFDP		$\mathbf{67.3}$	58.7	74.9	64.19	$\mathbf{92.43}$
SGNMF	f_1	66.76 ± 0.8	$\mathbf{65.58 \pm 0.55}$	81.88 ± 1.67	$\mathbf{68.06 \pm 0.59}$	90.04 ± 0.25
	f_2	$\mathbf{67.36 \pm 0.95}$	$\mathbf{65.43 \pm 0.55}$	82.85 ± 0.8	$\mathbf{68.04 \pm 0.35}$	90.08 ± 0.29
	f_3	66.94 ± 0.51	59.64 ± 0.26	$\mathbf{83.24 \pm 0.72}$	66.81 ± 0.43	89.97 ± 0.59
	f_4	67 ± 0.89	65.28 ± 0.97	$\mathbf{83.15 \pm 0.65}$	66.66 ± 0.55	89.81 ± 0.71
	f_5	67.11 ± 0.76	$\mathbf{65.35 \pm 1.12}$	$\mathbf{83.3 \pm 0.62}$	$\mathbf{68.08 \pm 0.19}$	$\mathbf{90.11 \pm 0.32}$

ranks in the top three on JAFFE and UMIST, especially on JAFFE, where it achieves a 7%–8% higher ACC than others. For NMI, SGNMF ranks in the top three on UMIST and LIBRAS, especially on UMIST, where it is almost 15%–17% higher than others.

- SGNMF has a more stable result. Among the five functions used in SGNMF, at least three have a standard error less than 1%, while for comparison algorithms, the standard errors are almost higher than 1%.

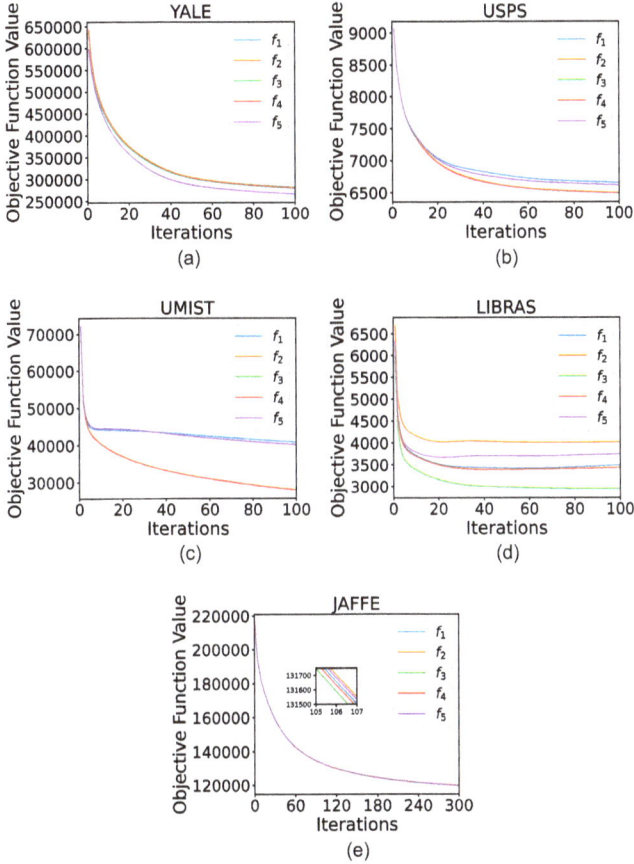

Figure 5.3   Convergence behaviors of the objective function value on five datasets
(a) YALE (b) USPS (c) UMIST (d) LIBRAS (e) JAFFE

- From Figure 5.3, the objective function values decrease with the increase in iterations.

5.3.5   Sparsity discussion

Sparsity can eliminate noise, increase the interpretability of data, and ensure NMF to learn part of object. Sparsity performance is discussed as follows.

To observe the performance on sparsity, we plot $\boldsymbol{B}$ as a grayscale image, factorized by NMF, GNMF, and SGNMF. To better illustrate sparsity, 20×20 grayscale patches of the original images are shown in Figures 5.4–5.8. The original images can be accessed via the link in footnote.** Furthermore, the sparsity of the matrices shown in the plots is given in Table 5.4. Sparsity is calculated as follows:

**https://github. com/chen12304/SGNMF/tree/main/pic_spar.

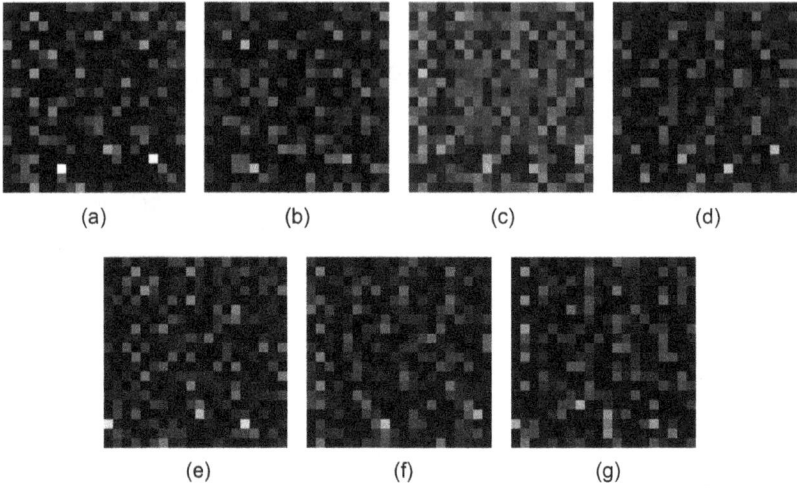

Figure 5.4   Comparison of sparsity performance on YALE (a) NMF (b) GNMF (c) SGNMF with f_1 (d) SGNMF with f_2 (e) SGNMF with f_3 (f) SGNMF with f_4 (g) SGNMF with f_5

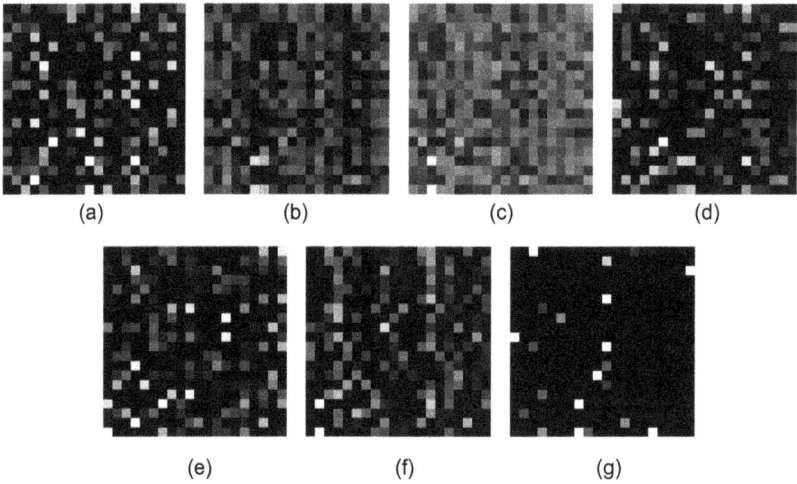

Figure 5.5   Comparison of sparsity performance on USPS (a) NMF (b) GNMF (c) SGNMF with f_1 (d) SGNMF with f_2 (e) SGNMF with f_3 (f) SGNMF with f_4 (g) SGNMF with f_5

$$Sparsity(\boldsymbol{X}) = \frac{SF(\boldsymbol{X})}{mn} \tag{5.32}$$

$SF(\boldsymbol{X})$ denotes the sparseness factor of $\boldsymbol{X}$, which was used in [11]. It is described as follows:

$$SF(\boldsymbol{X}) = \sum_{i=1}^{m} \sum_{j=1}^{n} m(x_{ij}),$$

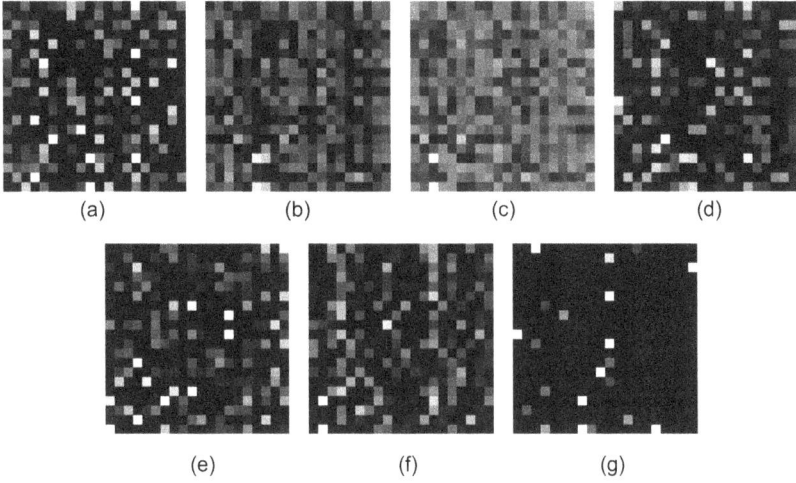

Figure 5.6   Comparison of sparsity performance on UMIST (a) NMF (b) GNMF (c) SGNMF with f_1 (d) SGNMF with f_2 (e) SGNMF with f_3 (f) SGNMF with f_4 (g) SGNMF with f_5

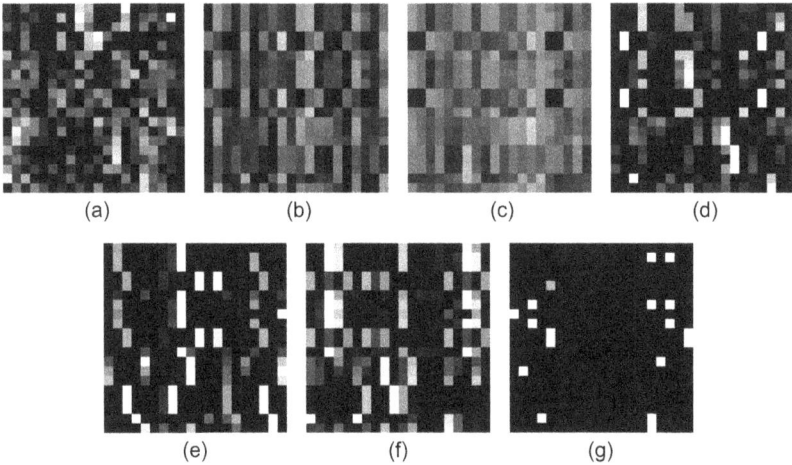

Figure 5.7   Comparison of sparsity performance on LIBRAS (a) NMF (b) GNMF (c) SGNMF with f_1 (d) SGNMF with f_2 (e) SGNMF with f_3 (f) SGNMF with f_4 (g) SGNMF with f_5

$$m(x) = \begin{cases} 1 \ (x < \tau) \\ 0 \ (x \geqslant \tau) \end{cases}.$$

where τ is the threshold value used to decide whether an element can be regarded as zero.

For $\boldsymbol{B}$ shown in Figures 5.4–5.8, both β and λ are set to 5, and σ is set to 0.001. In Figure 5.4, it is obvious that $\boldsymbol{B}$ of SGNMF with f_1, f_2, f_3, f_4, and f_5 are

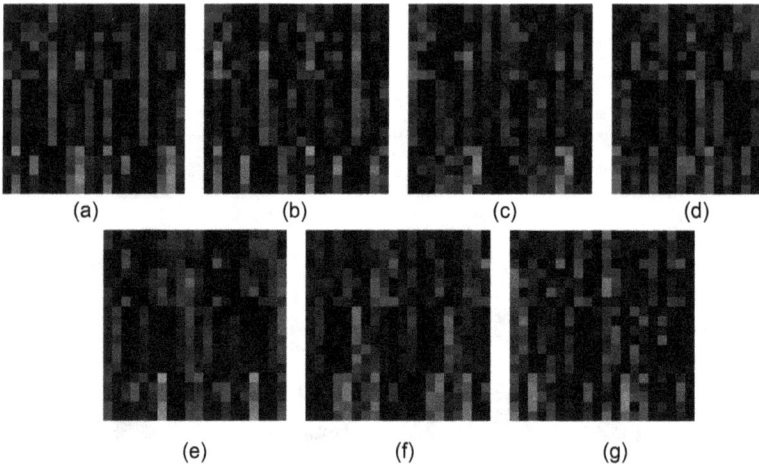

Figure 5.8   Comparison of sparsity performance on JAFFE (a) NMF (b) GNMF (c) SGNMF with f_1 (d) SGNMF with f_2 (e) SGNMF with f_3 (f) SGNMF with f_4 (g) SGNMF with f_5

Table 5.4   The Sparsity of the algorithms' results

Dataset		YALE(%)	USPS(%)	UMIST(%)	LIBRAS(%)	JAFFE(%)
NMF		6.91	42.88	9.70	7.59	2.95
GNMF		8.57	2.20	1.17	0.33	3.33
SGNMF	f1	7.72	1.40	1.71	0.46	2.86
	f2	8.40	33.5	11.73	37.89	3.28
	f3	9.25	24.45	12.17	27.04	3.66
	f4	9.05	38.03	16.10	55.04	4.69
	f5	**15.19**	**95.50**	**86.96**	**97.04**	**13.29**

Note: The bold values represent the best results in the comparison method.

smoother than those of NMF and GNMF. In Figure 5.5, only SGNMF with f_1 learns a smoother result, while SGNMF with f_5 yields a much sparser $\boldsymbol{B}$ on USPS. In Figure 5.6, SGNMF with the proposed f_5 also learns a much sparser matrix, but with $f_1, f_2, f_3,$ and f_4, it learns a smoother matrix. In Figure 5.7, only SGNMF with f_1 learns a smoother matrix $\boldsymbol{B}$, while others shown in Figures 5.7(d)–5.7(g) learn sparser $\boldsymbol{B}$.

It is concluded that SGNMF with f_{1-4} may lead smoother results rather than sparser results. However, using our proposed function f_5 as a regularizer, the smoother results can be avoided, and sparser result can be obtained. Besides, it is shown in Table 5.4 that SGNMF with the proposed f_5 always obtains the sparsest $\boldsymbol{B}$.

5.3.6   Parameter setting

GNMF has two parameters (p and λ): p is used to construct the graph, and λ is used to ensure local invariance. Two more parameters (β and σ) are introduced than GNMF.

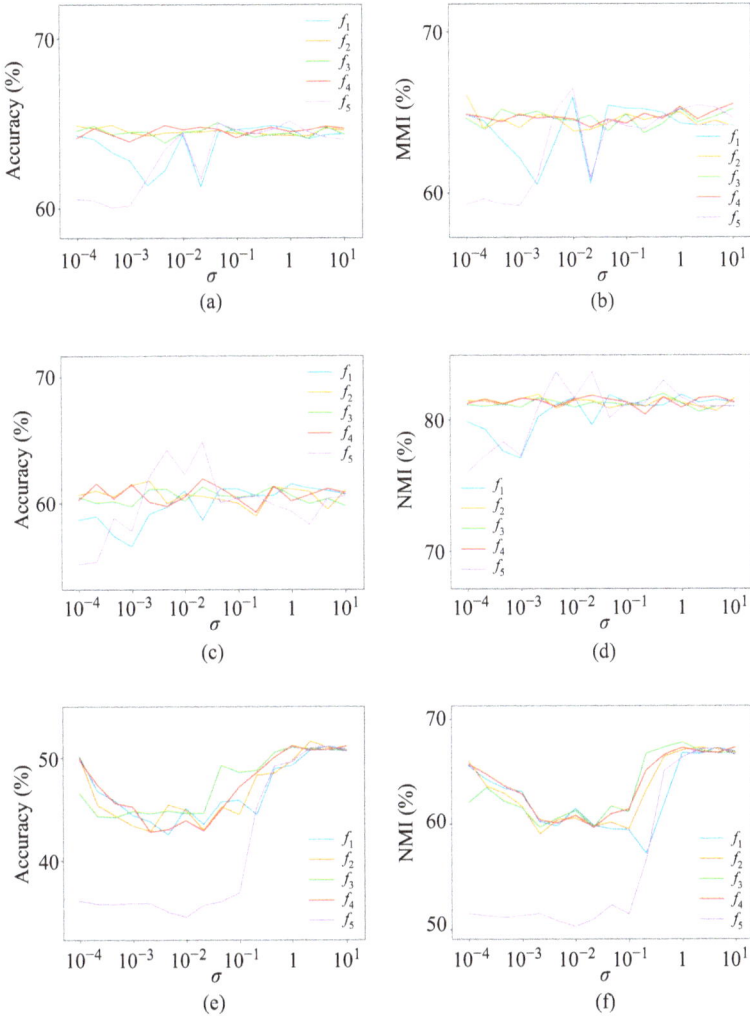

Figure 5.9   *β is set to $\{10^{-3}, 4 \times 10^{-3}, 7 \times 10^{-3}, 10^{-2}, \ldots, 100\}$ to show the effect on accuracy and NMI (a) Accuracy of USPS, (b) NMI of USPS, (c) Accuracy of USPS, (d) NMI of UMIST, (e) Accuracy of LIBRAS, (f) NIMI of LIBRAS*

β is used to ensure the sparsity of the result, and σ is used to ensure that $f(x, \sigma)$ is close to the l_0 norm. The impact of β and σ on performance across different datasets is shown in Figures 5.9 and 5.10. The ACC and NMI plotted in the figure are the mean result of 20 times.

For β, it is shown in Figure 5.9 that performance decreases with larger β on the whole. But, in Figures 5.9(d) and 5.9(b), when $\beta \in (10^{-2}, 10^{-1})$, performance increases with larger β and achieves the best performance.

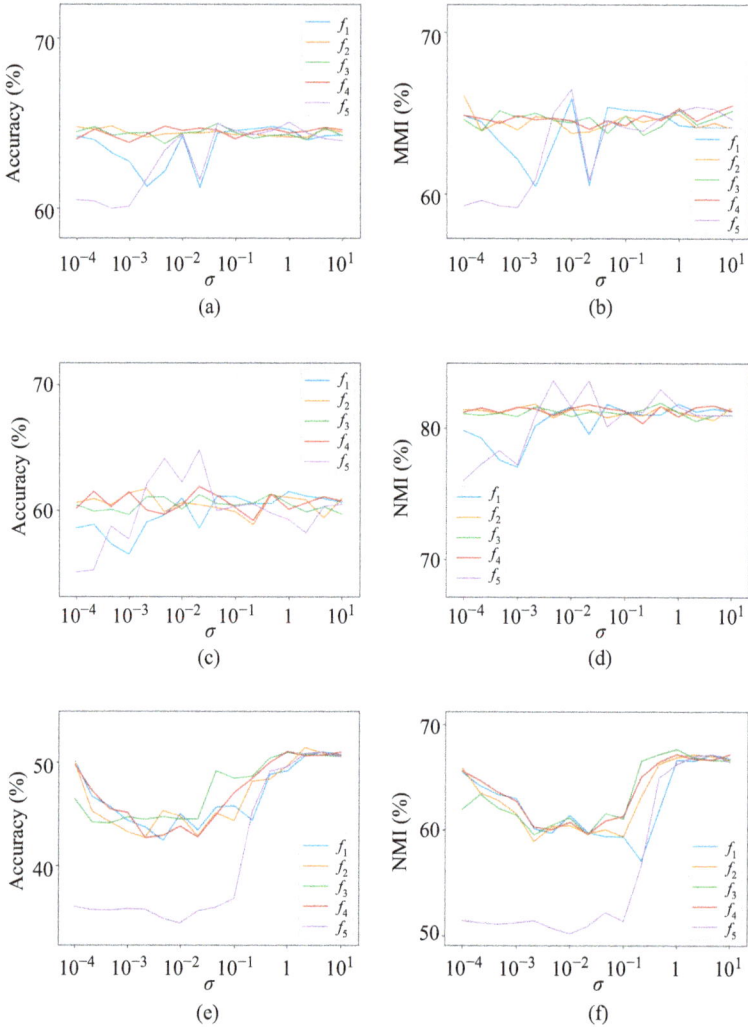

Figure 5.10   σ is set to {10⁻⁴, 4 × 10⁻⁴, 7 × 10⁻⁴, 10⁻³, ..., 10} to show the effect on accuracy and NMI (a) Accuracy of USPS, (b) NMI of USPS, (c) ACC of UMIST, (d) NMI of UMIST, (e) Accuracy of LIBRAS, (f) NIMI of LIBRAS

For σ, it is shown in Figures 5.10(e) and 5.10(f) that when $\sigma \in [10^{-4}, 10^{-3}]$ or $\sigma \in [1, 10]$, better performance can be obtained. When $\sigma \in [10^{-4}, 1]$, SGNMF with f_5 performs much worse. Similarly, in Figures 5.10(a)–5.10(d), when $\sigma \in [10^{-4}, 10^{-1}]$, SGNMF with f_5 performs much worse, but SGNMF with f_5 attains the best performance when σ is set to an appropriate value in these figures, such as $\sigma = 1$ in Figure 5.10(a), $\sigma = 10^{-2}$ in Figure 5.10(b), and $\sigma = 4 \times 10^{-2}$ in Figures 5.10(c) and 5.10(d). In summary, when using SGNMF with f_5, σ can be set within $(10^{-2}, 10^{-1})$

or larger than 1. For f_1, f_2, f_3, and f_4, it is better to set σ to larger than 1 or smaller than 10^{-2}.

5.4   Chapter summary

In this chapter, SGNMF is formulated as a global optimization problem using the sum of the different smooth functions to approximate the l_0 norm. A general algorithm with guaranteed convergence is designed. The clustering results on five public datasets show that the proposed approach can enhance robustness of GNMF with high sparsity.

References

[1]   Mohimani H., Babaie-Zadeh M., Jutten C.: "A fast approach for overcomplete sparse decomposition based on smoothed l_0 norm." *IEEE Trans. Signal Process.* 2008;57(1):289–301.

[2]   Guo Z., Wang J.: "A neurodynamic optimization approach to constrained sparsity maximization based on alternative objective functions." in *The 2010 International Joint Conference Neural Networks (IJCNN)*; 2010. pp. 1–8.

[3]   Wang L., Ye P., Xiang J.: "A modified algorithm based on smoothed L_0 norm in compressive sensing signal reconstruction." in *2018 25th IEEE International Conference on Image Process. (ICIP)*; 2018. pp. 1812–16.

[4]   Xiang J., Yue H., Yin X. Ruan G.: "A reweighted symmetric smoothed function approximating L_0-norm regularized sparse reconstruction method." *Symmetry.* 2018;10(11):583.

[5]   Cai D., He X., Han J., Huang T.S: "Graph regularized nonnegative matrix factorization for data representation." *IEEE Trans. Pattern Anal. Mach Intell.* 2011;33(8):1548–60.

[6]   Boutsidis C., Gallopoulos E.: "SVD based initialization: A head start for nonnegative matrix factorization." *Pattern Recognit.* 2008;41(4):1350–62.

[7]   Dua D., Graff C.: UCI Machine Learning Repository; 2017.

[8]   Huang HC., Chuang Y. Y., Chen C. S.: "Affinity aggregation for spectral clustering." in *2012 IEEE Conference on Computer Vision and Pattern Recognition*; 2012. pp. 773–80.

[9]   Du L., Zhou P., Shi L., *et al.*: "Robust Multiple Kernel K-Means Using $L_{2,1}$-Norm." in *Proceedings of the 24th International Conference on Artificial Intelligence, IJCAI*; 2015. pp. 3476–82.

[10] Rodriguez A., Laio A.: "Clustering by fast search and find of density peaks." *Science.* 2014;344(6191):1492–96.

[11] Peharz R., Pernkopf F.: "Sparse nonnegative matrix factorization with l_0-constraints." *Neurocomputing.* 2012;80:38–46 Special Issue on Machine Learning for Signal Processing 2010.

Chapter 6
Self-paced regularized matrix factorization for clustering

Non-negative matrix factorization (NMF) is a popular approach to extract intrinsic features from the original data. Due to the non-convexity of NMF formulation, it always leads to degrade the performance. To alleviate the defect, in this chapter, self-paced regularization is introduced to find better factorized matrices by sequentially selecting data in the learning process. Additionally, to find the low-dimension manifold embedded in the high-dimension space, an adaptive graph is introduced using dynamic neighbors assignment. An alternating iterative algorithm is designed to solve the proposed factorization mathematical formulation. Experimental results are given to show the effectiveness of the proposed approach in comparison with state-of-the-art algorithms on six public datasets.

6.1 Preliminaries

6.1.1 Self-paced non-negative matrix factorization

Self-paced learning (SPL) is proposed to learn a weight variable $w = [w_1, \cdots, w_1]^T$ and the model parameter θ. The objective function of SPL [1] is as follows:

$$\min_{\theta, w} J(\theta, w; \eta) = \sum_{i=1}^{n} w_i l_i + f(\eta, w), \tag{6.1}$$

where l_i denotes the reconstruction error of the ith sample, which is computed by a loss function, and θ is the model parameter of the loss function. η denotes a regular term coefficient. Traditional SPL usually lets $w \in \{0, 1\}^n$ and defines $f(\eta, w)$ as

$$f(\eta, w) = -\eta \sum_{i=1}^{n} w_i, \tag{6.2}$$

and the optimal w^* can be calculated by

$$w_i^* = \begin{cases} 1, & \text{if } l_i < \eta \\ 0, & \text{otherwise.} \end{cases} \tag{6.3}$$

η is used to determine which data points are selected for training. If the value of η is small, the objective function optimization process tends to choose data points with small loss values. As the number of iterations increases, the value of η is increased. Therefore, the process of SPL can be understood as starting with a small number of "simple" data points and gradually selecting more data points until all the data points are selected into the model.

To realize the advantages of SPL, in [1], a novel NMF model called SPLNMF is proposed by minimizing the following objective:

$$\min_{A,B,w} \left\| \text{diag}(w) \left(X - AB^T\right) \right\|_{2,1} + f(\eta, w)$$
$$\text{s.t.} \quad A \geq 0, B \geq 0, B^T B = I, w \in [0,1]^n, \tag{6.4}$$

where $\text{diag}(w)$ denotes a diagonal matrix with the ith diagonal element w_i. Equation (6.4) can be reformulated by optimizing the problem as follows:

$$\min_{A,B,w} \sum_{i=1}^{n} d_i \left\| x_i - Ab_i \right\|_2^2 + f(\eta, w)$$
$$\text{s.t.} \quad A \geq 0, B \geq 0, B^T B = I, w \in [0,1]^n, \tag{6.5}$$

where

$$d_i = \frac{w_i}{2 \left\| x_i - Ab_i \right\|}. \tag{6.6}$$

With simple algebra, (6.5) can be written as

$$\min_{A,B,w} \text{tr}\left(\left(X - AB^T\right) D \left(X - AB^T\right)^T \right) + f(\eta, w)$$
$$\text{s.t.} \quad A \geq 0, B \geq 0, B^T B = I, w \in [0,1]^n, \tag{6.7}$$

where D is the diagonal matrix, and $D_{ii} = d_i$.
In [1], a novel SPL regularization term is utilized.

$$f(\eta, w) = -\sum_{i=1}^{n} \zeta \ln(w_i + \zeta/\eta), \tag{6.8}$$

the optimal w^* can be computed by

$$w_i^* = \begin{cases} 1, & \text{if } l_i \leq \zeta\eta/(\zeta + \eta) \\ 0, & \text{if } l_i \geq \eta \\ \zeta/l_i - \zeta/\eta, & \text{otherwise.} \end{cases} \tag{6.9}$$

It is clear that (6.9) is a soft weighting strategy, and ζ can be set to 0.5η for simplicity in experiments.

Meanwhile, in [1], an iterative updating algorithm is proposed to optimize the objective function, and it is proven that the value of the objective function is nonincreasing under the updating rules.

$$A_{ij} \leftarrow A_{ij} \sqrt{\frac{(XDB)_{ij}}{(AB^T DB)_{ij}}}. \tag{6.10}$$

$$B_{ij} \leftarrow B_{ij} \sqrt{\frac{(DX^TA)_{ij}}{(DBB^TX^TA)_{ij}}}. \tag{6.11}$$

6.1.2   The assignment of adaptive neighbors

NMF or SPLNMF may mislead the factorization because data graphs used in these studies are usually constructed by the k-nearest neighbors (KNN), which has a problem that the nearest neighbors may belong to different clusters. In [2], a method to solve the above problem is proposed by exploring the local connectivity of the data.

Given a data matrix $X \in \mathbb{R}^{m \times n}$, let $B \in \mathbb{R}^{n \times c}$ be a low-dimensional matrix. For each data point data point x_i, S_{ij} denotes the probability of all the data point x_j connected to x_i as a neighbor. The smaller distance $\|x_i - x_j\|_2^2$ is, the larger the probability S_{ij} will be. The problem can be formulated as follows:

$$\min_{S,B} \mu \sum_{i,j=1}^{n} \left(\|x_i - x_j\|_2^2 S_{ij} + \gamma S_{ij}^2 \right) + \lambda \operatorname{tr} \left(B^T L_S B \right) \tag{6.12}$$

$$\text{s.t.} \quad s_i^T \mathbf{1} = 1, \ 0 \leq s_i \leq 1, \ B \geq 0,$$

$$\min_{S} \mu \sum_{i,j=1}^{n} \left(\|x_i - x_j\|_2^2 S_{ij} + \gamma S_{ij}^2 \right) + \frac{\lambda}{2} \sum_{i,j=1}^{n} \|b_i - b_j\|_2^2 S_{ij} \tag{6.13}$$

where γ, λ, and μ are positive regularization parameters balancing the reconstruction error of clustering, $L_s = D_s - W_s$ is called the Laplacian matrix in the graph theory, where W_s is the symmetric similarity matrix and $W_s = \frac{S+S^T}{2}$, and the degree matrix $D_s \in \mathbb{R}^{n \times n}$ is defined as a diagonal matrix, where the ith diagonal element is $(D_s)_{ii} = \sum_j (W_s)_{ij}$.

6.2   Main result

Considering that exploring the local connectivity of data is a successful strategy for clustering task, we incorporate adaptive neighbors methodology into the SPLNMF model called SPLNMFAN. It ensures that the neighbors assignment is an adaptive process and alleviates the non-convexity of the NMF model.

6.2.1   Proposed model

The objective function of SPLNMFAN can be obtained by combining (6.4) with (6.12) as follows:

$$\min_{S,A,B,w} \mu \sum_{i,j=1}^{n} \left(\|x_i - x_j\|_2^2 S_{ij} + \gamma S_{ij}^2 \right) + \lambda \operatorname{tr} \left(B^T L_S B \right)$$
$$+ \left\| \operatorname{diag}(w) \left(X - AB^T \right) \right\|_{2,1} + f(\eta, w) \tag{6.14}$$

$$\text{s.t.} \quad s_i^T \mathbf{1} = 1, 0 \leq s_i \leq 1, \ A \geq 0, \ B \geq 0, B^T B = I, \ w \in [0,1]^n.$$

Note that $l_{2,1}$ norm is used to measure the cost of factorization to guarantee the robustness of the algorithm. Meanwhile, the function enforces the orthogonal constraint on B, which can guarantee the uniqueness of the solution and make the clustering results easier to interpret. The SPL regularization term $f(\eta, w)$ is the same as (6.8), employing the soft weighting strategy.

According to [1], (6.14) can be written as

$$
\min_{S,A,B,w} \mu \sum_{i,j=1}^{n} \left(\|x_i - x_j\|_2^2 S_{ij} + \gamma S_{ij}^2 \right) + \lambda \operatorname{tr} \left(B^T L_S B \right)
$$
$$
+ \operatorname{tr} \left(\left(X - AB^T \right) D \left(X - AB^T \right)^T \right) + f(\eta, w)
\tag{6.15}
$$

s.t. $s_i^T \mathbf{1} = 1, 0 \le s_i \le 1, A \ge 0, B \ge 0, B^T B = I, w \in [0,1]^n.$

The first two items of the model are adaptive neighbors regularization, while the last term of the model is SPL regularization. SPLNMFAN eventually converts the input X to B, which can be regarded as the local structure preservation of X. Meanwhile, the ith row of B can be regarded as the low-dimensional representation of the ith data point with respect to the new basis A. In this process, the probability matrix S is proposed, and we assume that the data points with smaller distance are more likely to become neighbors. Based on the local distance, the adaptive optimal neighbor learning data is allocated for each data point, which improves the robustness of the model. Furthermore, with the participation of SPL methodology, the proposed model starts with a small number of "simple" data points and gradually selects more data points until all the data points are selected into the model. This strategy, which is similar to curriculum learning, alleviates the non-convexity of the NMF model.

6.2.2 Optimization algorithm

In (6.15), variables w, A, B, and S should be optimized with respect to one variable while fixing the other variables. As the SPL regularization term $f(\eta, w)$ is the same as (6.8), w can be computed by (6.9). Furthermore, note that the updating rule of A is the same as SPLNMF, and A can be updated by (6.10).

- **Updating S with fixed A and B:**

  Optimizing (6.15) w.r.t. S is equal to solving the problem as follows:

  $$
  \min_S \sum_{i,j=1}^{n} \left(\|x_i - x_j\|_2^2 S_{ij} + \gamma S_{ij}^2 \right) + \bar{\lambda} \operatorname{tr} \left(B^T L_S B \right)
  \tag{6.16}
  $$

  s.t. $s_i^T \mathbf{1} = 1, \quad 0 \le s_i \le 1$

  where $\bar{\lambda} = \frac{\lambda}{\mu}$. According to [2], the problem (6.16) can be written as

  $$
  \min_{s_i^T \mathbf{1}=1, 0 \le s_i \le 1} \left\| s_i + \frac{1}{2\gamma} d_i \right\|_2^2,
  \tag{6.17}
  $$

  where $d_{ij}^x = \|x_i - x_j\|_2^2$, $d_{ij}^b = \frac{1}{2} \|b_i - b_j\|_2^2$, and $d_i \in \mathbb{R}^{n \times 1}$ is a vector with the jth element as $d_{ij} = d_{ij}^x + \bar{\lambda} d_{ij}^b$.

Nie *et al.* [3] has proved that (6.17) can be solved with a closed-form solution. Without loss of generality, supposed $d_{i1}^x, d_{i2}^x, \cdots, d_{in}^x$ are ordered from small to large. If the optimal s_i has only k nonzero elements, then we have

$$\mathbf{S}_{ij} = \begin{cases} -\frac{1}{2\gamma}d_{ik}^x + \eta > 0 \\ -\frac{1}{2\gamma}d_{i,k+1}^x + \eta \leq 0. \end{cases} \tag{6.18}$$

To obtain an optimal solution s_i to the problem (6.17) that has exact k nonzero values, we could set γ_i to be

$$\gamma_i = \frac{k}{2}d_{i,k+1}^x - \frac{1}{2}\sum_{j=1}^{k} d_{ij}^x. \tag{6.19}$$

The overall γ could be set to the mean of $\gamma_1, \gamma_2, \cdots, \gamma_n$, i.e.,

$$\gamma = \frac{1}{n}\sum_{i=1}^{n}\left(\frac{k}{2}d_{i,k+1}^x - \frac{1}{2}\sum_{j=1}^{k} d_{ij}^x\right). \tag{6.20}$$

The number of neighbors k is much easier to tune than the regularization parameter γ as k is an integer and has explicit meaning.

- **Updating B with fixed w, S and A:**
  When w, S, and A are fixed, optimizing (6.15) w.r.t. V is equivalent to minimizing

$$\text{tr}\left((X - AB^T) D (X - AB^T)^T\right) + \lambda \text{tr}(B^T L_S B) \tag{6.21}$$
$$\text{s.t.} \quad B \geq 0, B^T B = I.$$

With simple algebra, (6.21) can be written as

$$\text{tr}(XDX^T) - 2\text{tr}(XDBA^T) + \text{tr}(AB^T DBA^T)$$
$$+\lambda \text{tr}(B^T L_S B) \tag{6.22}$$
$$\text{s.t. } B \geq 0, B^T B = I.$$

Let ϕ and ψ be the Lagrange multiplier for constraints $B \geqslant 0$ and $B^T B = I$, respectively. Thus the Lagrange function is

$$J_2 = \text{tr}(XDX^T) - 2\text{tr}(XDBA^T) + \text{tr}(AB^T DBA^T)$$
$$+ \text{tr}(\Phi B^T) + \text{tr}\left(\Psi (B^T B - I)^T\right) + \lambda \text{tr}(B^T L_S B). \tag{6.23}$$

The partial derivation of J_2 w.r.t. B is

$$\frac{\partial J_2}{\partial B} = 2\lambda L_S B - 2DX^T A + 2DBA^T A + 2B\Psi + \Phi. \tag{6.24}$$

Setting $\frac{\partial J_1}{\partial A} = 0$, substituting $\Psi = -B^T DBA^T A + B^T DX^T A - B^T \lambda L_S B$, and using the (KKT) conditions [4] $\phi_{ij}B_{ij} = 0$, we have the following updating rule:

$$B_{ij} \leftarrow B_{ij}\sqrt{\frac{(DX^T A + \lambda W_S B)_{ij}}{(DBB^T X^T A + \lambda BB^T W_S B)_{ij}}}. \tag{6.25}$$

The whole algorithm of SPLNMFAN is described in Algorithm 1.

Algorithm 1 SPLNMFAN

Input: X: data matrix $X \in \mathbb{R}^{m \times n}$, where n is the number of data points and m is the
    data dimension; Number of clusters c; Controlling parameters k, λ, μ, η;
Output: matrix B;
 1: Initialize matrices B and A
 2: **repeat**
 3:     **Step 1:** Fix B, A and S, update w according to Eq. (6.9)
 4:     **repeat**
 5:         **Step 2:** Fix w, update B, A and S
 6:         Update each row of S by solving the problem Eq. (6.17)
 7:         Update D by Eq. (6.6): $d_i = \frac{w_i}{2\|x_i - Ab_i\|}$.
 8:         Update A by Eq. (6.10): $A_{ij} \leftarrow A_{ij}\sqrt{\frac{(XDB)_{ij}}{(AB^TDB)_{ij}}}$.
 9:         Update B by Eq. (6.25): $B_{ij} \leftarrow B_{ij}\sqrt{\frac{(DX^TA + \lambda W_s B)_{ij}}{(DBB^TX^TA + \lambda BB^TW_s B)_{ij}}}$.
10:     **until** convergence
11:     **until** All the instances are chosen

6.2.3   *Complexity analysis*

Here, we discuss the computational cost of NMF [5], $l_{2,1}$-NMF [6], NMFAN [2], SPLNMF [1], and our proposed method. The computational cost is recorded in Table 6.1.

The overall time cost for NMF is $O(mnct)$, where n denotes the number of data points, m denotes the number of features, t is the number of iterations, and c denotes the number of clusters. The overall time cost for $l_{2,1}$-NMF is $O(mn^2t)$. The overall time cost for NMFAN is $O(cn^2t)$. The overall time cost for SPLNMF is $O(mn^2tp)$, where p is the number of SPL steps for selecting the data points into the factorization process. While the overall computational cost of SPLNMFAN is $O(n^3tp)$. Generally speaking, m is smaller than n, so the computational cost of SPLNMFAN is higher than SPLNMF. However, the clustering performance of SPLNMFAN is better than that of SPLNMF, which can be seen in experiments.

6.3   Convergence analysis

In this section, the convergence of the iterative updating algorithm is investigated. Previous works have demonstrated the effectiveness of SPL in various models [7], [8]. Furthermore, (6.17) can be solved with a closed-form solution, which has been proved in [3]. The updating rule of A is the same as SPLNMF, and the nonincreasing property of the updating is proven in [1].

Thus, we only need to prove the value of the objective function in (6.15) is nonincreasing under the updating rules in (6.25) for each iteration. Specifically, the

Table 6.1 *Algorithm complexity analysis*

Methods	Variables	Addition	Multiplication	Division	Overall
NMF [5]	A	$3mnct$	$3mnct + mct$	mct	$O(mnct)$
	B	$3mnct$	$3mnct + nct$	nct	$O(mnct)$
$l_{2,1}$-NMF [6]	A	$2mn^2t + 3mnct$	$2mn^2t + 3mnct + mct$	mct	$O(mn^2t)$
	B	$2cn^2t + 3mnct$	$2cn^2t + 3mnct + nct$	nct	$O(cn^2t)$
NMFAN [2]	A	$3mnct$	$3mnct + mct$	mct	$O(mnct)$
	B	$3mnct + 2cn^2t$	$3mnct + 2cn^2t + 3nct$	nct	$O(cn^2t)$
SPLNMF [1]	A	$2mn^2tp + 3mnctp$	$2mn^2tp + 3mnctp + mctp$	$mctp$	$O(mn^2tp)$
	B	$2mn^2tp + 2mnctp + cn^2tp + n^2c^2tp$	$2mn^2tp + 2mnctp + cn^2tp + n^2c^2tp + nctp$	$nctp$	$O(mn^2tp)$
SPLNMFAN	A	$2mn^2tp + 3mnctp$	$2mn^2tp + 3mnctp + mctp$	$mctp$	$O(mn^2tp)$
	B	$2mn^2tp + 2mnctp + 3cn^2tp + 2n^2c^2tp + n^3tp$	$2mn^2tp + 2mnctp + 3cn^2tp + 2n^2c^2tp + n^3tp + 3nctp$	$nctp$	$O(n^3tp)$

auxiliary function [5] is used to prove the convergence. Here, we first introduce the definition of an auxiliary function.

Definition 1. *[5] $X(h, h')$ can be defined as an auxiliary function for $Y(h)$ if the conditions*

$$X(h, h') \geq Y(h), \quad X(h, h) = Y(h), \tag{6.26}$$

are satisfied.

Lemma 1. *If X is an auxiliary function for Y, then Y is nonincreasing under the updating formula as follows:*

$$h^{t+1} = \arg\min_h X(h, h'). \tag{6.27}$$

Proof. $Y(h^{t+1}) \leq X(h^{t+1}, h^t) \leq X(h^t, h^t) = Y(h^t)$ □

According to (6.15), the objective function with fixed w, S, and A can be rewritten as

$$\lambda \operatorname{tr} \left(B^T L_S B \right) + \sum_{i=1}^n d_i \|x_i - Ab_i\|_2^2. \tag{6.28}$$

To prove that the objective in (6.15) is nonincreasing under the updating rule in (6.25), we must prove Lemma 2.

Lemma 2. *Updating B using (6.25) while fixing A, the following inequality holds:*

$$\begin{aligned}
\lambda \operatorname{tr} \left(B^{T(t+1)} L_S B^{(t+1)} \right) &+ \sum_{i=1}^n d_i \left\| x_i - Ab_i^{t+1} \right\|_2^2 \\
&\leq \lambda \operatorname{tr} \left(B^{T(t)} L_S B^{(t)} \right) + \sum_{i=1}^n d_i \left\| x_i - Ab_i^t \right\|_2^2.
\end{aligned} \tag{6.29}$$

Proof.   To prove the constrained problem in Lemma 2, we need to prove the following Lagrangian function:

$$\begin{aligned}
J(B) &= \operatorname{tr} \left(XDX^T - 2XDBA^T \right) + \operatorname{tr} \left(AB^T DBA^T \right) \\
&\quad + \operatorname{tr} \left(\Psi \left(B^T B - I \right)^T \right) + \lambda \operatorname{tr} \left(B^T L_s B \right).
\end{aligned} \tag{6.30}$$

The auxiliary function is as follows:

$$\begin{aligned}
J(B, B') &= \operatorname{tr} \left(XDX^T - \Psi \right) + \sum_{j=1}^c \sum_{i=1}^n \frac{\left(DB'A^T A + B'\Psi \right)_{ij} B_{ij}^2}{B'_{ij}} \\
&\quad - 2 \sum_{j=1}^c \sum_{i=1}^n \left(DX^T A \right)_{ij} B'_{ij} \left(1 + \log \frac{B_{ij}}{B'_{ij}} \right) + \lambda \sum_{j=1}^c \sum_{i=1}^n \frac{\left(L_S B' \right)_{ij} B_{ij}^2}{B'_{ij}}.
\end{aligned} \tag{6.31}$$

As the following equality holds [9],

$$\sum_{i=1}^n \sum_{j=1}^k \frac{\left(AC'B \right)_{ij} C_{ij}^2}{C'_{ij}} \geq \operatorname{tr} \left(C^T AC B \right), \tag{6.32}$$

where A, B, and C are non-negative matrices, and both A and B are symmetric. Furthermore, we know the inequality, $w \geq 1 + \log(w)$ for all $w > 0$. Thus, we have

$$
\begin{aligned}
\operatorname{tr}\left(B^T D B A^T A^T\right) + \operatorname{tr}\left(\Psi B^T B\right) &\leq \sum_{j=1}^{c} \sum_{i=1}^{n} \frac{\left(DB'A^T A\right)_{ij} B_{ij}^2}{B'_{ij}} \\
&+ \sum_{j=1}^{c} \sum_{i=1}^{n} \frac{\left(B'\Psi\right)_{ij} B_{ij}^2}{B'_{ij}} = \sum_{j=1}^{c} \sum_{i=1}^{n} \frac{\left(DB'A^T A + B'\Psi\right)_{ij} B_{ij}^2}{B'_{ij}},
\end{aligned}
\tag{6.33}
$$

and

$$
\sum_{j=1}^{c} \sum_{i=1}^{n} \frac{\left(L_s B'\right)_{ij} B_{ij}^2}{B'_{ij}} \geq \operatorname{tr}\left(B^T L_s B\right).
\tag{6.34}
$$

It can be seen that (6.31) is a valid auxiliary function, and we can find the stationary point of $J\left(B, B'\right)$. As defined in (6.31), taking the derivative of $J\left(B, B'\right)$ w.r.t. B

$$
\frac{\partial J\left(B, B'\right)}{\partial B_{ij}} = 2\frac{\left(DB'A^T A + B'\Psi + \lambda L_s B'\right)_{ij} B_{ij}}{B'_{ij}} - 2\left(DX^T A\right)_{ij} \frac{B'_{ij}}{B_{ij}}.
\tag{6.35}
$$

Setting (6.35) to zero and substituting $\Psi = -B^T D B A^T A + B^T D X^T A - B^T \lambda L_s B$, we have the following stationary point:

$$
B_{ij} \leftarrow B'_{ij} \sqrt{\frac{\left(DX^T A + \lambda W_s B'\right)_{ij}}{\left(DBB^T X^T A + \lambda B' B'^T W_s B\right)_{ij}}}.
\tag{6.36}
$$

To verify that the stationary point is the minimum of $J\left(B, B'\right)$, we need to check that whether the Hessian matrix is a positive semidefinite matrix. Taking the second derivative B

$$
\begin{aligned}
\frac{\partial^2 J\left(B, B'\right)}{\partial B_{ij} \partial B_{kl}} &= \left(2\left(DX^T A\right)_{ij} \frac{B'_{ij}}{B_{ij}^2}\right) \delta_{ik} \delta_{jl} \\
&+ \left(2\frac{\left(DB'A^T A + B'\Psi + \lambda L_s B'\right)_{ij} B_{ij}}{B'_{ij}}\right) \delta_{ik} \delta_{jl}.
\end{aligned}
\tag{6.37}
$$

It is clear that the Hessian matrix is a positive semidefinite matrix, thus indicating that $J\left(B, B'\right)$ is a convex function and the stationary point in (6.36) is the unique global minima of $J\left(B, B'\right)$. According to Lemma 1, Lemma 2 is established. Consequently, Theorem 1 has also been proven. Note that by substituting $B = B^{t+1}$ and $B' = B^t$ into (6.36), we obtain the updating rule in (6.25). $\qquad \square$

Table 6.2   Summary of the datasets

Dataset	# Samples	# Features	# Classes
EOOLDAT	2111	16	7
YALE	165	77760	15
HCVDAT	615	12	5
HFCRDAT	299	12	2
UMIST	564	2576	20
ESDRPDAT	520	15	2

6.4   Experiments

6.4.1   Description of dataset

The information of datasets will be given in the following section, and the summary of the datasets is provided in Table 6.2.

- EOOLDAT:[*] This dataset includes data for the estimation of obesity levels in individuals from the countries of Mexico, Peru, and Colombia, based on their eating habits and physical conditions. The data contains 16 attributes and 2111 records. The records are labeled with the class variable NObesity (Obesity Level), which allows classification of the data using the values of Insufficient Weight, Normal Weight, Overweight Level I, Overweight Level II, Obesity Type I, Obesity Type II, and Obesity Type III.
- YALE:[†] It contains 165 grayscale image of 15 persons, each with different facial expression or configurations. In Figure 6.1, we can see some typical images of YALE.
- HCVDAT:[‡] It is a dataset from the UCI dataset, which consists of 5 classes of 612 instances. The dataset contains laboratory values of blood donors and Hepatitis C patients and demographic values like age.
- HFCRDAT:[§] This dataset contains the medical records of 299 patients with heart failure, collected during their follow-up period, where each patient profile has 12 clinical features.
- UMIST:[|] It consists of 564 images of 20 persons, each shown in a range of poses from profile to frontal views. Each image is resized to 46×56 pixels. In Figure 6.2, we can see some typical images of UMIST.
- ESDRPDAT:[¶] It is a dataset from the UCI dataset, which contains the sign and symptom data of newly diagnosed or would be diabetic patients.

[*] http://archive.ics.uci.edu/ml/datasets/Estimation+of+obesity+levels+based+on+eating+habits+ and+physical+condition+.
[†] http://www.cad.zju.edu.cn/home/dengcai/Data/FaceData.html.
[‡] http://archive.ics.uci.edu/ml/datasets/HCV+data.
[§] http://archive.ics.uci.edu/ml/datasets/Heart+failure+clinical+records.
[|] https://www.visioneng.org.uk/datasets/.
[¶] http://archive.ics.uci.edu/ml/datasets/Early+stage+diabetes+ris +prediction+dataset.

Figure 6.1   Some typical images of YALE

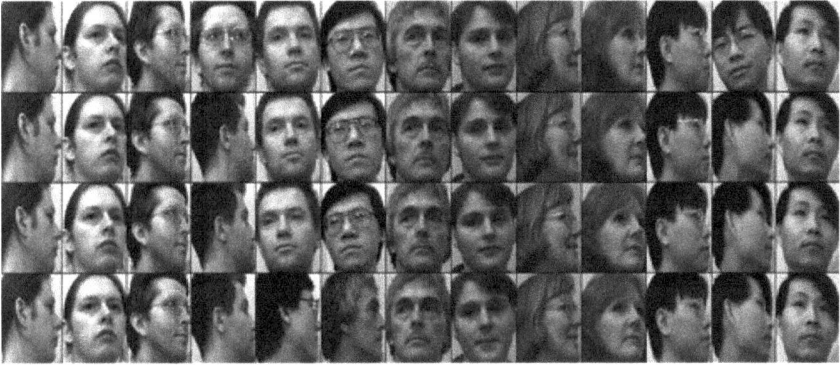

Figure 6.2   Some typical images of UMIST

6.4.2   Evaluation measure

To evaluate the clustering results, three widely used clustering performance measures are adopted. They are accuracy (ACC), normalized mutual information (NMI), and Purity. The specific definitions of these metrics are summarized as follows:

- Clustering ACC is a metric used to compare the obtained labels with the real labels provided by the data. It can be defined as

$$\text{ACC} = \frac{\sum_{i=1}^{n} \delta\left(s_i, \text{map}\left(r_i\right)\right)}{N}, \tag{6.38}$$

where r_i is the label after clustering, s_i is the real labels provided by the data, n is the sample number. δ is the indicator function, defined as follows:

$$\delta(x, y) = \begin{cases} 1 & \text{if } x = y \\ 0 & \text{otherwise} \end{cases}, \tag{6.39}$$

map represents the reproduction allocation of the best class object to ensure the correctness of statistics, which can generally be realized through the Kuhn–Munkres or Hungarian algorithm.

- NMI is often used in clustering to measure the similarity of two clustering results. It is an important measure of community detection, as it can objectively evaluate the ACC of a community division compared with the standard division. It can be defined as

$$\text{NMI}(X, Y) = \frac{2\text{MI}(X, Y)}{H(X) + H(Y)}, \tag{6.40}$$

where $H(X)$ and $H(Y)$ are the entropies of X and Y, respectively. MI can be obtained from the following formula

$$\text{MI}(X, Y) = \sum_{i=1}^{X} \sum_{j=1}^{Y} P(i,j) \log \left(\frac{P(i,j)}{P(i)P'(j)} \right). \tag{6.41}$$

- Purity is the proportion of correctly clustered samples in the total samples. It can be defined as

$$\text{Purity} = \sum_{i=1}^{K} \frac{m_i}{m} P_i, \tag{6.42}$$

where $p_i = \max(p_{ij})$ and $p_{ij} = \frac{m_{ij}}{m_i}$, m_i is the number of all members in cluster i, and k is the number of cluster.

6.4.3   Compared algorithms

To compare the performance of the proposed approach, we use comparison algorithms as follows:

- K-means [10]: It is the most classic clustering algorithm. The algorithm is a clustering algorithm based on partition. It takes K as the parameter and divides n data objects into K clusters, such that the similarity within clusters is high, and the similarity between clusters is low.
- NMF [5]: NMF is used to extract the features of each sample. Then, K-means is used to get the tag of the sample. When extracting the feature, the number of columns of the basis matrix in NMF is set to the number of items, and the number of iterations of the algorithm is 500.
- KKM (kernel K-means) [11]: The algorithm is almost the same with K-means, but it pays more attention on the kernel space rather than the Euclidean space.
- PALM-NMF [12]: The algorithm is an NMF method based on PALM for clustering. PALM is a minimization scheme for convex functions with non-differentiable constraints to solve the NMF problem with solutions that can be smooth and sparse.
- $l_{2,1}$-KKM [13]: The algorithm improves the performance of KKM using the $l_{2,1}$-norm.
- CANFS [14]: It is an UFS method via a convex non-negative matrix factorization (NMF) with an adaptive graph constraint.

- NMFAN [2]: The algorithm is an NMF method with adaptive neighbors for clustering.
- SPLNMF [1]: It is an NMF method based on SPL for clustering.

6.4.4 Parameter setting

To investigate the experimental results in terms of ACC, NMI, and Purity under different parameter settings, the results under different parameter settings are recorded. The parameter k is determined by the grid $\{5, 6, 7, 8, 9, 10\}$. When the value of k is varied, we set the value of λ to 1 and keep the other parameters constant. The regularization parameters λ are set by search the grid $\{0.01, 0.1, 1, 10, 50, 100, 500, 1000\}$. When the value of λ is varied, we set the value of k to 10 and keep the other parameters constant.

As shown in Figures 6.3–6.8, SPLNMFAN changes slightly with k and λ. It can be seen that, after adjusting parameters, the clustering results of SPLNMFAN are better than other algorithms.

Remark. As other comparison algorithms have no parameters k and λ, the curves are flat and shown as the baseline for comparison in the figures.

As described in Section 2.2, we increase the parameter η to select more instances to the process of SPL. In the first iteration, we set η such that half of the instances are selected. Then, η is increased such that 10% more data points is added in every following iteration. In addition, to investigate the experimental results under different ratios of added instances in each iteration, we show the experimental results in terms of ACC, NMI and Purity on dataset HCVDAT and ESDRPDAT under different ratios of added instances (5%, 10%, 25%, and 40%). Other datasets usually lead to similar tendency.

As shown in Figure 6.9, the clustering performance of SPLNMFAN generally decreases with a gradual increase in ratio of added instances in each iteration. Furthermore, the clustering results of SPLNMFAN are always better than NMF, which proves that the SPL strategy can improve the performance.

6.4.5 Clustering results

In the comparison experiments, the component number is set to the number of clusters for each dataset. To be fair, we use our algorithm under different parameter settings. Each parameter setting clusters on a dataset for 20 times, and the best average result is recorded for comparison. Furthermore, each compared algorithm clusters on a dataset for 20 times too, and the means of the ACC, NMI, and Purity are given.

The clustering results are recorded in Tables 6.3–6.5, where the best means of ACC, NMI, and Purity are highlighted in bold. The clustering results are analyzed as follows:

- ACC: On EOOLDAT, KKM performs best and SPLNMFAN is the second best algorithm. On UMIST, SPLNMF performs best and SPLNMFAN is the second best algorithm. SPLNMFAN performs best on YALE, HCVDAT, HFCRDAT and ESDRPDAT.

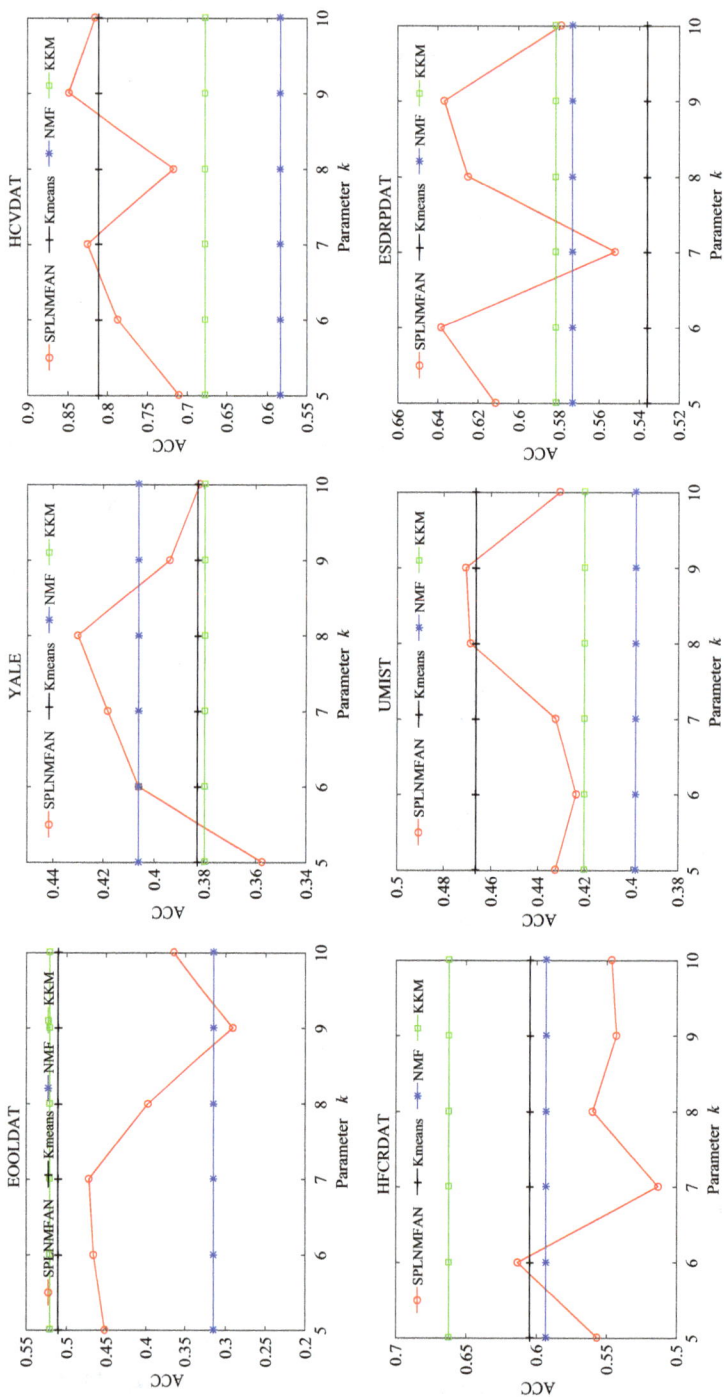

Figure 6.3   ACC with respect to the regularization parameter k

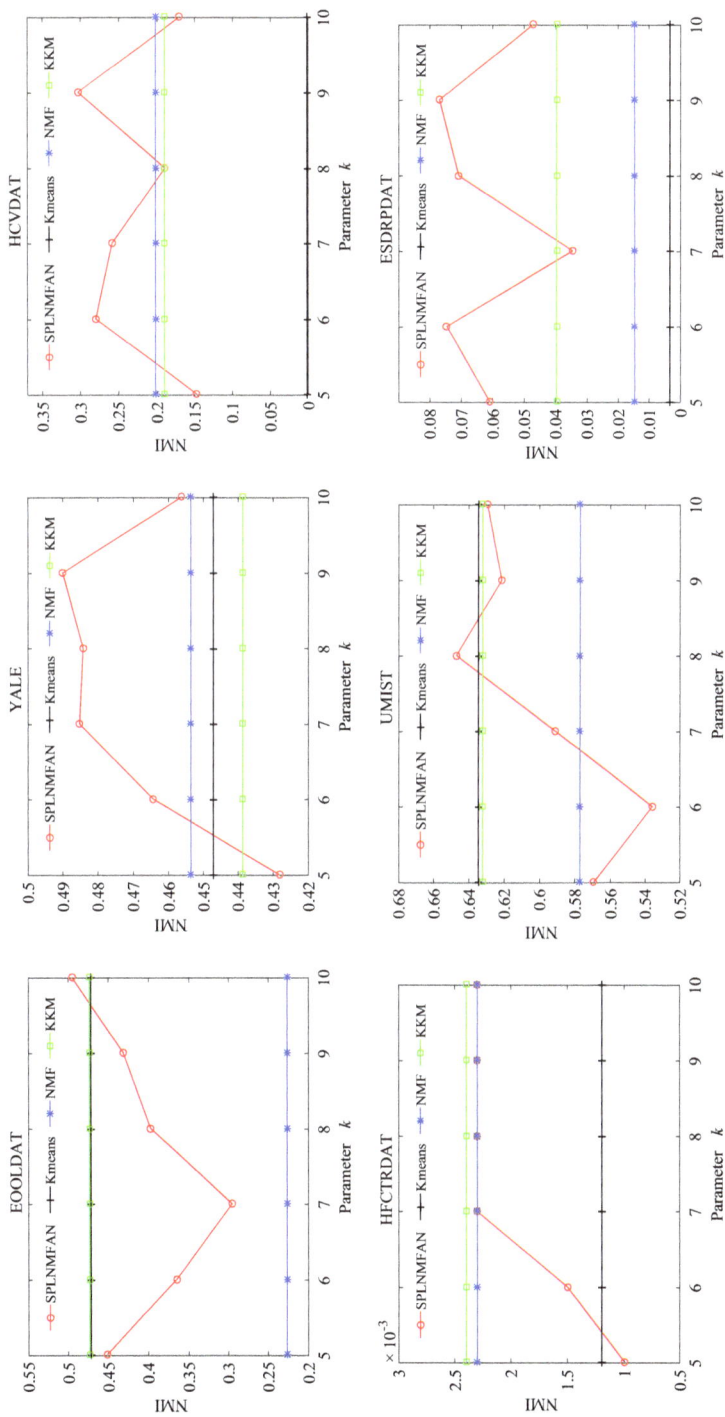

Figure 6.4   NMI with respect to the regularization parameter k

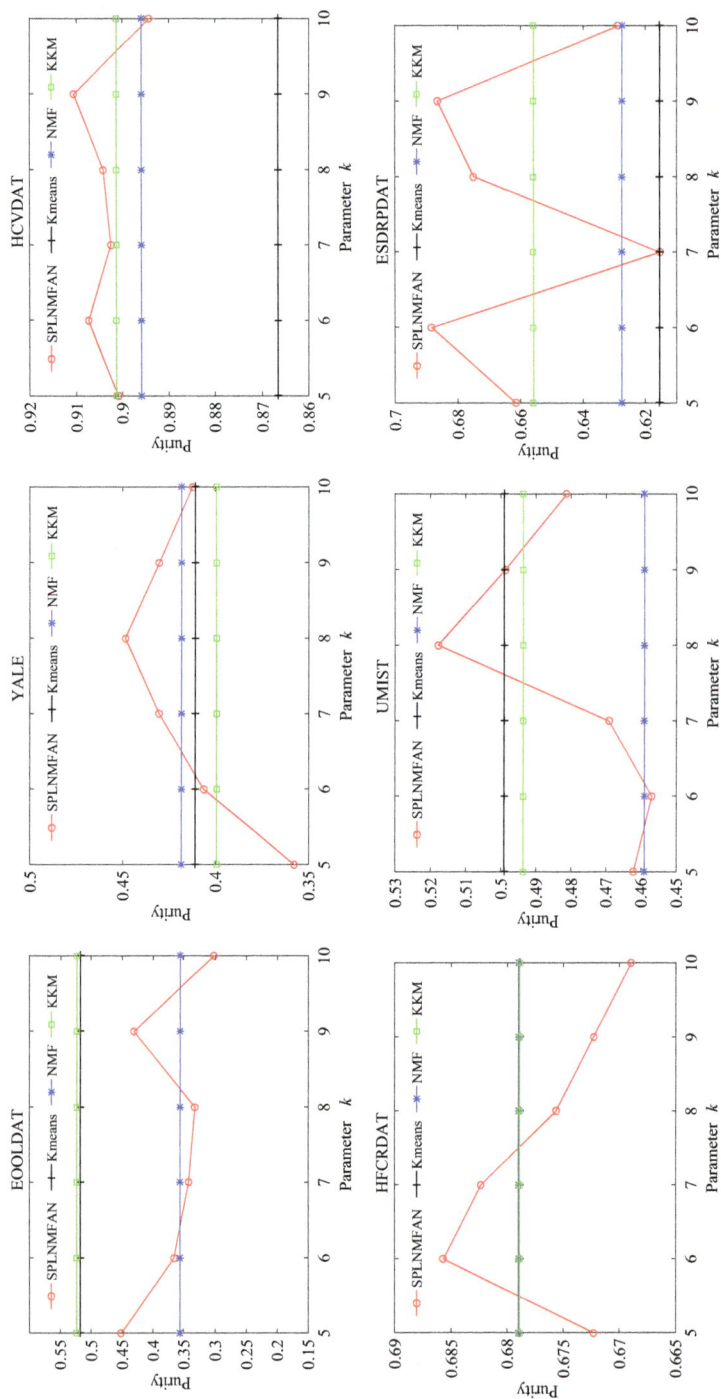

Figure 6.5   Purity with respect to the regularization parameter k

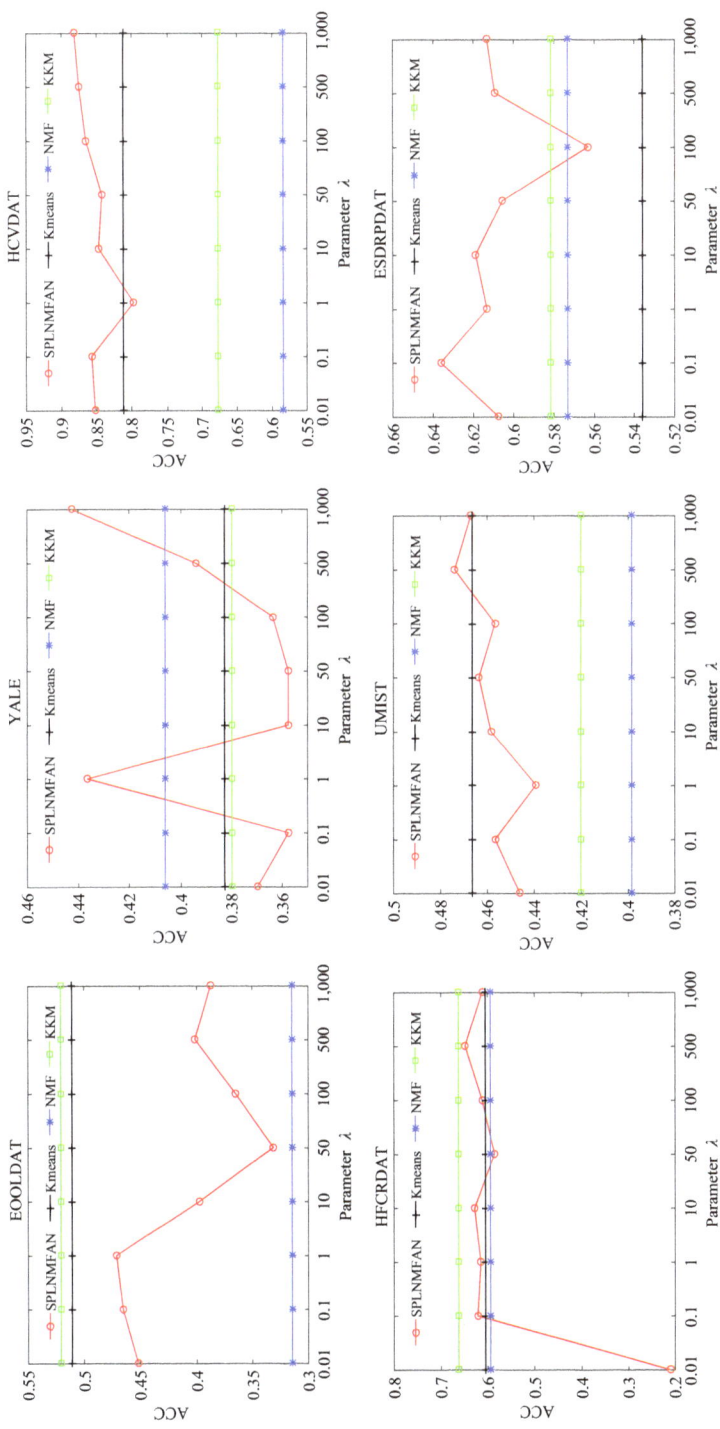

Figure 6.6   ACC with respect to the regularization parameter λ

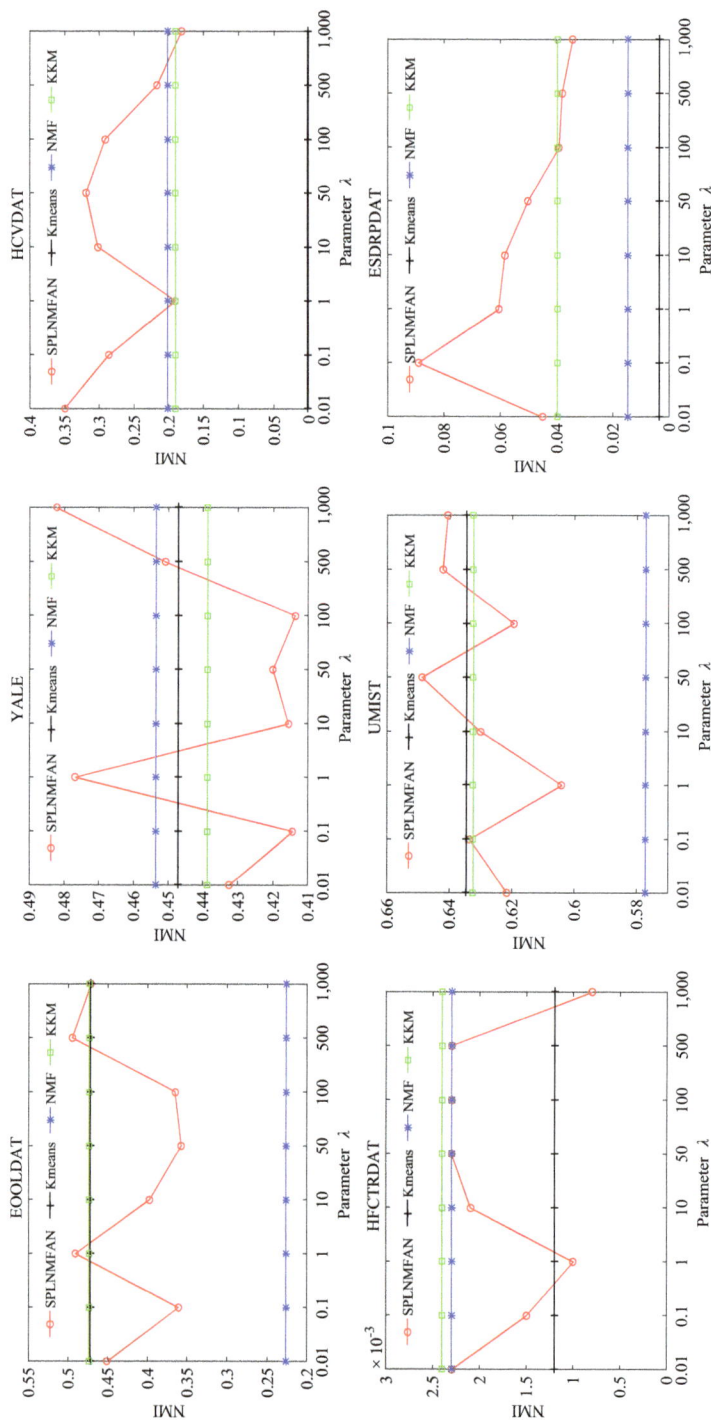

Figure 6.7 NMI with respect to the regularization parameter λ

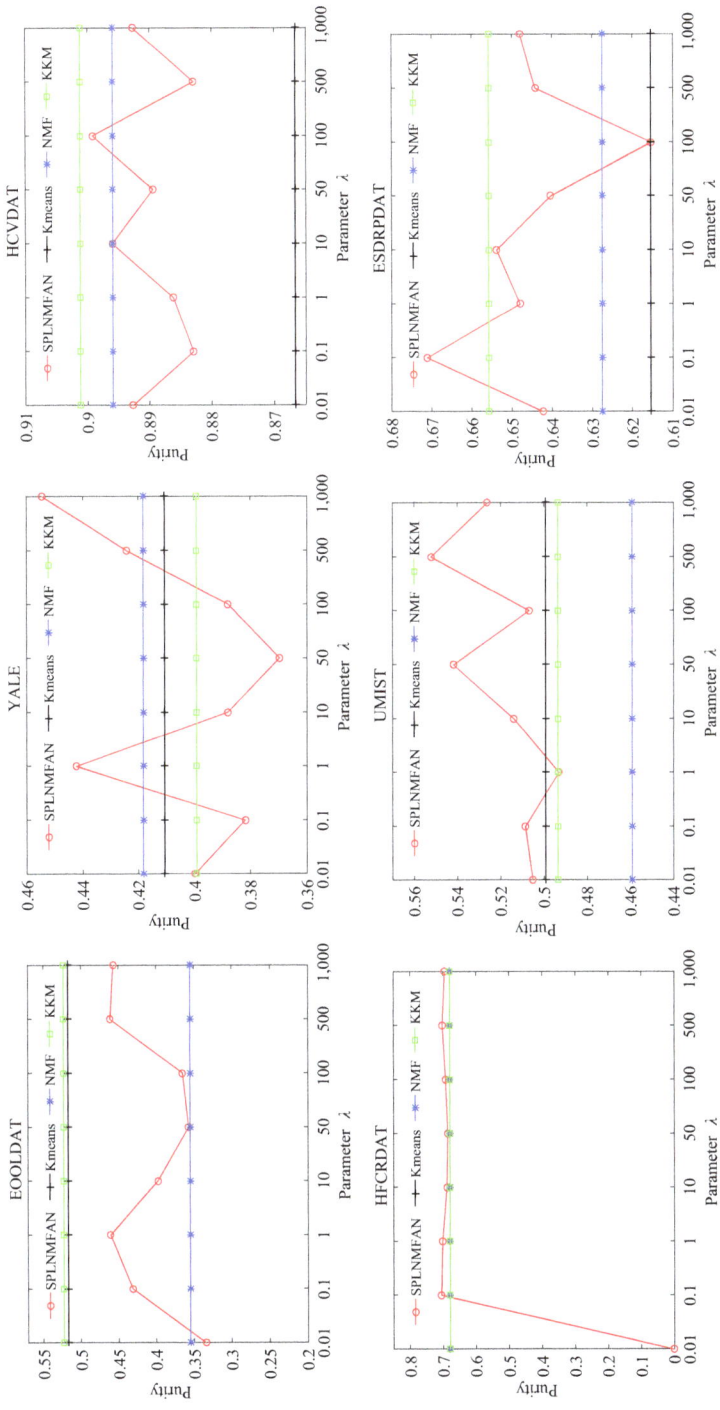

Figure 6.8 Purity with respect to the regularization parameter λ

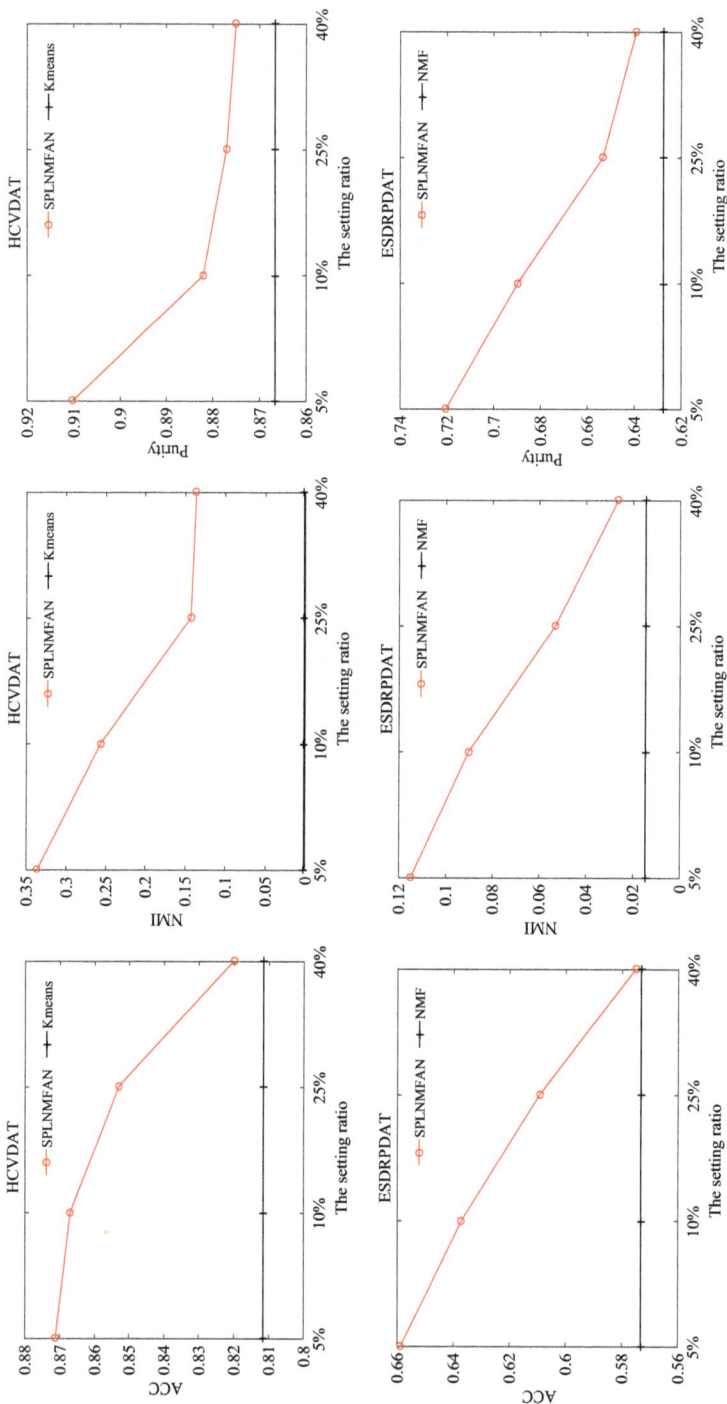

Figure 6.9 Clustering results with respect to different ratios of added instances in each iteration

Table 6.3   Clustering results measured by ACC

Dataset	K-means	NMF [10]	KKM [5]	PALM-NMF [11]	$l_{2,1}$-KKM [12]	CANFS [13]	NMFAN [14]	SPLNMF [2]	SPLNMFAN [1]
EOOLDAT	0.5111	0.3143	**0.5210**	0.4789	0.5012	0.3674	0.4612	0.4535	0.4712
YALE	0.3827	0.4061	0.3798	0.4121	0.3861	0.3879	0.4242	0.4213	**0.4401**
HCVDAT	0.8116	0.5837	0.6769	0.8394	0.8211	0.8211	0.8211	0.8593	**0.8712**
HFCRDAT	0.6050	0.5933	0.6622	0.5886	0.6289	0.5719	0.5886	0.6725	**0.6823**
UMIST	0.4664	0.3983	0.4202	0.4209	0.4241	0.3992	0.4673	**0.4931**	0.4799
ESDRPDAT	0.5358	0.5732	0.5815	0.5615	0.6221	0.5603	0.6173	0.6036	**0.6372**

Table 6.4   Clustering results measured by NMI

Dataset	K-means	NMF [10]	KKM [5]	PALM-NMF [11]	$l_{2,1}$-KKM [12]	CANFS [13]	NMFAN [14]	SPLNMF [2]	SPLNMFAN [1]
EOOLDAT	0.4717	0.2267	0.4735	0.4930	0.4573	0.3135	0.4728	0.4796	**0.4952**
YALE	0.4471	0.4536	0.4387	0.4593	0.4436	0.4432	0.4935	0.4756	**0.4966**
HCVDAT	0.0017	0.2021	0.1902	0.3128	0.1622	0.0026	0.2542	0.3016	**0.3499**
HFCRDAT	0.0012	0.0023	0.0024	0.0021	**0.0027**	0.0112	0.0019	0.0017	0.0023
UMIST	0.6346	0.5772	0.6324	0.6209	0.6327	0.5983	0.6890	**0.7132**	0.6516
ESDRPDAT	0.0034	0.0147	0.0397	0.0172	0.0398	0.0836	0.0822	0.0515	**0.0902**

Table 6.5   Clustering results measured by Purity

Dataset	K-means	NMF [10]	KKM [5]	PALM-NMF [11]	$l_{2,1}$-KKM [12]	CANFS [13]	NMFAN [14]	SPLNMF [2]	SPLNMFAN [1]
EOOLDAT	0.5171	0.3553	**0.5230**	0.5088	0.4712	0.3721	0.4924	0.4013	0.4614
YALE	0.4106	0.4182	0.3992	0.4424	0.4046	0.3939	0.4364	0.4271	**0.4576**
HCVDAT	0.8667	0.8959	0.9012	0.9024	0.9010	0.8728	0.9006	0.8862	**0.9102**
HFCRDAT	0.6789	0.6790	0.6789	0.6789	0.6790	0.6789	0.6789	0.6789	**0.6790**
UMIST	0.4991	0.4591	0.4936	4957	0.4937	0.5132	0.5183	0.5403	**0.5565**
ESDRPDAT	0.6154	0.6276	0.6558	0.6154	0.6542	0.6012	0.6672	0.6154	**0.6897**

- NMI: On HFCRDAT, $l_{2,1}$-KKM performs best and SPLNMFAN is the third best algorithm. On UMIST, SPLNMF performs best and SPLNMFAN is the third best algorithm. SPLNMFAN performs best on EOOLDAT, YALE, HCVDAT, and ESDRPDAT.
- Purity: On EOOLDAT, KKM performs best and SPLNMFAN is the fifth best algorithm. SPLNMFAN performs best on the other five datasets.

It can be seen that our method is very competitive, compared with other eight algorithms.

Table 6.6   Clustering results measured by ACC/NMI/Purity of EOOLDAT

Metric	ACC	NMI	Purity
Baseline	0.3923	0.3608	0.4129
+Adaptive neighbors	0.4416	0.4618	**0.5016**
+Self-paced learning	0.4535	0.4796	0.4013
SPLNMFAN	**0.4712**	**0.4952**	0.4614

Table 6.7   Clustering results measured by ACC/NMI/Purity of HCVDAT

Metric	ACC	NMI	Purity
Baseline	0.5613	0.1816	0.8576
+Adaptive neighbors	0.8211	0.2892	0.8972
+Self-paced learning	0.8593	0.3016	0.8862
SPLNMFAN	**0.8712**	**0.3499**	**0.9102**

Table 6.8   Clustering results measured by ACC/NMI/Purity of HFCRDAT

Metric	ACC	NMI	Purity
Baseline	0.6273	0.0023	0.6790
+Adaptive neighbors	0.6501	0.0023	0.6789
+Self-paced learning	0.6725	0.0017	0.6789
SPLNMFAN	**0.6823**	**0.0023**	**0.6790**

6.4.6   Ablation experiment

The proposed algorithm can be considered as a combination of $l_{2,1}$-NMF [6], adaptive neighbors regularization, and SPL regularization. To determine which component is related to the improvement of clustering performance, we conducted ablation studies on EOOLDAT, HCVDAT, and HFCRDAT.

$l_{2,1}$-NMF is used as the "Baseline" for the ablation experiment. The row "+Adaptive neighbors" lists the result of the direct combination of $l_{2,1}$-NMF and adaptive neighbors regularization. The row "+Self-paced learning" lists the result of SPLNMF [1], which is the direct combination of $l_{2,1}$-NMF and SPL regularization. Finally, the results of SPLNMFAN are listed for comparison with the other two algorithms.

The clustering results are recorded in Tables 6.6–6.8, where the best results of ACC, NMI, and Purity are highlighted in bold. It can be seen that both "+Adaptive neighbors" and "+Self-paced learning" perform better than $l_{2,1}$-NMF, and SPLN-MFAN perform better than the others in most cases. Thus, we know that both adaptive neighbors regularization and SPL regularization contribute to $l_{2,1}$-NMF's

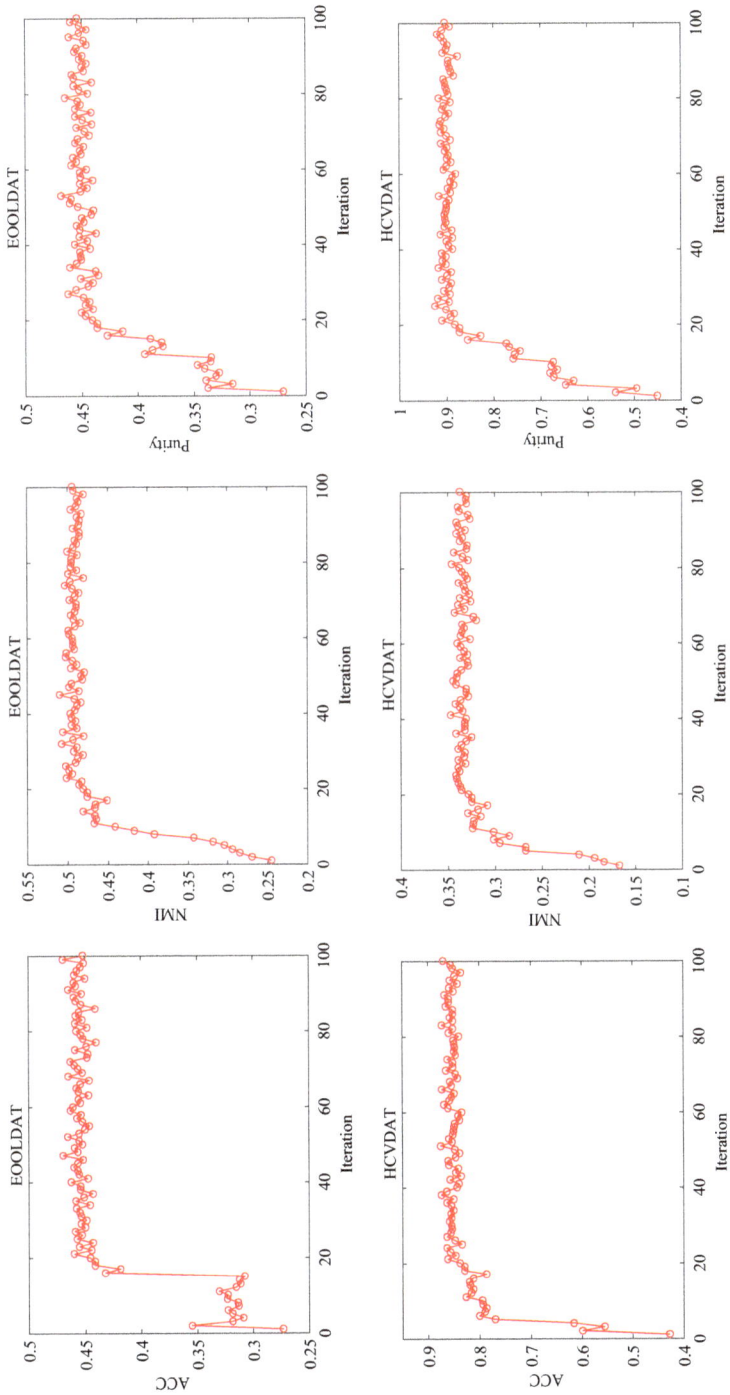

Figure 6.10 Convergence results of SPLNMFAN

performance improvement. SPLNMFAN's superior performance is the result of the combination of them.

6.4.7   Convergence curve of SPLNMFAN

In Section 6.4, the convergence of the iterative updating algorithm is proved theoretically. To show the convergence of the proposed algorithm more intuitively, the tendency curves of ACC, NMI, and Purity with respect to iterations for SPLNMFAN are plotted.

Figure 6.10 shows that the clustering results in terms of ACC, NMI, and Purity increase as the number of iterations increases in the first 20 iterations. The result indicates that the iterative updating rules for SPLNMFAN are convergent, and the proposed updating algorithm is effective.

6.5   Chapter summary

In this chapter, SPL and adaptive neighbors methodology are incorporated into the NMF model called SPLNMFAN. The adaptive neighbors can lead a better local structure and ensure that NMF learns parts of objects. Meanwhile, the SPL methodology can also improve the performance. An iterative updating algorithm is presented to solve the optimization problem of our model. The convergence of the alternating optimization rules is also theoretically guaranteed. Experiments on several datasets prove that the proposed method is very competitive.

References

[1]   Huang S., Zhao P., Ren Y., Li T., Xu Z.: "Self-paced and soft-weighted nonnegative matrix factorization for data representation." *Knowl.Based Syst.* 2019;164:29–37.

[2]   Huang S., Xu Z., Kang Z., Ren Y.: "Regularized nonnegative matrix factorization with adaptive local structure learning." *Neurocomputing.* 2020;382: 196–209.

[3]   Nie F., Wang X., Huang H.: "Clustering and projected clustering with adaptive neighbors." *Proceedings of the 20th ACM SIGKDD International Conference on Knowledge Discovery and Data Mining*; 2014.

[4]   Boyd S., Boyd S.P., Vandenberghe L.: *Convex Optimization* (Cambridge: Cambridge University Press; 2004).

[5]   Lee D., Seung H.S.: "Algorithms for non-negative matrix factorization." *Advances in Neural Information Processing Systems 13*; 2000.

[6]   D'iaz A.F, Steele D.: "Analysis of the robustness of NMF algorithms." in *Conference on Robot Learning.* PMLR, 2020, pp. 513–529.

[7]   Klink P., Abdulsamad H., Belousov B., Peters J.: "Self-Paced Contextual Reinforcement Learning." ArXiv. 2019;abs/1910.02826.

[8]   Ren Y., Que X., Yao D,. Xu Z.: "Self-paced multi-task clustering." *Neurocomputing.* 2019;350:212–220.

[9]   Ding C.H.Q., Li T., Jordan M.I.: "Convex and semi-nonnegative matrix factorizations." *IEEE Trans. Pattern Anal. Mach Intell.* 2010;32(1):45–55.

[10]   MacQueen J.: "Some methods for classification and analysis of multivariate observations." in Proceedings of the Fifth Berkeley Symposium on Mathematical Statistics and Probability. Oakland, CA, USA: University of California Press; 1967, Vol. 1. pp. 281–97.

[11]   Zhang R., Rudnicky A.I.: "A large scale clustering scheme for kernel K-means." in *2002 International Conference on Pattern Recognition*; 2002. Vol. 4. pp. 289–92.

[12]   Fabregat R., Pustelnik N., Gonçalves P., Borgnat P.: "Solving NMF with smoothness and sparsity constraints using PALM." ArXiv. 2019;abs/1910.14576.

[13]   Du L., Zhou P., Shi L., *et al.* "Robust multiple kernel k-means using l21-norm." in *Twenty-fourth International Joint Conference on Artificial Intelligence*; 2015.

[14]   Yuan A., You M., He D., Li X.: "Convex Non-Negative Matrix Factorization With Adaptive Graph for Unsupervised Feature Selection." *IEEE Trans. Cybern.* 2022;52:5522–34.

Chapter 7

Centric graph regularized log-norm sparse non-negative matrix factorization for clustering

Multi-view non-negative matrix factorization (NMF) provides a reliable method for analyzing multiple views of data for low-dimensional representation. A variety of multi-view learning methods have been developed in recent years, demonstrating successful applications in clustering. However, existing methods in multi-view learning often tend to overlook the nonlinear relationships among data and the significance of the similarity of internal views, both of which are essential in multi-view tasks. Meanwhile, the mapping between the obtained representation and the original data typically contains complex hidden information that deserves thorough exploration. In this chapter, a novel multi-view NMF is proposed that explores the local geometric structure among multi-dimensional data and learns the hidden representation of different attributes through centric graph regularization and pairwise co-regularization of the coefficient matrix. In addition, the proposed model is further sparsified with the $l_{2,\log}$-(pseudo) norm to efficiently generate sparse solutions. As a result, the model obtains a better parts-based representation, enhancing its robustness and applicability in complex noisy scenarios. An effective iterative update algorithm is designed to solve the proposed model, and the convergence of the algorithm is proven to be theoretically guaranteed. The effectiveness of the proposed method is verified by comparison with nine state-of-the-art methods in clustering tasks of eight public datasets.

7.1 Preliminaries

7.1.1 Propagation regularization

The graph Laplace regularization is widely used for its ability to effectively discover the nonlinear structural information of the data [1]. Moreover, to provide new supervisory signals to the nodes in the graph and supply additional information to improve model reliability, a propagation regularization is proposed based on the graph Laplacian regularization [2]. The propagation regularization is expressed as

$$L_{p-reg} = \frac{1}{q}\phi(V, \hat{A}V) \tag{7.1}$$

where $A = [a_{ij}] \in R^{q \times q}$ is the similarity matrix that describes the degree of similarity between data points, and $\hat{A} = D^{-1}A$ is a normalized similarity matrix, where $D = [d_{ij}] \in R^{q \times q}$ is a diagonal degree matrix with $d_{ij} = \sum_{j=1}^{q} a_{ij}$. $\hat{A}V$ is the further propagated output, and $\phi(V, \hat{A}V)$ is a function to measure the difference between V and $\hat{A}V$ directly. While using squared error as ϕ, denoted as ϕ_{SE}, there is

$$\phi_{SE}(V, \hat{A}V) = \frac{1}{2} \sum_{i=1}^{q} ||(\hat{A}V)_i^T - (V)_i^T||_2^2 = \frac{1}{2} ||\hat{A}V - V||_F^2 \tag{7.2}$$

where $(.)_i^T$ denotes the vector of the ith row in a matrix. $\phi_{SE}(V, \hat{A}V)$ is node-centric, which involves the aggregation of the information from a node's neighbors to serve as supervision targets [2]. This allows each node to acquire additional categorical information from its neighbors, aiding in better determining their positions and roles within the data, particularly in capturing complex nonlinear structures.

7.1.2   Sparsity-induction norm

In NMF, sparse solutions always lead to better parts-based representations and further improve the robustness [3]. Therefore, the $l_{2,1}$ norm with column-wise sparsity is used instead of the l_2 norm, which is the sum of the l_2 norms of all column vectors in the matrix. For a matrix $G = [g_{ij}] \in R^{p \times q}$, it is defined as

$$||G||_{2,1} = \sum_{j=1}^{q} ||g_j||_2. \tag{7.3}$$

However, the $l_{2,1}$ norm and l_1 norm exhibit similar limitations in achieving adequate column sparsity [4]. Specifically, as the size of the input matrix increases, the approximation error tends to increase, potentially leading to inaccurate approximations and non-optimal solutions. Hence, $||G||_{\log} = \sum_{i=1}^{p} \sum_{j=1}^{q} \log(1 + |g_{ij}|)$ is proposed to enhance the smoothness and reduce solving complexity. It is further extended to the $l_{2,1}$ norm by designing the following novel $l_{2,\log}$-(pseudo) norm:

$$||G||_{2,\log} = \sum_{j=1}^{q} \log(1 + ||g_j||_2). \tag{7.4}$$

In terms of denoising, the $l_{2,\log}$-(pseudo) norm can lead to more sparseness than the $l_{2,1}$ norm [4]. Due to the log-based value being closer to 0 than the l_2-based value, it provides a more accurate approximation of the actual sparsity. To visually compare the robustness of the l_1 norm, l_2 norm, $l_{2,1}$ norm, and $l_{2,\log}$-(pseudo) norm to noise, each norm is used to normalize a matrix with added noise, respectively. The norms-based loss functions are employed to measure the norm value under a certain noise intensity, and the variation of the norm value with noise intensity is shown in Figure 7.1. It can be observed that the $l_{2,\log}$-(pseudo) norm is significantly more robust to noise than the other norms.

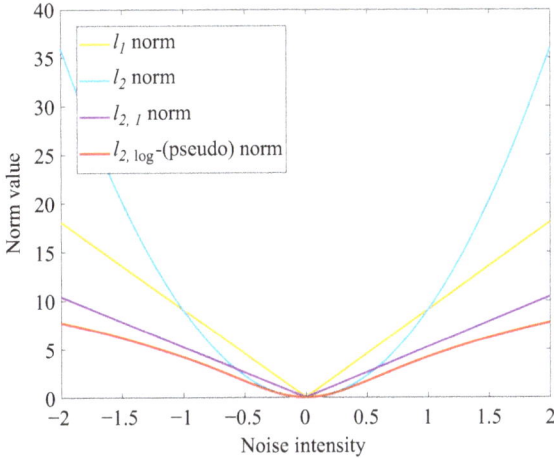

Figure 7.1   Robust performance of the l_1 norm, l_2 norm, $l_{2,1}$ norm, and $l_{2,log}$-(pseudo) norm against noise

7.2   Main results

In this section, the centric graph regularized log-norm sparse NMF for multi-view clustering is formulated as an optimization problem in detail. Then, an iterative algorithm is designed, and its convergence behavior and computational complexity are analyzed.

7.2.1   Centric graph regularized NMF for multi-view clustering

Let $X^{(m)} \in R^{p^{(m)} \times q}$ represent the mth view of the matrix, where $m = 1, 2, \dots, n_m$. The data matrix for each view is factorized into $U^{(m)} \in R^{p^{(m)} \times r}$ and $V^{(m)} \in R^{q \times r}$, which are non-negative low-rank matrices. Thus, the problem of multi-view clustering based on NMF can be described as follows:

$$\min_{U^{(m)}, V^{(m)}} \sum_{m=1}^{n_m} ||X^{(m)} - U^{(m)} V^{(m)^T}||_F^2, \quad \text{s.t.} \quad U^{(m)}, V^{(m)} \geq 0, \ m = 1, \dots, n_m.$$

$$(7.5)$$

To capture the structures among distinct views, pairwise co-regularization is introduced to evaluate the similarity of the coefficient matrices of the paired views [5] [6]. The method aims to minimize $||V^{(m)} - V^{(n)}||_F^2$ for $m, n = 1, \dots, n_m$ and $n \neq m$, to pursue the maximum similarity between $V^{(m)}$ and $V^{(n)}$. Higher coefficient matrix similarity serves as a more important effect in clustering, and the following cost function is adopted to measure the similarity between views:

$$\min_{V^{(m)}} \sum_{m,n=1,n\neq m}^{n_m} ||V^{(m)} - V^{(n)}||_F^2, \quad \text{s.t.} \quad V^{(m)} \geq 0, \; m = 1, \ldots, n_m. \tag{7.6}$$

The similarity of paired views captures the clustering structure and facilitates the parts-based representation. However, it fails to fully consider non-linear associations among data. To solve the problem, a novel graph regularization is designed based on the metric employed by propagation regularization in (7.2), which is named the centric graph regularization. The expression is as follows:

$$\frac{1}{2n_m} \sum_{m=1}^{n_m} ||\hat{A}^{(m)} V^{(m)} - V^{(m)}||_F^2, \quad \text{s.t.} \quad V^{(m)} \geq 0, \; m = 1, \ldots, n_m. \tag{7.7}$$

In the above term, for each mth view, the geometrical information of multi-view data is measured with $\phi_{SE}(V^{(m)}, \hat{A}^{(m)} V^{(m)})$ to obtain information from more distant nodes. In addition, it is normalized by the number of views, which aims to maintain multi-view spatial consistency. By incorporating centric graph regularization and pairwise co-regularization into the multi-view NMF framework, the problem (7.5) is reconstructed as follows:

$$\min_{U^{(m)},V^{(m)}} \sum_{m=1}^{n_m} ||X^{(m)} - U^{(m)} V^{(m)^T}||_F^2 + \beta \sum_{m=1}^{n_m} \sum_{n=1,n\neq m}^{n_m} ||V^{(m)} - V^{(n)}||_F^2$$
$$+ \frac{\gamma}{2n_m} \sum_{m=1}^{n_m} ||\hat{A}^{(m)} V^{(m)} - V^{(m)}||_F^2, \tag{7.8}$$
$$\text{s.t.} \quad U^{(m)}, V^{(m)} \geq 0, \; m = 1, \ldots, n_m$$

where $\beta \geq 0$ and $\gamma \geq 0$ are the balancing parameters, which give the model greater degrees of freedom. The first term in the optimization problem represents multi-view NMF. The second term corresponds to the pairwise co-regularization, which constrains the similarity between distinct views. The last term is the centric graph regularization, which enhances the nonlinear properties of the data within the transformed low-dimensional space while incorporating additional remote node information to facilitate the model in capturing the spatial structure more efficiently.

7.2.2   Problem formulation

Due to the noises in data, sparse representation is needed for enhancing the robustness of the formulation (7.8), and the optimization problem is expanded as:

$$
\min_{U^{(m)},V^{(m)}} \sum_{m=1}^{n_m} ||X^{(m)} - U^{(m)} V^{(m)^T}||_{2,1} + \beta \sum_{m=1}^{n_m} \sum_{n=1,n\neq m}^{n_m} ||V^{(m)} - V^{(n)}||_F^2
$$

$$
+ \frac{\gamma}{2n_m} \sum_{m=1}^{n_m} ||\hat{A}^{(m)} V^{(m)} - V^{(m)}||_F^2, \tag{7.9}
$$

$$
\text{s.t.} \quad U^{(m)}, V^{(m)} \geq 0, \ m = 1, \ldots, n_m
$$

where $||\cdot||_{2,1}$ is the $l_{2,1}$ norm in (7.3). The $l_{2,1}$ norm remains fixed, ensuring the preservation of spatial information in the examples. However, optimizing the $l_{2,1}$ norm under the non-negativity constraint presents significant challenges. To facilitate the optimization process, the data matrix is commonly further factorized considering noise [4]. In the mth dimension, it is factorized as $X^{(m)} = U^{(m)} V^{(m)^T} + S^{(m)}$, where $S^{(m)}$ is a matrix with column-wise sparsity to interpret noise. Based on the above assumption, a closed-form solution is employed [4], and the optimization problem is relaxed as follows:

$$
\min_{U^{(m)},V^{(m)},S^{(m)}} \sum_{m=1}^{n_m} ||(X^{(m)} - S^{(m)}) - U^{(m)} V^{(m)^T}||_F^2 + \alpha \sum_{m=1}^{n_m} ||S^{(m)}||_{2,1}
$$

$$
+ \beta \sum_{m=1}^{n_m} \sum_{n=1,n\neq m}^{n_m} ||V^{(m)} - V^{(n)}||_F^2 + \frac{\gamma}{2n_m} \sum_{m=1}^{n_m} ||\hat{A}^{(m)} V^{(m)} - V^{(m)}||_F^2, \tag{7.10}
$$

$$
\text{s.t.} \quad U^{(m)}, V^{(m)} \geq 0, \ m = 1, \ldots, n_m
$$

where $\alpha \geq 0$ is a balancing parameter. It can be observed that the relaxed function is easier to solve. However, it should be noted that the $l_{2,1}$ norm is computed in a closely related way to the l_1 norm, which sums the l_2 norm of all columns. Therefore it can be judged that the column-wise sparsity property of the $l_{2,1}$ norm has the same problem as the l_1 norm, which means that the regularization may be less efficient in approximating the real sparsity. Therefore, the $l_{2,\log}$-(pseudo) norm begins to be applied, which enhances the column sparsity property and better takes into account the noise impact [4]. The log-norm regularized sparse multi-view NMF model is obtained by utilizing the $l_{2,\log}$-(pseudo) norm in (7.4) to measure the matrix $S^{(m)}$ and is formulated as follows:

$$
\min_{U^{(m)},V^{(m)},S^{(m)}} \sum_{m=1}^{n_m} ||(X^{(m)} - S^{(m)}) - U^{(m)} V^{(m)^T}||_F^2 + \alpha \sum_{m=1}^{n_m} ||S^{(m)}||_{2,\log}
$$

$$
+ \beta \sum_{m=1}^{n_m} \sum_{n=1,n\neq m}^{n_m} ||V^{(m)} - V^{(n)}||_F^2 + \frac{\gamma}{2n_m} \sum_{m=1}^{n_m} ||\hat{A}^{(m)} V^{(m)} - V^{(m)}||_F^2, \tag{7.11}
$$

$$
\text{s.t.} \quad U^{(m)}, V^{(m)} \geq 0, \ m = 1, \ldots, n_m.
$$

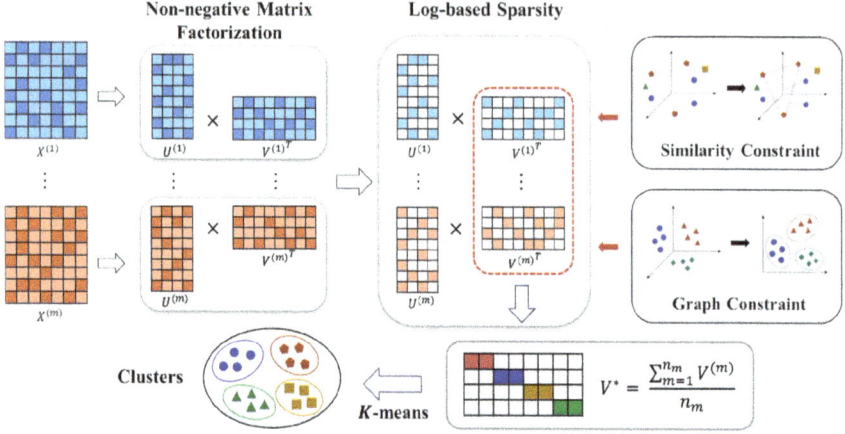

Figure 7.2   *The illustration of the proposed method. First, NMF is performed on the input matrix. Second, a novel graph constraint is applied to the coefficient matrix by centric graph regularization. Third, a similarity constraint is implemented on the coefficient matrix through pairwise co-regularization. Then, the sparseness of factorized matrices is enforced by the $l_{2,\log}$-(pseudo) norm. Finally, clustering results are obtained by performing K-means on the consensus coefficient matrix V^*.*

Since the log-based approximation is closer to 0 than the l_2 norm, the elements of the $S^{(m)}$ matrix contain only essentially small values. It indicates that the matrix $S^{(m)}$ represents noise and is indeed sparse. The flowchart of the proposed method is shown in Figure 7.2.

7.2.3   *The proposed optimization algorithm*

In this section, the optimization problem of the centric graph regularized log-norm sparse NMF for multi-view clustering is addressed.

7.2.3.1 $S^{(m)}$ **minimization**

In the mth dimension, $m = 1, \ldots, n_m$, for the minimization problem of the matrix $S^{(m)}$, the sub-problem is

$$\min_{S^{(m)}} ||(X^{(m)} - S^{(m)}) - U^{(m)} V^{(m)^T}||_F^2 + \alpha ||S^{(m)}||_{2,\log}. \tag{7.12}$$

According to the $l_{2,\log}$ shrinkage operator theorem [4], in the mth dimension, given the matrix $H^{(m)} = X^{(m)} - U^{(m)} V^{(m)^T}$ and the non-negative parameter $\sigma = \frac{\alpha}{2}$, the problem is converted as follows:

$$\min_{S^{(m)}} \frac{1}{2} ||H^{(m)} - S^{(m)}||_F^2 + \sigma ||S^{(m)}||_{2,\log}. \tag{7.13}$$

The closed-form solution of $s_i^{(m)}$ is

$$s_i^{(m)} = \begin{cases} \frac{\psi}{||h_i^{(m)}||_2} h_i^{(m)}, & \text{if } f_i^{(m)}(\psi) \leq \frac{1}{2}||h_i^{(m)}||_2^2, \ (1+||h_i^{(m)}||_2)^2 > 4\sigma, \ \psi > 0 \\ 0, & \text{otherwise,} \end{cases}$$

(7.14)

where $f_i^{(m)}(t) = \frac{1}{2}(t - ||h_i^{(m)}||_2)^2 + \sigma \log(1+t)$ and $\psi = \frac{||h_i^{(m)}||_2 - 1}{2} + \sqrt{\frac{(1+||h_i^{(m)}||_2)^2}{4} - \sigma}$.

7.2.3.2 Lagrange function construction

In the optimization problem (7.11), fixing $S^{(m)}$ and considering $U^{(m)}$ and $V^{(m)}$, the associated sub-problem of each view is formulated as follows:

$$\min_{U^{(m)}, V^{(m)}} ||(X^{(m)} - S^{(m)}) - U^{(m)} V^{(m)^T}||_F^2 + \beta \sum_{n=1, n \neq m}^{n_m} ||V^{(m)} - V^{(n)}||_F^2$$

$$+ \frac{\gamma}{2n_m} ||\hat{A}^{(m)} V^{(m)} - V^{(m)}||_F^2,$$

(7.15)

s.t. $U^{(m)}, V^{(m)} \geq 0, \ m = 1, \ldots, n_m.$

Previous study has shown that all columns of $X^{(m)} - S^{(m)}$ are the non-negative values, so the matrix $X^{(m)} - S^{(m)}$ is non-negative [4]. Therefore, the variables can be updated iteratively using the multiplication strategy. Let $\delta^{(m)} = [\delta_{ij}^{(m)}]$ and $\eta^{(m)} = [\eta_{ij}^{(m)}]$ be the Lagrange multipliers of constraints $U^{(m)} \geq 0$ and $V^{(m)} \geq 0$, respectively. The following Lagrange function L is obtained according to problem (7.15):

$$L = \mathrm{tr}((X^{(m)} - S^{(m)})(X^{(m)} - S^{(m)})^T - 2U^{(m)} V^{(m)^T} (X^{(m)} - S^{(m)})^T$$

$$+ U^{(m)} V^{(m)^T} V^{(m)} U^{(m)^T}) + \beta \sum_{n=1, n \neq m}^{n_m} \mathrm{tr}(V^{(n)} V^{(n)^T} - 2V^{(n)} V^{(m)^T} + V^{(m)} V^{(m)^T})$$

$$+ \frac{\gamma}{2n_m} \mathrm{tr}(\hat{A}^{(m)} V^{(m)} V^{(m)^T} \hat{A}^{(m)^T} - 2V^{(m)} V^{(m)^T} \hat{A}^{(m)^T} + V^{(m)} V^{(m)^T})$$

$$+ \mathrm{tr}(\delta^{(m)} U^{(m)}) + \mathrm{tr}(\eta^{(m)} V^{(m)}).$$

(7.16)

The iterative updating of U and V is discussed in the subsequent content.

7.2.3.3 Fix $V^{(m)}$ and update $U^{(m)}$

Let the partial derivative of L with regard to $U^{(m)}$ be 0, which gives

$$\delta^{(m)} = 2(X^{(m)} - S^{(m)})V^{(m)} - 2U^{(m)} V^{(m)^T} V^{(m)}.$$

(7.17)

Following the Karush–Kuhn–Tucker (KKT) condition [7] $\delta_{ij}^{(m)} u_{ij}^{(m)} = 0$, the equation is rewritten as:

$$(2(X^{(m)} - S^{(m)})V^{(m)} - 2U^{(m)} V^{(m)^T} V^{(m)})u_{ij}^{(m)} = 0.$$

(7.18)

Then, we can obtain the updating rule of $u_{ij}^{(m)}$:

$$u_{ij}^{(m)} \leftarrow u_{ij}^{(m)} \frac{((X^{(m)} - S^{(m)})V^{(m)})_{ij}}{(U^{(m)} V^{(m)^T} V^{(m)})_{ij}}. \tag{7.19}$$

7.2.3.4   Fix $U^{(m)}$ and update $V^{(m)}$

Let the partial derivative of L with regard to $V^{(m)}$ be 0, which gives

$$\eta^{(m)} = 2(X^{(m)} - S^{(m)})^T U^{(m)} - 2V^{(m)} U^{(m)^T} U^{(m)} + 2\beta \sum_{n=1, n \neq m}^{n_m} V^{(n)} \tag{7.20}$$
$$- 2\beta(n_m - 1)V^{(m)} - \frac{\gamma}{n_m}(\hat{A}^{(m)^T} \hat{A}^{(m)} V^{(m)} - 2\hat{A}^{(m)^T} V^{(m)} + V^{(m)}).$$

Equivalently make $\eta_{ij}^{(m)} v_{ij}^{(m)} = 0$, the following equation for $v_{ij}^{(m)}$ is obtained:

$$(2(X^{(m)} - S^{(m)})^T U^{(m)} - 2V^{(m)} U^{(m)^T} U^{(m)} + 2\beta \sum_{n=1, n \neq m}^{n_m} V^{(n)} \tag{7.21}$$
$$- 2\beta(n_m - 1)V^{(m)} - \frac{\gamma}{n_m}(\hat{A}^{(m)^T} \hat{A}^{(m)} V^{(m)} - 2\hat{A}^{(m)^T} V^{(m)} + V^{(m)}))v_{ij}^{(m)} = 0.$$

The following updating rule is derived:

$$v_{ij}^{(m)} \leftarrow v_{ij}^{(m)} \frac{((X^{(m)} - S^{(m)})^T U^{(m)} + \beta \sum_{n=1, n \neq m}^{n_m} V^{(n)} + \frac{\gamma}{n_m} \hat{A}^{(m)^T} V^{(m)})_{ij}}{(V^{(m)} U^{(m)^T} U^{(m)} + \beta(n_m - 1)V^{(m)} + \frac{\gamma}{2n_m}(\hat{A}^{(m)^T} \hat{A}^{(m)} V^{(m)} + V^{(m)}))_{ij}}. \tag{7.22}$$

Algorithm 1 summarizes the optimization process with the convergence condition defined as iter $\leq k_{\max}$, where iter represents the number of iterations, and $k_{\max}$ is the maximum allowed number of iterations.

7.2.4   Convergence analysis

In (7.15), the second and third terms relate only to $V^{(m)}$. Moreover, it is known that $X^{(m)} - S^{(m)}$ is non-negative if the initial values of $U^{(m)}$ and $V^{(m)}$ are non-negative. Therefore, the update formula for $U^{(m)}$ is treated in the method the same as in [8] by replacing $X^{(m)}$ with $X^{(m)} - S^{(m)}$. Now, it needs to be shown that the objective function of (7.15) is nonincreasing under the updating rule (7.22). Following the proof in [8], an auxiliary function is first defined as follows:

Definition 1. *If the functions $G(v, v')$ and $F(v)$ satisfy the following conditions:*

$$G(v, v') \geq F(v), \quad G(v, v) = F(v), \tag{7.23}$$

$G(v, v')$ is an auxiliary function of $F(v)$.

Algorithm 1 The description of the proposed multi-view clustering algorithm

---

Input:

Multi-view datasets $X^{(1)}, X^{(2)}, \ldots, X^{(n_m)}$.

Balancing parameters α, β, γ.

Maximum iteration k_{max}.

1: **for** $m = 1$ to n_m **do**
2:     Normalize $X^{(m)}$.
3:     Initialize $U^{(m)}, V^{(m)}, S^{(m)}$.
4: **end for**
5: **while** *iter* $\leq k_{max}$ **do**
6:     **for** $m = 1$ to n_m **do**
7:         Fix $V^{(m)}$, update $U^{(m)}$ by Eq. (7.19).
8:         Fix $U^{(m)}$, update $V^{(m)}$ by Eq. (7.22).
9:     **end for**
10: **end while**
11: Calculate the consensus coefficient matrix by $V^* = \frac{\sum_{m=1}^{n_m} V^{(m)}}{n_m}$.

Output:

Consensus coefficient matrix V^*. Execute K-means on V^* to accomplish clustering.

Lemma 1. *When $G(v, v')$ is an auxiliary function of $F(v)$, optimize the variable v according to the following rule:*

$$v^{t+1} = \arg \min_v G(v, v'), \tag{7.24}$$

and $F(v)$ is nonincreasing.

Proof. The proof can be easily verified via following inequalities:

$$F(v^{t+1}) \leq G(v^{t+1}, v^t) \leq G(v^t, v^t) = F(v^t). \tag{7.25}$$

The next step is to construct a suitable auxiliary function such that the updating rule in (7.22) is equivalent to the update step in (7.24). The objective function of problem (7.15) is expressed in the following component form:

$$O_m = ||(X^{(m)} - S^{(m)}) - U^{(m)} V^{(m)^T}||_F^2 + \beta \sum_{n=1, n \neq m}^{n_m} ||V^{(m)} - V^{(n)}||_F^2$$

$$+ \frac{\gamma}{2n_m} ||\hat{A}^{(m)} V^{(m)} - V^{(m)}||_F^2$$

$$= \sum_{i=1}^{p^{(m)}} \sum_{j=1}^{q} \left(x_{ij}^{(m)} - s_{ij}^{(m)} - \sum_{k=1}^{r} u_{ik}^{(m)} v_{kj}^{(m)} \right)^2 + \beta \sum_{n=1, n \neq m}^{n_m} \sum_{j=1}^{q} \sum_{k=1}^{r} (v_{jk}^{(m)} - v_{jk}^{(n)})^2$$

$$+ \frac{\gamma}{2n_m} \sum_{j=1}^{q} \sum_{k=1}^{r} (\hat{a}_{jj}^{(m)} v_{jk}^{(m)} - v_{jk}^{(m)})^2. \tag{7.26}$$

Given an element $v_{ab}^{(m)}$ in $V^{(m)}$, $F_{ab}^{(m)}$ represents the part of (7.16) that is only relevant to $v_{ab}^{(m)}$. The first- and second-order derivatives of $F_{ab}^{(m)}$ with respect to $v_{ab}^{(m)}$ can be obtained directly:

$$F_{ab}' = \left(\frac{\partial O_m}{\partial V^{(m)}}\right)_{ab} = (-2(X^{(m)} - S^{(m)})^T U^{(m)} + 2V^{(m)} U^{(m)^T} U^{(m)})_{ab}$$

$$+ 2\beta((n_m - 1)V^{(m)} - \sum_{n=1,n\neq m}^{n_m} V^{(n)})_{ab} \tag{7.27}$$

$$+ \frac{\gamma}{n_m}(\hat{A}^{(m)^T}\hat{A}^{(m)} V^{(m)} - 2\hat{A}^{(m)^T} V^{(m)} + V^{(m)})_{ab},$$

$$F_{ab}'' = \left(\frac{\partial F_{ab}^{(m)'}}{\partial V^{(m)}}\right)_{ab} = (2U^{(m)^T} U^{(m)})_{bb} + (2\beta(n_m - 1) + \frac{\gamma}{n_m})I_{bb}$$

$$+ \frac{\gamma}{n_m}(\hat{A}^{(m)^T}\hat{A}^{(m)} - 2\hat{A}^{(m)^T})_{aa}. \tag{7.28}$$

As the updates are element-wise, it is adequate to establish that $F_{ab}^{(m)}$ remains nonincreasing under the updating rule presented in (7.22). $\qquad\square$

Lemma 2. *The function*

$$G(v^{(m)}, v_{ab}^{(m)^t}) = F_{ab}(v_{ab}^{(m)^t}) + F_{ab}'(v_{ab}^{(m)^t})(v^{(m)} - v_{ab}^{(m)^t})$$

$$+ \frac{(V^{(m)} U^{(m)^T} U^{(m)})_{ab} + (\beta(n_m - 1) + \frac{\gamma}{2n_m})V_{ab}^{(m)} + \frac{\gamma}{2n_m}(\hat{A}^{(m)^T}\hat{A}^{(m)} V^{(m)})_{ab}}{v_{ab}^{(m)^t}}$$

$$(v^{(m)} - v_{ab}^{(m)^t})^2$$

$$\tag{7.29}$$

is an auxiliary function of F_{ab}. It is a component of O_m and only relevant for $v_{ab}^{(m)}$.

Proof.   It is obvious that $G(v^{(m)}, v^{(m)}) = F_{ab}(v^{(m)})$. Therefore, it is only necessary to prove that $G(v^{(m)}, v^{(m)^t}) \geq F_{ab}(v^{(m)})$. The Taylor series expansion of $F_{ab}(v^{(m)})$ is

$$F_{ab}(v^{(m)}) = F_{ab}(v_{ab}^{(m)^t}) + F_{ab}'(v^{(m)} - v_{ab}^{(m)^t}) + F_{ab}''(v^{(m)} - v_{ab}^{(m)^t})^2. \tag{7.30}$$

Substituting (7.27) and (7.28) into (7.30), the proof of $G(v^{(m)}, v^{(m)^t}) \geq F_{ab}(v^{(m)})$ can be reformulated as the demonstration of the following inequality:

$$\frac{(V^{(m)} U^{(m)^T} U^{(m)})_{ab} + (\beta(n_m - 1) + \frac{\gamma}{2n_m})V_{ab}^{(m)} + \frac{\gamma}{2n_m}(\hat{A}^{(m)^T}\hat{A}^{(m)} V^{(m)})_{ab}}{v_{ab}^{(m)^t}}$$

$$\geq (U^{(m)^T} U^{(m)})_{bb} + \left(\beta(n_m - 1) + \frac{\gamma}{2n_m}\right)I_{bb} + \frac{\gamma}{2n_m}\left(\hat{A}^{(m)^T}\hat{A}^{(m)} - 2\hat{A}^{(m)^T}\right)_{aa}. \tag{7.31}$$

As a result, there are

$$(V^{(m)}U^{(m)^T}U^{(m)})_{ab} = \sum_{k=1}^{r} v_{ak}^{(m)^t}(U^{(m)^T}U^{(m)})_{kb} \geq v_{ab}^{(m)^t}(U^{(m)^T}U^{(m)})_{bb}, \quad (7.32)$$

$$\left(\beta(n_m - 1) + \frac{\gamma}{2n_m}\right)V_{ab}^{(m)} = \left(\beta(n_m - 1) + \frac{\gamma}{2n_m}\right)\sum_{j=1}^{q} v_{aj}^{(m)^t}I_{jb}$$

$$\geq v_{ab}^{(m)^t}\left(\beta(n_m - 1) + \frac{\gamma}{2n_m}\right)I_{bb} \quad (7.33)$$

and

$$\frac{\gamma}{2n_m}(\hat{A}^{(m)^T}\hat{A}^{(m)}V^{(m)})_{ab} = \frac{\gamma}{2n_m}\sum_{j=1}^{q}(\hat{A}^{(m)^T}\hat{A}^{(m)})_{aj}v_{jb}^{(m)^t}$$

$$\geq \frac{\gamma}{2n_m}(\hat{A}^{(m)^T}\hat{A}^{(m)})_{aa}v_{ab}^{(m)^t} \geq \frac{\gamma}{2n_m}(\hat{A}^{(m)^T}\hat{A}^{(m)} - 2\hat{A}^{(m)^T})_{aa}v_{ab}^{(m)^t}. \quad (7.34)$$

Therefore, (7.31) holds, which leads to $G(v^{(m)}, v^{(m)^t}) \geq F_{ab}(v^{(m)})$.   □

Theorem 1. *The objective function of (7.15) is nonincreasing under the updating rule (7.22).*

Proof. Replacing $G(v^{(m)}, v_{ab}^{(m)^t})$ in (7.24) by (7.29) results in the following iterative updating rule:

$$v_{ab}^{(m)^{t+1}} = v_{ab}^{(m)^t} - v_{ab}^{(m)^t}$$

$$\frac{F'_{ab}(v_{ab}^{(m)^t})}{2(V^{(m)}U^{(m)^T}U^{(m)})_{ab} + (2\beta(n_m-1) + \frac{\gamma}{n_m})V_{ab}^{(m)} + \frac{\gamma}{n_m}(\hat{A}^{(m)^T}\hat{A}^{(m)}V^{(m)})_{ab}}$$

$$= v_{ab}^{(m)^t}\frac{2((X^{(m)} - S^{(m)})^T U^{(m)})_{ab} + 2\beta\sum_{n=1, n\neq m}^{n_m}V_{ab}^{(n)} + \frac{2\gamma}{n_m}(\hat{A}^{(m)^T}V^{(m)})_{ab}}{2(V^{(m)}U^{(m)^T}U^{(m)})_{ab} + (2\beta(n_m-1) + \frac{\gamma}{n_m})V_{ab}^{(m)} + \frac{\gamma}{n_m}(\hat{A}^{(m)^T}\hat{A}^{(m)}V^{(m)})_{ab}}.$$

$$(7.35)$$

This is essentially the updating rule of (7.22). As (7.29) is an auxiliary function of $F_{ab}(v^{(m)})$, according to Lemma 1, it can be concluded that $F_{ab}(v^{(m)})$ is nonincreasing under (7.22). Combining the previously proven property that $U^{(m)}$ remains nonincreasing during updates, it is evident that the proposed algorithm ensures the convergence of the objective function for problem (7.15).   □

7.2.5 *Computational complexity analysis*

This section discusses the computational complexity of the proposed model. The main computational cost of the model lies in the iterative updates of $U^{(m)}$ and $V^{(m)}$, where $m = 1, 2, \ldots, n_m$. The essential step involves solving the optimization problem in (7.19), which is performed for each column of $U^{(m)}$. The computational cost of the updating rule (7.19) is $O(p^{(m)}q)$, resulting in a total cost of $O(rp^{(m)}q)$ for $U^{(m)}$. Similarly, the computational cost of $V^{(m)}$ is $O(rp^{(m)}q)$.

In conclusion, the computational cost of optimizing the mth view objective function is $O(rp^{(m)}q)$ in combination with $U^{(m)}$ and $V^{(m)}$. Therefore, the total computational complexity of the proposed model in all views is $O(rn_m pq)$, where $p = \max\{p^{(1)}, p^{(2)}, \ldots, p^{(n_m)}\}$.

7.3 Experimental results

Extensive experiments are presented in this section to substantiate the effectiveness of the proposed method. The datasets and codes are available at https://github.com/dyz200219/CRLSNMF.

7.3.1 Description of datasets

The experiments utilize eight real-world datasets. These benchmark datasets serve as the basis for evaluating the method's performance, and the summary of significant statistics is presented in Table 7.1.

- **Yale:**[*]. The dataset consists of 165 black and white facial images representing 15 distinct individuals, resulting in 15 different clusters. It contains facial features captured from three distinct perspectives.
- **3Sources:**[†] The data comes from three different news sources, reporting a total of 169 stories. The stories are categorized into six subject tags.
- **BBCSport:**[‡]. The dataset consists of 544 documents fetched from websites, and each document is divided into two parts. The subject of each news item is assigned to one of five topic tags, resulting in five different clusters.

Table 7.1   The statistics for eight datasets

Dataset	Instances (N)	Views (P)	Cluster (C)
Yale	165	3	15
3Sources	169	3	6
BBCSport	544	2	5
Wisconsin	265	2	5
Handwritten	2000	5	10
20NewsGroups	500	3	5
Caltech20	2386	5	20
Scene	2688	3	8

[*] https://cvc.yale.edu/projects/yalefaces/yalefaces.html
[†] http://mlg.ucd.ie/datasets/3sources.html
[‡] https://mlg.ucd.ie/datasets/segment.html

- **Wisconsin:**[§]. The dataset consists of 265 web documents categorized into five groups. Each document is expressed by two feature bags.
- **Handwritten:**[|]. The dataset contains 2000 instances of decimal numbers from 0 to 9, resulting in 10 different clusters. The data encompasses feature information from five different aspects.
- **20NewsGroups:**[¶]. This is a multi-view dataset of newsgroups, consisting of three views. Each view contains 500 instances, which are divided into five clusters.
- **Caltech20:**[**]. The dataset contains 2386 images of objects belonging to 20 classes. All images are described using five types of features, which are Gabor, CENTRIST, HOG, GIST, and LBP.
- **Scene:**[††]. The dataset comprises 2688 images, divided into eight groups. For each image, three different feature vectors are used, including GIST, color moment, and HOG.

7.3.2   Compared methods

The proposed method is compared with the following state-of-the-art clustering methods to demonstrate its effectiveness.

- **NMF** [8]: The standard NMF achieves dimensionality reduction of the original matrix by seeking two non-negative matrices, resulting in a reduced-dimensional matrix of data features. We perform NMF on each view of the dataset and record the best results as the final experimental outcomes.
- **CoRegSPC**[‡‡]. [5]: This method makes different views appear to have a common consensus, by normalizing their view-specific feature vectors. The graph Laplacian operators of all views are also combined so that each Laplacian produces a close to consistent underlying structure. We set the range for the weight parameter from 0.01 to 0.05, with an interval of 0.01.
- **GNMF**[§§]. [9]: GNMF is an improved model based on NMF that constructs an affine graph to encode geometric information in pursuit of matrix factorization with graph structure constraints. Execute GNMF on each view of the dataset, where the balancing parameter is selected from $\{10^{-3}, 10^{-2}, 10^{-1}, 1, 10, 10^2, 10^3\}$, and record the best results as the final results.
- **MVKKM** [10]: The method executes the multi-view clustering task through unsupervised multi-kernel learning. It assigns different weights to each view's kernel matrix according to the view quality. According to the original paper, the value of parameter p is chosen from the set $\{1, 1.3, 1.5, 2, 4, 6\}$.

[§] https://lig-membres.imag.fr/grimal/data.html
[|] http://archive.ics.uci.edu/ml/datasets/Multiple+Features
[¶] https://lig-membres.imag.fr/grimal/data.html
[**] https://github.com/sudalvxin/2019-PR-Sparse-Multi-view-clustering/tree/master/Data
[††] https://github.com/sudalvxin/SMSC/tree/master/data
[‡‡] https://sites.google.com/site/feipingnie/publications
[§§] http://www.cad.zju.edu.cn/home/dengcai/Data/GNMF.html

- **MultiNMF**[||] [11]: This is a manifold-based multi-view NMF method that explores the correlation among internal views and incorporates local graph regularization. Therefore, MultiNMF integrates the local geometric information for each view. In each view, the regularization parameter is set to 0.01, which is the parameter value recommended in the original paper.

- **RMKMC**[¶¶] [12]: RMKMC extends the traditional K-means clustering to a robust multi-view K-means clustering. It integrates heterogeneous representations of large-scale data. The parameter γ can be configured, and according to the original paper, $\log_{10} \gamma$ varies from 0.1 to 2 with an incremental step of 0.2.

- **DiNMF** [13]: The purpose of DiNMF is to enhance the diversity of data. It explores the diversity from different views and reduces redundancy between multi-view representations. Additionally, it makes the learning process in a linear execution time. For parameters α and β, values are chosen from $\{10^{-4}, 10^{-3}, 10^{-2}, 10^{-1}, 1, 10, 10^2, 10^3\}$ for each parameter.

- **AMvDMD**[***] [14]: This method unveils the hierarchical semantics in data through a layered approach and captures hidden representations of distinct attributes. Consequently, it generates a new deep multi-view clustering model. We conduct experiments using the layer sizes as set in the original paper and record the best experimental results.

- **DMFPA**[†††] [15]: The method employs deep matrix factorization to gain the partition representation for each view and combines it with the optimal partition representation to achieve partition alignment, thereby integrating multi-view information. The parameters are set according to the original paper.

To perform a comprehensive assessment, three distinct evaluation metrics are employed: accuracy (ACC), normalized mutual information (NMI), and Purity. The detailed definitions for these metrics are given in [4]. Higher values for all three metrics indicate better clustering performance. Using different measurements, various aspects of the clustering performance are evaluated, allowing for a comprehensive assessment. Each comparison experiment is performed 10 times, and the mean values and standard deviations are recorded.

7.3.3   Comparison of clustering performance

Tables 7.2–7.9 present the clustering performance measured in terms of ACC, NMI, and Purity. The bold values indicate the best performance among the 10 advanced approaches. Through comparison, it can be observed that the proposed method is

---

[||] http://jialu.info/.
[¶¶] https://sites.google.com/site/feipingnie/publications.
[***] https://github.com/huangsd/DeepMVC,
[†††] https://github.com/zhangchen234/MVC-DMF-PA

Table 7.2   *Mean values and standard deviations of ACC, NMI, and Purity for clustering results with the proposed method and nine baseline methods on Yale (%)*

Method	ACC	NMI	Purity
NMF	50.18(3.97)	53.39(3.15)	51.58(3.49)
CoRegSPC	60.24(5.61)	63.75(4.31)	61.58(5.41)
GNMF	46.85(2.37)	52.33(2.07)	48.18(2.56)
MVKKM	58.18(0.00)	61.99(0.00)	60.00(0.00)
MultiNMF	59.64(1.65)	61.97(1.40)	59.64(1.65)
RMKMC	44.61(4.01)	50.67(3.64)	45.70(3.88)
DiNMF	59.21(3.23)	61.72(2.87)	59.39(3.26)
AMvDMD	43.76(5.68)	48.93(5.73)	45.39(4.59)
DMFPA	56.42(6.33)	61.04(4.37)	57.52(5.65)
Ours	**64.36(3.54)**	**65.88(3.01)**	**64.85(3.37)**

Table 7.3   *Mean values and standard deviations of ACC, NMI, and Purity for clustering results with the proposed method and nine baseline methods on 3Sources (%)*

Method	ACC	NMI	Purity
NMF	59.05(3.84)	54.25(2.34)	74.02(0.76)
CoRegSPC	55.86(3.65)	50.74(1.88)	69.76(1.56)
GNMF	58.17(3.83)	51.73(2.74)	72.25(1.54)
MVKKM	35.50(0.00)	6.58(0.00)	39.05(0.00)
MultiNMF	50.36(3.53)	45.99(2.34)	61.18(2.54)
RMKMC	46.75(6.82)	32.59(6.00)	59.11(3.38)
DiNMF	54.97(6.78)	49.40(4.81)	68.34(4.13)
AMvDMD	56.75(9.67)	35.96(15.52)	60.53(9.70)
DMFPA	56.33(2.10)	55.81(3.11)	75.27(2.57)
Ours	**76.92(5.37)**	**66.62(4.91)**	**81.83(3.14)**

competitive among a series of advanced methods and outperforms other comparative methods in most cases. Based on the information presented in these tables, the following conclusions can be drawn.

- As shown in Table 7.3, on the 3Sources, the improvement of the method over the second best method is about 17.87%, 12.37%, and 7.81% for ACC, NMI, and Purity, respectively. In Table 7.7, on the 20NewsGroups, the improvement is about 21.40%, 23.13%, and 20.24%. Despite a 0.19% decrease in NMI on the Wisconsin dataset and a 0.53% decrease in Purity on the Caltech20 dataset compared to the second best methods, the differences are small, and the other two

Table 7.4   Mean values and standard deviations of ACC, NMI, and Purity for clustering results with the proposed method and nine baseline methods on BBCSport (%)

Method	ACC	NMI	Purity
NMF	66.08(6.48)	48.16(5.71)	70.57(2.90)
CoRegSPC	48.92(1.97)	28.33(1.37)	52.39(0.61)
GNMF	72.21(2.65)	54.71(2.26)	75.62(2.52)
MVKKM	35.66(0.00)	1.23(0.00)	36.21(0.00)
MultiNMF	62.94(7.48)	45.43(3.91)	67.32(4.14)
RMKMC	65.13(6.03)	53.79(6.25)	70.96(4.88)
DiNMF	70.22(5.95)	53.74(4.82)	72.96(4.81)
AMvDMD	56.36(9.39)	41.95(9.11)	63.46(6.49)
DMFPA	56.89(1.63)	39.71(0.58)	63.36(1.36)
Ours	**78.03(3.69)**	**63.28(2.34)**	**79.08(1.68)**

Table 7.5   Mean values and standard deviations of ACC, NMI, and Purity for clustering results with the proposed method and nine baseline methods on Wisconsin (%)

Method	ACC	NMI	Purity
NMF	56.83(3.68)	35.83(4.47)	72.26(3.70)
CoRegSPC	55.36(2.55)	33.28(3.74)	71.70(2.55)
GNMF	57.32(1.20)	**42.64(1.64)**	74.08(1.31)
MVKKM	52.45(0.00)	13.45(0.00)	54.72(0.00)
MultiNMF	46.91(1.87)	11.48(3.55)	53.13(1.12)
RMKMC	45.21(4.69)	16.93(2.53)	60.38(2.97)
DiNMF	47.74(5.85)	18.67(6.93)	58.68(4.26)
AMvDMD	45.55(4.85)	16.08(6.41)	56.11(6.51)
DMFPA	44.79(0.84)	1.09(0.59)	46.19(0.48)
Ours	**60.60(1.84)**	42.45(3.42)	**75.92(2.64)**

metrics remain the best results as well. Overall, the proposed model generally outperforms the comparison methods.

- By comparing with the CoRegSPC and GNMF methods, which also use graph regularization, evidently the proposed method demonstrates the best overall performance across all metrics. This indicates that the innovative utilization of the graph regularization variant, centric graph regularization, actually provides more valid information.
- On the majority of datasets, the proposed method outperforms other comparative approaches, providing evidence for the superiority of log-based regularization. In contrast to the Frobenius norm employed by most methods, the novel and

Table 7.6 Mean values and standard deviations of ACC, NMI, and Purity for clustering results with the proposed method and nine baseline methods on Handwritten (%)

Method	ACC	NMI	Purity
NMF	68.57(5.74)	62.53(4.77)	70.66(4.59)
CoRegSPC	74.00(5.18)	70.36(2.57)	75.18(4.36)
GNMF	85.63(8.29)	82.69(5.10)	87.18(6.53)
MVKKM	73.15(0.00)	68.31(0.00)	73.15(0.00)
MultiNMF	79.02(4.37)	70.95(2.51)	79.38(3.73)
RMKMC	74.65(4.16)	72.98(2.93)	77.72(3.41)
DiNMF	71.35(4.84)	65.19(3.30)	72.07(4.46)
AMvDMD	79.57(7.46)	75.30(3.73)	80.70(5.39)
DMFPA	69.04(3.85)	64.06(1.43)	70.21(2.12)
Ours	**93.22(0.57)**	**86.96(0.91)**	**93.22(0.57)**

Table 7.7 Mean values and standard deviations of ACC, NMI, and Purity for clustering results with the proposed method and nine baseline methods on 20NewsGroups (%)

Method	ACC	NMI	Purity
NMF	60.48(6.47)	42.54(2.71)	61.68(5.62)
CoRegSPC	28.22(3.33)	4.85(2.47)	29.16(3.76)
GNMF	58.50(4.19)	38.37(2.42)	58.66(3.88)
MVKKM	21.00(0.00)	1.03(0.00)	21.00(0.00)
MultiNMF	23.40(1.48)	3.37(1.38)	23.92(1.73)
RMKMC	41.04(6.93)	15.32(6.30)	42.10(6.81)
DiNMF	52.66(10.08)	37.94(9.08)	55.54(8.75)
AMvDMD	39.60(7.38)	28.75(11.42)	40.58(8.02)
DMFPA	40.38(3.28)	17.32(3.69)	41.16(3.37)
Ours	**81.88(5.68)**	**65.67(4.33)**	**81.92(5.56)**

meaningful log-based sparse representation of the original objective function yields a more parts-based representation, which is of practical interest for NMF.

In addition, a two-sample t-test is used to determine if the proposed method significantly outperforms other clustering methods [16]. When the significance level is set at 5%, the null hypothesis states that "there is no difference between the proposed method and other methods," while the alternative hypothesis posits that "the proposed method is superior to other methods." The statistical test results for ACC, NMI, and Purity are displayed in Tables 7.10–7.12, respectively.

From Table 7.10, it can be observed that there is no significant difference between the proposed method and CoRegSPC on the Yale dataset. However, apart from this case, the p-values between the proposed method and each compared method

Table 7.8   Mean values and standard deviations of ACC, NMI, and Purity for clustering results with the proposed method and nine baseline methods on Caltech20 (%)

Method	ACC	NMI	Purity
NMF	36.70(1.65)	46.37(0.57)	69.58(0.80)
CoRegSPC	35.57(2.03)	41.09(0.66)	65.27(0.72)
GNMF	36.65(1.87)	39.42(0.91)	62.20(1.98)
MVKKM	40.53(0.00)	53.07(0.00)	**74.43(0.00)**
MultiNMF	37.26(1.93)	46.45(1.79)	69.91(1.30)
RMKMC	41.58(4.12)	45.18(2.61)	66.27(1.96)
DiNMF	33.09(1.93)	42.38(1.73)	67.92(1.35)
AMvDMD	41.04(2.92)	50.49(1.56)	71.75(2.10)
DMFPA	35.93(2.91)	15.66(4.70)	45.69(3.40)
Ours	**46.24(3.33)**	**53.78(1.35)**	73.90(1.55)

Table 7.9   Mean values and standard deviations of ACC, NMI, and Purity for clustering results with the proposed method and nine baseline methods on Scene (%)

Method	ACC	NMI	Purity
NMF	61.54(0.95)	44.90(0.88)	61.54(0.95)
CoRegSPC	64.04(1.08)	49.62(0.60)	64.14(0.99)
GNMF	41.03(2.22)	32.76(0.55)	44.90(2.03)
MVKKM	57.92(0.00)	45.26(0.00)	57.92(0.00)
MultiNMF	59.23(6.80)	46.54(3.25)	60.52(5.08)
RMKMC	48.31(5.22)	37.33(3.94)	50.41(4.57)
DiNMF	51.63(2.47)	39.27(1.29)	53.87(2.02)
AMvDMD	57.50(6.33)	45.65(3.40)	58.65(5.06)
DMFPA	52.93(1.45)	40.10(0.86)	56.48(1.41)
Ours	**67.23(2.24)**	**50.34(1.89)**	**67.23(2.24)**

are all less than 0.05, indicating that the proposed method achieves higher ACC on these eight datasets. In Table 7.11, the NMI of the proposed method is lower than CoRegSPC on the Wisconsin dataset. Nevertheless, in most cases, the proposed method obtains higher NMI compared to the compared methods. In Table 7.12, except for cases where there is no significant difference with specific comparison methods on the Yale, Wisconsin, and Caltech20 datasets, the proposed method achieves superior Purity in most cases.

Table 7.10   P-values of comparisons between the proposed method and other clustering methods in terms of ACC

Comparisons	Yale	3Sources	BBCSport	Wisconsin	Handwritten	20NewsGroups	Caltech20	Scene
				Datasets				
NMF	1.15e−07	9.31e−08	1.61e−04	1.22e−02	2.30e−07	3.13e−07	1.98e−07	3.24e−05
CoRegSPC	6.52e−02	6.05e−09	1.80e−14	7.55e−13	7.93e−07	1.16e−15	7.97e−08	7.37e−04
GNMF	8.08e−10	4.45e−08	7.39e−04	1.69e−04	1.78e−02	4.34e−09	2.75e−07	8.48e−16
MVKKM	3.72e−04	1.57e−09	4.48e−11	2.05e−07	1.91e−15	8.34e−11	4.21e−04	3.56e−07
MultiNMF	2.18e−03	1.27e−10	2.00e−05	2.64e−12	2.36e−06	3.37e−17	7.65e−07	4.70e−03
RMKMC	7.87e−10	2.05e−09	1.81e−05	1.49e−08	1.42e−07	2.49e−11	1.23e−02	1.76e−07
DiNMF	3.22e−03	2.34e−07	3.02e−03	4.12e−05	1.37e−07	2.51e−07	2.70e−09	1.62e−11
AMvDMD	1.34e−08	1.82e−05	2.18e−05	1.21e−06	2.57e−04	2.68e−11	1.61e−03	7.41e−04
DMFPA	2.78e−03	1.22e−07	2.37e−12	5.06e−12	5.96e−09	9.49e−14	7.68e−07	1.64e−12

Table 7.11   P-values of comparisons between the proposed method and other clustering methods in terms of NMI

Comparisons	Yale	3Sources	BBCSport	Wisconsin	Handwritten	20NewsGroups	Caltech20	Scene
				Datasets				
NMF	3.95e−08	7.41e−06	5.38e−06	1.55e−03	3.03e−08	2.76e−11	1.67e−09	3.02e−02
CoRegSPC	2.16e−01	7.82e−07	2.20e−16	1.99e−05	5.88e−10	9.17e−19	6.44e−16	2.74e−01
GNMF	7.36e−10	1.26e−07	1.40e−07	8.77e−01	2.70e−02	1.05e−12	3.02e−16	3.10e−11
MVKKM	2.76e−03	2.57e−11	2.50e−14	6.68e−10	2.44e−13	4.27e−12	1.33e−01	1.37e−05
MultiNMF	2.69e−03	5.07e−10	3.08e−10	1.07e−13	6.13e−10	1.14e−19	5.47e−09	4.96e−03
RMKMC	6.88e−09	4.7e−11	8.23e−04	2.34e−13	2.34e−08	4.78e−14	2.95e−08	2.24e−08
DiNMF	5.42e−03	2.83e−07	2.43e−05	2.28e−07	1.22e−09	7.03e−08	2.92e−12	9.32e−12
AMvDMD	1.51e−07	1.03e−04	2.75e−05	2.03e−08	2.18e−06	7.99e−07	8.64e−05	1.87e−03
DMFPA	9.90e−03	1.44e−05	2.44e−11	1.05e−11	1.53e−19	5.54e−16	1.29e−10	6.81e−12

Table 7.12   P-values of comparisons between the proposed method and other clustering methods in terms of Purity

Comparisons	Yale	3Sources	BBCSport	Wisconsin	Handwritten	20NewsGroups	Caltech20	Scene
				Datasets				
NMF	7.92e−08	1.72e−05	1.08e−06	2.02e−02	6.33e−08	2.06e−07	2.29e−06	2.41e−07
CoRegSPC	1.22e−01	5.87e−08	2.54e−20	1.85e−03	2.84e−07	2.18e−15	9.09e−10	8.75e−04
GNMF	2.75e−10	8.89e−07	2.01e−03	6.24e−02	1.69e−02	2.51e−09	1.78e−11	6.47e−15
MVKKM	1.38e−03	9.87e−12	3.53e−14	1.08e−09	1.91e−15	6.84e−11	3.07e−01	3.56e−07
MultiNMF	7.14e−04	3.74e−12	1.38e−07	2.89e−05	6.85e−07	3.37e−17	7.03e−06	2.30e−03
RMKMC	6.69e−10	6.85e−12	4.06e−04	3.02e−10	1.04e−07	2.78e−11	1.55e−08	1.01e−07
DiNMF	1.71e−03	1.66e−07	2.87e−03	2.36e−09	8.59e−08	2.25e−07	3.18e−08	4.08e−11
AMvDMD	2.69e−09	3.35e−06	2.15e−05	1.32e−06	4.03e−05	8.38e−11	1.80e−02	3.33e−04
DMFPA	2.42e−03	7.24e−05	8.63e−15	1.89e−11	8.47e−12	1.12e−13	7.12e−12	1.68e−10

7.3.4   Experiments of robustness

In this section, the proposed method is further evaluated on datasets with Gaussian and Poisson noise. Specifically, all methods are tested under different noise level conditions on the BBCSport dataset. Regarding the synthetic noise dataset for BBCSport, here is the provided information.

- **BBCSportG1**: This is a synthetic dataset where Gaussian noise with a mean of 0 and a variance of 0.005 is incorporated into each view of the original BBCSport dataset.
- **BBCSportG2**: This dataset introduces Gaussian noise to the original BBCSport. In this dataset, the Gaussian noise has an intensity characterized by a mean of 0 and a variance of 0.01.
- **BBCSportG3**: This dataset similarly incorporates Gaussian noise into the original BBCSport, with the Gaussian noise intensity characterized by a mean of 0 and a variance of 0.015.
- **BBCSportP**: This is a synthetic dataset where Poisson noise is added to each view of the original BBCSport dataset using functions from the MATLAB toolbox.

Tables 7.13–7.16 present the experimental results for four synthetic noise datasets. For all four different types of noise, the proposed method exhibits better performance compared to the other methods. It can be observed that the proposed method is less affected by both Gaussian and Poisson noise. With increasing Gaussian noise, the performance of all methods generally decreases, confirming the adverse effects of noise. However, the proposed method is relatively less affected by the increase in noise. Therefore, the experiments on the four noise-inclusive datasets validate the robustness of the proposed method.

Table 7.13   Mean values and standard deviations of ACC, NMI, and Purity for clustering results with the proposed method and nine baseline methods on BBCSportG1 (%)

Method	ACC	NMI	Purity
NMF	69.30(6.59)	48.73(6.49)	71.86(5.02)
CoRegSPC	54.61(7.52)	38.83(8.91)	63.86(8.56)
GNMF	56.45(8.82)	45.85(8.00)	65.72(7.60)
MVKKM	36.03(0.00)	1.11(0.00)	36.58(0.00)
MultiNMF	64.96(2.60)	50.37(1.98)	69.56(2.50)
RMKMC	63.71(9.27)	50.11(7.69)	69.89(6.37)
DiNMF	68.24(6.95)	48.08(4.32)	70.31(4.10)
AMvDMD	54.30(9.93)	30.74(12.55)	57.61(8.73)
DMFPA	56.64(3.17)	29.63(1.50)	60.70(0.83)
Ours	**77.28(2.69)**	**60.28(2.95)**	**78.31(2.14)**

Table 7.14   Mean values and standard deviations of ACC, NMI, and Purity for clustering results with the proposed method and nine baseline methods on BBCSportG2 (%)

Method	ACC	NMI	Purity
NMF	66.78(5.81)	45.24(5.65)	70.53(4.55)
CoRegSPC	56.71(6.46)	42.66(5.22)	67.19(5.99)
GNMF	56.38(8.20)	42.48(4.93)	64.96(6.43)
MVKKM	36.03(0.00)	1.11(0.00)	36.58(0.00)
MultiNMF	64.19(1.26)	50.43(0.97)	68.84(1.27)
RMKMC	62.13(9.52)	43.61(11.24)	64.43(8.08)
DiNMF	66.47(8.46)	48.46(5.38)	69.23(8.30)
AMvDMD	54.61(9.03)	33.95(8.81)	59.26(7.32)
DMFPA	57.35(3.06)	36.32(1.30)	63.97(2.37)
Ours	**77.13(5.00)**	**62.84(2.65)**	**79.17(2.47)**

Table 7.15   Mean values and standard deviations of ACC, NMI, and Purity for clustering results with the proposed method and nine baseline methods on BBCSportG3 (%)

Method	ACC	NMI	Purity
NMF	68.44(6.23)	48.20(4.84)	71.31(5.26)
CoRegSPC	55.22(6.64)	40.20(7.76)	65.72(7.42)
GNMF	54.52(5.65)	44.92(3.51)	65.04(4.14)
MVKKM	36.03(0.00)	1.11(0.00)	36.58(0.00)
MultiNMF	63.81(5.89)	49.42(6.76)	68.93(4.65)
RMKMC	59.61(9.80)	39.32(8.60)	63.62(7.62)
DiNMF	64.08(7.49)	46.72(6.79)	67.21(7.15)
AMvDMD	51.51(7.77)	28.36(7.79)	55.02(7.61)
DMFPA	57.28(1.78)	39.53(0.54)	66.01(0.52)
Ours	**74.94(5.71)**	**59.20(4.37)**	**77.48(2.29)**

Table 7.16   Mean values and standard deviations of ACC, NMI, and Purity for clustering results with the proposed method and nine baseline methods on BBCSportP (%)

Method	ACC	NMI	Purity
NMF	67.32(6.09)	46.12(6.60)	69.69(4.98)
CoRegSPC	58.73(1.39)	44.60(1.13)	69.15(0.70)
GNMF	62.13(4.29)	42.58(3.92)	66.89(3.85)
MVKKM	38.24(0.00)	4.03(0.00)	38.42(0.00)
MultiNMF	65.75(0.17)	51.19(0.52)	69.85(0.17)
RMKMC	64.89(7.89)	49.63(9.08)	69.98(7.97)
DiNMF	66.87(6.57)	47.95(4.83)	69.01(5.29)
AMvDMD	53.92(5.82)	35.67(8.55)	59.85(5.38)
DMFPA	62.17(2.44)	40.67(0.93)	66.73(1.21)
Ours	**75.09(3.25)**	**57.69(3.38)**	**75.96(2.82)**

7.3.5   *Visualization of the evolution of $V^{(m)}$*

To demonstrate the effectiveness of the coefficient matrix $V^{(m)}$, where $m = 1, 2, \ldots, n_m$, the coefficient matrix $V^{(m)}$ is visualized to evaluate its learning effect. Therefore, the t-SNE algorithm is performed on $V^{(m)}$ [17]. Based on data labels, clusters with different colors are generated.

Figure 7.3 shows the comparative effect of $V^{(m)}$ in the proposed method and DiNMF. 3Sources, BBCSport, Handwritten, and 20NewsGroups are used in this experiment. The visualizations demonstrate that the coefficient matrix $V^{(m)}$ of the proposed method acquires significant and clear clustering structures. Compared to DiNMF, the coefficient matrix of the proposed method is more centralized for categories and has less overlapping. Such results clearly show the usefulness of the learned $V^{(m)}$ in clustering.

7.3.6   *Convergence experiments*

In Figure 7.4, the evolution of the objective values during the iterations is plotted. It is evident that for the majority of datasets, the objective function values decrease dramatically within 100 iterations and then exhibit slight decrease after 200 iterations. However, for data with complex features, such as 3Sources, the model costs more iterations to find the solution. Therefore, it shows that the proposed method converges effectively on most datasets.

7.3.7   *Parameter sensitivity*

In practical applications, determining the optimal parameters for unsupervised learning methods can be challenging. Therefore, the insensitivity of the performance of unsupervised methods to parameter settings is crucial. The sensitivity to balancing parameters of the proposed method is demonstrated in this experiment. While preserving generality, the results for four datasets, including Yale, 3Sources, BBCSport, and Handwritten, are displayed. Similar patterns can be observed in other datasets as well.

The proposed model consists of three essential parameters, α, β, and γ. The sensitivity analysis of a parameter is conducted by first fixing the other two parameters and varying the value of the parameter within a range. Due to the transformation relationship of the balancing parameter between the formulation (7.12) and (7.13), the values of $\frac{\alpha}{2}$, β, and γ are modified within the range $\{1, 10, 10^2, 10^3, 10^4, 10^5, 10^6, 10^7, 10^8\}$. Figures 7.5–7.7 display the experimental results.

The outcomes indicate that the proposed method exhibits improved performance when α is relatively larger. This indicates that a larger value of α means that the model can eliminate noises better. For β, the model achieves higher performance over a wider range of parameter choices. The parameter γ obtains better performance at larger values. This indicates that the graph structure has an important role in the clustering task. Similar patterns can be observed on other datasets, which suggests that larger values may be set for the balancing parameters in practical applications.

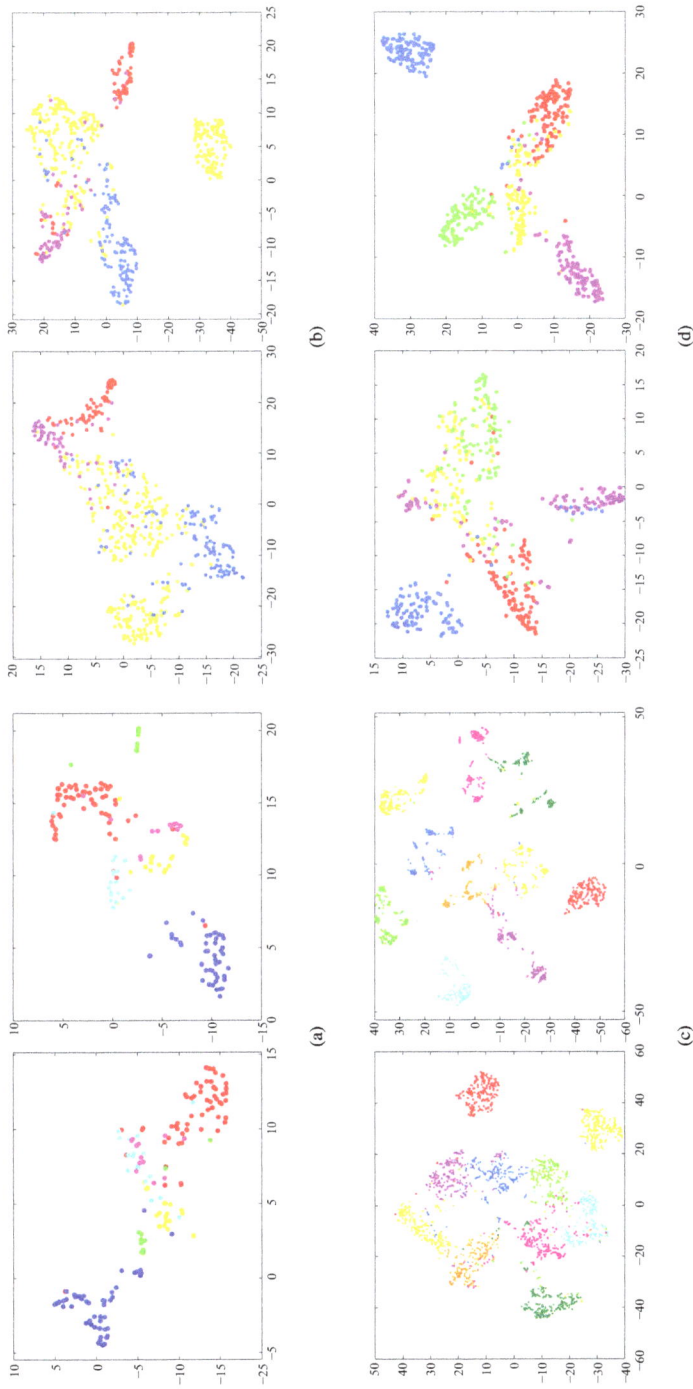

Figure 7.3   The proposed method and DiNMF use t-SNE [17] on (a) 3Sources, (b) BBCSport, (c) Handwritten and (d) 20NewsGroups. In each subfigure, the left part shows the effect of DiNMF visualized using t-SNE, and the right part shows the visualization of the proposed method. Different clusters for each dataset are indicated by different colors.

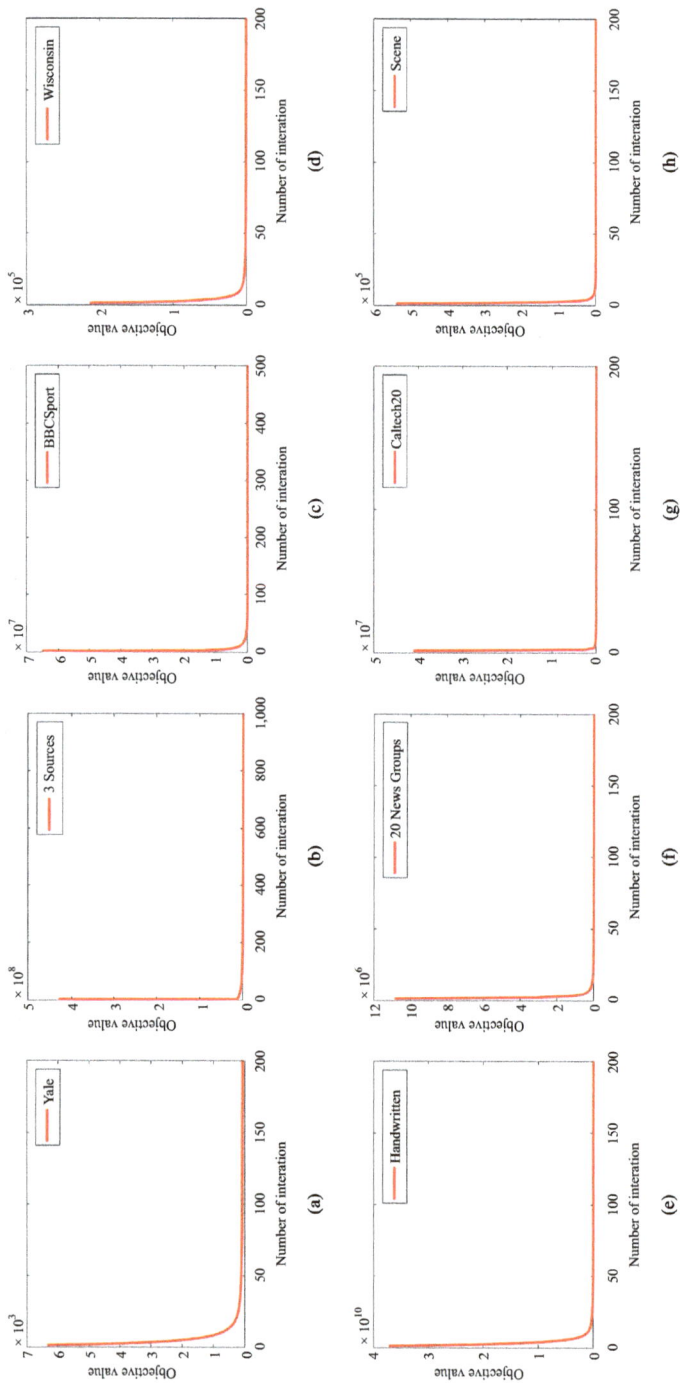

Figure 7.4 Convergent results on eight datasets. (a) Yale, (b) 3Sources, (c) BBCSport, (d) Wisconsin, (e) Handwritten, (f) 20NewsGroups, (g) Caltech20, and (h) Scene.

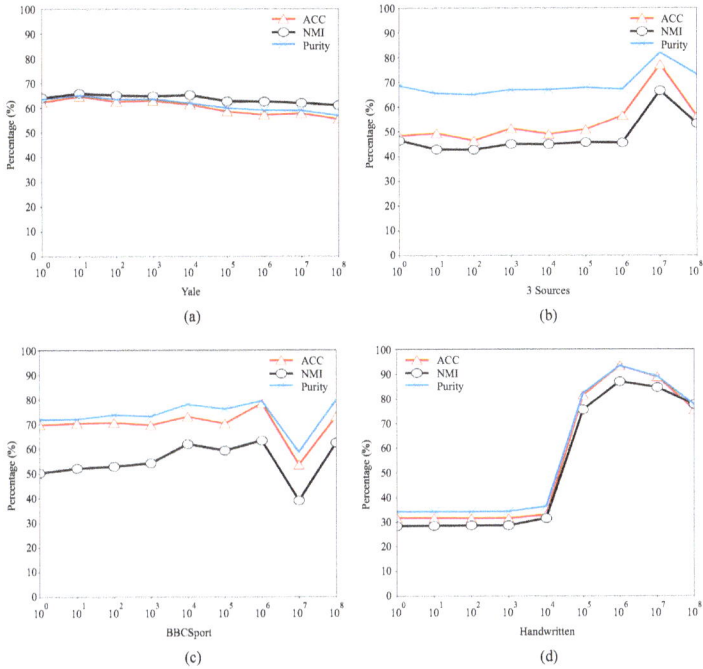

Figure 7.5 *The sensitivity analysis of $\frac{\alpha}{2}$ on four datasets. (a) Yale, (b) 3Sources, (c) BBCSport, and (d) Handwritten.*

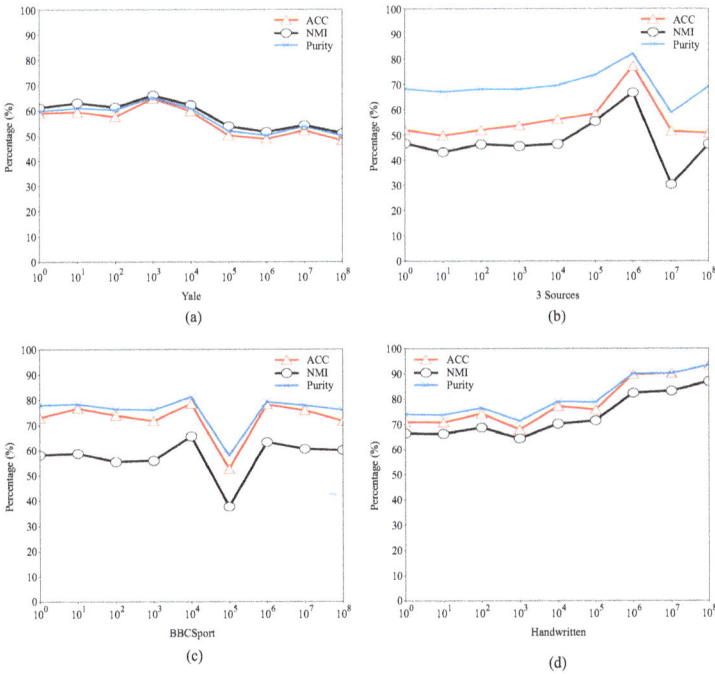

Figure 7.6 *The sensitivity analysis of β on four datasets. (a) Yale, (b) 3Sources, (c) BBCSport, and (d) Handwritten.*

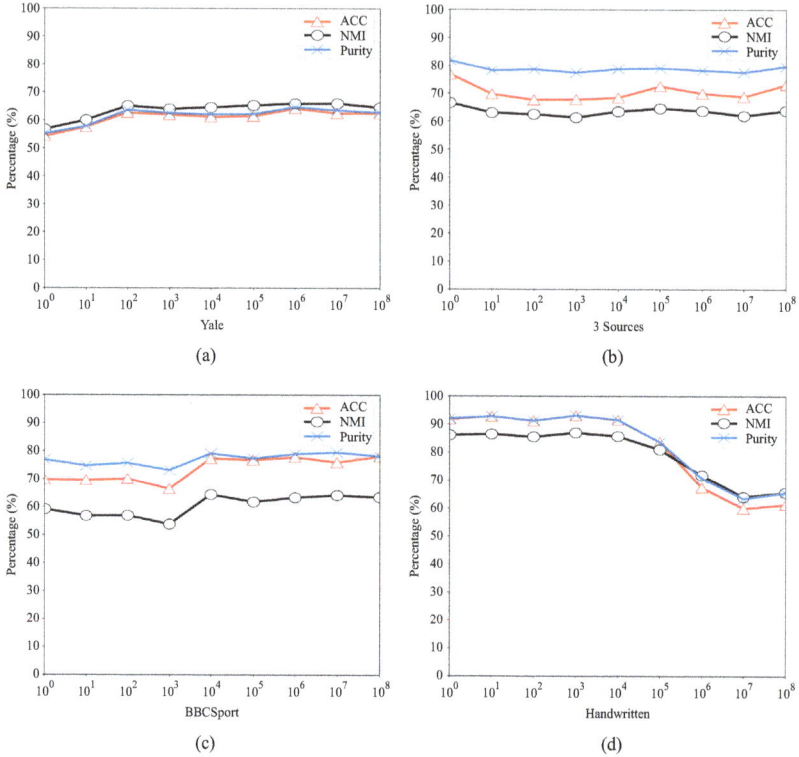

Figure 7.7   The sensitivity analysis of γ on four datasets. (a) Yale, (b) 3Sources, (c) BBCSport, and (d) Handwritten.

7.4   Chapter summary

In this chapter, a centric graph-regularized log-norm sparse NMF is proposed for multi-view clustering. To reliably learn the underlying geometric structure that is embedded in multi-view data, the graph structure of the multi-view coefficient matrix is extracted using centric graph regularization, which obtains more information about the spatial structure than using traditional graph regularization. Additionally, the pairwise co-regularization is used to reduce the redundant information within views. Finally, the log-based sparsification is introduced to improve the robustness of the model. An efficient update algorithm is derived for the formulated optimization problem, while its convergence and complexity are theoretically analyzed. Comparative experiments on eight real-world datasets with nine state-of-the-art methods demonstrate the effectiveness of the model.

References

[1]   Chen K., Che H., Li X., Leung M.F.: "Graph non-negative matrix factorization with alternative smoothed L_0 regularizations." *Neural Comput. Appl.* 2022;35(14):9995–10009.

[2]   Yang H., Ma K., Cheng J.: "Rethinking graph regularization for graph neural networks." in *Proceedings of the AAAI Conference on Artificial Intelligence*; 2021. Vol. 35. pp. 4573–81.

[3]   Che H., Wang J., Cichocki A.: "Bicriteria sparse nonnegative matrix factorization via two-timescale duplex neurodynamic optimization." *IEEE Trans. Neural Netw. Learn. Syst.* 2023;34(8):4881–91.

[4]   Peng C., Zhang Y., Chen Y., Kang Z., Chen C., Cheng Q.: "Log-based sparse nonnegative matrix factorization for data representation." *Knowl.Based Syst.* 2022;251:109127.

[5]   Kumar A., Rai P., Daumé H.: "Co-regularized multi-view spectral clustering." in *Proceedings of the 24th International Conference on Neural Information Processing Systems, NIPS'11*. Red Hook, NY, USA: Curran Associates Inc.; 2011. pp. 1413–21.

[6]   Wang X., Zhang T., Gao X.: "Multiview Clustering Based on Non-Negative Matrix Factorization and Pairwise Measurements." *IEEE Trans. Cybern.* 2019;49(9):3333–46.

[7]   Chen W.S., Zeng Q., Pan B.: "A survey of deep nonnegative matrix factorization." *Neurocomputing.* 2022;491:305–20.

[8]   Lee D.D., Seung H.S.: "Algorithms for non-negative matrix factorization." in *Proceedings of the 13th International Conference on Neural Information Processing Systems, NIPS'00*. Cambridge, MA, USA: MIT Press; 2000. pp. 535–41.

[9]   Cai D., He X., Han J., Huang T.S: "Graph regularized nonnegative matrix factorization for data representation." *IEEE Trans. Pattern Anal. Mach. Intell.* 2011;33(8):1548–60.

[10]   Tzortzis G., Likas A.: "Kernel-based weighted multi-view clustering." in *2012 IEEE 12th International Conference on Data Mining*; 2012. pp. 675–84.

[11]   Liu J., Wang C., Gao J., Han J.: "Multi-view clustering via joint nonnegative matrix factorization." in *Proceedings of the 2013 SIAM International Conference on Data Mining*. Philadelphia, PA: SIAM; 2013. pp. 252–60.

[12]   Cai X., Nie F., Huang H.: "Multi-view K-means clustering on big data." in *Proceedings of the Twenty-Third International Joint Conference on Artificial Intelligence, IJCAI '13*. Menlo Park, CA: AAAI Press; 2013. pp. 2598–604.

[13]   Wang J., Tian F., Yu H., Liu C. H., Zhan K., Wang X.: "Diverse non-negative matrix factorization for multiview data representation." *IEEE Trans. Cybern.* 2018;48(9):2620–32.

[14]   Huang S., Kang Z., Xu Z.: "Auto-weighted multi-view clustering via deep matrix decomposition." *Pattern Recogn.* 2020;97:107015.

[15]   Zhang C., Wang S., Liu J., *et al.* "Multi-view clustering via deep matrix factorization and partition alignment." in *Proceedings of the 29th ACM International Conference on Multimedia, MM '21*. New York, NY, USA: Association for Computing Machinery; 2021. pp. 4156–64.

[16]   Huang Y., Shen Z., Cai F., Li T., Lv F.: "Adaptive graph-based general-
       ized regression model for unsupervised feature selection." *Knowl.Based Syst.*
       2021;227:107156.
[17]   Zhong G., Pun C.M.: "Improved normalized cut for multi-view clustering."
       IEEE Trans. Pattern Anal. Mach. Intell. 2022;44(12):10244–51.

Chapter 8
Diversity-constrained matrix factorization for clustering

Multi-view clustering (MVC) has received extensive attention due to its efficient processing of high-dimensional data. Most of the existing MVC methods are based on non-negative matrix factorization (NMF), which can achieve dimensionality reduction and interpretable representation. However, there are following issues in the existing research: (1) The existing methods based on NMF using the Frobenius norm are sensitive to noises and outliers. (2) Many methods use only the information shared by multi-view data while ignoring the diverse information between views. (3) The data graph constructed by the conventional K-Nearest Neighbors (KNN) method may misclassify neighbors and degrade the clustering performance. To address the above problems, we propose a novel robust MVC method. Specifically, an $l_{2,1}$-norm is introduced to measure the factorization error to improve the robustness of NMF. Additionally, a diversity constraint is utilized to learn the diverse relationship of multi-view data, and an adaptive graph method via information entropy is designed to overcome the shortcomings of misclassifying neighbors. Finally, an iterative updating algorithm is developed to solve the optimization model, which can make the objective function monotonically nonincreasing. The effectiveness of the proposed method is substantiated by comparing with eleven state-of-the-art methods on five real-world and four synthetic multi-view datasets for clustering tasks.

8.1 The proposed method

Suppose that $\mathscr{X} = \{X^1, X^2, \ldots, X^P\}$ is a multi-view dataset containing P views. The data matrix corresponding to the pth view is $X^p = \{x_1^p, x_2^p, \ldots, x_n^p\} \in R^{m_p \times n}$, $x_i^p \in R^{m_p} (i = 1, 2, \ldots, n), (p = 1, 2, \ldots, P)$. Then, robust multi-view NMF using the $l_{2,1}$-norm is expressed as

$$\min_{U^p, V^p} \sum_{p=1}^{P} ||X^p - U^p V^p||_{2,1} \tag{8.1}$$

$$\text{s.t.} \quad U^p \geq 0, V^p \geq 0, p \in \{1, 2, \ldots, P\}.$$

The basis matrix and the coefficient matrix of the pth view are $U^p \in R^{m^p \times k}$ and $V^p \in R^{k \times n}$, respectively.

Multi-view data is richer in content than single-view data, that is, it has diverse features. To obtain the diverse coefficient matrix, we need to constrain the learning of the coefficient matrix. Let the ith coefficient vector corresponding to the pth view be $v_i^p \in R^k$, and the ith coefficient vector of the wth view be $v_i^w \in R^k$. Stronger orthogonality between two vectors always means having more diverse information [1]. Therefore, we can extract diverse information by minimizing the inner product between coefficient vectors of two different views. For n vectors, the formula is as follows:

$$\min_{V^p} \sum_{i=1}^{n} (v_i^p)^T v_i^w = \min_{V^p} \mathrm{tr}(V^p (V^w)^T), \tag{8.2}$$

where $\mathrm{tr}(\cdot)$ represents the trace operation of the matrix. To learn the diverse information between the coefficient matrix of the pth view and the other views, the diversity constraint can be expressed as

$$\min_{V^p} \sum_{p=1}^{P} \sum_{w=1}^{P} \mathrm{tr}(V^p (V^w)^T). \tag{8.3}$$

As data is sampled from low-dimensional manifolds embedded in high-dimensional spaces [2], preserving the intrinsic geometric structure of the data is significant. The expression of the graph regularization is

$$\min_{V^p} \frac{1}{2} \sum_{i=1}^{n} \sum_{j=1}^{n} ||v_i^p - v_j^p||_2^2 s_{ij}^p = \min_{V^p} tr(V^p L^p (V^p)^T), \tag{8.4}$$

where S^p is the similarity matrix, which describes the degree of similarity between data points, $L^p = \hat{W}^p - W^p$ denotes the graph Laplacian matrix, and $\hat{W}^p$ is a diagonal matrix with $\hat{w}_{jj}^p = \sum_{i=1}^{n} w_{ij}^p$, $W^p = \frac{S^p + (S^p)^T}{2}$.

For similarity matrix learning, the KNN method is usually used. However, if most of data points are close to the intersection of multiple subspaces, KNN fails to properly partition the subspaces, and the KNN method needs to adjust the number of neighbors frequently [3]. Therefore, another method for learning the similarity matrix is adopted. In information theory, information entropy is a physical quantity that describes the unpredictability of information content. Let the information $q = [q_1, q_2, \ldots, q_n]$, which consists of n sources, and q_i be the probability of the ith source. The information entropy of q can be described as

$$y = \sum_{i=1}^{n} q_i \log \frac{1}{q_i}. \tag{8.5}$$

In (8.5), higher y corresponds to a more stable state. For graph learning, if two samples are very similar, there is a high probability that they will be placed in the same category [4]. However, a more rigorous similarity matrix represents a more unstable state, which reduces the generalization ability of the model. Consequently, the learning of the similarity matrix S can be realized by maximizing entropy [5]. The mathematical expression is expressed as

$$\max_{S} \sum_{i=1}^{n} \sum_{j=1}^{n} s_{ij}^{p} \log\left(\frac{1}{s_{ij}^{p}}\right)$$

$$\text{s.t.} \quad \sum_{j=1}^{n} s_{ij}^{p} = 1, \; s_{ij}^{p} \geq 0.$$

(8.6)

Since S^p is an asymmetric matrix, let $W^p = \frac{S^p + (S^p)^T}{2}$.

Finally, we consider utilizing diversity and adaptive graph constraints based on the multi-view $l_{2,1}$-norm NMF, and the optimization model of the proposed method is

$$\min_{U^p, V^p, S^p} \sum_{p=1}^{P} ||X^p - U^p V^p||_{2,1} + 2\alpha \sum_{p=1}^{P} \sum_{w=1}^{P} \text{tr}[V^p (V^w)^T]$$

$$+ \gamma \sum_{p=1}^{P} [\text{tr}(V^p L^p (V^p)^T) + \lambda \sum_{i=1}^{n} \sum_{j=1}^{n} s_{ij}^{p} \log(s_{ij}^{p})]$$

(8.7)

$$\text{s.t.} \; U^p \geq 0, \; V^p \geq 0, \; \sum_{j=1}^{n} s_{ij}^{p} = 1, \; s_{ij}^{p} \geq 0, \; \forall p \in \{1, 2, \ldots, P\}.$$

In Problem (8.7), the first term is a multi-view $l_{2,1}$-norm NMF, the second term is a diversity constraint, and the last part is an adaptive graph constraint. $\alpha, \gamma,$ and $\lambda \geq 0$ are parameters, which adjust the weight relationship between these parts. α measures the importance of the diversity constraint, while γ and λ adjust the weight of the adaptive graph constraint. The coefficient matrix V^p for each view can be obtained by solving the above optimization problem. The consensus representation matrix V^* can then be calculated as $V^* = \frac{1}{P} \sum_{p=1}^{P} V^p$. The flowchart of the proposed model is shown in Figure 8.1.

8.2 Optimization

In this section, an alternate updating technique is employed to solve the optimization problem (8.7). Specifically, we update each variable while keeping the other variables constant. The detailed optimization algorithm is outlined in Algorithm 1.

8.2.1 *Fixing V^p and S^p and updating U^p*

With fixed V^p and S^p, the objective function with respect to U^p can be written as follows:

$$\min_{U^p} ||X^p - U^p V^p||_{2,1}$$

$$\text{s.t.} \quad U^p \geq 0.$$

(8.8)

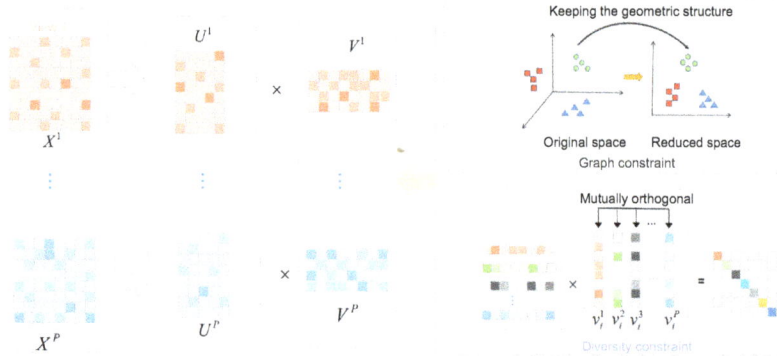

Figure 8.1   Flowchart of the proposed method. (a) Diversity constraint: The diversity constraint obtains the diverse information of the data by making the coefficient vectors of different views orthogonal. (b) Adaptive graph constraint: The adaptive graph constraint makes the data after dimensionality reduction has the same geometric structure as the data in the original space.

We can use the following method to solve problem (8.8). Let the error between the real value and the reconstructed value of each sample be e_i, and the function $\Delta(e_i)$ be an increasing function with regard to $|e_i|$. Then, the general reconstruction problem can be expressed as the following form:

$$\min \sum_i \Delta(e_i). \tag{8.9}$$

Suppose that there are c variables $[g_1, g_2, \ldots, g_c]$ in the problem (8.9), then the problem can be solved by setting the derivative value to 0.

$$\sum_i \frac{\partial \Delta(e_i)}{\partial e_i} \frac{\partial e_i}{\partial g_j} = 0 \qquad (j = 1, 2, \ldots, c). \tag{8.10}$$

Equation (8.10) is equivalent to the below equation:

$$\sum_i \frac{1}{e_i} \frac{\partial \Delta(e_i)}{\partial e_i} e_i \frac{\partial e_i}{\partial g_j} = 0 \qquad (j = 1, 2, \ldots, c). \tag{8.11}$$

Let $w(e_i) = \frac{1}{e_i} \frac{\partial \Delta(e_i)}{\partial e_i}$, it is easy to find that problem (8.9) can be transformed into the following iterative problem:

$$\min \sum_i \frac{1}{2} w(e_i^t) e_i^2, \tag{8.12}$$

where e_i^t denotes the reconstruction error of the tth iteration of the ith sample, and $w(e_i^t)$ is regarded as a constant during the $(t+1)$th iteration. For problem (8.8), $\Delta(e_i) = ||x_i^p - U^p v_i^p||_2$, so we transform problem (8.8) into the following problem:

$$\min_{U^p} \sum_i^n d_{ii}^p ||x_i^p - U^p v_i^p||_2^2 = \min_{U^p} tr[(X^p - U^p V^p)D^p(X^p - U^p V^p)^T] \tag{8.13}$$

$$\text{s.t.} \quad U^p \geq 0,$$

where D^p is a diagonal matrix and

$$d_{ii}^p = \frac{1}{2}w(x_i^p - U^p v_i^p) = \frac{1}{2||x_i^p - U^p v_i^p||_2}. \tag{8.14}$$

By introducing the Lagrange multiplier ψ, the Lagrange function of problem (8.13) is

$$L_1 = tr[(X^p - U^p V^p)D^p(X^p - U^p V^p)^T] + tr(\psi^T U^p). \tag{8.15}$$

By taking the partial derivative of the Lagrange function L_1 with respect to the variable U^p, we get

$$\left(\frac{\partial L_1}{\partial U^p}\right)_{ij} = [-2X^p D^p(V^p)^T + 2U^p V^p D^p(V^p)^T + \psi)]_{ij} = 0. \tag{8.16}$$

According to Karush–Kuhn–Tucker (KKT) condition [6] of the optimization theory, $\psi_{ij} u_{ij}^p = 0$, we can get

$$[-2X^p D^p(V^p)^T + 2U^p V^p D^p(V^p)^T]_{ij} u_{ij}^p = 0. \tag{8.17}$$

By organizing (8.17), we can get the multiplicative iterative formula of U^p:

$$u_{ij}^p \leftarrow u_{ij}^p \times \frac{[X^p D^p(V^p)^T]_{ij}}{[U^p V^p D^p(V^p)^T]_{ij}}. \tag{8.18}$$

8.2.2   *Fixing U^p and S^p and updating V^p*

With fixed U^p and S^p, the objective function with respect to V^p can be expressed as

$$\min_{V^p} ||X^p - U^p V^p||_{2,1} + 2\alpha \sum_{w=1}^P tr[V^p(V^w)^T] + \gamma tr(V^p L^p (V^p)^T \tag{8.19}$$

$$\text{s.t.} \quad V^p \geq 0.$$

Similarly, we transform problem (8.19) into the following problem:

$$\min_{V^p} tr[(X^p - U^p V^p)D^p(X^p - U^p V^p)^T]$$

$$+ 2\alpha \sum_{w=1}^P tr[V^p(V^w)^T] + \gamma\, tr[V^p L^p(V^p)^T] \tag{8.20}$$

$$\text{s.t.} \quad V^p \geq 0,$$

where D^p is a diagonal matrix, and $d_{ii}^p = \frac{1}{2||x_i^p - U^p v_i^p||_2}$. Set ϕ to be the Lagrange multiplier of the inequality constraint. The Lagrange function of problem (8.20) is

$$
\begin{aligned}
L_2 &= \text{tr}[(X^p - U^p V^p)D^p(X^p - U^p V^p)^T] \\
&\quad + 2\alpha \sum_{w=1}^{P} \text{tr}[V^p(V^w)^T] + \gamma\, \text{tr}[V^p L^p(V^p)^T] + \text{tr}(\phi^T V^p).
\end{aligned}
\tag{8.21}
$$

The partial derivative of L_2 with respect to the variable matrix V^p is

$$
\left(\frac{\partial L_2}{\partial V^p}\right)_{ij} = \left[-2(U^p)^T X^p D^p + 2(U^p)^T U^p V^p D^p \right.
$$

$$
\left. +2\alpha \sum_{w=1, w \neq p}^{P} V^w + 4\alpha V^p + 2\gamma V^p(\hat{W}^p - W^p) + \phi \right]_{ij} = 0.
\tag{8.22}
$$

According to the KKT condition of the optimization theory, $\phi_{ij} v_{ij}^p = 0$, we can get

$$
\left[-2(U^p)^T X^p D^p + 2(U^p)^T U^p V^p D^p \right.
$$

$$
\left. +2\alpha \sum_{w=1, w \neq p}^{P} V^w + 4\alpha V^p + 2\gamma V^p(\hat{W}^p - W^p) \right]_{ij} v_{ij}^p = 0.
\tag{8.23}
$$

By operating (8.23), we can get the multiplicative iterative formula of V^p:

$$
v_{ij}^p \leftarrow v_{ij}^p
$$

$$
\times \frac{[(U^p)^T X^p D^p + \gamma V^p W^p]_{ij}}{[(U^p)^T U^p V^p D^p + \alpha \sum_{w=1, w \neq p}^{P} V^w + 2\alpha V^p + \gamma V^p \hat{W}^p]_{ij}}.
\tag{8.24}
$$

8.2.3   *Fixing U^p and V^p and updating S^p*

With fixed U^p and V^p, the objective function with respect to S^p can be written as

$$
\min_{S^p} \; 2\, \text{tr}(V^p L^p(V^p)^T) + 2\lambda \sum_{i=1}^{n} \sum_{j=1}^{n} s_{ij}^p \log(s_{ij}^p)
$$

$$
\text{s.t.} \quad \sum_{j=1}^{n} s_{ij}^p = 1, \; s_{ij}^p \geq 0.
\tag{8.25}
$$

By introducing the Lagrange multiplier π_{ij}, ξ_i, we can get the Lagrange function of problem (8.25):

$$
\begin{aligned}
L_3 &= 2\mathrm{tr}(V^p L^p (V^p)^T) + 2\lambda \sum_{i=1}^{n} \sum_{j=1}^{n} s_{ij}^p \log(s_{ij}^p) \\
&\quad - \sum_{i=1}^{n} \xi_i \left(\sum_{j=1}^{n} s_{ij}^p - 1 \right) - \sum_{i=1}^{n} \sum_{j=1}^{n} \pi_{ij} s_{ij}^p \\
&= \sum_{i=1}^{n} \sum_{j=1}^{n} ||v_i^p - v_j^p||_2^2 s_{ij}^p + 2\lambda \sum_{i=1}^{n} \sum_{j=1}^{n} s_{ij}^p \log(s_{ij}^p) \\
&\quad - \sum_{i=1}^{n} \xi_i \left(\sum_{j=1}^{n} s_{ij}^p - 1 \right) - \sum_{i=1}^{n} \sum_{j=1}^{n} \pi_{ij} s_{ij}^p .
\end{aligned}
\tag{8.26}
$$

The partial derivative of L_3 with respect to S^p is

$$
\frac{\partial L_3}{\partial s_{ij}^p} = ||v_i^p - v_j^p||_2^2 + 2\lambda(\log s_{ij}^p + 1) - \xi_i - \pi_{ij} = 0.
\tag{8.27}
$$

According to the KKT condition of optimization theory, $\pi_{ij} s_{ij}^p = 0$. When $s_{ij}^p > 0$, $\pi_{ij} = 0$, we have

$$
||v_i^p - v_j^p||_2^2 + 2\lambda(\log s_{ij}^p + 1) - \xi_i = 0,
\tag{8.28}
$$

$$
s_{ij}^p = e^{\frac{\xi_i - 2\lambda}{2\lambda}} e^{-\frac{||v_i^p - v_j^p||_2^2}{2\lambda}} = \rho_i e^{-\frac{||v_i^p - v_j^p||_2^2}{2\lambda}},
\tag{8.29}
$$

where $\rho_i = e^{\frac{\xi_i - 2\lambda}{2\lambda}}$. Due to $\sum_{j=1}^{n} s_{ij}^p = 1$, we can calculate ρ_i by

$$
\sum_{j=1}^{n} s_{ij}^p = \sum_{j=1}^{n} \rho_i e^{-\frac{||v_i^p - v_j^p||_2^2}{2\lambda}} = 1,
\tag{8.30}
$$

$$
\rho_i = \frac{1}{\sum_{j=1}^{n} e^{-\frac{||v_i^p - v_j^p||_2^2}{2\lambda}}}.
\tag{8.31}
$$

Combining the above equation, we can get the updating formula for S^p:

$$
s_{ij}^p \leftarrow \frac{e^{-\frac{||v_i^p - v_j^p||_2^2}{2\lambda}}}{\sum_{j=1}^{n} e^{-\frac{||v_i^p - v_j^p||_2^2}{2\lambda}}}.
\tag{8.32}
$$

8.2.4   Computational complexity analysis

In this section, we analyze the computational complexity of Algorithm 1. Let the number of samples in the dataset containing P views be n, the dimension of data matrix in the pth view be m_p, and the dimension of subspace be k. The number of iterations is t. Then, the complexities of the updating formulas for U^p and V^p are

---

Algorithm 1 Robust multi-view non-negative matrix factorization with adaptive graph and diversity constraints

---

Input: Multi-view datasets $\mathscr{X} = \{X^1, X^2, ..., X^P\}$. Parameters α, γ and λ.
Output: Consensus representation matrix V^*
  1: **for** $p = 1$ to P **do**
    2:    Normalize X^p
    3:    Initialize V^p and U^p
    4:    Initialize S^p based on Eq. (8.32)
  5: **end for**
  6: **while** not converging **do**
    7:    **for** $p = 1$ to P **do**
    8:      Update V^p based on Eq. (8.24)
    9:      Update U^p based on Eq. (8.18)
  10:     Update S^p based on Eq. (8.32)
  11:   **end for**
 12: **end while**
 13: Calculate consensus representation matrix by $V^* = \frac{1}{P}\sum_{p=1}^{P} V^p$, and normlize V^*.

$O(m_p nk + (m + n)k^2 + n^2 k + mk)$ and $O(m_p nk + (m + n)k^2 + n^2 k + nk)$, respectively. When $n \gg k$, $m_p \gg k$, and $m_p \gg n$, the overall complexity of updating U^p and V^p is $O(t\sum_{p=1}^{P} m_p nk)$. Furthermore, the complexity of the constructing data graph for each view is $O(n^2)$. Therefore, the computational complexity of the proposed method is $O(t\sum_{p=1}^{P} m_p nk)$. The complexity of other comparison algorithms is shown in Table 8.1. For those algorithms whose updating formulas are not matrix multiplications, we only give the final computational complexity.

8.3 Convergence analysis

The mathematical proof of convergence of the proposed algorithm is given in this section. We only give the convergence analysis about V^p, and it can be extended to the proof of U^p.

Definition 1. *$G(h, h^{'})$ is an auxiliary function of $F(h)$, if the following conditions are satisfied.*

$$F(h) \leq G(h, h^{'}), \quad F(h) = G(h, h). \tag{8.33}$$

Lemma 1. *If G is an auxiliary function of $F(h)$, then $F(h)$ is nonincreasing under the following updating rule.*

$$h^{t+1} = \arg\min_{h} G(h, h^{'}). \tag{8.34}$$

Proof.

$$F(h^{t+1}) \leq G(h^{t+1}, h^t) \leq G(h^t, h^t) = F(h^t). \tag{8.35}$$

Table 8.1   Algorithm complexity analysis

Methods	Variables	Addition	Multiplication	Division	Overall
NMF [7]	U	$mnk + (m+n)k^2$	$mnk + (m+n)k^2 + mk$	mk	$O(mnk)$
	V	$mnk + (m+n)k^2$	$mnk + (m+n)k^2 + nk$	nk	
GNMF [2]	U	$mnk + (m+n)k^2$	$mnk + (m+n)k^2 + mk$	mk	$O(mnk)$
	V	$mnk + (m+n)k^2 + 2n^2k + 2nk$	$mnk + (m+n)k^2 + 2n^2k + 3nk$	nk	
ColNMF [8]	U^p	$m_pnk + (m_p+n)k^2$	$m_pnk + (m_p+n)k^2 + m_pk$	m_pk	$O(\sum_{p=1}^{P} m_pnk)$
	V^*	$\sum_{p=1}^{P}(m_pnk + m_pk^2) + n^2k + Pk^2 + nk^2$	$\sum_{p=1}^{P}(m_pnk + m_pk^2) + nk + nk^2$	nk	
MultiNMF [9]	U^p	$m_pnk + (m_p+n)k^2 + (2n+3m-3)k$	$m_pnk + (m_p+n)k^2 + (2n+3)k$	m_pk	$O(\sum_{p=1}^{P} m_pnk)$
	V^p	$m_pnk + (m_p+n)k^2 + 2nk$	$m_pnk + (m_p+n)k^2 + 2nk$	nk	
RMKMC [10]	—	—	—	—	$O(\sum_{p=1}^{P} m_pnk)$
CoregSPC [11]	—	—	—	—	$O(Pn^3)$
KMLRSSC [12]	—	—	—	—	$O(Pn^3)$
GBS-KO [13]	—	—	—	—	$O(Pn^3)$
2CMV [14]	U^p	$2m_pnk + 2(m_p+n)k^2 + 2m_pk$	$2m_pnk + 2(m_p+n)k^2 + 2m_pk$	m_pk	$O(\sum_{p=1}^{P} m_pnk)$
	V^p	$m_pnk + (m_p+n)k^2 + 3nk + 2n^2k$	$m_pnk + (m_p+n)k^2 + 4nk + 2n^2k$	nk	
	V^*	$\sum_{p=1}^{P}(m_pnk + m_p^2) + nk^2 + (2P+1)nk$	$\sum_{p=1}^{P}(m_pnk + m_pk^2) + nk^2 + 2nk$	nk	
Ours	U^p	$m_pnk + (m_p+n)k^2 + 2n^2k$	$m_pnk + (m_p+n)k^2 + m_pk + n^2k$	m_pk	$O(\sum_{p=1}^{P} m_pnk)$
	V^p	$m_pnk + (m_p+n)k^2 + (P+3)nk + 4n^2k$	$m_pnk + (m_p+n)k^2 + 5nk + 4n^2k$	nk	

Equation (8.35) shows that $F(h)$ is nonincreasing under the updating rule (8.34). Therefore, if we can find a suitable auxiliary function, the convergence with respect to V^p can be proved.

Let $F(V^p)$ be the objective function of problem (8.20).

$$F(V^p) = \mathrm{tr}[(X^p - U^p V^p)D^p(X^p - U^p V^p)^T]$$
$$+ 2\alpha \sum_{w=1}^{P} \mathrm{tr}[V^p(V^w)^T] + \gamma\,\mathrm{tr}[V^p L^p(V^p)^T]. \tag{8.36}$$

The first and second partial derivatives of $F(V^p)$ with respect to the variable v_{ij}^p can be calculated.

$$F'_{ij} = \frac{\partial F}{\partial v_{ij}^p} = [-2(U^p)^T X^p D^p + 2(U^p)^T U^p V^p D^p$$
$$+ 2\alpha \sum_{w=1,w\neq p}^{P} V^w + 4\alpha V^p + 2\gamma V^p(\hat{W}^p - W^p)]_{ij}. \tag{8.37}$$

$$F''_{ij} = \frac{\partial F'_{ij}}{\partial v_{ij}^p} = 2d_{jj}^p[(U^p)^T U^p]_{ii} + 4\alpha + 2\gamma(\hat{W}^p - W^p)_{jj}. \tag{8.38}$$

The Taylor series expansion of $F(v_{ij}^p)$ is expressed as

$$F(v_{ij}^p) = F(v_{ij}^{p'}) + F_{ij}'(v_{ij}^{p'})(v_{ij}^p - v_{ij}^{p'}) + \frac{1}{2}F_{ij}''(v_{ij}^{p'})(v_{ij}^p - v_{ij}^{p'})^2. \tag{8.39}$$

$\square$

Lemma 2. *The function*

$$G(v_{ij}^p, v_{ij}^{p'}) = F_{ij}(v_{ij}^{p'}) + F_{ij}'(v_{ij}^{p'})(v_{ij}^p - v_{ij}^{p'}) + \frac{h_{ij}}{v_{ij}^{p'}}(v_{ij}^p - v_{ij}^{p'})^2 \tag{8.40}$$

is an auxiliary function for $F(v_{ij}^p)$, where

$$h_{ij} = \left[(U^p)^T U^p V^{p'} D^p + \alpha \sum_{w=1, w \neq p}^{P} V^w + 2\alpha V^{p'} + \gamma V^{p'} \hat{W}^p \right]_{ij}. \tag{8.41}$$

Proof.   It is easy to verify that $F_{ij}(v_{ij}^{p'}) = G(v_{ij}^{p'}, v_{ij}^{p'})$. Then, proving $F_{ij}(v_{ij}^p) \leq G(v_{ij}^p, v_{ij}^{p'})$ is equivalent to prove

$$\frac{h_{ij}}{v_{ij}^{p'}} \geq d_{jj}^p[(U^p)^T U^p]_{ii} + 2\alpha + \gamma(\hat{W}^p - W^p)_{jj}. \tag{8.42}$$

It is obvious that the following formulas are satisfied.

$$[(U^p)^T U^p V^p D^p]_{ij} = \sum_{q=1}^{n} d_{qj}^p \sum_{l=1}^{k} [(U^p)^T U^p]_{il} v_{lq}^{p'} \geq d_{jj}^p[(U^p)^T U^p]_{ii} v_{ij}^{p'}. \tag{8.43}$$

$$(V^{p'} \hat{W}^p)_{ij} = \sum_{l=1}^{n} v_{il}^{p'} \hat{w}_{lj}^p \geq v_{ij}^{p'} \hat{w}_{jj}^p \geq v_{ij}^{p'}(\hat{W}^p - W^p)_{jj}. \tag{8.44}$$

Therefore, $G(v_{ij}^p, v_{ij}^{p'})$ is an auxiliary function for $F(v_{ij}^p)$.

We can calculate the optimal solution of v_{ij}^p by minimizing $G(v_{ij}^p, v_{ij}^{p'})$. Since $G(v_{ij}^p, v_{ij}^{p'})$ is a convex function with respect to v_{ij}^p, setting $\frac{\partial G(v_{ij}^p, v_{ij}^{p'})}{\partial v_{ij}^p} = 0$, we obtain

$$v_{ij}^{p'+1} = v_{ij}^{p'} - \frac{v_{ij}^{p'} F_{ij}'}{2h_{ij}}. \tag{8.45}$$

Equation (8.45) is the same as the updating formula for V^p. Consequently, under the updating formula (8.24), the objective function $F(V^p)$ is nonincreasing and achieves convergence, i.e., $F(V^{p'+1}) \leq F(V^{p'})$.

Let $J(V^p)$ be the objective function of problem (8.19).

$$J(V^p) = ||X^p - U^p V^p||_{2,1} + \sum_{w=1}^{P} \text{tr}[V^p(V^w)^T] + \gamma \, \text{tr}(V^p L^p (V^p)^T. \tag{8.46}$$

In problem (8.20), D^p is a diagonal matrix and

$$d_{ii}^p = \frac{1}{2||x_i^p - U^p v_i^{p'}||_2}. \tag{8.47}$$

$$F(V^p) = \sum_{i=1}^n d_{ii}^p ||x_i^p - U^p v_i^p||_2^2 + \sum_{w=1}^P \mathrm{tr}[V^p (V^w)^T] + \gamma \, \mathrm{tr}(V^p L^p (V^p)^T. \tag{8.48}$$

□

Lemma 3. *The function $J(V^p)$ is nonincreasing under the updating formula (8.24).*

Proof.

$$
\begin{aligned}
&[J(V^{p^{t+1}}) - J(V^{p^t})] - [F(V^{p^{t+1}}) - F(V^{p^t})] \\
&= \sum_{i=1}^n \left(||x_i^p - U^p v_i^{p^{t+1}}||_2 - ||x_i^p - U^p v_i^{p^{t+1}}||_2^2 d_{ii}^p - \frac{1}{4d_{ii}^p} \right) \\
&= \sum_{i=1}^n d_{ii}^p \left(\frac{1}{d_{ii}^p} ||x_i^p - U^p v_i^{p^{t+1}}||_2 - ||x_i^p - U^p v_i^{p^{t+1}}||_2^2 - \frac{1}{4d_{ii}^{p^2}} \right) \\
&= \sum_{i=1}^n (-d_{ii}^p) \left[-\frac{1}{d_{ii}^p} ||x_i^p - U^p v_i^{p^{t+1}}||_2 + ||x_i^p - U^p v_i^{p^{t+1}}||_2^2 + \frac{1}{(2d_{ii}^p)^2} \right] \\
&= \sum_{i=1}^n (-d_{ii}^p)(-||x_i^p - U^p v_i^{p^{t+1}}||_2 + \frac{1}{2d_{ii}^p})^2 \le 0.
\end{aligned}
\tag{8.49}
$$

According to (8.3), we can obtain $J(V^{p^{t+1}}) \le J(V^{p^t})$. Therefore, the function $J(V^p)$ is nonincreasing under the updating formula (8.24).

The same approach can be applied to the proof of convergence with respect to U^p. In general, the proposed algorithm enables the objective function of problem (8.7) to converge.

8.4 Experiments

In this section, we perform extensive experiments to demonstrate the effectiveness and robustness of the proposed method.

8.4.1 Datasets descriptions

We conduct experiments on five real-world and four synthetic multi-view datasets. The brief information of each dataset is listed in Table 8.2.

- ORL* [15]: The dataset contains facial information from 40 different people, and each person has 10 images taken under different lighting conditions and at

---

* https://www.cl.cam.ac.uk/research/dtg/attarchive/facedatabase.html.

Table 8.2   Datasets used in experiments

Dataset	Views	Samples	Class
ORL	3	400	40
ORLG	3	400	40
ORLSP	3	400	40
ORLB	3	400	40
ORLP	3	400	40
Cornell	2	195	4
Texas	2	187	4
Washington	2	230	4
Wisconsin	2	265	4

different times. These images show facial expressions and facial details. The dataset describes each face from three different perspectives: the pixel value of the image and two different features of the original image. Sample images of this dataset are shown in Figure 8.2(a).

- ORLG: Gaussian noise with a mean of 0 and a variance of 0.01 is loaded onto the image view of the original ORL dataset, while the other two views remain unchanged. The sample images of ORLG are expressed in Figure 8.2(b).

- ORLSP: We add salt and pepper noise with a density of 0.1 to the image view of the original ORL dataset, while the other two views are unaltered. The sample images of ORLSP are shown in Figure 8.2(c).

- ORLB: For the image view of the ORL dataset, we generate occlusion patches of size 15×15 for each image, while the other two views remain unchanged. The sample images of ORLB can be seen in Figure 8.2(d).

- ORLP: We use the function "imnoise()" in the MATLAB® toolbox to add Poisson noise to each image in ORL. This function automatically adds Poisson noise based on the pixel value of the image. The images with Poisson noise are shown in Figure 8.2(e).

- WebKB[†] [15]: This is a web page dataset that contains data from four different universities. The data for these universities is separated into four datasets: Cornell, Texas, Washington, and Wisconsin. The dataset for each university is divided into five categories: student, project, course, staff, and faculty. Each dataset has information about two views. One represents the content contained in the web page, and the other represents the various links within the text content.

8.4.2   Compared methods

We describe the details of 11 different compared methods, which include single-view and multi-view methods.

[†] http://lig-membres.imag.fr/grimal/data.html.

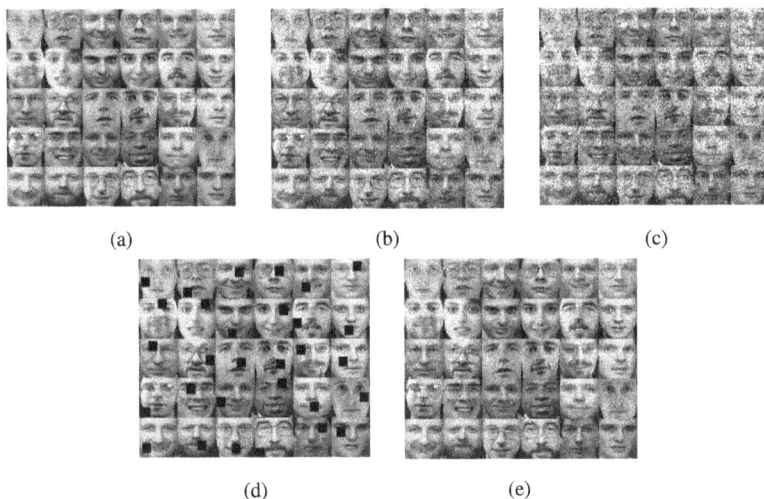

Figure 8.2   ORL sample images. (a) ORL, (b) ORLG, (c) ORLSP, (d) ORLB, and (e) ORLP.

- **NMF** (non-negative matrix factorization) [7]: We execute NMF on each view of the datasets and then record the best results from all views as the final experimental results.
- **GNMF** (graph regularized non-negative matrix factorization)[‡] [2]: The method imposes a graph constraint on the coefficient matrix in NMF. There is one trade-off parameter in GNMF, which we choose from $\{10^{-3}, 10^{-2}, 10^{-1}, 1, 10, 10^2, 10^3\}$. We execute GNMF on each view of the datasets and then record the best results from all views as the final experimental results.
- **FCNMF** (feature concatenation non-negative matrix factorization) [7]: The method first concatenates the data matrices of all views to form a new dataset and then performs NMF on this new dataset.
- **ColNMF** (collective NMF) [8]: This method extends NMF to the multi-view method. The idea is to decompose multi-view data matrices into a consistency matrix and multiple basis matrices.
- **MultiNMF** (MVC via joint NMF)[§] [9]: It learns the consensus representation by narrowing the gap between all coefficient matrices and the consensus matrix. We set parameters according to the original paper.
- **RMKMC** (robust multi-view k-means clustering)[|] [10]: This is the multi-view k-means method using the $l_{2,1}$-norm, which uses a shared cluster indicator for clustering. In this method, by adjusting a parameter, each view is given various weights. We choose this parameter according to the original paper.

[‡] http://www.cad.zju.edu.cn/home/dengcai/Data/GNMF.html.
[§] http://jialu.info/.
[|] https://sites.google.com/site/feipingnie/publications.

- **CoRegSPC** (co-regularized multi-view spectral clustering)¶ [11]: This approach utilizes co-regularization for spectral clustering. We set the weighting parameters in the range of 0.01 to 0.05.
- **KMLRSSC** (kernel multi-view low-rank sparse subspace clustering)** [12]: This is an MVC method with sparsity and low-rank constraints. By applying the centroid-based method, a consistent representation matrix can be obtained. Each parameter in this method is adjusted according to the description in the original paper.
- **GBS-KO** (a study of graph-based system for MVC)†† [13]: This is an MVC approach, which can effectively construct graph matrices based on manifold learning and sparse representation and automatically weight each graph matrix to learn the unified graph.
- **2CMV** (a novel approach to learning consensus and complementary information for multi-view data clustering)‡‡ [14]: This method simultaneously learns two factor matrices, encoding the consensus and complementary information in multi-view data using the coupled matrix factorization. A diversity constraint is imposed on these two matrices to obtain complementary information. An optimal graph is constructed to protect the geometric structure information of the data.
- **MVCDMFPA** (MVC via deep matrix factorization and partition alignment)§§ [16]: The method utilizes deep semi-NMF to obtain the hierarchical information of the data. The partition learning and late fusion stages interact to obtain the final common matrix.
- **Ours**: There are three parameters within the proposed method, and we choose each parameter value from the set $\{10^{-4}, 10^{-3}, 10^{-2}, 10^{-1}, 1, 10, 10^2, 10^3\}$ before fine-tuning.

To verify the sensitivity of each method to noise, for the NMF and GNMF single-view methods, we only execute the methods on the first view of ORLG, ORLSP, ORLB, and ORLP datasets. We set the number of neighbors to 5 for the method that involves constructing a graph using KNN. The subspace dimension of each method based on NMF is set to the number of dataset categories. For all methods, we execute the clustering experiment ten times and record the average result and standard deviation.

8.4.3 Results

The clustering results are evaluated by three extensive evaluation metrics, including accuracy (ACC) [17], normalized mutual information (NMI) [17], and Purity [18]. Each metric represents a different clustering performance. Moreover, a two-sample

---

¶ https://github.com/areslp/matlab/tree/master.
** https://github.com/mbrbic/Multi-view-LRSSC.
†† https://github.com/cswanghao/gbs.
‡‡ https://github.com/khanhluongds/Multi-view-Clustering-2CMV.
§§ https://github.com/zhangchen234/MVC-DMF-PA.

t-test [19] is used to check whether the performance of the proposed method is significantly different from that of the compared methods. Given the significance level of 5%, let the null hypothesis be "there is no significant difference between the proposed method and the compared methods," and let the alternative hypothesis be "the proposed method is significantly different from the compared methods."

Tables 8.3–8.7 provide the experimental results on five real-world datasets. In each table, the best result is highlighted in boldface. From these tables, we can find that the clustering performance of the proposed method outperforms most existing methods. On the ORL dataset, the proposed method and 2CMV achieve high results compared to other methods. This is because the proposed method and 2CMV can capture the diversity information of the data, illustrating that using diversity constraints

Table 8.3   The results of ORL

Method	ACC	NMI	Purity
NMF	67.63 (2.44)	82.77 (1.51)	72.23 (1.88)
GNMF	70.68 (2.55)	84.45 (1.49)	74.70 (2.11)
FCNMF	56.85 (3.31)	75.11 (1.80)	62.62 (2.51)
ColNMF	68.65 (2.68)	84.05 (1.65)	73.82 (1.85)
MultiNMF	67.10 (3.38)	82.46 (1.74)	72.38 (2.60)
RMKMC	58.53 (3.13)	76.36 (1.78)	62.37 (2.59)
CoRegSPC	72.53 (2.76)	86.01 (1.65)	76.38 (2.34)
KMLRSSC	70.49 (2.59)	84.33 (1.06)	74.33 (2.14)
GBS-KO	63.25 (0.00)	80.35 (0.00)	71.50 (0.00)
2CMV	73.31 (2.43)	**88.31 (0.66)**	77.98 (1.73)
MVCDMFPA	71.00 (1.99)	85.61 (1.19)	74.98 (1.82)
Ours	**74.13 (1.52)**	86.84 (0.71)	**78.20 (1.35)**

Table 8.4   The results of Cornell

Method	ACC	NMI	Purity
NMF	53.08 (3.35)	37.35 (1.19)	69.23 (1.18)
GNMF	51.90 (2.45)	38.27 (1.28)	67.08 (1.87)
FCNMF	52.87 (3.80)	40.86 (1.20)	70.00 (1.21)
ColNMF	36.41 (0.00)	13.55 (0.00)	45.64 (0.00)
MultiNMF	38.72 (3.02)	9.85 (1.60)	44.67 (0.66)
RMKMC	36.82 (2.29)	15.01 (3.21)	49.69 (2.41)
CoRegSPC	52.56 (4.79)	34.55 (2.53)	63.54 (1.94)
KMLRSSC	57.28 (1.19)	42.51 (3.90)	70.64 (4.40)
GBS-KO	44.10 (0.00)	6.86 (0.00)	46.15 (0.00)
2CMV	53.59 (5.66)	27.55 (3.50)	58.66 (3.79)
MVCDMFPA	43.69 (3.25)	23.73 (3.92)	58.15 (4.27)
Ours	**70.10 (0.35)**	**44.61 (1.00)**	**73.95 (0.53)**

Table 8.5   The results of Texas

Method	ACC	NMI	Purity
NMF	50.27 (2.14)	32.54 (3.05)	72.67 (2.41)
GNMF	52.94 (3.18)	31.70 (2.35)	71.60 (0.92)
FCNMF	55.03 (3.80)	33.07 (2.52)	72.83 (1.69)
ColNMF	51.50 (0.26)	16.92 (0.05)	58.82 (0.00)
MultiNMF	59.41 (2.66)	18.74 (3.46)	60.70 (1.99)
RMKMC	46.74 (5.62)	15.67 (3.32)	60.86 (2.44)
CoRegSPC	62.73 (2.17)	28.50 (3.48)	69.84 (3.64)
KMLRSSC	53.24 (3.16)	27.55 (2.33)	70.24 (2.44)
GBS-KO	59.36 (0.00)	12.24 (0.00)	62.57 (0.00)
2CMV	56.89 (5.14)	21.33 (1.09)	63.47 (0.35)
MVCDMFPA	47.17 (3.98)	19.94 (1.73)	62.57 (1.87)
Ours	**66.20 (0.66)**	**37.02 (0.42)**	**73.26 (0.00)**

Table 8.6   The results of Washington

Method	ACC	NMI	Purity
NMF	50.78 (1.40)	31.94 (1.64)	70.00 (0.85)
GNMF	65.26 (2.51)	**40.64 (1.60)**	71.35 (0.66)
FCNMF	50.39 (0.93)	29.79 (1.23)	68.65 (1.13)
ColNMF	62.61 (0.00)	32.75 (0.00)	69.57 (0.00)
MultiNMF	64.26 (0.18)	22.43 (0.46)	65.52 (0.21)
RMKMC	55.87 (5.08)	28.33 (4.07)	68.78 (2.16)
CoRegSPC	54.13 (2.65)	30.27 (2.68)	68.70 (0.07)
KMLRSSC	55.85 (2.98)	37.51 (4.04)	71.74 (1.88)
GBS-KO	64.78 (0.00)	24.29 (0.00)	66.52 (0.00)
2CMV	59.34 (1.04)	21.54 (2.14)	63.76 (0.45)
MVCDMFPA	54.57 (1.39)	19.22 (0.95)	64.91 (0.54)
Ours	**67.87 (0.14)**	39.24 (0.35)	**73.09 (0.14)**

Table 8.7   The results of Wisconsin

Method	ACC	NMI	Purity
NMF	57.13 (4.11)	36.17 (4.27)	72.38 (3.64)
GNMF	58.42 (1.06)	**43.21 (1.02)**	**74.42 (0.77)**
FCNMF	56.49 (5.33)	36.17 (5.58)	72.83 (4.55)
ColNMF	45.96 (0.24)	23.26 (0.26)	66.34 (0.24)
MultiNMF	46.49 (1.91)	10.92 (3.25)	52.64 (0.54)
RMKMC	47.02 (4.79)	29.44 (4.46)	68.30 (2.91)
CoRegSPC	58.19 (3.39)	35.86 (2.33)	71.25 (2.26)
KMLRSSC	56.49 (0.64)	33.40 (0.70)	69.21 (0.70)
GBS-KO	47.92 (0.00)	5.07 (0.00)	51.32 (0.00)
2CMV	49.15 (1.64)	14.96 (1.05)	58.56 (1.25)
MVCDMFPA	38.75 (1.14)	10.54 (0.92)	57.06 (1.39)
Ours	**61.36 (0.19)**	35.56 (0.37)	71.55 (0.19)

to obtain comprehensive representations can improve clustering performance. On the Cornell and the Texas datasets, the proposed method performs better than all the compared methods. A major reason for this is that the proposed method considers diverse information and preserves the geometrical structure of the data with adaptive graph constraints. On the Washington dataset, the proposed method exceeds other methods in terms of ACC and Purity. On the Wisconsin dataset, the proposed method outperforms other methods in terms of ACC only. However, GNMF achieves higher NMI on both the Washington and the Wisconsin datasets.

Tables 8.8–8.11 provide the experimental results of four synthetic datasets. For four different noises, the proposed method achieves better performance than the compared methods. It is easy to find that the clustering performance of some compared methods is greatly affected by noise, such as NMF, GNMNF, KMLRSSC, and 2CMV. However, the proposed method is less affected by four different noises. Experiments on four datasets containing noise verify the robustness of the proposed method.

Tables 8.12–8.14 show the statistical test results with regards to ACC, NMI, and Purity, respectively. If the p-value is less than 0.05, the performance of the proposed method is significantly different from that of the compared methods. Table 8.12 exhibits the p-value with respect to ACC. As seen from Table 8.12, the proposed method on ORL is not significantly different from CoregSPC and 2CMV. The p-value between the proposed method and each compared method, except for CoregSPC and 2CMV, is less than 0.05, which illustrates that the proposed method is able to achieve higher ACC on these five datasets. In Table 8.13, the NMI of the proposed method on ORL is lower than 2CMV, and the NMI on the Washington and Wisconsin is lower than GNMF. However, for most cases, the NMI obtained by the proposed method is higher than the compared methods. In Table 8.14, except that the Purity obtained by the proposed method on Washington and Wisconsin is lower than GNMF, the proposed method can achieve higher Purity than comparison methods in most cases.

According to the results of Tables 8.3–8.14, we can see that the performance of the proposed method on all datasets surpass most of the compared methods. Hence, these experimental results demonstrate the effectiveness of the proposed method.

8.4.4 Ablation study

In this section, to verify the validity of the adaptive graph and diversity constraints, we record the clustering results for three cases: (1) without diversity and adaptive graph constraints, (2) with only the diversity constraint, and (3) with only the adaptive graph constraint. The results are presented in Tables 8.15–8.17. By comparing Table 8.15 with Table 8.16, it is revealed that the values of metrics increase after adding the diversity constraint. Furthermore, a comparison between Table 8.15 and Table 8.17 shows that the metrics on Texas, Washington, and Wisconsin increase significantly due to the adaptive graph constraint. According to the results of the proposed method presented in Tables 8.3–8.7 and the three cases shown in Tables 8.15–8.17, after utilizing diversity and adaptive graph constraints on multi-view $l_{2,1}$-norm NMF, the performance on all five datasets is highly improved. This illustrates that the addition of diversity constraints and adaptive graphs can result in better clustering performance.

Table 8.8   The results of ORLG

Method	ACC	NMI	Purity
NMF	56.33 (2.34)	74.89 (1.06)	62.20 (1.72)
GNMF	56.83 (2.01)	74.99 (1.06)	62.00 (1.62)
FCNMF	55.73 (1.87))	73.99 (1.19)	61.63 (1.58)
ColNMF	67.28 (3.91)	82.92 (2.17)	72.83 (2.99)
MultiNMF	68.02 (3.44)	82.57 (2.69)	72.90 (3.49)
RMKMC	57.40 (3.49)	75.47 (2.47)	60.92 (2.72)
CoRegSPC	72.22 (4.71)	85.97 (2.40)	75.82 (3.95)
KMLRSSC	70.81 (3.37)	83.56 (1.60)	73.52 (2.71)
GBS-KO	62.75 (0.00)	78.88 (0.00)	71.50 (0.00)
2CMV	67.86 (1.90)	85.94 (0.65)	72.66 (1.63)
MVCDMFPA	70.00 (3.45)	85.24 (1.47)	74.20 (2.77)
Ours	**74.78 (1.17)**	**87.28 (0.66)**	**78.82 (1.03)**

Note: The bold values represent the best results in the comparison method.

Table 8.9   The results of ORLSP

Method	ACC	NMI	Purity
NMF	51.60 (1.90)	70.64 (1.58)	57.02 (1.89)
GNMF	55.63 (1.82)	72.75 (1.14)	60.53 (1.37)
FCNMF	52.68 (1.83)	71.03 (1.45)	57.93 (1.23)
ColNMF	69.55 (2.63)	84.54 (1.50)	75.35 (1.94)
MultiNMF	66.95 (1.08)	82.57 (0.80)	72.22 (0.92)
RMKMC	57.13 (3.29)	74.88 (1.75)	60.98 (1.80)
CoRegSPC	**73.88 (5.86)**	**87.27 (2.20)**	77.63 (4.45)
KMLRSSC	67.69 (3.47)	81.03 (1.67)	70.65 (2.90)
GBS-KO	59.25 (0.00)	74.80 (0.00)	68.50 (0.00)
2CMV	67.93 (2.48)	84.54 (0.98)	72.57 (1.86)
MVCDMFPA	72.23 (2.88)	86.31 (1.25)	75.98 (1.89)
Ours	73.48 (2.74)	87.04 (1.15)	**77.70 (2.01)**

Note: The bold values represent the best results in the comparison method.

Table 8.10   The results of ORLB

Method	ACC	NMI	Purity
NMF	20.27 (1.00)	42.53 (0.94)	21.55 (0.92)
GNMF	21.60 (1.48)	43.18 (1.07)	22.87 (1.27)
FCNMF	21.28 (0.98)	42.93 (0.70)	22.55 (0.99)
ColNMF	69.60 (1.72)	82.73 (0.76)	73.40 (0.94)
MultiNMF	62.05 (3.13)	76.99 (2.11)	66.17 (2.88)
RMKMC	54.68 (2.73)	73.17 (1.60)	58.15 (2.24)
CoRegSPC	67.95 (3.81)	81.72 (1.92)	71.45 (3.08)
KMLRSSC	27.04 (1.51)	48.79 (1.11)	29.42 (1.60)
GBS-KO	59.25 (0.00)	74.96 (0.00)	68.00 (0.00)
2CMV	61.08 (3.88)	80.32 (1.30)	65.76 (2.86)
MVCDMFPA	72.38 (3.52)	86.21 (2.06)	76.52 (2.83)
Ours	**75.42 (1.77)**	**87.33 (0.88)**	**79.10 (1.65)**

Note: The bold values represent the best results in the comparison method.

Table 8.11   The results of ORLP

Method	ACC	NMI	Purity
NMF	57.75 (2.70)	75.37 (1.59)	62.98 (2.39)
GNMF	59.45 (3.36)	76.27 (1.97)	64.55 (2.57)
FCNMF	56.10 (3.35)	74.24 (1.87)	61.45 (2.70)
ColNMF	57.37 (3.43)	75.52 (2.24)	61.67 (2.38)
MultiNMF	67.73 (3.56)	82.42 (1.76)	72.38 (2.41)
RMKMC	58.00 (2.26)	76.21 (1.13)	62.13 (2.00)
CoRegSPC	72.43 (2.49)	86.26 (1.09)	76.35 (1.73)
KMLRSSC	69.30 (2.12)	83.73 (1.08)	73.63 (1.87)
GBS-KO	60.50 (0.00)	77.85 (0.00)	70.00 (0.00)
2CMV	**73.67 (3.21)**	**88.61 (0.09)**	**77.87 (2.15)**
MVCDMFPA	70.53 (2.10)	85.35 (1.43)	74.87 (1.71)
Ours	73.05 (2.37)	86.54 (1.05)	77.02 (2.02)

Note: The bold values represent the best results in the comparison method.

Table 8.12   p-Values between the proposed method and other clustering methods according to ACC

	ORL	Cornell	Texas	Washington	Wisconsin
NMF	1.19e−06	5.12e−08	2.38e−10	1.92e−11	9.94e−03
GNMF	1.72e−03	7.02e−15	1.84e−07	9.51e−03	8.11e−06
FCNMF	1.27e−11	1.47e−07	3.38e−08	2.15e−13	1.80e−02
ColNMF	3.56e−11	1.09e−08	4.31e−05	5.33e−04	1.01e−05
MultiNMF	5.22e−05	7.42e−11	1.34e−05	9.74e−21	1.13e−09
RMKMC	9.61e−11	4.82e−13	2.49e−08	1.27e−05	2.68e−06
CoRegSPC	1.26e−01	9.82e−07	5.63e−04	4.96e−08	1.61e−02
KMLRSSC	2.05e−03	2.27e−09	3.48e−08	6.25e−06	1.17e−08
GBS−KO	3.04e−09	2.11e−18	1.08e−10	1.10e−13	4.58e−18
2CMV	6.67e−01	1.46e−05	2.35e−04	1.29e−10	1.19e−13
MVCDMFPA	9.35e−04	7.34e−10	6.68e−08	1.77e−10	9.93e−14

Table 8.13   p-Values between the proposed method and other clustering methods according to NMI

	ORL	Cornell	Texas	Washington	Wisconsin
NMF	3.83e−06	1.63e−11	1.18e−03	6.28e−11	6.63e−01
GNMF	2.39e−04	3.19e−10	4.51e−05	2.17e−02	1.52e−14
FCNMF	3.26e−10	5.16e−07	7.42e−04	1.24e−10	7.36e−01
ColNMF	9.43e−09	2.58e−12	1.18e−03	1.64e−04	7.82e−05
MultiNMF	7.62e−07	5.63e−22	3.40e−08	4.94e−25	1.32e−09
RMKMC	3.81e−15	1.38e−19	4.11e−09	1.14e−04	1.40e−04
CoRegSPC	1.70e−01	8.09e−08	2.59e−05	4.46e−09	6.69e−01
KMLRSSC	1.66e−05	1.11e−05	5.85e−08	8.80e−03	1.20e−05
GBS−KO	3.40e−10	1.02e−15	1.69e−17	1.79e−15	1.03e−18
2CMV	2.75e−05	2.05e−07	2.53e−13	7.16e−11	1.33e−20
MVCDMFPA	1.17e−02	3.10e−12	3.24e−11	2.55e−22	1.24e−17

Table 8.14   p-Values between the proposed method and other clustering methods according to Purity

	ORL	Cornell	Texas	Washington	Wisconsin
NMF	1.79e−07	9.98e−10	4.60e−01	1.15e−09	4.90e−01
GNMF	3.35e−04	1.56e−09	3.06e−04	1.18e−05	1.15e−09
FCNMF	1.20e−12	2.21e−08	4.43e−01	4.74e−07	3.96e−01
ColNMF	1.26e−11	3.16e−07	5.17e−07	3.14e−04	2.36e−05
MultiNMF	6.17e−06	7.16e−27	9.16e−09	6.65e−23	3.37e−18
RMKMC	2.01e−12	4.17e−11	2.40e−06	7.99e−04	8.05e−03
CoRegSPC	4.66e−02	2.98e−12	1.56e−02	7.75e−09	6.84e−01
KMLRSSC	6.96e−04	7.51e−05	2.29e−04	6.61e−03	1.21e−04
GBS−KO	7.51e−08	5.33e−17	9.52e−266	1.25e−16	1.15e−19
2CMV	7.82e−01	2.11e−06	2.65e−14	3.39e−14	9.09e−10
MVCDMFPA	2.75e−04	7.85e−07	2.20e−08	4.07e−13	5.76e−11

Table 8.15   The results without diversity and adaptive graph constraints

Dataset	ACC	NMI	Purity
ORL	71.60 (2.67)	84.82 (1.14)	75.83 (1.62)
Cornell	51.23 (0.61)	32.32 (1.01)	63.33 (0.36)
Texas	48.93 (0.28)	23.86 (0.29)	70.05 (0.00)
Washington	51.65 (0.27)	21.75 (0.33)	54.48 (0.31)
Wisconsin	46.53 (0.25)	25.52 (0.16)	66.15 (0.25)

Table 8.16   The results with only the diversity constraint

Dataset	ACC	NMI	Purity
ORL	71.63 (2.71)	84.84 (1.18)	75.85 (1.65)
Cornell	51.69 (0.40)	33.70 (0.97)	63.49 (0.40)
Texas	66.31 (0.67)	37.07 (0.41)	73.26 (0.00)
Washington	53.87 (0.14)	22.82 (0.17)	67.35 (0.14)
Wisconsin	55.85 (0.00)	33.44 (0.32)	71.32 (0.00)

Table 8.17   The results with only the adaptive graph

Dataset	ACC	NMI	Purity
ORL	71.17 (2.67)	84.78 (1.12)	75.70 (1.58)
Cornell	51.13 (0.54)	32.24 (0.78)	63.38 (0.26)
Texas	55.78 (2.43)	27.43 (1.06)	70.64 (0.47)
Washington	62.70 (1.84)	33.43 (1.74)	68.78 (0.98)
Wisconsin	47.47 (0.16)	23.50 (0.19)	65.96 (0.16)

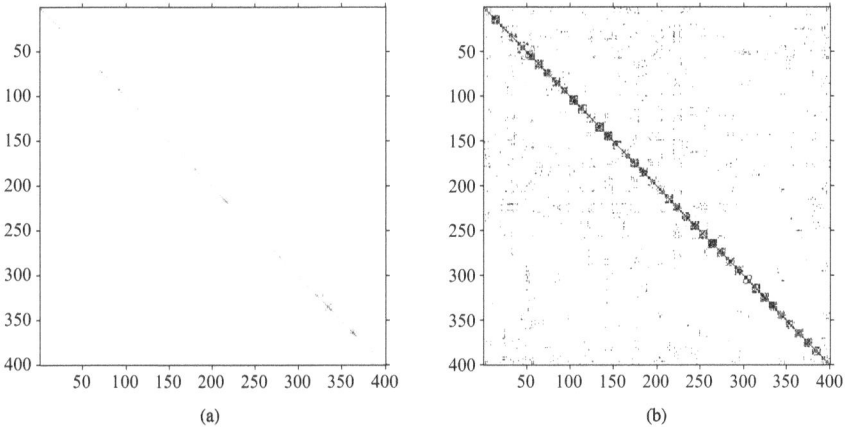

Figure 8.3 *Similarity matrix constructed by two different methods. (a) Adaptive graph method and (b) KNN method.*

8.4.5 Visualization on the ORL dataset

To validate the effectiveness of the adaptive graph constraint, we visualize the similarity matrices of the first view of the ORL dataset. Figures 8.3(a) and 8.3(b) present the similarity matrices constructed by the adaptive graph method and the KNN method, respectively. As seen from Figure 8.3(b), there exists neighbor relationship between many samples belonging to different classes, in other words, there is high similarity between samples belonging to different classes. Such similarity matrices are not conducive to clustering. In Figure 8.3(a), the similarity between samples belonging to same class is high, and the similarity between samples belonging to different classes is very low. This can facilitate data clustering. Consequently, the adaptive graph method is superior to the KNN method in constructing the similarity matrix.

8.4.6 Parameter investigation

In this section, we analyze the parameter sensitivity of the proposed method. The method involves three parameters, i.e., α, γ, and $\lambda \geq 0$. α measures the importance of the diversity constraint, while γ and λ adjust the weight of the adaptive graph constraint. We vary one of these parameters while keeping the others constant to investigate the sensitivity. Clustering experiments are repeated ten times, and the average values of ACC, NMI, and Purity on five real-world datasets are shown in Figures 8.4–8.8.

Here, we take ORL and Cornell datasets as examples. Figure 8.4 presents the sensitivity to parameters α, γ, and λ on the ORL dataset. It can be observed that the ACC, NMI, and Purity decrease as α, γ, and λ increase. As α and λ vary, the fluctuating range of each metric is low, indicating that the performance is not sensitive to α and λ. For the Cornell dataset, the parameter sensitivity analysis is shown in Figure 8.5. The three metrics increase with increasing α. As γ increases, the three metrics increase first and then decrease. The clustering performance is not sensitive to λ.

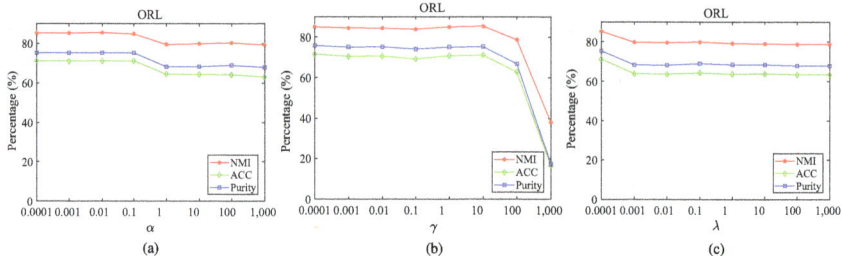

Figure 8.4   Parameter analysis for ORL. (a) Fix $\gamma = 10$, $\lambda = 0.0001$, and vary α.
(b) Fix $\alpha = 0.0001$, $\lambda = 0.0001$, and vary γ. (c) Fix $\alpha = 0.0001$,
$\gamma = 10$, and vary λ.

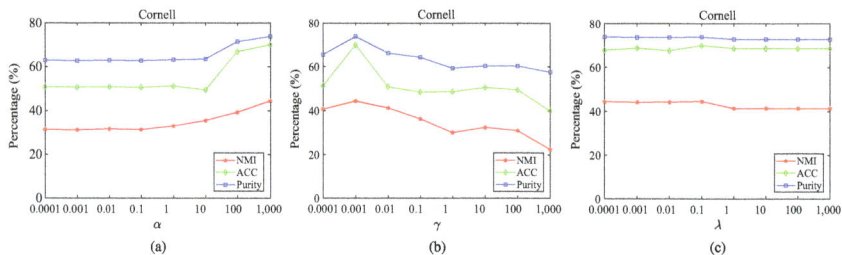

Figure 8.5   Parameter analysis for Cornell. (a) Fix $\gamma = 0.001$, $\lambda = 0.1$, and vary
α. (b) Fix $\alpha = 1,000$, $\lambda = 0.1$, and vary γ. (c) Fix $\alpha = 1,000$,
$\gamma = 0.001$, and vary λ.

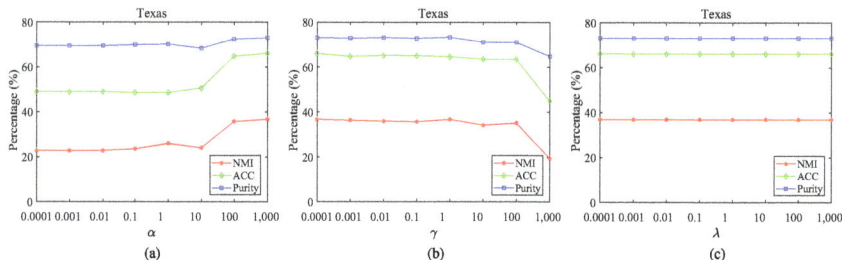

Figure 8.6   Parameter analysis for Texas. (a) Fix $\gamma = 0.0001$, $\lambda = 0.1$, and vary α.
(b) Fix $\alpha = 1,000$, $\lambda = 0.1$, and vary γ. (c) Fix $\alpha = 1,000$,
$\gamma = 0.0001$, and vary λ.

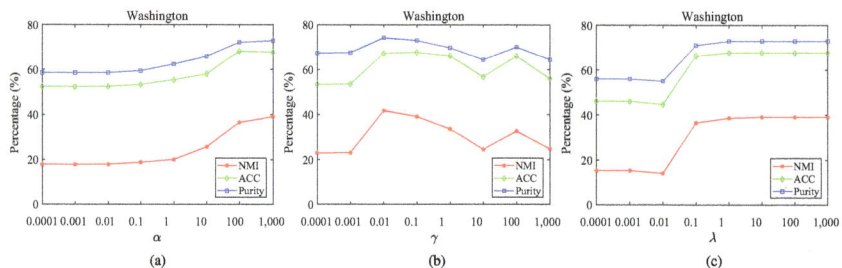

Figure 8.7   Parameter analysis for Washington. (a) Fix $\gamma = 0.0001$, $\lambda = 1$, and
vary α. (b) Fix $\alpha = 1,000$, $\lambda = 1$, and vary γ. (c) Fix $\alpha = 1,000$,
$\gamma = 0.0001$, and vary λ.

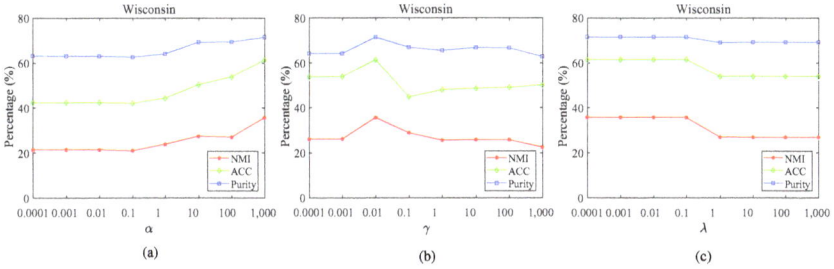

Figure 8.8   *Parameter analysis for Wisconsin. (a) Fix $\gamma = 0.001$, $\lambda = 0.1$, and vary α. (b) Fix $\alpha = 1,000$, $\lambda = 0.1$, and vary γ. (c) Fix $\alpha = 1,000$, $\gamma = 0.01$, and vary λ.*

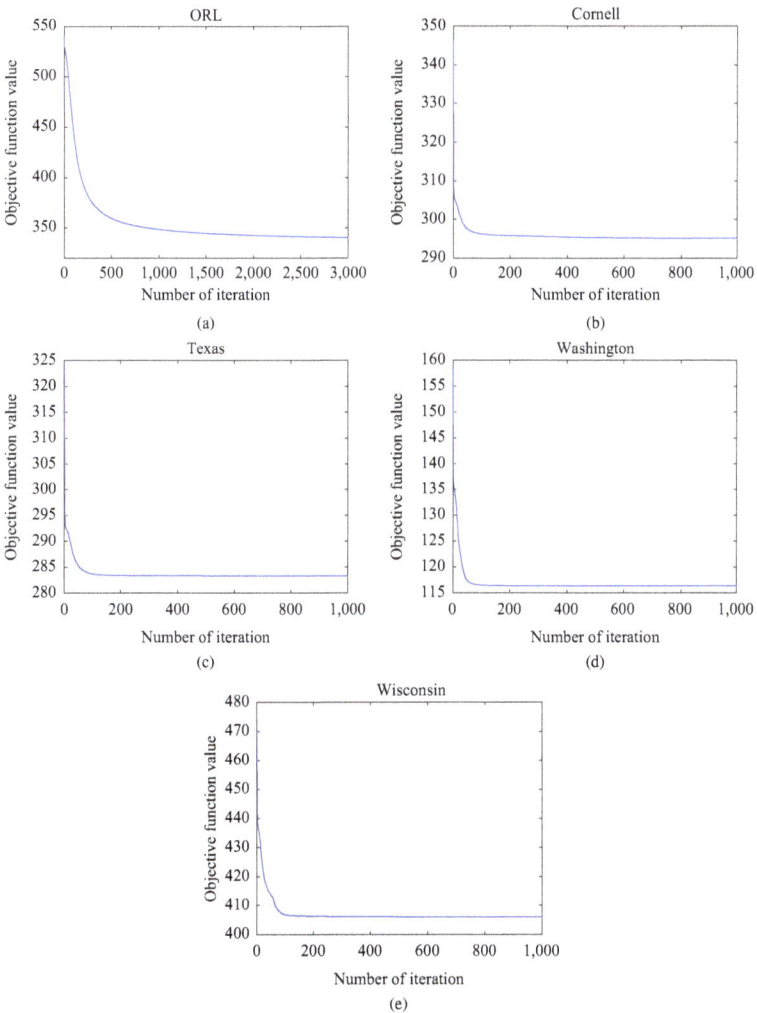

Figure 8.9   *Convergence results for five datasets. (a) ORL, (b) Cornell, (c) Texas, (d) Washington, and (e) Wisconsin.*

Table 8.18   Running time (second)

	ORL	Cornell	Texas	Washington	Wisconsin
NMF	3.04	0.19	0.17	0.19	0.22
GNMF	4.34	0.32	0.28	0.16	0.18
FCNMF	19.93	0.63	0.74	0.71	1.03
ColNMF	25.98	0.62	0.54	0.73	0.91
MultiNMF	266.04	6.45	7.86	9.07	8.12
RMKMC	6.29	0.23	0.05	0.43	0.40
CoRegSPC	2.16	0.41	0.36	0.26	0.50
KMLRSSC	1.48	0.71	0.46	0.51	0.81
GBS-KO	0.53	0.19	0.15	0.22	0.20
2CMV	93.68	6.16	5.76	6.93	8.37
MVCDMFPA	148.63	4.39	4.16	2.33	1.32
Ours	119.27	6.41	6.18	8.95	11.06

Therefore, we can obtain better clustering performance by adjusting the parameters appropriately.

8.4.7   Convergence study

As shown in Figure 8.9, we present the convergence curve of the proposed updating algorithm on each dataset. Overall, the updating algorithm on all datasets converges after finite iterations. For a small dataset such as WebKb, the proposed algorithm on each sub-dataset can converge after 100 iterations. However, on a large image dataset such as ORL, the algorithm requires more iterations to converge. Moreover, we record the running time of each method from initialization to convergence, with the results shown in Table 8.18. As observed, since the updating formulas of MultiNMF, 2CMV, MVCDMFPA, and the proposed method are matrix multiplications, the running time on each dataset is relatively long.

8.5   Chapter summary

In this chapter, a novel MVC method is proposed, which enhances the robustness of NMF by utilizing the $l_{2,1}$-norm and captures the diverse information between views using a diversity constraint. Furthermore, the proposed method constructs a data graph based on information entropy, which makes the data after dimensionality reduction to retain the geometric structure of the original data. An efficient iterative updating algorithm is developed to solve the proposed optimization model, and the convergence and complexity are both analyzed theoretically and experimentally. Finally, the effectiveness of the proposed method is demonstrated by comparing it with 11 state-of-the-art methods in clustering experiments. In future work, we will focus on improving the robustness of deep matrix factorization, enhancing the ability to eliminate noise, and exploring novel data graph construction methods.

References

[1]   Wang J., Tian F., Yu H., Liu C.H., Zhan K., Wang X.: "Diverse non-negative matrix factorization for multiview data representation." *IEEE Trans. Cybern.* 2017;48(9):2620–32.

[2]   Cai D., He X., Han J., Huang T. S.: "Graph regularized nonnegative matrix factorization for data representation." *IEEE Trans. Pattern Anal. Mach. Intell.* 2010;33(8):1548–60.

[3]   Luo P., Peng J., Guan Z., Fan J.: "Dual regularized multi-view non-negative matrix factorization for clustering." *Neurocomputing.* 2018;294:1–11.

[4]   Jia Y., Liu H., Hou J., Kwang S.: "Pairwise constraint propagation with dual adversarial manifold regularization." *IEEE Trans. Neural Networks Learn. Syst.* 2020;31(12):5575–87.

[5]   Li X., Zhang H., Zhang R., Liu Y., Nie F.: "Generalized uncorrelated regression with adaptive graph for unsupervised feature selection." *IEEE Trans. Neural Networks Learn. Syst.* 2018;30(5):1587–95.

[6]   Chen W.S., Zeng Q., Pan B.: "A survey of deep nonnegative matrix factorization." *Neurocomputing.* 2022;491:305–20.

[7]   Lee D., Seung H.S.: "Algorithms for non-negative matrix factorization." in *Proceedings of the 14th International Conference on Neural Information Processing Systems.* Cambridge, MA, USA: MIT Press; 2000. pp. 535–541.

[8]   Singh A.P., Gordon G.J.: "Relational learning via collective matrix factorization." in *Proceedings of the 14th ACM SIGKDD International Conference on Knowledge Discovery and Data Mining;* 2008. pp. 650–8.

[9]   Liu J., Wang C., Gao J., Han J.: "Multi-view clustering via joint nonnegative matrix factorization." in *Proceedings of the 2013 SIAM International Conference on Data Mining.* Philadelphia: SIAM; 2013. pp. 252–60.

[10]   Cai X., Nie F., Huang H.: "Multi-view k-means clustering on big data." in *Twenty-Third International Joint conference on Artificial Intelligence.* Citeseer; 2013.

[11]   Kumar A., Rai P., Daume H.: "Co-regularized multi-view spectral clustering." *Advances in Neural Information Processing Systems*; 2011. p. 24.

[12]   Brbić M., Kopriva I.: "Multi-view low-rank sparse subspace clustering." *Pattern Recogn.* 2018;73:247–58.

[13]   Wang H., Yang Y., Liu B., Fujita H.: "A study of graph-based system for multi-view clustering." *Knowl. Based Syst.* 2019;163:1009–19.

[14]   Luong K., Nayak R.: "A novel approach to learning consensus and complementary information for multi-view data clustering." in *2020 IEEE 36th International Conference on Data Engineering (ICDE);* 2020. pp. 865–76.

[15]   Liang N., Yang Z., Li Z., Sun W., Xie S.: "Multi-view clustering by nonnegative matrix factorization with co-orthogonal constraints." *Knowl. Based Syst.* 2020;194:105582.

[16]   Zhang C., Wang S., Liu J., Zhou S.: "Multi-view clustering via deep matrix factorization and partition alignment." in *Proceedings of the 29th ACM International Conference on Multimedia*; 2021. pp. 4156–64.

[17]   Liu H., Wu Z., Li X., Cai D., Huang T. S.: "Constrained nonnegative matrix factorization for image representation." *IEEE Trans. Pattern Anal. Mach. Intell.* 2011;34(7):1299–311.

[18]   Feng L., Liu W., Meng X., Zhang Y.: "Re-weighted multi-view clustering via triplex regularized non-negative matrix factorization." *Neurocomputing.* 2021;464:352–63.

[19]   Huang Y., Shen Z., Cai F., Li T., Lv F.: "Adaptive graph-based generalized regression model for unsupervised feature selection." *Knowl. Based Syst.* 2021;227:107156.

Chapter 9

Dual hyper-graph regularized non-negative matrix tri-factorization for clustering

Non-negative matrix factorization (NMF) has been an ideal tool for machine learning. Non-negative matrix tri-factorization (NMTF) is a generalization of NMF that incorporates a third non-negative factorization matrix and has shown impressive clustering performance by imposing simultaneous orthogonality constraints on both the sample and feature spaces. However, the performance of NMTF dramatically degrades when the data is contaminated with noises and outliers. Furthermore, the high-order geometric information is rarely considered. In this chapter, a robust NMTF with dual hyper-graph regularization (RDHNMTF) is introduced. First, to enhance the robustness of NMTF, an improvement is made by utilizing the $l_{2,1}$-norm to evaluate the reconstruction error. Second, a dual hyper-graph is established to uncover the higher-order inherent information within the sample and feature spaces for clustering. Furthermore, an alternating iteration algorithm is devised, and its convergence is thoroughly analyzed. Additionally, computational complexity is analyzed among comparison algorithms. The effectiveness of RDHNMTF is verified by benchmarking it against ten cutting-edge algorithms across seven datasets corrupted with four types of noise.

9.1 Robust NMTF with dual hyper-graph regularization

In this section, the novel RDHNMTF is introduced. The convergence and the complexity analysis of RDHNMTF are discussed subsequently.

9.1.1 Problem formulation

First, the $l_{2,1}$-norm is applied to improve the robustness of RDHNMTF. Specifically, the $l_{2,1}$-norm calculates the residual error of sample point x_i as $\|x_i - Uv_i\|$ without squaring them, while the Frobenius norm used in traditional NMF squares the residual error of sample point x_i as $\|x_i - Uv_i\|^2$. Therefore, when the sample point x_i is an outlier, the $l_{2,1}$-norm can decrease the loss of x_i. Besides, the $l_{2,1}$-norm makes the basis matrix sparser. RDHNMTF also utilizes the dual hyper-graph regularization.

The dual hyper-graph regularization approach employs two nearest-neighbor hyper-graphs to capture the geometric structure of both the sample space and feature space in a lower-dimensional space. Ultimately, RDHNMTF is formulated as follows:

$$\min_{U,B,V} \left\| X - UBV^T \right\|_{2,1} + \mu(\text{tr}(V^T L^V_{\text{hyper}} V) + \text{tr}(U^T L^U_{\text{hyper}} U))$$

$$+ \nu(\left\| I_K - U^T U \right\|^2_F + \left\| I_K - V^T V \right\|^2_F) \tag{9.1}$$

$$\text{s.t.} \quad U \geq 0, \ B \geq 0, \ V \geq 0.$$

In problem (9.1), $\left\| X - UBV^T \right\|_{2,1}$ indicates using the $l_{2,1}$-norm to measure the reconstruction error. Besides, $\mu(\text{Tr}(V^T L^V_{\text{hyper}} V) + \text{Tr}(U^T L^U_{\text{hyper}} U))$ denotes the dual hyper-graph regularization, where $\mu \geq 0$ denotes the dual hyper-graph regularization parameter. $\nu(\left\| U^T U - I_K \right\|^2_F + \left\| V^T V - I_K \right\|^2_F)$ indicates the orthogonality constraints, and $\nu \geq 0$ denotes the orthogonality parameter. Orthogonality constraints is vital to HNMTF, as orthogonality constraints can lead to a better clustering inter-pretation [1]. Specifically, orthogonality constraints $\nu \left\| V^T V - I_K \right\|^2_F$ lead to a better clustering interpretation, while orthogonality constraint $\nu \left\| U^T U - I_K \right\|^2_F$ helps to clus-ter the rows and columns of the data matrix simultaneously and prevent the mapping $U \leftarrow UB$, without which the proposed NMTF algorithms may degenerate into an NMF method with only one orthogonal constraint imposed on the matrix V. The flowchart of the proposed method is shown in Figure 9.1.

9.1.2   Optimization of RDHNMTF

It is evident that the optimization problem (9.1) is non-convex, making it challenging to directly solve the problem. To facilitate the optimization process, the optimization problem is formulated as follows:

$$\min_{U,B,V} \text{tr} \left((X - UBV^T) D (X - UBV^T)^T \right) + \alpha(\text{tr}(V^T L^V_{\text{hyper}} V)$$

$$+ \text{tr}(U^T L^U_{\text{hyper}} U)) + \beta(\left\| I_k - U^T U \right\|^2_F + \left\| I_k - V^T V \right\|^2_F) \tag{9.2}$$

$$\text{s.t.} \quad U \geq 0, \ B \geq 0, \ V \geq 0.$$

where $\alpha = 2\mu$, $\beta = 2\nu$, and D is a diagonal matrix with its ith diagonal element calculated as follows:

$$D_{ii} = \frac{1}{\left\| (X - UBV^T)_i \right\|} \tag{9.3}$$

Theorem 1. *The updates rules derived from optimization problem (9.2) are able to optimize the optimization problem (9.1):*

To prove Theorem 1, Lemmas 1–3 must be proved first. We define U^t as the value of U at the tth iteration, so are B^t and V^t.

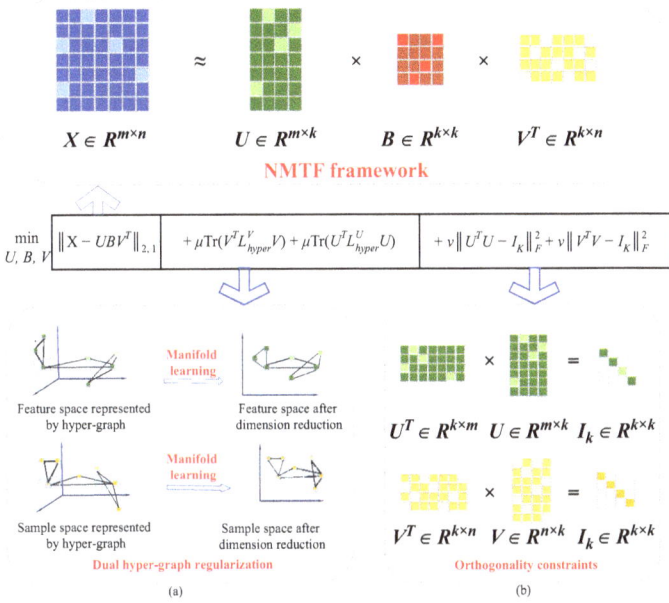

$X \in R^{m \times n}$ $U \in R^{m \times k}$ $B \in R^{k \times k}$ $V^T \in R^{k \times n}$

NMTF framework

$$\min_{U,\,B,\,V} \left\| X - UBV^T \right\|_{2,1} \quad + \mu \mathrm{Tr}(V^T L^V_{hyper} V) + \mu \mathrm{Tr}(U^T L^U_{hyper} U) \quad + \nu \left\| U^T U - I_k \right\|_F^2 + \nu \left\| V^T V - I_k \right\|_F^2$$

Feature space represented by hyper-graph   Manifold learning   Feature space after dimension reduction

$U^T \in R^{k \times m}$ $U \in R^{m \times k}$ $I_k \in R^{k \times k}$

Sample space represented by hyper-graph   Manifold learning   Sample space after dimension reduction

$V^T \in R^{k \times n}$ $V \in R^{n \times k}$ $I_k \in R^{k \times k}$

Dual hyper-graph regularization   Orthogonality constraints

(a)   (b)

Figure 9.1   *The flowchart of the proposed RDHNMTF. (a) Dual hyper-graph regularization: It helps to discover the low-dimensional geometric structure embedded in the high-dimensional sample space and feature space. (b) Orthogonality constraints: The use of orthogonality constraints allows the proposed algorithm to capture the most distinctive components and enhance the uniqueness of the decomposed outcomes.*

Lemma 1.

$$\left\| X - U^{t+1} BV^T \right\|_{2,1} - \left\| X - U^t BV^T \right\|_{2,1}$$
$$\leq \frac{1}{2} \left(\mathrm{tr}\left((X - U^{t+1} BV^T) D (X - U^{t+1} BV^T)^T \right) \right.$$
$$\left. - \mathrm{tr}\left((X - U^t BV^T) D (X - U^t BV^T)^T \right) \right) \quad (9.4)$$

Proof. Considering $D_{ii} = \frac{1}{\|X_i - (UBV)_i\|}$. The left-hand-side (LHS) of (9.4) is equal to:

$$\mathrm{LHS} = \sum_{i=1}^{n} \left(\left\| X_i - (U^{t+1} BV)_i \right\| - \left\| X_i - (U^t BV)_i \right\| \right)$$
$$= \sum_{i=1}^{n} \left(\left\| X_i - (U^{t+1} BV)_i \right\| - \frac{1}{D_{ii}} \right) \quad (9.5)$$

The right-hand-side (RHS) of (9.4) is equal to:

$$RHS = \frac{1}{2}\sum_{i=1}^{n}\left(\left\|X_i - (U^{t+1}BV)_i\right\|^2 D_{ii} - \left\|X_i - (U^tBV)_i\right\|^2 D_{ii} \right)$$

$$= \frac{1}{2}\sum_{i=1}^{n}\left(\left\|X_i - (U^{t+1}BV)_i\right\|^2 D_{ii} - \frac{1}{D_{ii}} \right) \tag{9.6}$$

Hence, we derive the following equations:

LHS $-$ RHS

$$= \sum_{i=1}^{n}\left(\left\|X_i - (U^{t+1}BV)_i\right\| - \frac{1}{2}\left\|X_i - (U^{t+1}BV)_i\right\|^2 D_{ii} - \frac{1}{2D_{ii}} \right)$$

$$= \sum_{i=1}^{n}\frac{D_{ii}}{2}\left(\frac{2\left\|X_i - (U^{t+1}BV)_i\right\|}{D_{ii}} - \left\|X_i - (U^{t+1}BV)_i\right\|^2 - \frac{1}{D_{ii}^2} \right)$$

$$= \sum_{i=1}^{n}\frac{-D_{ii}}{2}\left(\left\|X_i - (U^{t+1}BV)_i\right\| - \frac{1}{D_{ii}} \right)^2 \le 0 \tag{9.7}$$

The proof of Lemma 1 is completed.   □

Lemma 2.

$$\left\|X - UB^{t+1}V^T\right\|_{2,1} - \left\|X - UB^tV^T\right\|_{2,1}$$

$$\le \frac{1}{2}\left(\operatorname{tr}\left((X - UB^{t+1}V^T)D(X - UB^{t+1}V^T)^T \right) \right.$$

$$\left. -\operatorname{tr}\left((X - UB^tV^T)D(X - UB^tV^T)^T \right) \right) \tag{9.8}$$

The proof of Lemma 2 is similar to the proof of Lemma 1, so it is omitted.

Lemma 3.

$$\left\|X - UB(V^T)^{t+1}\right\|_{2,1} - \left\|X - UB(V^T)^t\right\|_{2,1}$$

$$\le \frac{1}{2}\left(Tr\left((X - UB(V^T)^{t+1})\, D\, (X - UB(V^T)^{t+1})^T \right) \right.$$

$$\left. -\operatorname{tr}\left((X - UB(V^T)^t)\, D\, (X - UB(V^T)^t)^T \right) \right) \tag{9.9}$$

The proof of Lemma 3 is similar to the proof of Lemma 1, so it is omitted.

The proof of Theorem 1 :

Proof.   Assume that the proposed updating rules are able to optimize the optimization problem (9.2). Therefore, we can derive the following inequalities:

$$
\begin{aligned}
&\operatorname{tr}\left((X - U^{t+1}BV^T)D(X - U^{t+1}BV^T)^T\right) \\
&+ 2\mu\operatorname{tr}\left((U^{t+1})^T L^U_{\text{hyper}} U^{t+1}\right) + 2\nu\left\|(U^{t+1})^T U^{t+1} - I_K\right\|^2_F \\
&\leq \operatorname{tr}\left((X - U^t BV^T)D(X - U^t BV^T)^T\right) \\
&+ 2\mu\operatorname{tr}\left((U^t)^T L^U_{\text{hyper}} U\right) + 2\nu\left\|(U^t)^T U^t - I_K\right\|^2_F
\end{aligned}
\tag{9.10}
$$

$$
\begin{aligned}
&\operatorname{tr}\left((X - UB^{t+1}V^T)D(X - UB^{t+1}V^T)^T\right) \\
&\leq \operatorname{tr}\left((X - U^t B^t V^T)D(X - U^t B^t V^T)^T\right)
\end{aligned}
\tag{9.11}
$$

$$
\begin{aligned}
&\operatorname{tr}\left((X - UB(V^{t+1})^T) D (X - UB(V^{t+1})^T)^T\right) \\
&+ 2\mu\operatorname{tr}\left((V^{t+1})^T L^V_{\text{hyper}} V^{t+1}\right) + 2\nu\left\|(V^{t+1})^T V^{t+1} - I_K\right\|^2_F \\
&\leq \operatorname{tr}\left((X - UB(V^t)^T) D (X - UB(V^t)^T)^T\right) \\
&+ 2\mu\operatorname{tr}\left((V^t)^T L^V_{\text{hyper}} V^t\right) + 2\nu\left\|(V^t)^T V^t - I_K\right\|^2_F
\end{aligned}
\tag{9.12}
$$

Substituting inequality (9.10) into Lemma 1, inequality (9.11) into Lemma 2, inequality (9.12) into Lemma 3, we get:

$$
\begin{aligned}
&\left\|X - U^{t+1}BV^T\right\|_{2,1} + \mu\operatorname{tr}\left((U^{t+1})^T L^U_{\text{hyper}} U^{t+1}\right) \\
&+ \nu\left\|(U^{t+1})^T U^{t+1} - I_K\right\|^2_F \\
&\leq \left\|X - U^t BV^T\right\|_{2,1} + \mu\operatorname{tr}\left((U^t)^T L^U_{\text{hyper}} U^t\right) + \nu\left\|(U^t)^T U^t - I_K\right\|^2_F
\end{aligned}
\tag{9.13}
$$

$$
\left\|X - UB^{t+1}V^T\right\|_{2,1} \leq \left\|X - UB^t V^T\right\|_{2,1}
\tag{9.14}
$$

$$
\begin{aligned}
&\left\|X - UB(V^T)^{t+1}\right\|_{2,1} + \mu\operatorname{tr}\left((V^{t+1})^T L^V_{\text{hyper}} V^{t+1}\right) \\
&+ \nu\left\|(V^{t+1})^T V^{t+1} - I_K\right\|^2_F \\
&\leq \left\|X - UB(V^T)^{t+1}\right\|_{2,1} + \mu\operatorname{tr}\left((V^t)^T L^V_{\text{hyper}} V^t\right) + \nu\left\|(V^t)^T V^t - I_K\right\|^2_F
\end{aligned}
\tag{9.15}
$$

Inequalities (9.13), (9.14), and (9.15) show that the updating rules on optimization problem (9.2) are able to decrease the optimization problem (9.1).

According to Theorem 1, the optimization problem (9.1) can be solved by optimizing intermediate problem (9.2). Thus, we subsequently design an optimization strategy for solving (9.2).

9.1.3   Updating rules of RDHNMF

Considering $||X||_F^2 = \text{tr}(XX^T)$, the optimization problem (9.2) can be rewritten in the following manner:

$$
\begin{aligned}
\min_{U,B,V} \text{tr}\,&\left(XDX^T - 2UBV^TDX^T + UBV^TDVB^TU^T\right) \\
&+ \alpha(\text{tr}(V^TL_{\text{hyper}}^V V) + \text{tr}\left(U^TL_{\text{hyper}}^U U\right)) \\
&+ \beta(\text{tr}\left(I_k - 2U^TU + U^TUU^TU\right) + \text{tr}\left(I_k - 2V^TV + V^TVV^TV\right))
\end{aligned} \tag{9.16}
$$

Optimization problem (9.16) can be solved by the multiplicative iteration method. Let $\phi = [\phi_{jk}] \in R_{\geq 0}^{m \times k}$, $\omega = [\omega_{kk'}'] \in R_{\geq 0}^{k \times k}$, and $\psi = [\psi_{ik}] \in R_{\geq 0}^{n \times k}$ be the Lagrange multipliers for U, B, and V respectively, and Lagrange function $\mathscr{L}$ is obtained as follows:

$$
\begin{aligned}
\mathscr{L} = \text{tr}\,&\left(XDX^T - 2UBV^TDX^T + UBV^TDVB^TU^T\right) \\
&+ \alpha(\text{tr}\left(V^TL_{\text{hyper}}^V V\right) + \text{tr}\left(U^TL_{\text{hyper}}^U U\right)) \\
&+ \beta(\text{tr}\left(I_k - 2U^TU + U^TUU^TU\right) \\
&+ \text{tr}(I_k - 2V^TV + V^TVV^TV)) + \text{tr}\left(\phi U^T\right) + \text{tr}\left(\omega B^T\right) + \text{tr}\left(\psi V^T\right)
\end{aligned} \tag{9.17}
$$

Next, we can derive the partial derivatives of $\mathscr{L}$ with respect to U, B, and V as follows:

$$
\begin{aligned}
\frac{\partial\mathscr{L}}{\partial U} = {}&-2XDVB^T + 2UBV^TDVB^T \\
&+ \phi + 4\beta(UU^TU - U) + 2\alpha L_{\text{hyper}}^U
\end{aligned} \tag{9.18}
$$

$$
\frac{\partial\mathscr{L}}{\partial B} = -2U^TXDV + \omega + 2U^TUBV^TDV \tag{9.19}
$$

$$
\begin{aligned}
\frac{\partial\mathscr{L}}{\partial V} = {}&-2DX^TUB + 2DVB^TU^TUB \\
&+ \psi + 4\beta(VV^TV - V) + 2\alpha L_{\text{hyper}}^V
\end{aligned} \tag{9.20}
$$

Given that L_{hyper} is not a non-negative matrix, we refer to $L = D - S$, let $L_{\text{hyper}} = D_{\text{hyper}} - S_{\text{hyper}}$, where D_{hyper} and S_{hyper} are non-negative matrices. Using the Karush–Kuhn–Tucker (KKT) condition, the multiplicative update rules of RDHNMTF are obtained as follows:

$$
u_{jk} \leftarrow u_{jk}\frac{(XDVB^T + \alpha S_{\text{hyper}}^U U + 2\beta U)_{jk}}{(UBV^TDVB^T + \alpha D_{\text{hyper}}^U U + 2\beta UU^TU)_{jk}} \tag{9.21}
$$

$$
b_{kk'} \leftarrow b_{kk'}\frac{(U^TXDV)_{kk'}}{(U^TUBV^TDV)_{kk'}} \tag{9.22}
$$

$$
v_{ik} \leftarrow v_{ik}\frac{(DX^TUB + \alpha S_{\text{hyper}}^V V + 2\beta V)_{ik}}{(DVB^TU^TUB + \alpha D_{\text{hyper}}^V V + 2\beta VV^TV)_{ik}} \tag{9.23}
$$

Algorithm 1 Iterative algorithm for RDHNMTF

Input: Data matrix $X \in R^{m \times n}$, parameter α, β, k.
Output: Decomposed matrices $U \in R^{m \times k}$, $V \in R^{n \times k}$
 1: Initialize matrices $U \geq 0, B \geq 0, V \geq 0$ randomly
 2: Initialize matrix D based on equation (9.3)
 3: Repeat:
 4: Calculate matrix D based on equation (9.3)
 5: Update U using equation (9.21)
 6: Update B using equation (9.22)
 7: Update V using equation (9.23)
 8: Until Converges
 9: Return decomposed matrices V
 10: Utilize the K-means to obtain learned cluster label information for matrices V.

9.1.4 *Computational complexity analysis*

In this section, the computational complexity analysis for the mentioned algorithms is presented. It is widely adopted to analyze the computational complexity with big O notation. However, big O notation is not precise enough to differentiate the computational complexity between RDHNMTF and its comparison algorithms. To enhance the accuracy (ACC) of computational complexity analysis, three arithmetic operations, namely addition, multiplication, and division, are utilized. Table 9.1 displays the computational complexity of each algorithm during each iteration. From Table 9.1, it can be observed that NMTF-based algorithms (i.e., DNMTF and CNMTF) require more arithmetic operations than NMF-based algorithms (i.e., DNMF and CHNMF) due to the extra decomposed matrix and orthogonality constraints. When assessed using big O notation, the overall costs for all algorithms amount to $O(mnk)$. In addition, RDHNMTF requires the feature hyper-graph and sample hyper-graph to capture the manifold structure, whose computational complexities are $O(mn^2)$ and $O(n^2m)$, respectively. The total computational complexity of *RDHNMTF* can be expressed as $O(tmnk + mn^2 + nm^2)$. We can draw the conclusion that RDHNMTF can achieve a better clustering performance without much increase in run time, the reasons are as follows:

(1) Given that $k << \min(m, n)$, the term *mnk* dominates the computational analysis and is considered to estimate the computational complexity. As shown in Table 9.1, the coefficient of the *mnk* terms in RDHNMTF is 3, which is not large, as the coefficient of *mnk* terms in comparison algorithms varies from 2 to 5.

(2) Some NMF methods, such as CHNMF and CNMTF, require exponential operations when calculating similarity, whereas RDHNMTF does not require exponential arithmetic operations, which also save run time.

(3) As feature hyper-graph and sample hyper-graph are constructed only once in the initial phase, the extra run time to construct the hyper-graph is not large.

Table 9.1 Computational complexity comparison

	Floating point addition	Floating point multiplication	Floating point division	Denoted by big O
RDHNMTF	$3mnk + 8mk^2 + 5nk^2 + 6k^3 + 5mk + 11nk + (m+n)pk$	$3mnk + 8mk^2 + 5nk^2 + 6k^3 + 2mk + 8nk + k^2 + (m+n)pk$	$mk + nk + k^2$	$O(mnk)$
HNMF	$2mnk + 2mk^2 + 2nk^2 + mk + 3nk + mpk$	$2mnk + 2mk^2 + 2nk^2 + mk + 2nk + npk$	$mk + nk$	$O(mnk)$
CNMTF	$5mnk + 9mk^2 + 6nk^2 + 2k^3 + 11mk + 5nk + (m+n)pk$	$5mnk + 9mk^2 + 6nk^2 + 2k^3 + 8mk + 2nk + k^2 + (m+n)pK$	$mk + nk + k^2$	$O(mnk)$
CHNMF	$2mnk + 2mk^2 + 4mk + 3nk + npk$	$2mnk + 2mk^2 + 2nk^2 + 5mk + 2nk + npk$	$mk + nk$	$O(mnk)$
HGSNMF	$2mnk + 2mk^2 + 3mk + 3nk + mpk$	$2mnk + 2mk^2 + 2nk^2 + mk + 3nk + npk$	$mk + nk$	$O(mnk)$
DNMF	$2mnk + 2mk^2 + 3mk + 3nk + (m+n)pk$	$2mnk + 2mk^2 + 2nk^2 + 2mk + 2nk + (m+n)pk$	$mk + nk$	$O(mnk)$
SHNMF-MCC	$2mnk + 2mk^2 + 4mk + 4nk + npk$	$2mnk + 2mk^2 + 2nk^2 + 5mk + 3nk + npk$	$mk + nk$	$O(mnk)$
RHNMF	$2mnk + 2mk^2 + 7nk + npk$	$2mnk + 2mk^2 + 2nk^2 + mk + 6nk + npp$	$mk + nk$	$O(mnk)$
RDGDNMF	$2mnk + 2mk^2 + 3mk + 3nk + (m+n)pk$	$2mnk + 2mk^2 + 2nk^2 + 2mk + 2nk + (m+n)pk$	$mk + nk$	$O(mnk)$
SDGNMF-BO	$2mnk + 2mk^2 + 2k^3 + 4mk + 3nk + (m+n)pk$	$2mnk + 2mk^2 + 2nk^2 + 2k^3 + mk + 2nk + (m+n)pk$	$mk + nk + k^2$	$O(mnk)$

9.1.5 Convergence analysis

The convergence of RDHNMTF is analyzed in this section, and the following theorem is derived.

Theorem 2. *The optimization problem (9.2) is monotonically decreasing under the updating rules (9.21), (9.22), and (9.23).*

To prove Theorem 2, we first introduce the definition of auxiliary function as follows:

Definition. $G(v, v')$ is an auxiliary function for $F(v)$ if it satisfies the following conditions [2]:

$$G(v, v') \geq F(v), \quad G(v, v) = F(v) \tag{9.24}$$

Lemma 4. *If G is an auxiliary function for F, then F is nonincreasing under the following updates steps from iteration t to t + 1 [2]:*

$$v^{t+1} = \arg \min_V G(v, v') \tag{9.25}$$

Proof.

$$F(v^{t+1}) \leq G(v^{t+1}, v^t) \leq G(v^t, v^t) = F(v^t) \tag{9.26}$$

From optimization problem (9.3), we define $\mathscr{O}$ as follows:

$$
\begin{aligned}
\mathscr{O} = \mathrm{tr}\left(XDX^T\right) &- 2\mathrm{tr}\left(UBV^TDX^T\right) \\
&+ \mathrm{tr}\left(UBV^TDVB^TU^T\right) + \alpha\mathrm{tr}\left(V^TL^V_{\mathrm{hyper}}V\right) + \alpha\mathrm{tr}\left(U^TL^U_{\mathrm{hyper}}U\right) \\
&+ \beta\mathrm{tr}\left(U^TUU^TU - 2U^TU + I_k\right) + \beta\mathrm{tr}\left(V^TVV^TV - 2V^TV + I_k\right)
\end{aligned}
\tag{9.27}
$$

Next, we will show that the updating rules, which can minimize the auxiliary function G of the function $\mathscr{O}$, are exactly the update rules (9.21), (9.22), and (9.23).

We define F_{jk}, $F_{kk'}$, and $F_{ik'}$ to be the part of $\mathscr{O}$, which only involve the u_{jk}, $b_{kk'}$, and v_{ik} terms, respectively. The first and second partial derivatives of O with respect to U, B, V are defined as follows:

$$
\begin{aligned}
F'_{jk} = \left(\frac{\partial \mathscr{O}}{\partial U}\right)_{jk} &= \left(-2XDVB^T + 2UBV^TDVB^T\right)_{jk} \\
&+ 2\alpha\left(L^U_{\mathrm{hyper}}U\right)_{jk} + 4\beta\left(UU^TU - U\right)_{jk}
\end{aligned}
\tag{9.28}
$$

$$
\begin{aligned}
F''_{jk} = \left(\frac{\partial^2 \mathscr{O}}{\partial U^2}\right)_{jk} &= 2\left(BV^TDVB^T\right)_{kk} + 2\alpha\left(L^U_{\mathrm{hyper}}\right)_{jj} \\
&+ 4\beta\left(J^{jk}U^TU + U(J^{jk})^TU + UU^TJ^{jk} - J^{jk}\right)_{jk}
\end{aligned}
\tag{9.29}
$$

$$
F'_{kk'} = \left(\frac{\partial \mathscr{O}}{\partial B}\right)_{kk'} = \left(2U^TUBV^TDV\right)_{kk'} - \left(2U^TXDV\right)_{kk'} \tag{9.30}
$$

$$F''_{kk'} = \left(\frac{\partial^2 \mathcal{O}}{\partial B^2}\right)_{kk'} = \left(2U^T U\right)_{kk}\left(V^T DV\right)_{k'k'} \tag{9.31}$$

$$F'_{ik} = \left(\frac{\partial \mathcal{O}}{\partial V}\right)_{ik} = \left(-2DX^T UB + 2DVB^T U^T UB\right)_{ik}$$
$$+ 2\alpha \left(L^V_{\text{hyper}} V\right)_{ik} + 4\beta \left(VV^T V - V\right)_{ik} \tag{9.32}$$

$$F''_{ik} = \left(\frac{\partial^2 \mathcal{O}}{\partial V^2}\right)_{ik} = 2D_{ii}\left(B^T U^T UB\right)_{kk} + 2\alpha \left(L^V_{\text{hyper}}\right)_{ii}$$
$$+ 4\beta \left(J^{ik} V^T V + V(J^{ik})^T V + VV^T J^{ik} - J^{ik}\right)_{ik} \tag{9.33}$$

where J^{jk} denotes an $m \times k$ single-element matrix, whose element is 1 at coordinate (j, k) and 0 elsewhere, so are $J^{kk'}$ and J^{ik}. □

Apparently, we are required to prove that F_{jk}, $F'_{kk'}$, and $F_{i,k}$ are monotonically decreasing under the updating rules (9.21), (9.22), (9.23).

Lemma 5. *The functions constructed below are auxiliary functions for $F_{ik}(u)$, $F_{kk'}(b)$, and $F_{jk}(v)$:*

$$G(u, u^t_{jk}) = F_{jk}(u^t_{jk}) + F'_{jk}(u^t_{jk})(u - u^t_{jk})$$
$$+ \frac{\left(UBV^T DVB^T + \alpha D^U_{\text{hyper}} U + 2\beta UU^T U\right)_{jk}}{u^t_{jk}}(u - u^t_{jk})^2 \tag{9.34}$$

$$G(b, b^t_{kk'}) = F_{kk'}(b^t_{kk'}) + F'_{kk'}(b^t_{kk'})(b - b^t_{kk'})$$
$$+ \frac{\left(U^T UBV^T DV\right)_{kk'}}{b^t_{kk'}}(b - b^t_{kk'})^2 \tag{9.35}$$

$$G(v, v^t_{ik}) = F_{ik}(v^t_{ik}) + F'_{ik}(v^t_{ik})(v - v^t_{ik})$$
$$+ \frac{\left(DVB^T U^T UB + \alpha D^V_{\text{hyper}} V + 2\beta VV^T V\right)_{ik}}{v^t_{ik}}(v - v^2_{ik}) \tag{9.36}$$

Proof. We perform Taylor expansion on $F_{jk}(u)$, $F_{kk'}(b)$, and $F_{ik}(v)$ and get:

$$F_{jk}(u) = F_{jk}(u^t_{jk}) + F'_{jk}(u^t_{jk})(u - u^t_{jk}) + \frac{1}{2}F''_{jk}(u - u^t_{jk})^2 \tag{9.37}$$

$$F_{kk'}(b) = F_{kk'}(b^t_{kk'}) + F'_{kk'}(b^t_{kk'})(b - b^t_{kk'}) + \frac{1}{2}F''_{kk'}(b - b^t_{kk'})^2 \tag{9.38}$$

$$F_{ik}(v) = F_{ik}(v^t_{ik}) + F'_{ik}(v^t_{ik})(v - v^t_{ik}) + \frac{1}{2}F''_{ik}(v - v^t_{ik})^2 \tag{9.39}$$

It can be easily obtained that $G(u, u) = F_{jk}(u)$, $G(b, b) = F_{kk'}(b)$, $G(v, v) = F_{ik}(v)$. Next, we need to prove $G(u, u^t_{jk}) \geq F_{jk}(u)$, $G(b, b^t_{kk'}) \geq F_{kk'}(b)$, $G(v, v^t_{ik}) \geq F_{ik}(v)$, respectively. To guarantee $G(u, u^t_{jk}) \geq F_{jk}(u)$, we combine (9.37) and (9.34) and learn that proving the following inequality is needed:

$$\frac{\left(UBV^TDVB^T + \alpha D^U_{\text{hyper}}U + 2\beta UU^TU\right)_{jk}}{u^t_{jk}}$$

$$\geq \left(BV^TDVB^T\right)_{kk} + \alpha \left(L^U_{\text{hyper}}\right)_{jj} \tag{9.40}$$

$$+ 2\beta \left(J^{jk}U^TU + U(J^{jk})^TU + UU^TJ^{jk} - J^{jk}\right)_{jk}$$

Since $\alpha > 0$, $\beta > 0$, we have:

$$\left(UBV^TDVB^T\right)_{jk} = \sum_{x=1}^{k} u^t_{jx}\left(BV^TDVB^T\right)_{xk} \geq u^t_{jk}\left(BV^TDVB^T\right)_{kk} \tag{9.41}$$

$$\left(D^U_{\text{hyper}}U\right)_{jk} = \sum_{x=1}^{M} \left(D^U_{\text{hyper}}\right)_{jx} u^t_{xk}$$

$$\geq \left(D^U_{\text{hyper}}\right)_{jj} u_{jk} \geq \left(D^U_{\text{hyper}} - S^U_{\text{hyper}}\right)_{jj} u_{jk} \tag{9.42}$$

$$\left(UU^TU\right)_{jk} = \sum_{x=1}^{M}\sum_{y=1}^{K} u_{jy}u_{yx}u_{xk}$$

$$\geq \left(J^{jk}U^TU + U(J^{jk})^TU + UU^TJ^{jk}\right)_{jk} u^t_{jk} \tag{9.43}$$

$$\geq \left(J^{jk}U^TU + U(J^{jk})^TU + UU^TJ^{jk} - J^{jk}\right)_{jk} u^t_{jk}$$

Equations (9.41), (9.42), and (9.43) prove that $G(u, u^t_{jk}) \geq F_{jk}(u)$ holds. Similarly, to guarantee $G(b, b^t_{kk'}) \geq F_{kk'}(b)$, we combine (9.38) and (9.35) and prove the following inequality:

$$\frac{\left(U^TUBV^TDV\right)_{kk'}}{b^t_{kk'}} \geq \left(U^TU\right)_{kk}\left(V^TDV\right)_{k'k'} \tag{9.44}$$

We have

$$\left(U^TUBV^TDV\right)_{kk'} = \sum_{x=1}^{K} \left(U^TU\right)_{kk} b^t_{kx}\left(V^TDV\right)_{xk'}$$

$$\geq \left(U^TU\right)_{kk} b^t_{kk'}\left(V^TDV\right)_{k'k'} \tag{9.45}$$

Hence, $G(b, b^t_{kk'}) \geq F_{kk'}(b)$ holds. The proof for $G(v, v^t_{ik}) \geq F_{ik}(v)$ is similar to the proof for $G(u, u^t_{jk}) \geq F_{jk}(u)$, so we omit it here.

The proof of Theorem 2: Considering Lemma 4, we obtain the updating rules for auxiliary functions $G(u, u_{jk}^t)$, $G(b, b_{kk'}^t)$, and $G(v, v_{ik}^t)$:

$$u_{jk}^{t+1} - u_{jk}^t = -u_{jk}^t \frac{F'_{jk}(u_{jk}^t)}{2\left(UBV^TDVB^T + \alpha D_{\text{hyper}}^U U + 2\beta UU^TU\right)_{jk}}$$

$$u_{jk}^{t+1} = \frac{\left(XDVB^T + \alpha S_{\text{hyper}}^U U + 2\beta U\right)_{jk}}{\left(UBV^TDVB^T + \alpha D_{\text{hyper}}^U U + 2\beta UU^TU\right)_{jk}} \qquad (9.46)$$

$$b_{kk'}^{t+1} - b_{kk'}^t = -b_{kk'}^t \frac{F'_{kk'}(b_{kk'}^t)}{2\left(U^TUBV^TDV\right)_{kk'}}$$

$$b_{kk'}^{t+1} = b_{kk'} \frac{\left(U^TXDV\right)_{kk'}}{\left(U^TUBV^TDV\right)_{kk'}} \qquad (9.47)$$

$$v_{ik}^{t+1} - v_{ik}^t = -v_{ik}^t \frac{F'_{ik}(v_{ik}^t)}{2\left(DVB^TU^TUB + \alpha D_{\text{hyper}}^V V + 2\beta VV^TV\right)_{ik}}$$

$$v_{ik}^{t+1} = \frac{\left(DX^TUB + \alpha S_{\text{hyper}}^V V + 2\beta V\right)_{ik}}{\left(DVB^TU^TUB + \alpha D_{\text{hyper}}^V V + 2\beta VV^TV\right)_{ik}} \qquad (9.48)$$

It can be seen that the updating rules (9.21), (9.22), and (9.23) derived from the KKT condition are exactly the updating rules for minimizing the auxiliary function G. According to Lemma 4, $\mathcal{O}$ is monotonically decreasing under the updating rules (9.21), (9.22), and (9.23).

9.2   Experiments

RDHNMTF algorithm is compared with ten state-of-the-art algorithms across seven datasets (i.e., COIL20,* ORL,† YALE,‡ PIE,§ MSRA25,| PENDIGITS,¶ and Mpeg7) to demonstrate the efficacy and robustness of the introduced methods.

9.2.1   Experiments setting

9.2.1.1   Datasets description

A variety of datasets are utilized in the experiment, and Table 9.2 summarizes the details of the used datasets.

---

*https://www.cs.columbia.edu/CAVE/software/softlib/coil-20.php.
†http://www.cl.cam.ac.uk/Research/DTG/attarchive:pub/data/att_faces.tar.Z.
‡http://cvc.cs.yale.edu/cvc/projects/yalefaces/yalefaces.html.
§https://www.ri.cmu.edu/publications/the-cmu-pose-illumination-and-expression-pie-database-of-human-faces/.
|http://www.escience.cn/people/fpnie/index.html.
¶http://archive.ics.uci.edu/ml/datasets/pen-based+recognition+of+handwritten+digits.

Table 9.2   The description of the used datasets

Datasets	Sample	Feature	Class	Data types
COIL20	1440	1024	20	Object image
ORL	400	10304	40	Face image
YALE	165	1024	15	Face image
PIE	1166	1024	53	Face image
MSRA	1799	256	12	Face image
PENDIGITS	10992	16	10	Handwritten digit
MPEG7	1400	6000	70	Shape image

9.2.1.2   Comparison algorithms

RDHNMTF is compared with ten state-of-the-art algorithms to demonstrate the superior performance and robustness of RDHNMTF.

1. GNMF [3]. Graph regularized non-negative matrix factorization adopts graph regularization with the aim of constructing an affinity graph to capture the geometric information of the datasets.
2. HNMF [4]. Hyper-graph regularized non-negative matrix factorization constructs a hyper-graph to learn geometrical structure.
3. CNMTF [5]. Correntropy-based orthogonal non-negative matrix tri-factorizaion uses correntropy to measure the similarity.
4. CHNMF [6]. Correntropy-based hyper-graph regularized non-negative matrix factorization integrates hyper-graph regularization and the correntropy method into the NMF algorithm.
5. HGSNMF [7]. Hyper-graph regularized l_p smooth NMF adds hyper-graph regularization terms and an l_p smoothing constraint term to conventional NMTF.
6. DNMF [8]. Graph dual regularization non-negative matrix factorization simultaneously considers the data manifolds and feature manifolds.
7. SHNMF-MCC [9]. Maximizing correntropy is utilized in sparse hyper-graph regularized non-negative matrix factorization to measure similarity, while hyper-graph regularization and sparse constraint are employed to enhance clustering performance.
8. RHNMF [10]. Robust hyper-graph regularized non-negative matrix factorization uses the $l_{2,1}$-norm instead of the Euclidean distance to calculate the difference, and it absorbs hyper-graph regularization.
9. SDGNMF-BO [12]. SDGNMF-BO is a semi-supervised dual graph regularized NMF with biorthogonal constraints. In our unsupervised task experiment, the label matrix of SDGNMF-BO is fixed as the identity matrix.
10. RDGDNMF [11]. RDGDNMF is a robust supervised NMF algorithm with dual graph regularization. The coefficient of the label information terms is set to 0 for the unsupervised task.

9.2.1.3   Evaluation metrics

With the aim of evaluating the performance of the mentioned methods in a fair way, evaluation metrics purity (PUR), normalized mutual information (NMI), and ACC are introduced.

PUR measures the extent to which samples within each cluster belong to the same class and is defined as follows:

$$\text{Purity} = \frac{1}{N} \sum_{j=1}^{N} \max(n_i^j) \tag{9.49}$$

Here, n_i^j represents the sample in cluster i that also is a member of original class j.

The NMI evaluates the common information shared by two clusters and gauges the degree of consensus between them. Given the ground truth cluster C and the cluster obtained from the clustering algorithm result $\overline{C}$, NMI is defined as follows:

$$\text{NMI} = \frac{\text{MI}(C, \overline{C})}{\max(H(C), H(\overline{C}))} \tag{9.50}$$

Here, $\text{MI}(C, \overline{C})$ represents the mutual information between cluster C and $\overline{C}$, and $H(C)$ denotes the entropy of C.

The ACC explores the one-to-one relationship between the ground truth label l_i and the learned cluster label r_i and calculates the percentage of the correct label. ACC is defined as follows:

$$\text{ACC} = \frac{\sum_{n=1}^{N} \delta(l_n, \text{map}(r_n))}{n} \tag{9.51}$$

Here, $\delta(x, y) = 1$, if $x = y$ and $\delta(x, y) = 0$, otherwise. Map$(\cdot)$ is a mapping function, which can find a optimal match between l_n and r_n. In our experiments, the Hungarian algorithm is adopted [13], which is an effective mapping function to solve the mapping problem. For the mentioned evaluation metrics PUR, NMI, and ACC, a higher value indicates better performance of the clustering algorithm.

9.2.1.4   Experimental setup

In this section, the experimental setup is discussed comprehensively. The dimension k of the $\mathbf{B}^{k \times k}$ is set to match the real class in the datasets. In the graph regularized algorithms and hyper-graph regularized algorithms, we utilize the k-nearest neighbor method to construct the graph and the hyper-graph. The value of nearest neighbor p in the k-nearest neighbor method is empirically adjusted to be 5. After experimental verification, dual hyper-graph regularization parameter α of the proposed algorithm is set to 100, and orthogonality parameter β is adjusted to be 0.01. The parameters regarding the different compared algorithm are set as default. Matrices $\mathbf{U}, \mathbf{B}$, and $\mathbf{V}$ are randomly initialized, and each approach is executed 20 times on different datasets.

9.2.2 Experimental results

Tables 9.3, 9.4, and 9.5 show the ACC, PUR, and NMI of each algorithms on different datasets. The optimal values of the experiments are highlighted in bold. Figure 9.2 shows the convergent results of RDHNMTF on seven datasets, which confirms the convergence proof in the appendix. Overall, RDHNMTF demonstrates better clustering performance than other state-of-the-art algorithms. Specifically, three critical factors are summarized and explained as follows:

(1) Algorithms that combine hyper-graph regularization (e.g., HNMF, CHNMF, and RHNMF) outperform algorithms that combine conventional graph regularization (e.g., GNMF and DNMF). Moreover, the proposed RDHNMTF performs better than other single hyper-graph regularized algorithms (e.g., CHNMF and RHNMF) and graph regularized algorithms (e.g., GNMF). The above results show that the dual hyper-graph regularization is superior to single hyper-graph regularization and single graph regularization. The main reason is that dual hyper-graph regularization contributes to obtaining a better geometric information in the sample manifold and the feature manifold.

(2) $L_{2,1}$-norm based algorithms (e.g., RHNMF and RDHNMTF) have better performance than those using the Euclidean distance (e.g., NMF, GNMF, and DNMF) for measuring the reconstruction error. This indicates that the $l_{2,1}$ norm helps alleviate the influence of noise and outliers, thereby improving the clustering performance.

(3) The dual graph regularized algorithms without the NMTF framework (e.g., DNMF and SDGNMF-BO) performs similarly to the single-graph regularized algorithm (GNMF), whereas RDHNMTF outperforms other algorithms with single hyper-graph regularization, which indicates that the NMTF framework helps the proposed algorithm to obtain wider degrees of freedom. The adopted orthogonality condition contributes to find unique solution. Therefore, the used orthogonal NMTF framework improves the clustering performance of RDHNMTF.

9.2.3 Robustness analysis

To demonstrate the robustness of RDHNMTF, we further conducted additional experiments on contaminated datasets using the aforementioned state-of-the-art algorithms. The contaminated datasets include ORL, MSRA, and PIE datasets with four different noises, i.e., Salt and Pepper noise, block noise, Speckle noise, and Gaussian noise. Specifically, we add Salt and Pepper noise and block noise to the ORL dataset, Speckle noise to the MSRA dataset, and Gaussian noise to the PIE dataset. The intensity of several kinds of noises applied is gradually increased. Figure 9.3 shows the examples from the contaminated datasets. The clustering results on contaminated datasets are shown in Figures 9.4 and 9.5. The clustering results suggest that the robust M-estimator-based NMF methods (e.g., RHNMF, CNMF, CHNM, and RDHNMTF) can mitigate the adverse impact of noise and outliers. Additionally, the proposed RDHNMTF algorithm outperforms other state-of-the-art algorithms in most cases. This is due to the l_{21}-norm reducing the influence of noise and

Table 9.3 Accuracy on different datasets (accuracy ± standard deviation)

Datasets	COIL	ORL	YALE	PIE	MSRA25	PENDIGITS	Mpeg-7
GNMF [3]	73.64 ± 3.04	67.50 ± 2.31	43.07 ± 1.77	73.82 ± 2.21	58.68 ± 2.36	72.51 ± 4.54	53.01 ± 1.21
HNMF [4]	76.30 ± 3.35	67.38 ± 2.13	43.88 ± 2.53	77.24 ± 2.07	56.12 ± 2.41	74.00 ± 4.61	53.77 ± 1.24
CNMTF [5]	66.32 ± 2.51	64.11 ± 1.68	45.51 ± 3.47	67.75 ± 1.57	**59.66 ± 3.27**	71.53 ± 4.47	47.58 ± 2.29
CHNMF [6]	75.05 ± 3.18	68.59 ± 2.10	45.69 ± 2.58	73.13 ± 1.66	58.10 ± 2.48	71.43 ± 7.06	51.37 ± 2.17
HGSNMFF [7]	76.84 ± 3.22	72.17 ± 2.53	45.45 ± 2.14	76.63 ± 1.76	57.01 ± 2.19	73.37 ± 3.87	55.15 ± 0.86
DNMF [8]	66.11 ± 2.65	68.15 ± 1.01	43.55 ± 2.44	77.47 ± 1.50	57.98 ± 2.27	74.23 ± 3.84	52.61 ± 1.76
SHNMF-MCC [9]	69.87 ± 2.50	71.85 ± 1.91	46.97 ± 2.96	65.05 ± 1.32	58.27 ± 1.86	70.69 ± 7.75	54.51 ± 1.53
RHNMF [10]	77.34 ± 2.57	70.36 ± 1.94	44.85 ± 2.15	71.27 ± 3.01	53.93 ± 2.18	70.51 ± 5.43	54.87 ± 1.03
RDGDNMF [11]	66.04 ± 1.19	63.97 ± 2.45	45.57 ± 2.89	75.98 ± 1.85	56.89 ± 2.65	73.66 ± 2.44	56.02 ± 0.77
SDGNMF-BO [12]	71.09 ± 2.00	62.07 ± 2.55	40.06 ± 2.08	75.19 ± 2.02	56.08 ± 1.75	70.49 ± 4.70	51.97 ± 0.45
RDHNMTF	**78.12 ± 1.85**	**72.29 ± 2.66**	**47.96 ± 2.08**	**80.85 ± 2.10**	59.04 ± 3.80	**75.61 ± 3.11**	**58.41 ± 0.40**

Table 9.4 Purity on different datasets (purity ± standard deviation)

Datasets	COIL	ORL	YALE	PIE	MSRA25	PENDIGITS	Mpeg-7
GNMF [3]	75.97 ± 2.22	71.12 ± 2.03	43.99 ± 1.88	76.71 ± 1.53	61.56 ± 0.99	74.12 ± 2.65	56.77 ± 0.78
HNMF [4]	80.08 ± 2.45	71.01 ± 1.45	45.46 ± 2.16	80.83 ± 1.92	58.53 ± 2.80	75.22 ± 2.91	58.28 ± 0.80
CNMTF [5]	69.30 ± 2.24	67.19 ± 1.48	46.54 ± 3.29	71.69 ± 1.19	**63.26 ± 1.94**	73.72 ± 3.23	51.12 ± 1.34
CHNMF [6]	77.73 ± 2.58	73.11 ± 1.96	47.04 ± 2.31	76.68 ± 1.15	60.35 ± 3.96	73.21 ± 5.01	54.92 ± 1.84
HGSNMF [7]	79.16 ± 1.78	75.40 ± 1.80	46.12 ± 2.18	80.36 ± 1.30	60.14 ± 2.33	74.46 ± 2.28	59.27 ± 0.89
DNMF [8]	68.28 ± 2.27	71.65 ± 1.28	44.78 ± 2.11	81.35 ± 1.13	62.01 ± 3.36	74.76 ± 2.86	56.87 ± 1.20
SHNMF-MCC [9]	71.50 ± 1.76	75.55 ± 0.91	47.818 ± 2.42	68.11 ± 0.88	60.48 ± 1.29	72.37 ± 5.71	58.45 ± 0.63
RHNMF [10]	**81.39 ± 1.67**	74.02 ± 1.59	47.23 ± 1.97	75.27 ± 2.46	56.88 ± 1.61	72.48 ± 4.38	58.57 ± 0.70
RDGDNMF [11]	69.47 ± 1.33	67.5 ± 1.58	46.97 ± 2.38	79.75 ± 1.92	60.92 ± 1.42	70.00 ± 3.50	58.84 ± 0.37
SDGNMF-BO [12]	72.81 ± 2.02	66.97 ± 1.93	42.12 ± 2.05	79.14 ± 1.46	60.61 ± 0.57	72.26 ± 3.50	55.62 ± 0.35
RDHNMTF	80.31 ± 1.24	**75.98 ± 1.95**	**48.62 ± 2.46**	**83.71 ± 1.15**	60.24 ± 1.78	**75.65 ± 2.03**	**60.41 ± 0.36**

Table 9.5 NMI on different datasets (NMI ± standard deviation)

Datasets	COIL	ORL	YALE	PIE	MSRA25	PENDIGITS	Mpeg-7
GNMF [3]	83.16 ± 1.70	84.03 ± 1.31	47.81 ± 1.47	84.46 ± 0.90	73.11 ± 0.79	69.92 ± 1.23	73.03 ± 0.61
HNMF [4]	87.23 ± 1.81	83.60 ± 0.69	48.95 ± 1.75	87.98 ± 0.91	63.53 ± 3.445	70.01 ± 2.10	73.34 ± 0.539
CNMTF [5]	74.83 ± 2.95	81.43 ± 0.68	50.45 ± 2.99	82.04 ± 0.92	74.52 ± 1.82	70.23 ± 2.61	68.81 ± 0.49
CHNMF [6]	83.93 ± 2.61	85.41 ± 1.41	50.1 ± 1.83	85.03 ± 0.77	66.48 ± 3.06	67.22 ± 3.65	72.22 ± 1.24
HGSNMF [7]	87.82 ± 0.75	89.41 ± 0.77	47.78 ± 2.33	88.02 ± 0.74	68.75 ± 2.41	69.92 ± 1.42	74.00 ± 0.39
DNMF [8]	76.46 ± 1.12	83.73 ± 1.13	48.18 ± 1.71	88.85 ± 1.08	74.11 ± 2.23	68.37 ± 2.93	72.83 ± 0.52
SHNMF-MCC [9]	78.69 ± 1.19	89.69 ± 0.37	51.61 ± 2.41	78.69 ± 0.68	66.47 ± 1.97	67.90 ± 2.38	73.87 ± 0.06
RHNMF [10]	88.84 ± 1.28	85.76 ± 0.87	48.62 ± 2.46	84.67 ± 1.41	61.21 ± 1.61	66.96 ± 4.36	73.81 ± 0.46
RDGDNMF [11]	78.21 ± 1.22	81.12 ± 1.02	50.27 ± 2.30	87.89 ± 1.73	73.55 ± 1.28	65.47 ± 0.96	74.98 ± 0.32
SDGNMF-BO [12]	79.91 ± 1.39	80.30 ± 1.20	45.98 ± 2.44	87.35 ± 0.87	73.14 ± 0.72	67.78 ± 2.34	71.87 ± 0.15
RDHNMTF	84.30 ± 1.21	86.95 ± 0.58	51.65 ± 2.04	89.64 ± 0.82	65.30 ± 2.59	69.69 ± 2.15	76.24 ± 0.38

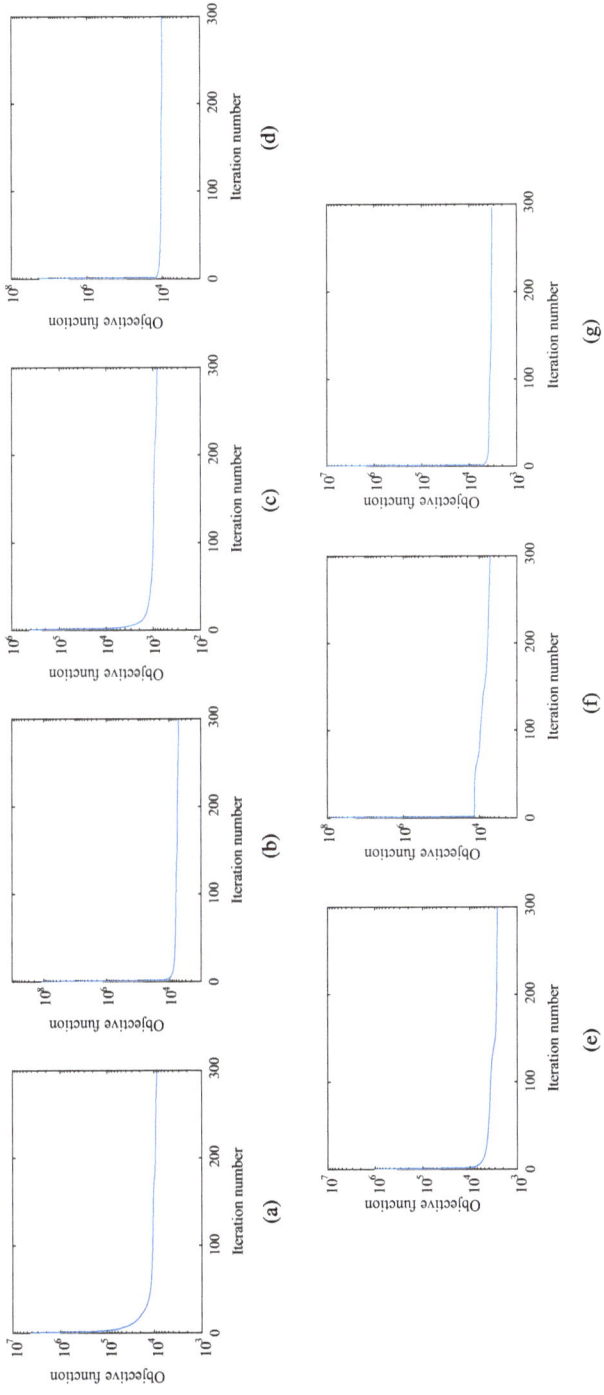

Figure 9.2   Convergence results on seven datasets. (a) COIL20, (b) ORL, (c) YALE, (d) PIE, (e) MSRA25, (f) PENDIGITS, (g) MPEG7.

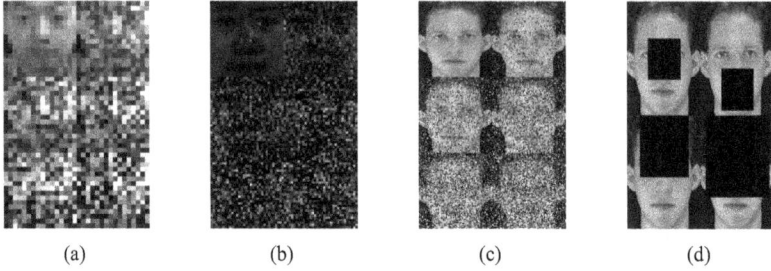

(a)   (b)   (c)   (d)

Figure 9.3   Sample images of different datasets in various noisy conditions: (a) an
illustrative image extracted from the MSRA25 dataset along with its
corrupted version by Speckle noise having a mean of 0 and variances
V = 0.04, 0.08, 0.12, 0.16, 0.2; (b) an illustrative image extracted from
the PIE dataset along with its corrupted version by Gaussian noise
having a mean of 0 and variance V = 0.01, 0.02, 0.03, 0.04, 0.05; (c)
an illustrative image from the ORL dataset along with its corrupted
version by Salt and Pepper noise having a density D = 10%, 20%,
30%, 40%, 50%; (d) an illustrative image from the ORL dataset along
with its corrupted version by a × a-block noise with a = 25, 30, 35, 40.

outliers, while orthogonality constrains and dual hyper-graph regularization improve the clustering performance.

9.2.4   Parameter selection

Parameter selection has a significant impact on the experimental results. The main parameters in RDHNMTF are α and β. Relatively small parameter values result in reduced impact of the dual hyper-graph regularization and orthogonality constraints. Also, comparatively large parameters may decrease the impact of the remaining terms in the optimization function and deteriorate the clustering performance. Unfortunately, it is hard to find optimal values for α and β. Hence, a grid searching method is adopted to find relatively ideal values for α and β within the range $\{10^{-3}, 10^{-2}, \ldots, 1, \ldots 10^{3}\}$. Although the gird searching method cannot find the optimal parameters for RDHNMTF, RDHNMTF with parameters found by gird searching can achieve a good clustering performance. Figure 9.6 demonstrates that DHNMTF achieves ideal performance when $\alpha = 100$ and $\beta = 0.01$. Hence, 100 and 0.01 are set as the default values of α and β, respectively.

9.2.5   Ablation study

An ablation study is conducted to illustrate the benefits of dual hyper-graph regularization and orthogonality constraints. The results of ablation study are recorded in Table 9.6 for four cases: (1) without dual hyper-graph regularization and orthogonality constraint, (2) with only dual hyper-graph regularization, (3) with only

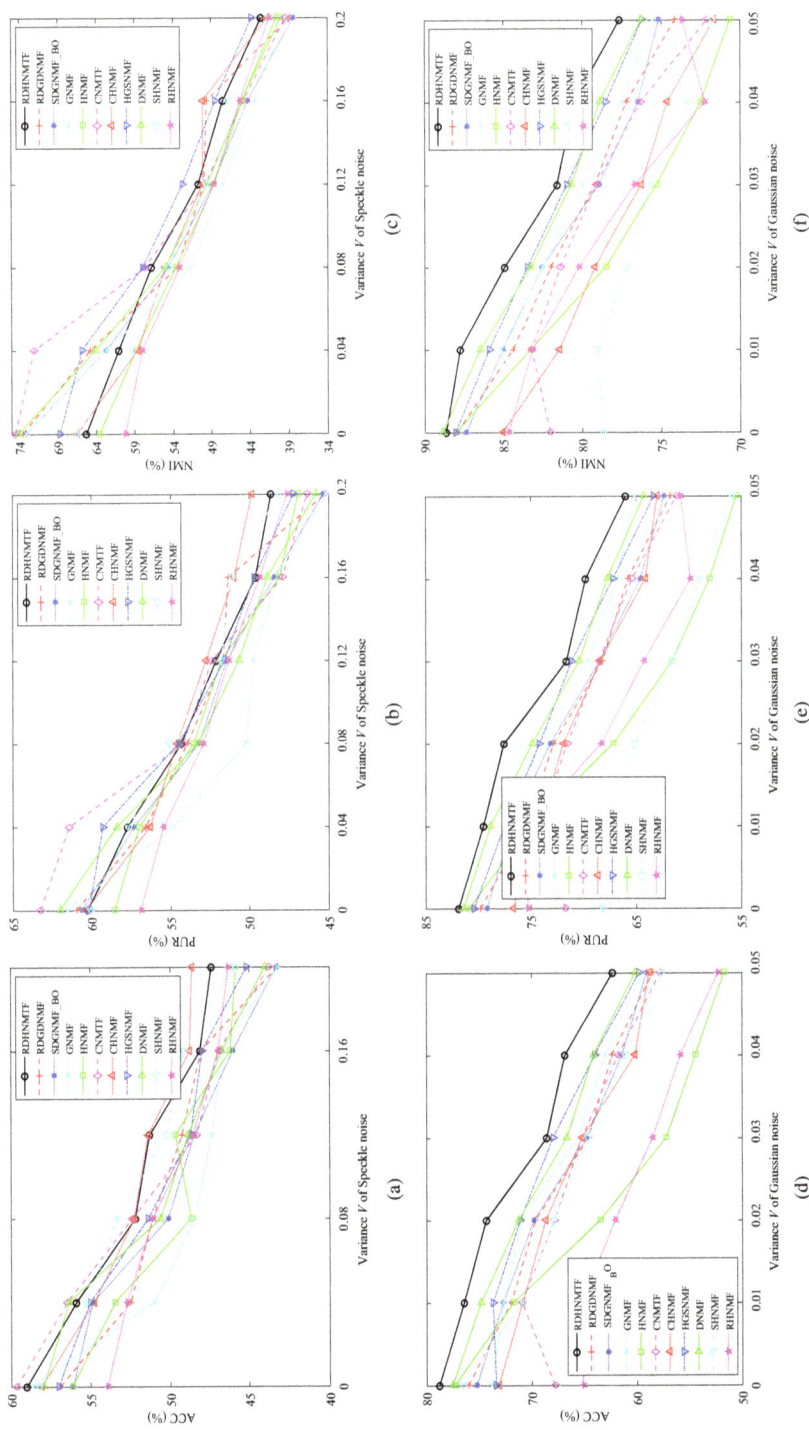

Figure 9.4 Panels (a), (b), and (c) show the clustering performance on the MSRA dataset corrupted by Speckle noise, while panels (d), (e), and (f) show the clustering performance on the PIE dataset corrupted by Gaussian noise

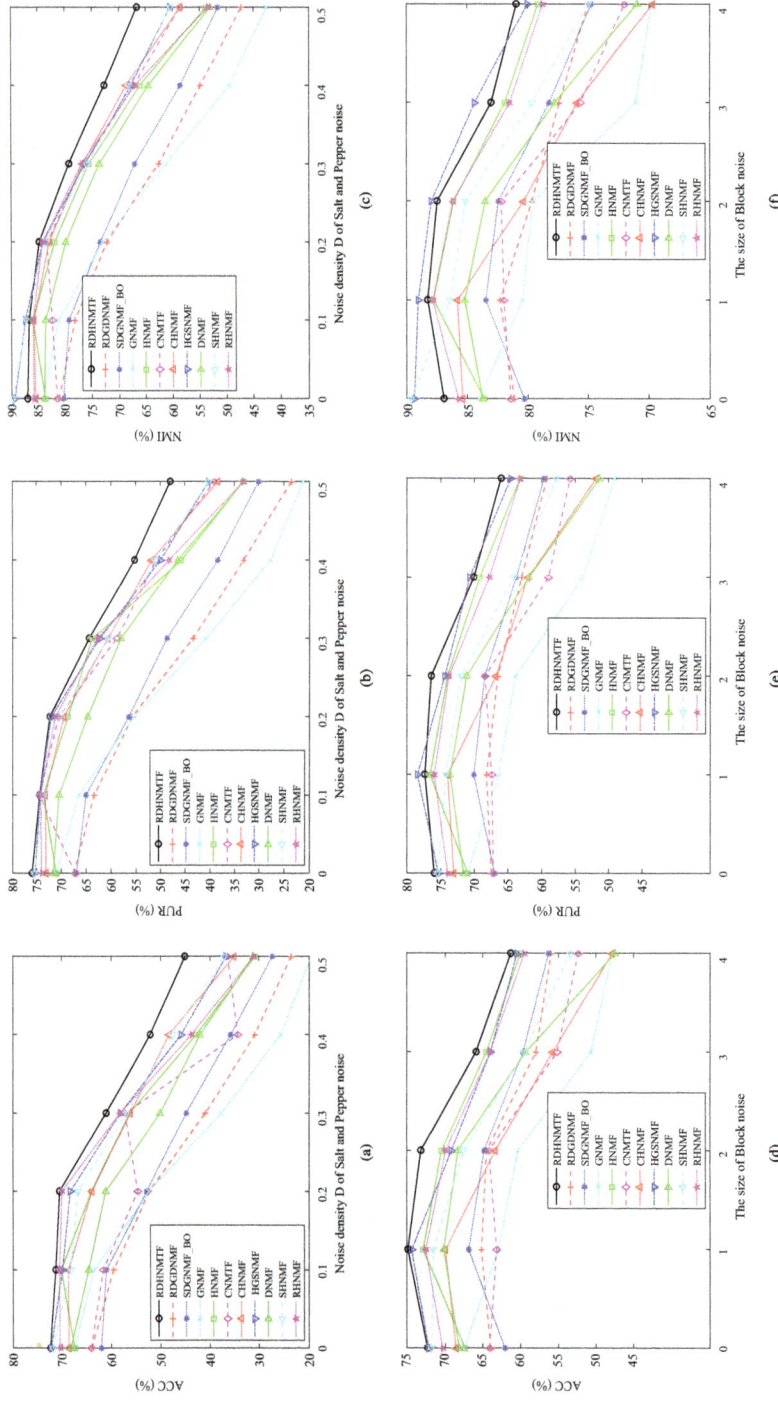

Figure 9.5   Panels (a), (b), and (c) show the clustering performance on the ORL dataset corrupted by Salt and Pepper noise, while panels (d), (e), and (f) show the clustering performance on the ORL dataset corrupted by block noise

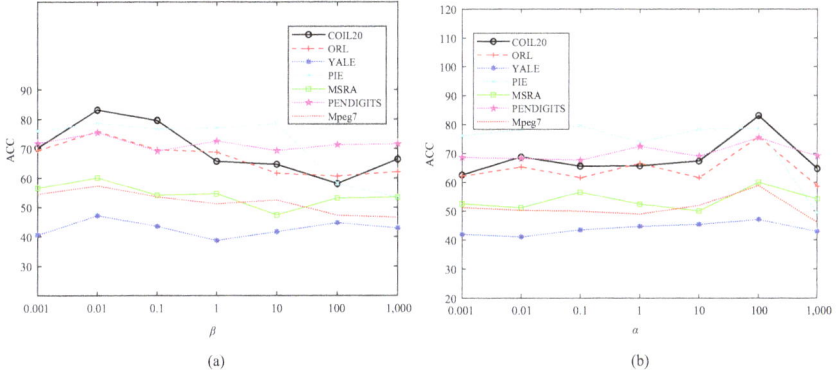

Figure 9.6   The performance of RDHNMTF with the regularization parameters. (a) Tuning β when α is fixed as 100. (b) Tuning α when β is fixed as 0.01.

Table 9.6   Ablation experiments

Datasets	ACC	PUR	NMI
(a) RDHNMTF without the use of dual hyper-graph regularization and constraints for orthogonality.			
COIL20	64.17 ± 1.64	67.44 ± 1.91	76.18 ± 1.41
ORL	65.00 ± 2.93	68.43 ± 2.80	81.63 ± 1.77
YALE	43.5 ± 2.49	44.97 ± 2.49	48.74 ± 1.71
PIE	76.03 ± 1.86	80.13 ± 1.86	88.48 ± 1.25
MSRA	52.26 ± 2.22	54.97 ± 2.37	57.08 ± 2.64
PENDIGITS	71.96 ± 5.77	66.80 ± 4.79	70.92 ± 6.46
Mpeg7	50.27 ± 0.79	53.75 ± 0.46	70.19 ± 0.51
(b) RDHNMTF solely utilizing dual hyper-graph regularization			
COIL20	50.94 ± 2.68	55.58 ± 0.98	64.26 ± 0.96
ORL	26.57 ± 3.51	30.43 ± 3.36	51.91 ± 4.54
YALE	21.02 ± 0.40	22.88 ± 0.62	27.17 ± 0.50
PIE	22.17 ± 2.55	27.93 ± 2.26	45.23 ± 3.59
MSRA	38.90 ± 7.23	42.51 ± 6.80	46.34 ± 9.44
PENDIGITS	70.28 ± 3.12	66.78 ± 2.91	68.22 ± 3.63
Mpeg7	22.20 ± 0.47	25.31 ± 0.71	50.15 ± 0.81
(c) RDHNMTF solely utilizing orthogonality constraints			
COIL20	66.05 ± 1.52	68.28 ± 1.29	76.06 ± 0.90
ORL	63.84 ± 1.65	67.11 ± 1.87	81.42 ± 1.15
YALE	45.89 ± 2.02	46.62 ± 2.17	49.96 ± 1.58
PIE	77.20 ± 1.78	80.56 ± 1.41	88.30 ± 0.71
MSRA	54.53 ± 1.63	56.67 ± 2.64	59.73 ± 3.44
PENDIGITS	71.73 ± 3.33	66.68 ± 2.56	69.91 ± 4.40
Mpeg7	$58.41 + 0.40$	60.41 ± 0.36	76.24 ± 0.38

Table 9.6   Continued

(d) **RDHNMTF with the use of dual hyper-graph regularization and orthogonality constraints**		
COIL20	78.12 ± 1.85	80.31 ± 1.24	84.30 ± 1.21
ORL	72.29 ± 2.66	75.98 ± 1.95	86.95 ± 0.58
YALE	47.96 ± 2.08	48.62 ± 2.46	51.65 ± 2.04
PIE	80.85 ± 2.10	83.71 ± 1.15	89.64 ± 0.82
MSRA	59.04 ± 3.80	60.24 ± 1.78	65.30 ± 2.59
PENDIGITS	75.61 ± 3.11	75.65 ± 2.03	69.69 ± 2.15
Mpeg7	49.38 ± 1.40	59.41 ± 0.36	56.97 ± 0.76

orthogonality constraints, and (4) with dual hyper-graph regularization and orthogonality constraints. To realize the above four cases, α and β are tuned, respectively, as follows: (1) 0 and 0, (2) 100 and 0, (3) 0 and 0.01, and (4) 100 and 0.01. Comparing Tables 9.6(a)–9.6(d), it can be seen that the performance of RDHNMTF with orthogonality constraints only is much better than the performance of RDHNMTF with dual hyper-graph regularization only (e.g., COIL20, YALE, PIE, and MSRA). Besides, when adding dual hyper-graph regularization, the performance of DHNMTF without dual orthogonality dramatically degrades on all datasets, whereas the performance of orthogonality constrained DHNMTF is greatly improved. The main reason to explain the experiment results is that the orthogonality constraints enable the proposed algorithms to have a distinct data representation. The dual hyper-graph regularization without orthogonality constraints makes the learned sample manifold and feature manifold to lose uniqueness and thus downgrade the performance. The ablation experiments suggest that the combination of dual hyper-graph regularization and orthogonality constraints is beneficial to the RDHNMTF model.

9.3   Chapter summary

In this paper, the robustness of NMTF is enhanced by introducing the $l_{2,1}$-norm to measure the construction error. Furthermore, hyper-graph is utilized to discover the high-order geometric information for improving clustering performance. To address the formulated optimization problem, an alternating optimization algorithm is designed and analyzed. Abundant experiments show the superiority of the proposed algorithm.

References

[1]   Ding C., Li T., Peng W., Park H.: "Orthogonal nonnegative matrix t-factorizations for clustering." in *Proceedings of the 12th ACM SIGKDD International Conference on Knowledge Discovery and Data Mining;* 2006. pp. 126–35.

[2]   Lee D., Seung H.S.: "Algorithms for non-negative matrix factorization." *Advances in Neural Information Processing Systems;* 2000. p. 13.

[3]   Cai D., He X., Han J., Huang T. S.: "Graph regularized nonnegative matrix factorization for data representation." *IEEE Trans. Pattern Anal. Mach. Intell.* 2010;33(8):1548–60.

[4]   Zeng K., Yu J., Li C., You J., Jin T.: "Image clustering by hyper-graph regularized non-negative matrix factorization." *Neurocomputing.* 2014;138:209–17.

[5]   Peng S., Ser W., Chen B., Lin Z.: "Robust orthogonal nonnegative matrix tri-factorization for data representation." *Knowl. Based Syst.* 2020;201:106054.

[6]   Yu N., Wu M. J., Liu J.X., Zhen C.H., Xu Y.: "Correntropy-based hyper-graph regularized NMF for clustering and feature selection on multi-cancer integrated data." *IEEE Trans. Cybern.* 2020;51(8):3952–63.

[7]   Xu Y., Lu L., Liu Q., Chen Z.: "Hypergraph-regularized Lp smooth nonnegative matrix factorization for data representation." *Mathematics.* 2023;11(13):2821.

[8]   Shang F., Jiao L., Wang F.: "Graph dual regularization non-negative matrix factorization for co-clustering." *Pattern Recognit.* 2012;45(6):2237–50.

[9]   Jiao C. N., Liu J. X., Gao Y. L., Kong X. Z., Zheng C. H., Yu X.: "Sparse hyper-graph non-negative matrix factorization by maximizing correntropy." in *2021 IEEE International Conference on Bioinformatics and Biomedicine (BIBM).* Piscataway, NJ: IEEE; 2021. pp. 418–23.

[10] Yu N., Gao Y. L., Liu J. X., Wang J., Shang J.: "Hypergraph regularized NMF by $L_{2,1}$-norm for clustering and Com-abnormal expression genes selection." in *2018 IEEE International Conference on Bioinformatics and Biomedicine (BIBM).* Piscataway, NJ: IEEE; 2018. pp. 578–82.

[11] Lu G., Leng C., Li B., Jiao L., Basu A.: "Robust dual-graph discriminative NMF for data classification." it Knowl. Based Syst. 2023;268:110465.

[12] Li S., Li W., Hu J., Li Y.: "Semi-supervised bi-orthogonal constraints dual-graph regularized NMF for subspace clustering." *Appl. Intell.* 2022; 52(3):3227–48.

[13] Lovász L., Plummer M.D.: *Matching Theory.* Providence, RI: American Mathematical Society; 2009. Vol. 367.

Chapter 10
Deep matrix factorization for disease detection

Multi-view clustering methods based on deep matrix factorization (DMF) play a vital role in data analysis within the healthcare sector. However, existing methods predominantly conduct DMF in the original data space, which is not conducive to addressing nonlinear and complex data patterns. To address this issue, the multi-kernel-based multi-view deep non-negative matrix factorization with optimal consensus graph (OGMKMDNMF) is introduced. This approach utilizes DMF after projecting the data matrix into a high-dimensional kernel space. Additionally, it employs an optimal consensus graph to alleviate the detrimental effects arising from misassigned nearest neighbors during the construction of the similarity matrix. An innovative iterative optimization algorithm is developed for OGMKMDNMF. The experimental results demonstrate the effectiveness and competitive advantage of OGMKMDNMF in addressing multi-view healthcare data clustering tasks.

10.1 Multi-kernel-based multi-view deep non-negative matrix factorization with optimal consensus graph

10.1.1 Kernel learning

Kernel learning plays a crucial role in enhancing the performance and applicability of various learning algorithms, particularly in scenarios where the input data exhibit complex nonlinear relationships. At its essence, kernel methods capitalize on the concept of implicitly mapping input data into high-dimensional feature spaces, where linear operations can effectively capture nonlinear relationships (as depicted in Figure 10.1). Commonly employed kernel functions include:

- RBF kernel: $K\left(x_i, x_j\right) = \exp\left(-\frac{\|x_i - x_j\|_2^2}{\sigma \rho^2}\right)$, where ρ denotes the maximum distance between samples, and σ is a predefined constant.
- Polynomial kernel: $K\left(x_i, x_j\right) = \left(1 + x_i^\top x_j\right)^p$.
- Linear kernel: $K\left(x_i, x_j\right) = x_i^\top x_j$.
- Cosine kernel: $K\left(x_i, x_j\right) = \frac{x_i^\top x_j}{\|x_i\|_2 \|x_j\|_2}$.

Central to kernel learning is the selection of appropriate kernel functions, which determine the similarity or distance between data points in the transformed feature

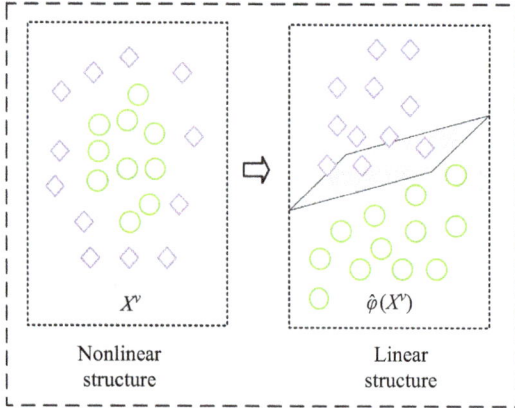

Figure 10.1　Mapping data points into the kernel space

space. This choice significantly impacts the learning process and the subsequent generalization ability of machine learning models.

10.1.2　Optimal consensus graph learning

Graph-based approaches leverage the principles of the graph theory to model data as networks of interconnected nodes, where each node represents a data point, and edges represent relationships or similarities between points [1,2]. Graph learning approaches can effectively capture both local and global structures in the data. By considering the connectivity between nodes, these methods can identify clusters that are closely related as well as more distant, leading to a more nuanced understanding of the underlying data distribution. In the context of multi-view methods, it is typical to construct similarity matrices for each individual view:

$$S_{ij}^v = \begin{cases} 1, & \text{if } \varphi(x_j^v) \in \mathcal{N}_k(x_i^v), \\ 0, & \text{otherwise,} \end{cases} \tag{10.1}$$

where S_{ij}^v represents the degree of similarity between x_i^v and x_j^v. The expression $x_j^v \in \mathcal{N}_k(x_i^v)$ signifies that x_j^v is among the k closest neighbors of x_i^v, as determined by the following proximity measure:

$$d\left(x_i^v, x_j^v\right) = \left\| x_i^v - x_j^v \right\|_2^2. \tag{10.2}$$

Nonetheless, in scenarios where several data points are in proximity to the intersection of multiple subspaces, (10.2) may fail to accurately delineate these subspaces, potentially leading to numerous incorrect assignments of neighboring points. To address this issue, the optimal consensus graph constraint is proposed [3]:

$$(S^*)_{ij} = \min \left\{ (S^1)_{ij}, (S^2)_{ij}, \ldots, (S^m)_{ij} \right\}. \tag{10.3}$$

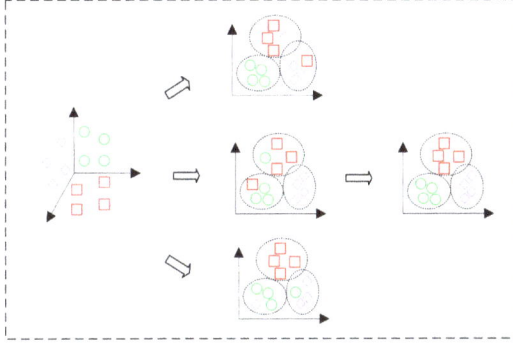

Figure 10.2   Averaging out inconsistencies and emphasizing consistent patterns observed across different views

It is evident that (10.3) imparts a significant degree of fault tolerance to the similarity matrix. Even if an incorrect neighbor assignment occurs in a particular view, (10.3) ensures that no misclassifications of neighboring samples are present in the similarity matrix of the final consensus optimal graph (as depicted in Figure 10.2). The consensus degree matrix can be computed using $\hat{S}^* = \text{diag}\left[\sum_{i=1}^{n}(S^*)_{i1}, \sum_{i=1}^{n}(S^*)_{i2}, \ldots, \sum_{i=1}^{n}(S^*)_{ij}\right]$, and the consensus Laplacian matrix can be derived using $L^* = \hat{S}^* - S^*$.

10.1.3   Objective formulation

Given the input multi-view data $X^v \in \mathbb{R}^{d_v \times n}$ $(v = 1, 2, \ldots, m)$, the multi-view DMF model can be formulated as follows:

$$\min_{A_r^v, B_R^v} \|X^v - A_1^v A_2^v \ldots A_R^v B_R^v\|_F^2,$$

$$\text{s.t. } B_R^v \geq 0, A_r^v \geq 0, (r = 1, 2, \ldots, R). \tag{10.4}$$

Although (10.4) achieves the expansion of a multi-layer decomposition structure, it overlooks the diversity among views, treating each view equally, which is evidently unreasonable. Consequently, dynamically allocating view weights to each view results in the following model:

$$\min_{A_r^v, B_R, \tau^v} \sum_{v=1}^{m} (\tau^v)^p \|X^v - A_1^v A_2^v \ldots A_R^v B_R\|_F^2,$$

$$\text{s.t. } B_R \geq 0, A_r^v \geq 0, (r = 1, 2, \ldots, R), \tau^v \geq 0, \sum_{v=1}^{m} \tau^v = 1, \tag{10.5}$$

where τ^v denotes the weight of the vth view, and p is a parameter adopted to circumvent trivial solutions. It can be observed that to facilitate more effective learning of the correlation information in multi-view data, B_R^v is constrained to be B_R.

To accurately capture intricate nonlinear structures within the dataset, we incorporate kernel learning techniques into the DMF framework. Considering that determining a kernel space suitable for the dataset at hand is a challenging task, the data is mapped into a consensus kernel space $\widehat{\varphi}(\boldsymbol{X}^v) = \left[\sqrt{\lambda_1^v}\varphi_1(\boldsymbol{X}^v), \ldots, \sqrt{\lambda_L^v}\varphi_l(\boldsymbol{X}^v)\right]$, which is composed of multiple kernel spaces. $\varphi_l(\cdot)$ denotes the lth kernel space, while λ_l^v represents the weight of the lth kernel space in the vth view. Multi-kernel learning allows the combination of multiple kernels, each capturing different aspects of the data. Automatic kernel weight updating enables the model to emphasize the most relevant kernels for the given task, adaptively leading to improved performance. This transformation leads to the development of the following model:

$$\min_{\substack{A_r^v, B_R, \\ \tau^v, \lambda_l^v}} \sum_{v=1}^m (\tau^v)^p \|\widehat{\varphi}(\boldsymbol{X}^v) - \boldsymbol{A}_1^v\boldsymbol{A}_2^v \ldots \boldsymbol{A}_R^v\boldsymbol{B}_R\|_F^2,$$

$$\text{s.t. } \boldsymbol{B}_R \geq 0, \boldsymbol{A}_r^v \geq 0, \ (r = 1, 2, \ldots, R), \ \tau^v \geq 0, \ \sum_{v=1}^m \tau^v = 1, \tag{10.6}$$

$$\lambda_l^v \geq 0, \quad \sum_{v=1}^m \sqrt{\lambda_l^v} = 1.$$

To maintain the intrinsic manifold structure inherent in the data, the model incorporates graph regularization. Considering that in kernel learning, complex mapped data can be implicitly computed as $\varphi(\widehat{\boldsymbol{X}})^{v\top}\varphi(\widehat{\boldsymbol{X}}^v) = \widehat{\boldsymbol{K}}^v$, the dot product method is utilized to establish the similarity graph [4]. $\widehat{\boldsymbol{K}}^v$ is the kernel function of the consensus kernel $\varphi(\widehat{\boldsymbol{X}}^v)$, computable via $\widehat{\boldsymbol{K}}^v = \sum_{l=1}^L \lambda_l^v\boldsymbol{K}_l^v$. The specific computation method for the similarity matrix is as follows:

$$S_{ij}^v = \begin{cases} \varphi(\boldsymbol{x}_i)^{v\top}\varphi(\boldsymbol{x}_j^v), & \text{if } \varphi(\boldsymbol{x}_j^v) \in \mathcal{N}_k(\varphi(\boldsymbol{x}_i^v)), \\ 0, & \text{otherwise}, \end{cases} \tag{10.7}$$

where S_{ij}^v represents the similarity between samples $\boldsymbol{x}_i^v$ and $\boldsymbol{x}_j^v$. The notation $\varphi(\boldsymbol{x}_j^v) \in \mathcal{N}_k(\varphi(\boldsymbol{x}_i^v))$ signifies that $\varphi(\boldsymbol{x}_j^v)$ is among the k-nearest neighbors of $\varphi(\boldsymbol{x}_i^v)$. According to the kernel matrix's definition, it follows that if $\varphi(\boldsymbol{x}_j^v)$ is a k-nearest neighbor of $\varphi(\boldsymbol{x}_i^v)$, then S_{ij}^v is equivalent to $\boldsymbol{K}_{ij}^v$. To address the issue of numerous incorrect assignments of neighboring points in multi-view graph learning, the optimal consensus graph constraint, as presented in (10.3), is incorporated into the model:

$$\frac{1}{2}\sum_{i,j}^n \|(\boldsymbol{B}_R)_i - (\boldsymbol{B}_R)_j\|^2 S_{ij}^* = \text{tr}\left(\boldsymbol{B}_R\boldsymbol{L}^*\boldsymbol{B}_R^\top\right). \tag{10.8}$$

The final model can be formulated as follows:

$$\min_{\substack{A_r^v, B_R, \\ \tau^v, \lambda_l^v}} \sum_{v=1}^m (\tau^v)^p \|\widehat{\varphi}(\boldsymbol{X}^v) - \boldsymbol{A}_1^v\boldsymbol{A}_2^v \ldots \boldsymbol{A}_R^v\boldsymbol{B}_R\|_F^2 + \alpha\,\text{tr}\left(\boldsymbol{B}_R\boldsymbol{L}^*\boldsymbol{B}_R^\top\right),$$

$$\text{s.t. } \boldsymbol{B}_R \geq 0, \boldsymbol{A}_r^v \geq 0, \ (r = 1, 2, \ldots, R), \ \tau^v \geq 0, \ \sum_{v=1}^m \tau^v = 1, \tag{10.9}$$

$$\lambda_l^v \geq 0, \quad \sum_{v=1}^m \sqrt{\lambda_l^v} = 1.$$

$\|\widehat{\varphi}(X^v) - A_1^v A_2^v \ldots A_R^v B_R\|_F^2$ is a DMF loss function based on multi-kernel learning, where the data matrix is projected into a consensus kernel space and decomposed into a product of multiple basis matrices A_r^v and a coefficient matrix B_R^v. $\mathrm{tr}\left(B_R L^* B_R^\top\right)$ preserves the data manifold structure, ensuring that the reduced-dimensional B_R^v retains the most essential information of the original data. The model automatically assigns weights τ^v to each view, accounting for the varying importance of different views. Furthermore, for different datasets, distinct weights λ_l^v are allocated to each kernel, enabling the model to adaptively emphasize the most relevant kernels for a given task, thereby enhancing performance.

10.2 Optimization

10.2.1 Alternate optimization

Due to the presence of $\widehat{\varphi}(X^v)$ in (10.9), optimizing (10.9) directly is challenging. Consequently, A_1^v is decomposed into $\widehat{\varphi}(X^v)Y^v$. With the aid of $\varphi(\widehat{X})^{v\top}\varphi(\widehat{X}^v) = \widehat{K}^v$, the formula for the matrix decomposition component of the model can be transformed into a more amenable optimization form as follows:

$$
\begin{aligned}
(\tau^v)^p &\|\widehat{\varphi}(X^v) - A_1^v A_2^v \ldots A_R^v B_R\|_F^2 \\
&= (\tau^v)^p \|\widehat{\varphi}(X^v) - \widehat{\varphi}(X^v)Y^v A_2^v \ldots A_R^v B_R\|_F^2 \\
&= (\tau^v)^p \, \mathrm{tr}(\widehat{K}^v (I - Y^v A_2^v \ldots A_R^v B_R^v)(I - Y^v A_2^v \ldots A_R^v B_R^v)^\top).
\end{aligned}
\tag{10.10}
$$

Optimizing (10.9) is equivalent to optimizing the following formula:

$$
\min_{\substack{A_r^v, B_R, \\ \tau^v, \lambda_l^v}} \sum_{v=1}^{m} (\tau^v)^p \, \mathrm{tr}(\widehat{K}^v (I - Y^v A_2^v \ldots A_R^v B_R^v)(I - Y^v A_2^v \ldots A_R^v B_R^v)^\top)
$$

$$
+ \alpha \, \mathrm{tr}\left(B_R L^* B_R^\top\right),
$$

$$
\text{s.t. } B_R \geq 0, \, A_r^v \geq 0, \, (r = 1, 2, \ldots, R), \, \tau^v \geq 0, \, \sum_{v=1}^{m} \tau^v = 1,
\tag{10.11}
$$

$$
\lambda_l^v \geq 0, \quad \sum_{v=1}^{m} \sqrt{\lambda_l^v} = 1.
$$

Subsequently, for the sake of simplicity, the following variables are defined:

$$
\widetilde{B_r^v} = \begin{cases} B_R, & r = R, \\ A_{r+1}^v A_{r+2}^v \ldots A_R^v B_R, & r < R, \end{cases}
\tag{10.12}
$$

$$
\pi_r^v = \begin{cases} Y^v, & r = 2, \\ Y^v A_2^v \ldots A_{r-1}^v, & r > 2, \end{cases}
\tag{10.13}
$$

$$
\varpi^v = A_2^v A_3^v \ldots A_R^v B_R.
\tag{10.14}
$$

$$
\sigma^v = Y^v A_2^v A_3^v \ldots A_R^v.
\tag{10.15}
$$

Update Y^v. When the remaining variables are held constant, optimizing equation (10.11) with respect to Y^v involves addressing the following problem:

$$\min_{Y^v} \text{ tr} \left(\widehat{K}^v (I - Y^v \varpi^v)(I - Y^v \varpi^v)^\top \right)$$

(10.16)

$$\text{s.t. } Y^v \geq 0.$$

Denote Θ_1 as the Lagrange multiplier, and the Lagrangian function is defined as follows:

$$L_1 = \text{tr} \left(\widehat{K}^v (I - Y^v \varpi^v)(I - Y^v \varpi^v)^\top \right) - \text{Tr} \left(\Theta_1 Y^{v\top} \right)$$

(10.17)

By setting the partial derivative of L_1 with respect to Y^v to zero and employing the Karush–Kuhn–Tucker (KKT) conditions, the update rule for Y^v can be obtained as follows:

$$Y_{ij}^v \leftarrow Y_{ij}^v \sqrt{\frac{(\widehat{K}^v \varpi^{v\top})_{ij}}{(\widehat{K}^v Y^v \varpi^v \varpi^{v\top})_{ij}}}.$$

(10.18)

Update B_R. When the other variables are held constant, optimizing (10.11) with respect to B_R entails solving the following problem:

$$\min_{B_R} \sum_{v=1}^{m} (\tau^v)^p \text{ tr} \left(\widehat{K}^v (I - \sigma^v B_R)(I - \sigma^v B_R)^\top \right) + \alpha \text{ tr} \left(B_R L^* B_R^\top \right),$$

(10.19)

$$\text{s.t. } B_R \geq 0.$$

Denote Θ_2 as the Lagrange multiplier, and the Lagrangian function for (10.19) is defined as follows:

$$L_2 = \sum_{v=1}^{m} (\tau^v)^p \text{ Tr} \left(\widehat{K}^v (I - \sigma^v B_R)(I - \sigma^v B_R)^\top \right)$$

$$+ \alpha \text{ tr} \left(B_R L^* B_R^\top \right) - \text{tr} \left(\Theta_2 B_R^\top \right)$$

(10.20)

To derive the updating rule for B_R, we first set the partial derivative of L_2 with respect to B_R to zero. Then, we apply the KKT conditions to obtain the rule:

$$(B_R)_{ij} \leftarrow (B_R)_{ij} \sqrt{\frac{(\sum_{v=1}^{m} (\tau^v)^p \sigma^{v\top} \widehat{K}^v + \alpha B_R S^*)_{ij}}{(\sum_{v=1}^{m} (\tau^v)^p \sigma^{v\top} \widehat{K}^v \sigma^v B_R + \alpha B_R \widehat{S}^*)_{ij}}}.$$

(10.21)

Update A_r^v ($2 \leq r \leq R$). When optimizing (10.11) with respect to A_r^v while keeping other variables constant, it is equivalent to solving the following problem:

$$\min_{A_r^v} \text{ tr} \left(\widehat{K}^v (I - \pi_r^v A_r^v \widetilde{B_r^v})(I - \pi_r^v A_r^v \widetilde{B_r^v})^\top \right).$$

(10.22)

$$\text{s.t. } A_r^v \geq 0, \ (r = 1, 2, \ldots, R).$$

Denote Θ_3 as the Lagrange multiplier, and the Lagrangian function for (10.22) is defined as follows:

$$L_3 = \text{tr} \left(\widehat{K}^v (I - \pi_r^v A_r^v \widetilde{B_r^v})(I - \pi_r^v A_r^v \widetilde{B_r^v})^\top \right) - \text{Tr} \left(\Theta_3 A_r^{v\top} \right).$$

(10.23)

By setting the partial derivative of L_3 with respect to A_r^v to zero and applying the KKT conditions, the updating rule for A_r^v can be derived as follows:

$$(A_r^v)_{ij} \leftarrow (A_r^v)_{ij} \sqrt{\frac{(\pi_r^{v\top} \widehat{K}^v \widetilde{B}_r^{v\top})_{ij}}{(\pi_r^{v\top} \widehat{K}^v \pi_r^v A_r^v \widetilde{B}_r^v \widetilde{B}_r^{v\top})_{ij}}}. \tag{10.24}$$

Ultimately, A_r^v is normalized to ensure that $(A_r^{v\top} A_r^v)_{ii} = 1$ for $i = 1, \ldots, c$ [5]. This normalization step addresses the issue of scale discrepancies among the features following dimensionality reduction.

Update λ_l^v. When optimizing (10.11) with respect to λ_l^v while keeping other variables constant, it is equivalent to solving the following problem:

$$\min_{\lambda_l^v} \sum_{l=1}^{L} \lambda_l^v \Omega_l^v \tag{10.25}$$

$$\text{s.t. } \lambda_l^v \geq 0, \quad \sum_{l=1}^{L} \sqrt{\lambda_l^v} = 1,$$

where

$$\Omega_l^v = (\tau^v)^p \operatorname{tr}\left(K_l^v (I - Y^v A_2^v \ldots A_R^v B_R)(I - Y^v A_2^v \ldots A_R^v B_R)^\top\right). \tag{10.26}$$

Denote Θ_4 as the Lagrange multiplier, and the Lagrangian function for (10.26) is defined as follows:

$$L_4 = \lambda^{v\top} \Omega^v + \Theta_4 \left(1 - \sum_{l=1}^{L} \sqrt{\lambda_l^v}\right), \tag{10.27}$$

where $\lambda^v = (\lambda_1^v, \ldots, \lambda_L^v)$ and $\Omega^v = (\Omega_1^v, \ldots, \Omega_L^v)$. By applying the KKT condition, setting $\frac{\partial L_4}{\partial \lambda_l^v} = 0$, and considering the constraint $\sum_{l=1}^{L} \sqrt{\lambda_l^v} = 1$, the updating rule for λ_l^v can be derived as follows:

$$\lambda_l^v = \left(\Omega_l^v \sum_{i=1}^{L} \frac{1}{\Omega_i^v}\right)^{-2}. \tag{10.28}$$

Update τ^v. When optimizing (10.11) with respect to τ^v while keeping other variables constant, it is equivalent to solving the following problem:

$$\min_{\tau} \sum_{v=1}^{m} (\tau^v)^p \Psi^v \tag{10.29}$$

$$\text{s.t. } \tau^v \geq 0, \quad \sum_{v=1}^{m} \tau^v = 1,$$

where

$$\Psi^v = \operatorname{tr}\left(\widehat{K}^v (I - Y^v A_2^v \ldots A_R^v B_R)(I - Y^v A_2^v \ldots A_R^v B_R)^\top\right). \tag{10.30}$$

Denote Θ_5 as the Lagrange multiplier, and the Lagrangian function for (10.30) is defined as follows:

$$L_5 = \sum_{v=1}^{m} (\tau^v)^p \Psi^v - \Theta_5 \left(\sum_{v=1}^{m} \tau^v - 1 \right), \tag{10.31}$$

By applying the KKT condition, setting $\frac{\partial L_5}{\partial \tau} = 0$, and considering the constraint $\sum_{v=1}^{m} \tau^v = 1$, the updating rule can be derived as follows:

$$\tau^v = \frac{(\Psi^v)^{1/(1-p)}}{\sum_{v=1}^{m} (\Psi^v)^{1/(p-1)}}. \tag{10.32}$$

The entire algorithm is detailed in Algorithm 1. The convergence criterion is set as $\left| \frac{obj(t+1)-obj(t)}{obj(t)} \right| \leq 10^{-5}$, where $obj(t)$ denotes the objective value at the tth iteration of (10.11).

Algorithm 1

Input: Pre-defined kernel matrices $\{K_l^v\}_{l=1}^{L}$. Number of clusters c. Number of nearest neighbors k. Regularization parameter α.

Output: Consensus coefficient matrix B_R.

1: Initialize A_r^v, B_r^v according to [6], Y^v as an identity matrix, $\lambda_l^v = \frac{1}{L}, \tau^v = \frac{1}{m}$.

2: **while** $\left| \frac{obj(t+1)-obj(t)}{obj(t)} \right| > 10^{-5}$ **do**

3:     **for** $v = 1$ to m **do**

4:         Calculate $\widehat{K}^v = \sum_{l=1}^{L} \tau_l^v K_l^v$.

5:         Construct similarity matrix S^*, degree matrix D^*, and Laplace matrix L^*.

6:         Calculate $\widetilde{B_r^v}, \pi_r^v, \varpi^v$ and σ^v.

7:         Update F^v by (10.18).

8:         Update A_r^v by (10.24).

9:         Update λ_l^v by (10.28).

10:        Update τ^v by (10.32).

11:     **end for**

12:     Update B_R by (10.21).

13: **end while**

10.2.2   Convergence analysis

In this section, the convergence analysis of the proposed optimization algorithm is explored. First, to facilitate further discussion, Definition 1 and Lemma 1 are presented initially.

Definition 1. *[7] If the following conditions hold:*

$$U(y, y') \geq g(y), U(y, y) = g(y), \tag{10.33}$$

$U(y, y')$ *is an auxiliary function to* $g(y)$.

Lemma 1. *If U is an auxiliary function of g, g is nonincreasing in the updating rule, which is shown as follows:*

$$y^{t+1} = \arg\min_{y} U\left(y, y^t\right). \tag{10.34}$$

Proof. $g\left(y^{t+1}\right) \le U\left(y^{t+1}, y^t\right) \le U\left(y^t, y^t\right) = g\left(y^t\right).$

Theorem 1. *By keeping other variables constant, the updating rule for Y^v as given in (10.18) guarantees that the objective function value in (10.11) does not increase.*
Proof.   Initially, J_1 is formulated as the term in (10.11) that incorporates Y^v:

$$J_1(Y^v) = \text{tr}\left(-Y^{v\top}\widehat{K}^v \varpi^{v\top} - \varpi^v \widehat{K}^v Y^v + Y^{v\top}\widehat{K}^v Y^v \varpi^v \varpi^{v\top}\right) \tag{10.35}$$

It is evident that to prove Theorem 1, it is adequate to confirm that $J_1(Y^v)$ does not increase with the updating rule in (10.18). The auxiliary function method [7] is utilized for a precise proof. Consider the following definition:

$$
\begin{aligned}
U\left(Y^v, Y^{v'}\right) = & -\sum_{ij} 2(\widehat{K}^v \varpi^{v\top})_{ij} Y_{ij}^{v'} \left(1 + \log \frac{Y_{ij}^{v'}}{Y_{ij}^{v'}}\right) \\
& + \sum_{ij} \frac{\left(\widehat{K}^v Y^{v'} \varpi^v \varpi^{v\top}\right)_{ij} Y_{ij}^{v2}}{Y_{ij}^{v'}}.
\end{aligned}
\tag{10.36}
$$

$U\left(Y^v, Y^{v'}\right)$ acts as an auxiliary function for $J_1(Y^v)$, as shown below.
Initially, we apply the inequality $y \ge 1 + \log y$, which is valid for any $y > 0$, to derive the bounds for the initial two terms of $J_1(Y^v)$:

$$
\begin{aligned}
\text{tr}\left(Y^{v\top}\widehat{K}^v \varpi^{v\top}\right) = \text{tr}\left(\varpi^v \widehat{K}^v Y^v\right) &= \sum_{ij} (\widehat{K}^v \varpi^{v\top})_{ij} Y_{ij}^v \\
&\ge \sum_{ij} (\widehat{K}^v \varpi^{v\top})_{ij} Y_{ij}^{v'} \left(1 + \log \frac{Y_{ij}^{v'}}{Y_{ij}^{v'}}\right).
\end{aligned}
\tag{10.37}
$$

Subsequently, we employ the inequality presented in [8] to establish the bound for the third term of $J_1(Y^v)$:

$$\sum_{ij} \frac{(AC'B)_{ij} C_{ij}^2}{C_{ij}'} \ge \text{tr}\left(C^T ACB\right). \tag{10.38}$$

By setting $C = Y^v, A = \widehat{K}^v Y^v$, and $B = \varpi^v \varpi^{v\top}$, the following relationship can be established:

$$\text{tr}\left(Y^{v\top}\widehat{K}^v Y^v \varpi^v \varpi^{v\top}\right) \le \sum_{ij} \frac{\left(\widehat{K}^v Y^{v'}\varpi^v \varpi^{v\top}\right)_{ij} Y_{ij}^{v2}}{Y_{ij}^{v'}}. \tag{10.39}$$

Collecting all bounds, we obtain $U\left(Y^v, Y^{v'}\right) \ge J_1(Y^v)$. Additionally, since $U\left(Y^{v'}, Y^{v'}\right) \ge J_1(Y^v)$, $U\left(Y^v, Y^{v'}\right)$ is an auxiliary function for $J_1(Y^v)$.   □

The proofs for B_R and A_r^v can be similarly derived using an analogous method. Furthermore, given that (10.28) and (10.32) are closed-form solutions, the convergence of the proposed algorithm is thereby demonstrated.

10.2.3   Computational complexity analysis

An analysis of computational complexity is conducted in this section. In DMF, the computational complexity of the algorithm depends on the sizes of the layers. The computational complexity for Y^v varies with the size of the first layer, amounting to $O(\sum_{v=1}^{m} n^2 l_1)$. For the last-layer coefficient matrix B_R, the complexity depends on the size of the last layer, amounting to $O(n^2 l_R)$. The computational complexity of the r-layer basis matrix A_r^v (for $2 \leq r \leq R$) is influenced by the sizes of both the $(r-1)$-layer and the r-layer, amounting to $O(\sum_{v=1}^{m} n^2 l_{r-1})$. Typically, n is much larger than l_1, which is in turn larger than l_r for $1 < r < R - 1$, and l_R. Hence, the most time-consuming step is the update of Y^v. The overall computational complexity of the algorithm is $O(\sum_{v=1}^{m} n^2 l_1)$.

10.3   Experimental analysis

10.3.1   Datasets descriptions and compared methods

To showcase the efficacy of the proposed method in handling data from medical diagnoses, comparative experiments are conducted across eight publicly available multi-view cancer datasets. The cancer datasets encompass Acute Myeloid Leukemia (**AML**), Colon Adenocarcinoma (**COAD**), Kidney Renal Clear Cell Carcinoma (**KIRC**), Liver Hepatocellular Carcinoma (**LIHC**), Lung Squamous Cell Carcinoma (**LUSC**), Skin Cutaneous Melanoma (**SKCM**), Ovarian serous cystadenocarcinoma (**OV**), and Sarcoma (**SARC**). These datasets* encompass three types of omics data: gene expression, DNA methylation, and miRNA expression. A comprehensive overview of these datasets is provided in Table 10.1.

The compared methods selected for the experiment included the robust deep K-means method (RDKM [9]), four innovative DMF-based multi-view clustering methods (AWDMD [10], DMFMVC [6], MVCDMFPA [11], and ODD-NMF [12]), a multi-kernel learning-based multi-view clustering method (MVCMK [13]†), and a novel NMF-based multi-view clustering method (RMVNMFGD [14]). Moreover, it is important to note that cancer databases do not specify the number of clusters. According to [15], the number of clusters is estimated by utilizing the rotation cost method in Table 10.2.

10.3.2   Performance comparison

The p-value derived from the Cox log-rank test [16] is utilized as an evaluation metric. This test evaluates the heterogeneity of survival curves among two or more groups, with a more favorable performance indicated by a lower p-value. The Cox log-rank test is detailed as follows [17]:

$$Q^2(\text{log-rank}) \approx \sum_{i=1}^{c}(o_i - e_i)^2/e_i, \tag{10.40}$$

---

*http://acgt.cs.tau.ac.il/multi_omic_benchmark/download.html.

†In this study, the proposed method, along with multi-kernel learning-based approaches such as MVCMK, utilizes a variety of kernels, including nine RBF kernels with σ values within the predefined range of $\{0.01, 0.05, 0.1, 0.2, 1, 5, 10, 50, 100\}$, two polynomial kernels with degrees $p = \{1, 2\}$, a linear kernel, and a cosine kernel. (The detailed description of these kernels can be found in Section 10.1.1.)

Table 10.1   Summary of cancer datasets

Datasets	Views	Samples	Features
AML	3	158	20531/5000/705
COAD	3	214	20531/5000/705
KIRC	3	205	20531/5000/1046
LIHC	3	404	20531/5000/1046
LUSC	3	337	20531/5000/1046
SKCM	3	439	20531/5000/1046
OV	3	289	20531/5000/705
SARC	3	260	20531/5000/1046

Table 10.2   The number of clusters based on different clustering methods

Methods	AML	COAD	KIRC	LIHC	LUSC	SKCM	OV	SARC
RDKM	5	5	2	5	5	5	5	4
AWDMD	4	5	4	5	5	5	5	4
DMFMVC	2	2	4	4	2	5	2	2
MVCDMFPA	5	5	5	5	5	5	5	5
ODDNMF	5	2	2	2	2	3	3	2
MVCMK	3	4	3	4	3	3	4	4
RMVNMFGD	4	4	4	5	2	5	4	4
OGMKMDNMF	2	3	5	5	3	5	3	5

where e_i represents the anticipated number of events for the ith group, o_i denotes the observed number of events for the ith group, and c signifies the total number of clusters.

Table 10.3 displays the Cox log-rank test p-values for various methods across eight cancer datasets, with the top results highlighted in bold. These findings reveal that the proposed model achieves the lowest p-values on datasets AML, COAD, KIRC, LIHC, LUSC, SKCM, and SARC, indicating superior performance. Furthermore, it attains the second-lowest p-value on the OV dataset. These results highlight the outstanding efficacy of the proposed approach when applied to analyze multi-view data from medical diagnoses.

To facilitate a more detailed comparison of the performance across all models on the cancer datasets, Kaplan–Meier survival curves for the different methods were plotted using MatSurv[‡] [18]. The results are depicted in Figures 10.3–10.10. The Kaplan–Meier probability is a widely utilized statistical method that evaluates the disparity in survival times between various groups. It is evident that the proposed method yields survival curves for cancer subgroups that are significantly more separated compared to most other methods.

[‡]https://github.com/aebergl/MatSurv.

Table 10.3 Clustering performance of different methods in terms of the Cox log-rank test p-value, and the bold numbers in this table indicate the best results

Methods	AML	COAD	KIRC	LIHC	LUSC	SKCM	OV	SARC
RDKM	0.279986	0.962380	0.423792	0.395042	0.161768	0.571322,	0.064436	0.724260
AWDMD	0.795960	0.456271	0.372606	0.136226	0.078131	0.616540	0.344812	0.314411
DMFMVC	0.946797	0.955950	0.404426	0.368811	0.263568	0.606355	0.910130	0.985808
MVCDMFPA	0.327618	0.333688	0.061958	0.524828	0.115361	0.285313	0.086758	0.755236
ODDNMF	0.077829	0.249050	0.666983	0.078522	0.147198	0.020235	**0.000062**	0.901295
MVCMK	0.321460	0.349334	0.721612	0.350749	0.582824	0.439122	0.023434	0.881000
RMVNMFGD	0.153135	0.439359	0.295295	0.398978	0.316992	0.669412	0.417100	0.483197
OGMKMDNMF	**0.020250**	**0.067249**	**0.020102**	**0.001530**	**0.006912**	**0.0043961**	0.001885	**0.002491**

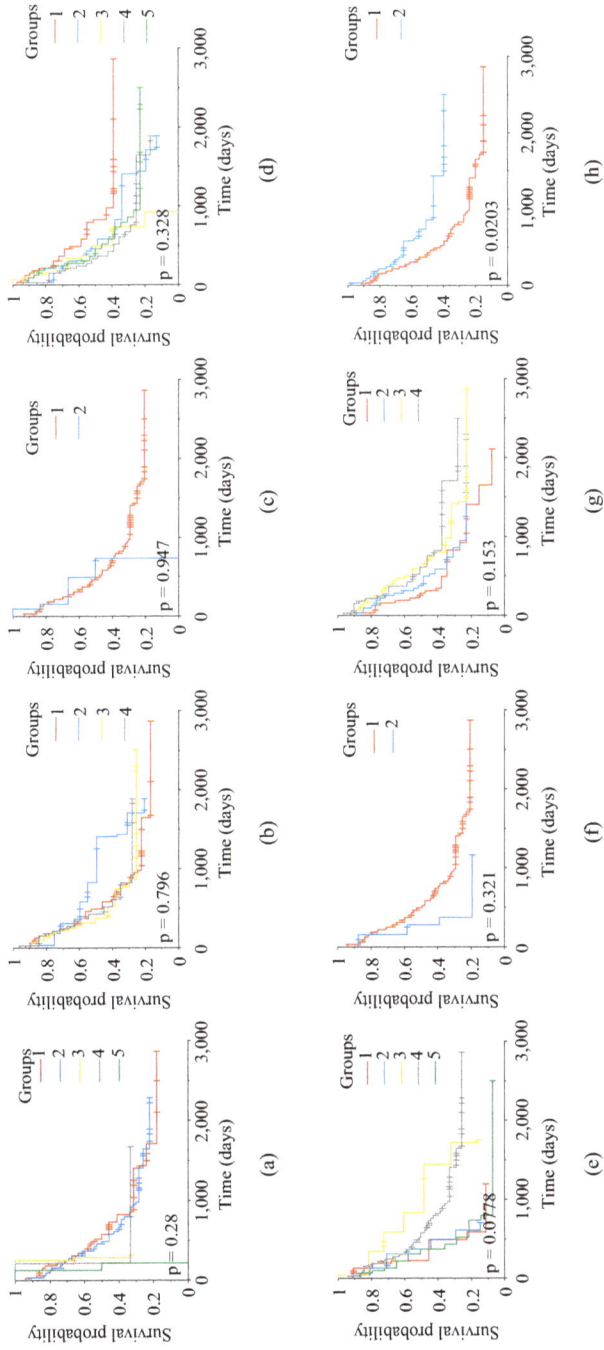

Figure 10.3   Kaplan–Meier survival curves of different methods on the AML dataset. (a) RDKM, (b) AWDMD, (c) DMFMVC, (d) MVCDMFPA, (e) ODDNMF, (f) MVCMK, (g) RMVNMFGD, and (h) OGMKMD-NMF.

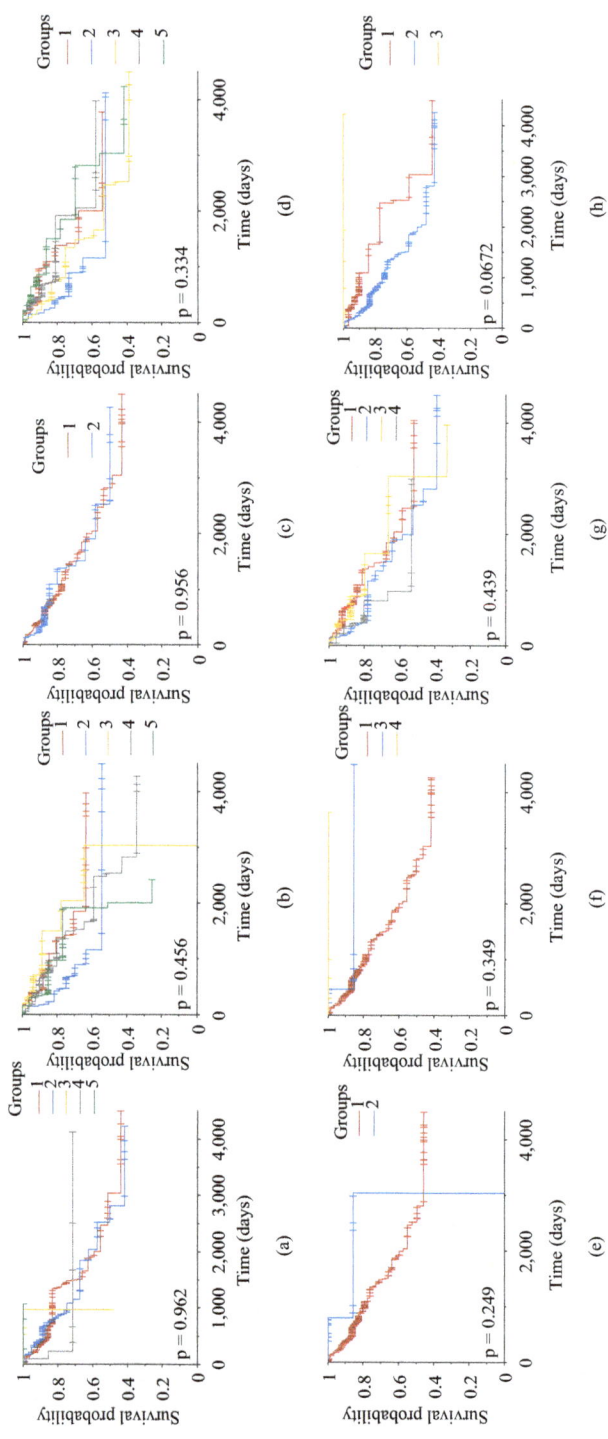

Figure 10.4 Kaplan–Meier survival curves of different methods on the COAD dataset. (a) RDKM, (b) AWDMD, (c) DMFMVC, (d) MVCDMFPA, (e) ODDNMF, (f) MVCMK, (g) RMVNMFGD, and (h) OGMKMD-NMF.

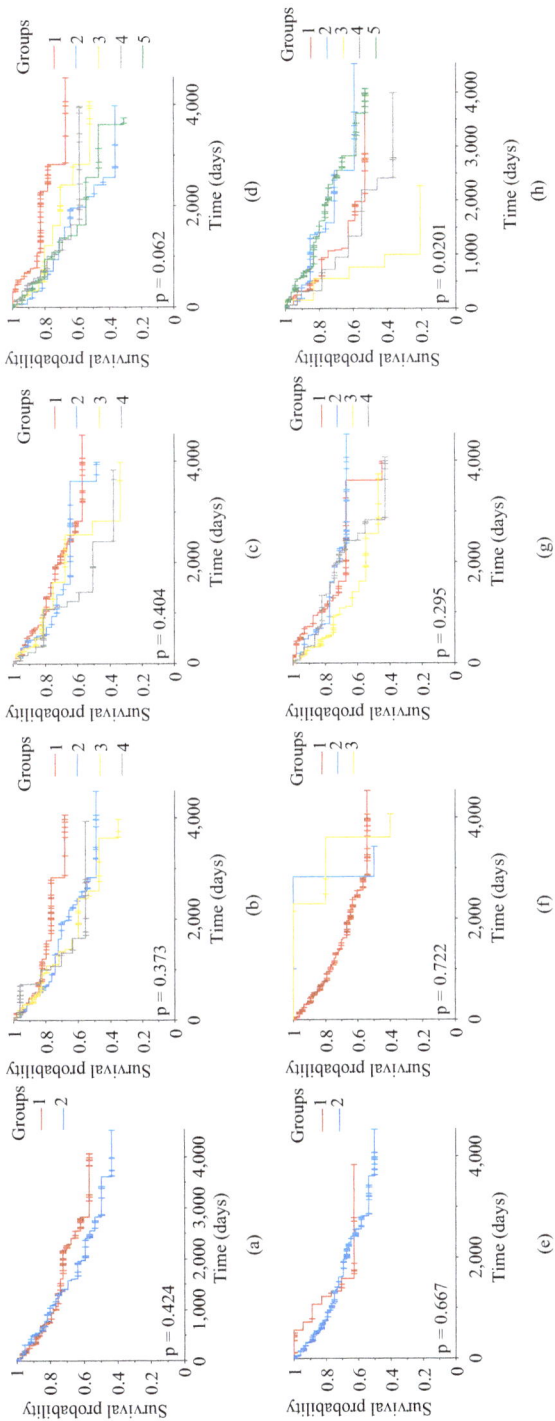

Figure 10.5   Kaplan–Meier survival curves of different methods on the KIRC dataset. (a) RDKM, (b) AWDMD, (c) DMFMVC, (d) MVCDMFPA, (e) ODDNMF, (f) MVCMK, (g) RMVNMFGD, and (h) OGMKMD-NMF.

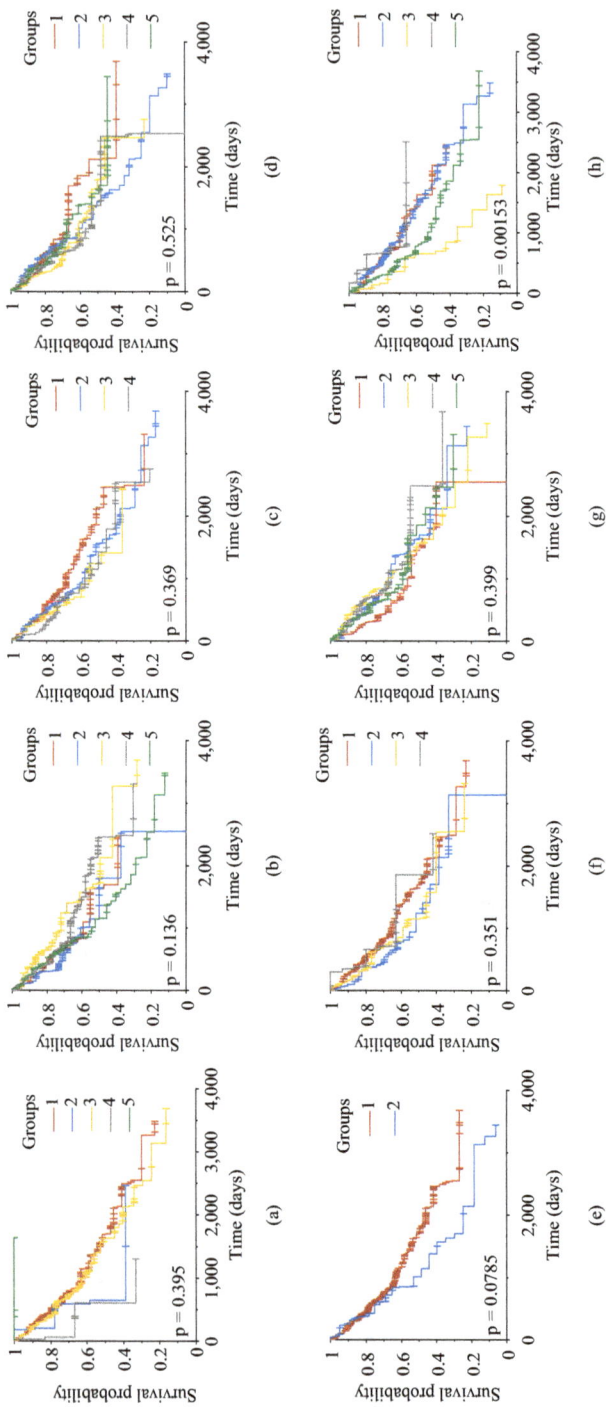

Figure 10.6 Kaplan–Meier survival curves of different methods on the LIHC dataset. (a) RDKM, (b) AWDMD, (c) DMFMVC, (d) MVCDMFPA, (e) ODDNMF, (f) MVCMK, (g) RMVNMFGD, and (h) OGMKMD-NMF.

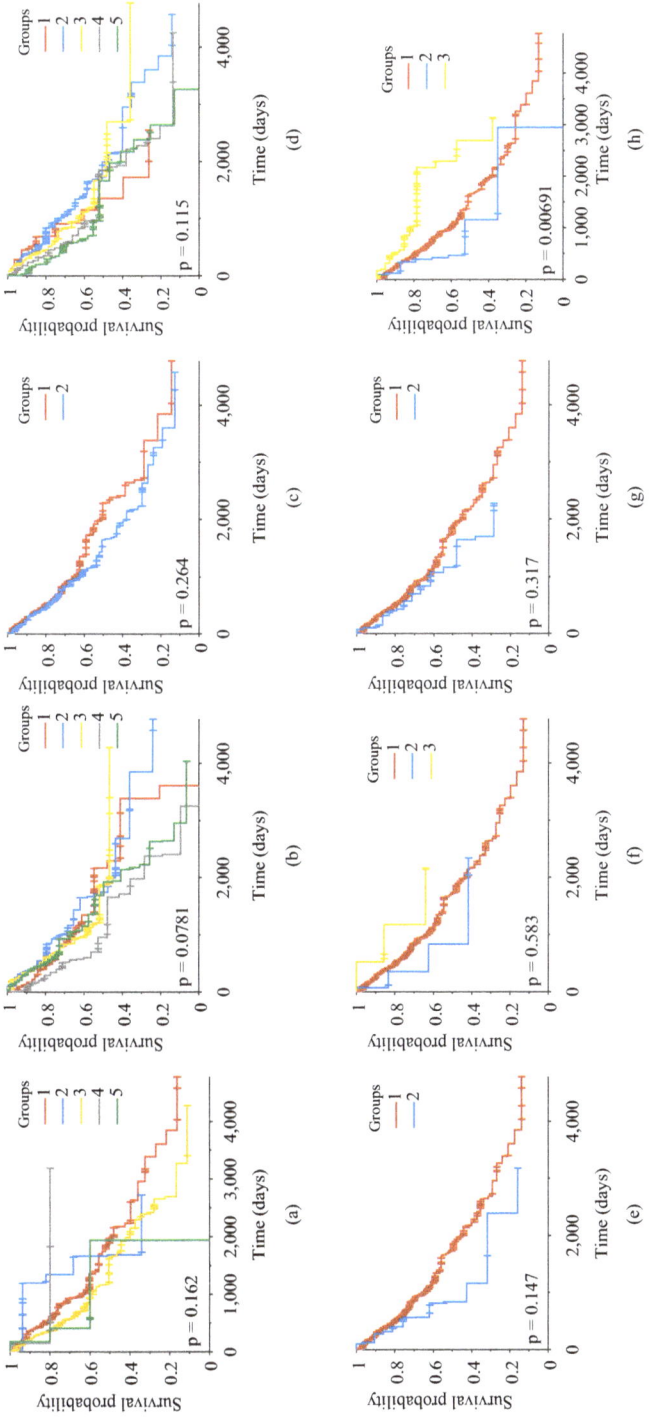

Figure 10.7   Kaplan–Meier survival curves of different methods on the LUSC dataset. (a) RDKM, (b) AWDMD, (c) DMFMVC, (d) MVCDMFPA, (e) ODDNMF, (f) MVCMK, (g) RMVNMFGD, and (h) OGMKMD-NMF.

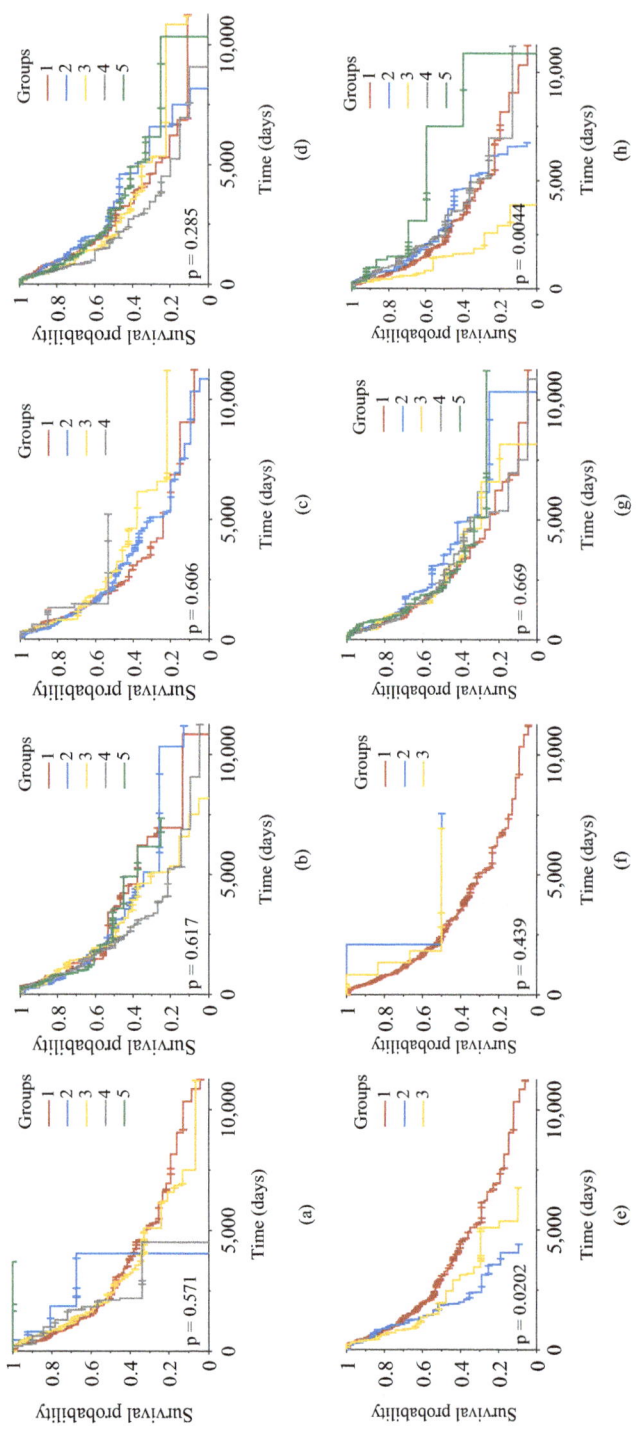

Figure 10.8   Kaplan–Meier survival curves of different methods on the SKCM dataset. (a) RDKM, (b) AWDMD, (c) DMFMVC, (d) MVCDMFPA, (e) ODDNMF, (f) MVCMK, (g) RMVNMFGD, and (h) OGMKMD-NMF.

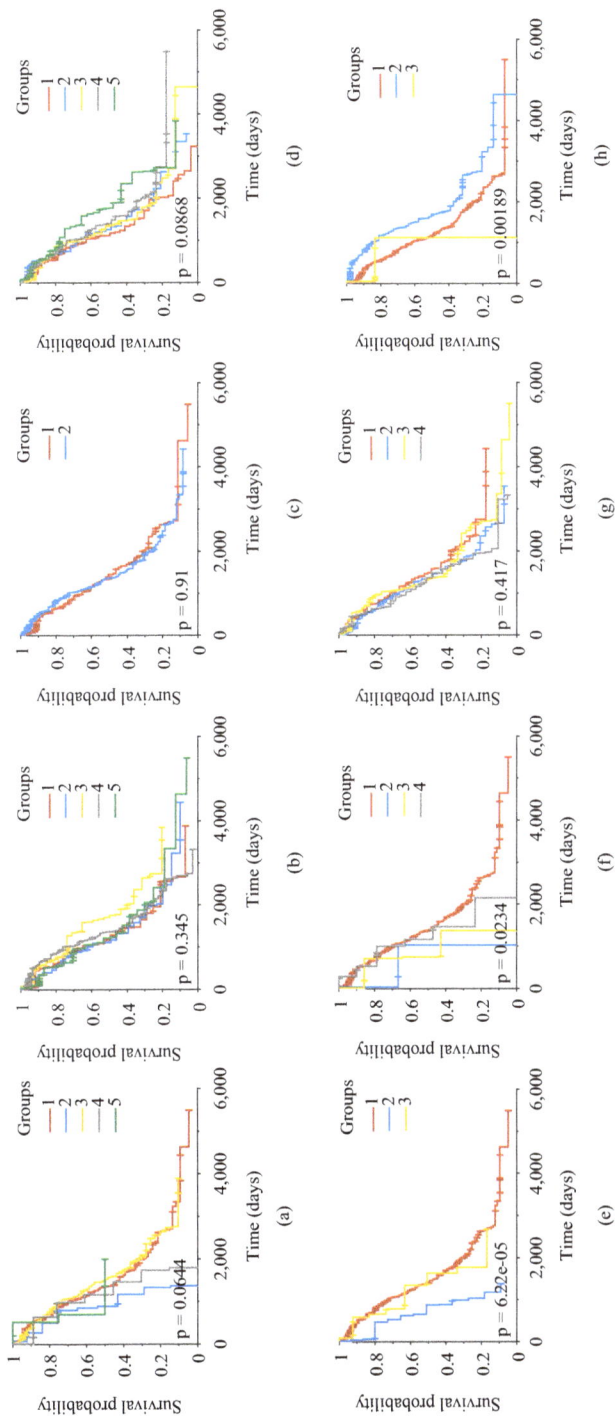

Figure 10.9   Kaplan–Meier survival curves of different methods on the OV dataset. (a) RDKM, (b) AWDMD, (c) DMFMVC, (d) MVCDMFPA, (e) ODDNMF, (f) MVCMK, (g) RMVNMFGD, and (h) OGMKMD-NMF.

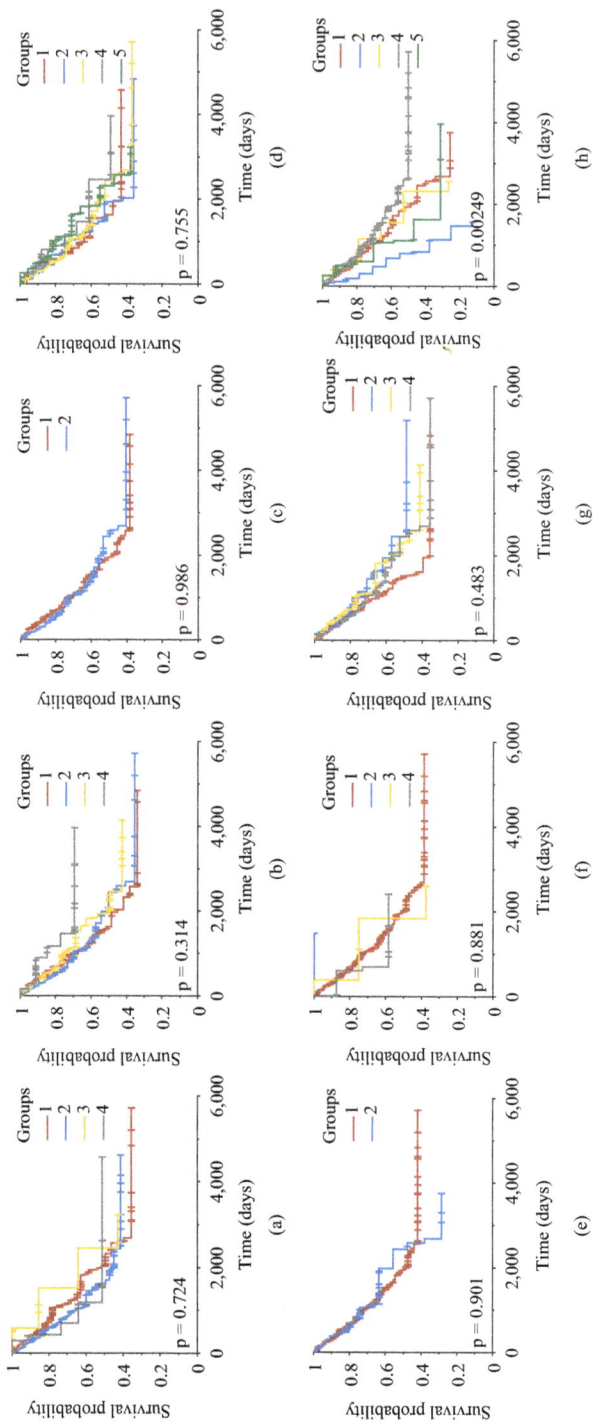

Figure 10.10 Kaplan–Meier survival curves of different methods on the SARC dataset. (a) RDKM, (b) AWDMD, (c) DMFMVC, (d) MVCDMFPA, (e) ODDNMF, (f) MVCMK, (g) RMVNMFGD, and (h) OGMKMD-NMF.

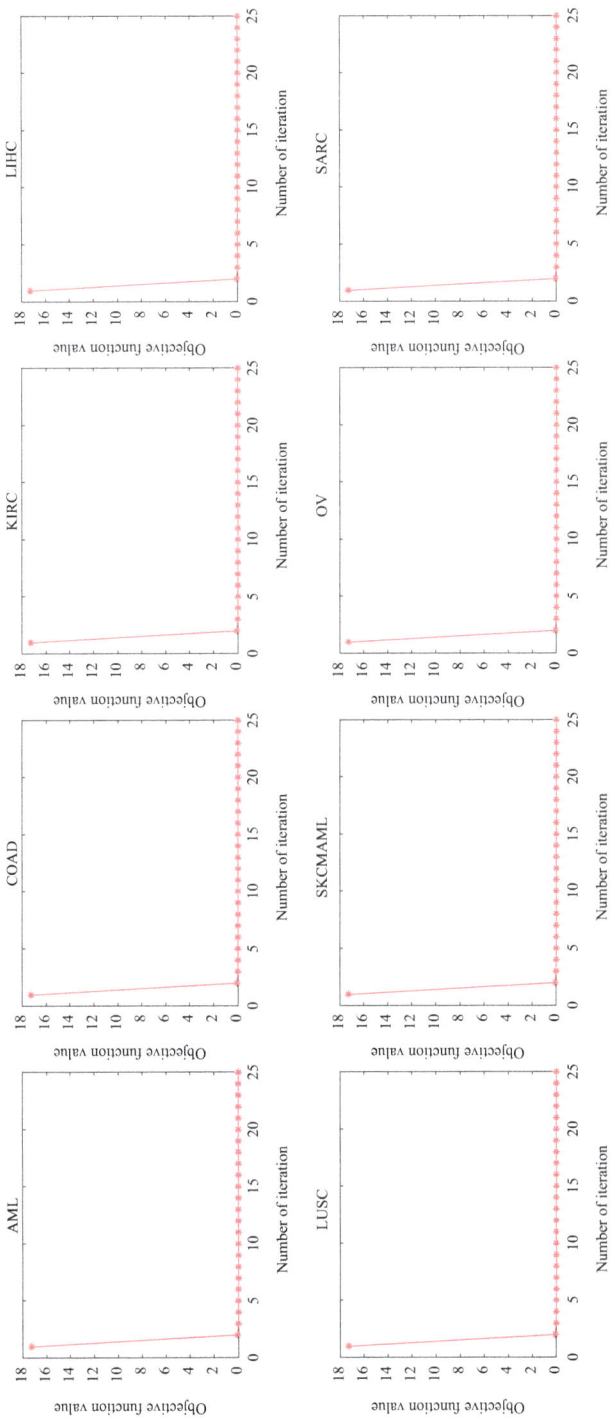

Figure 10.11   Convergence results of the proposed OGMKMDNMF on all datasets

10.3.3 Convergence study

In section 10.2.2, a theoretical analysis of the convergence of the proposed optimization algorithm is presented. In this section, experimental results are provided, including plots of the objective function values for OGMKMDNMF. As illustrated in Figure 10.11, the proposed optimization algorithm demonstrates excellent convergence characteristics.

10.4 Chapter summary

In this chapter, we introduce a multi-view clustering method termed OGMKMD-NMF, which incorporates multi-kernel learning into the framework of DMF. Moreover, an optimal consensus graph is integrated to enhance the fault tolerance in constructing similarity matrices within graph learning. We present an alternating iterative updating algorithm tailored for OGMKMDNMF. Through comparative experiments and in-depth analyses, the efficacy of OGMKMDNMF in managing multi-view data is demonstrated.

References

[1] Egilmez H.E., Pavez E., Ortega A.: "Graph learning from filtered signals: Graph system and diffusion kernel identification." *IEEE Trans. Signal Inf. Process. Netw.* 2018;5(2):360–74.

[2] Qu K., Li Z., Wang C., Luo F., Bao W.: "Hyperspectral Unmixing Using Higher-order Graph Regularized NMF With Adaptive Feature Selection." *IEEE Trans. Geosci. Remote Sens.* 2023;61:1–15.

[3] Luong K., Nayak R., Balasubramaniam T., Bashar M. A.: "Multi-layer manifold learning for deep non-negative matrix factorization-based multi-view clustering." *Pattern Recognit.* 2022;131:108815.

[4] Wang J.J.Y., Huang J.Z., Sun Y., Gao X.: "Feature selection and multi-kernel learning for adaptive graph regularized nonnegative matrix factorization." *Expert Syst. Appl.* 2015;42(3):1278–86.

[5] Feng Y., Xiao J., Zhuang Y., Liu X.: "Adaptive unsupervised multi-view feature selection for visual concept recognition." in *Computer Vision–ACCV 2012: 11th Asian Conference on Computer Vision*; Daejeon, Korea, November 5–9, 2012, Revised Selected Papers, Part I 11. Berlin: Springer; 2013. pp. 343–57.

[6] Zhao H., Ding Z., Fu Y.: "Multi-view clustering via deep matrix factorization." in *Proceedings of the AAAI Conference on Artificial Intelligence.* Vol. 31; 2017.

[7] Lee D., Seung H.S.: "Algorithms for Non-negative Matrix Factorization." in Leen T., Dietterich T., Tresp V. (ed.). *Advances in Neural Information Processing Systems.* Cambridge: MIT Press; 2000. Vol. 13.

[8] Ding C.H.Q., Li T., Jordan M.I.: "Convex and semi-nonnegative matrix factorizations." *IEEE Trans. Pattern Anal. Mach. Intell.* 2010;32(1): 45–55.

[9]   Huang S., Kang Z., Xu Z., Liu Q.: "Robust deep *k*-means: An effective and simple method for data clustering." *Pattern Recognit.* 2021;117:107996.

[10]   Huang S., Kang Z., Xu Z.: "Auto-weighted multi-view clustering via deep matrix decomposition." *Pattern Recognit.* 2020;97:107015.

[11]   Zhang C., Wang S., Liu J., *et al.* "Multi-view Clustering via Deep Matrix Factorization and Partition Alignment." in *Proceedings of the 29th ACM International Conference on Multimedia; MM '21.* New York, NY, USA: Association for Computing Machinery; 2021. pp. 4156–64.

[12]   Luong K., Nayak R., Balasubramaniam T., Bashar M.A.: "Multi-layer manifold learning for deep non-negative matrix factorization-based multi-view clustering." *Pattern Recognit.* 2022;131:108815.

[13]   Huang S., Kang Z., Tsang I.W., Xu Z.: "Auto-weighted multi-view clustering via kernelized graph learning." *Pattern Recognit.* 2019;88:174–84.

[14]   Li C., Che H., Leung M.F., Liu C., Yan Z.: "Robust multi-view non-negative matrix factorization with adaptive graph and diversity constraints." *Inf. Sci.* 2023;634:587–607.

[15]   Wang B., Mezlini A. M., Demir F., *et al.* "Similarity network fusion for aggregating data types on a genomic scale." *Nature Methods.* 2014;11(3):333–7.

[16]   Lemeshow S., May S., Hosmer Jr D.W.: "Applied Survival Analysis: Regression Modeling of Time-to-Event Data." New York: John Wiley & Sons; 2011.

[17]   Kleinbaum D. G., Klein M.: "Survival Analysis a Self-learning Text." Berlin: Springer; 1996.

[18]   Creed J.H., Gerke T.A., Berglund A.E.: "MatSurv: Survival analysis and visualization in MATLAB." *J. Open Source Softw.* 2020;5(46):1830.

Chapter 11

Matrix factorization for multi-view images clustering

With the rapid development of Internet of Things (IoT), data collected from different sensors and stored in distributed devices can be regarded as multi-view data. There are currently numerous clustering algorithms designed to handle multi-view data. However, most of these algorithms still suffer from the following problems: They are designed to operate directly on raw data, which preserves excessive redundant information and increases the computational burden for subsequent tasks. They primarily focus on pairwise relationships between views, neglecting the intricate high-order connections among multiple views. The prior information of singular values is not taken into account in multi-view. Different views are considered to have equal contributions for clustering. To efficiently address the above problems, adaptive multi-view subspace learning based on distributed optimization (AMSLDO) is proposed in this paper. Specifically, the original multi-view data is projected into a low-dimensional space for subspace representation, and multiple representation matrices are stacked into a tensor with a weighted tensor nuclear norm to obtain high-order correlations and discover the prior information of singular values. Furthermore, adaptive graph learning automatically assigns weights to obtain a consensus graph. Meanwhile, the samples are partitioned into the ideal number of clusters through the Laplacian rank constraint. An efficient distributed optimization algorithm based on the alternating direction method of multipliers (ADMM) framework is designed to solve the proposed model. Extensive experiments are conducted on six datasets, demonstrating the superiority of the proposed model over 11 state-of-the-art methods.

11.1 Adaptive multi-view subspace learning based on distributed optimization for multi-view clustering

Single-view data cannot fully depict the essential characteristics of the data. Therefore, in this work, the multi-view data is projected from the original space to a low-dimensional space. Suppose the multi-view data $\{X^{(v)}\}_{v=1}^{V} \in \mathbb{R}^{d_v \times N}$, where d_v is the number of features in the vth view, data projection can be expressed as follows:

$$\min_{P^{(v)}, H^{(v)}} \|X^{(v)} - P^{(v)} H^{(v)}\|_F^2,$$
$$\text{s.t. } P^{(v)^T} P^{(v)} = I, \tag{11.1}$$

where $P^{(v)} \in \mathbb{R}^{d_v \times k}(k < d_v)$ is the projection matrix, which is utilized to reduce the original data to k-dimension, $H^{(v)} \in \mathbb{R}^{k \times N}$ is the reduced-dimensional matrix that replaces the original high-dimensional data $X^{(v)} \in \mathbb{R}^{d_v \times N}$, and $P^{(v)^T} P^{(v)} = I$ is utilized to avoid trivial solutions. Model (11.1) aims to find a low-dimensional representation with a common d dimension, which is beneficial for exploring significant information from multi-view data. Then, subspace clustering based on self-representation is performed on the reduced-dimensional space as follows:

$$\min_{H^{(v)}, Z^{(v)}} \|H^{(v)} - H^{(v)} Z^{(v)}\|_F^2, \tag{11.2}$$

where $Z^{(v)}$ is the representation matrix learned from the reduced-dimensional matrix $H^{(v)}$.

Combining the projection of multi-view data and self-representation learning, a novel multi-view subspace clustering can be formulated as follows:

$$\min_{P^{(v)}, H^{(v)}, Z^{(v)}} \sum_{v=1}^{V} \Lambda(Z^{(v)}) + \alpha \sum_{v=1}^{V} \|X^{(v)} - P^{(v)} H^{(v)}\|_F^2$$
$$+ \beta \sum_{v=1}^{V} \|H^{(v)} - H^{(v)} Z^{(v)}\|_F^2 \tag{11.3}$$
$$\text{s.t. } P^{(v)^T} P^{(v)} = I,$$

where α and β are trade-off parameters, and $\Lambda(Z^{(v)})$ represents a certain constraint for the representation matrix $Z^{(v)}$.

However, the representation matrix obtained through self-expression inevitably contains redundant information, and a possible solution is to impose a low-rank constraint on the representation matrix. Due to the discrete nature of the rank function, the rank function is frequently substituted with the nuclear norm. Furthermore, Zhang *et al.* [1] proposed that the multi-view representation matrices can be stacked as a representation tensor. Thus, if all $Z^{(v)}$ are stacked as a tensor, model (11.3) is translated into the following:

$$\min_{Z^{(v)}, P^{(v)}, H^{(v)}} \|\mathcal{Z}\|_\circledast + \alpha \sum_{v=1}^{V} \|X^{(v)} - P^{(v)} H^{(v)}\|_F^2$$
$$+ \beta \sum_{v=1}^{V} \|H^{(v)} - H^{(v)} Z^{(v)}\|_F^2 \tag{11.4}$$
$$\text{s.t. } \mathcal{Z} = \Phi(Z^{(1)}, Z^{(2)}, \ldots, Z^{(V)}), \quad P^{(v)^T} P^{(v)} = I,$$

where $\Phi()$ represents stacking the multi-view representation matrices into a third-order tensor. However, regular tensor nuclear norm minimization assumes that larger singular values carry significant information, while smaller singular values contain insignificant information. However, for an image with substantial illumination variations, the initial larger singular values may contain lighting information, and it is advisable to shrink these larger singular values. Conversely, smaller singular values might still carry important information. For example, in an image with a considerable amount of noise, small singular values may represent crucial texture or edge features. In such cases, amplifying the smaller singular values is appropriate. Regular tensor nuclear norm minimization typically uses a threshold function to assign the same weight to each singular value, thereby ignoring the prior information encoded in the singular values. In this work, the weighted tensor nuclear norm [2] is employed to incorporate the prior information of singular values. Therefore, model (11.4) is transformed into the following:

$$
\min_{Z^{(v)}, P^{(v)}, H^{(v)}} ||\mathscr{Z}||_{\omega, \circledast} + \alpha \sum_{v=1}^{V} ||X^{(v)} - P^{(v)} H^{(v)}||_F^2
$$
$$
+ \beta \sum_{v=1}^{V} ||H^{(v)} - H^{(v)} Z^{(v)}||_F^2 \qquad (11.5)
$$
$$
\text{s.t. } \mathscr{Z} = \Phi(Z^{(1)}, Z^{(2)}, \ldots, Z^{(V)}), \ P^{(v)^T} P^{(v)} = I.
$$

Thus, representation matrices are expanded from second-order matrices to a third-order tensor, and a weighted tensor nuclear norm is imposed on the representation tensor to maintain a low-rank property and consider the prior information of singular values. To solve the problem of minimizing the weighted tensor nuclear norm, the tensor of size $N \times N \times V$ needs to be rotated to $N \times V \times N$. Singular value decomposition (SVD) is then applied to N slices of $N \times V$ tensors, which helps unveil the underlying connections between samples and views. Therefore, in the model, the weighted tensor nuclear norm can effectively capture high-order connections of multiple views. Furthermore, different representation matrices should tend toward an ideal consensus graph, which can be called consensus graph learning and is represented as follows:

$$
\min_{A} \sum_{v=1}^{V} ||A - Z^{(v)}||_F^2
$$
$$
\text{s.t. } a_i \geq 0, \ a_i^T 1 = 1, \qquad (11.6)
$$

where A is an ideal consensus graph matrix, a_i is the ith column of A, and $||A - Z^{(v)}||_F$ is the reconstruction error between A and $Z^{(v)}$.

In problem (11.6), for the consensus graph A, the reconstruction error with each similarity matrix $Z^{(v)}$ is treated equally. In practice, each view is expected to make distinct contributions for clustering. Thus, the target consensus graph A is expected to approximate each similarity matrix $Z^{(v)}$ with different weights [3], which can be formulated as follows:

$$
\min_{A} \sum_{v=1}^{V} \theta^{(v)} ||A - Z^{(v)}||_F^2
$$
$$
\text{s.t. } a_i \geq 0, \ a_i^T 1 = 1, \qquad (11.7)
$$

where

$$
\theta^{(v)} = 1/(2||Z^{(v)} - A||_F), \qquad (11.8)
$$

$\theta^{(v)}$ is the weight corresponding to vth reconstruction error of the similarity matrix $Z^{(v)}$. From problem (11.8), if the vth view is significant for clustering, reconstruction error $||Z^{(v)} - A||_F$ should be small, and $\theta^{(v)}$ for the reconstruction error should be large. Likewise, if the vth view is less important for clustering, reconstruction error $||Z^{(v)} - A||_F$ should be large, and $\theta^{(v)}$ for the reconstruction error should be small. Therefore, $\theta^{(v)}$ is automatically determined based on the contribution of the vth view for clustering, which enables the model to obtain a more ideal consensus graph A by considering the importance of views. Model (11.7) can be regarded as an adaptive consensus graph learning approach for clustering.

Theorem 1. *[4]. The number of connected components c in graph A is equal to the multiplicity of eigenvalue 0 of its Laplacian matrix L_A.*

Ideally, if the dataset has c clusters, the learned consensus graph A includes c distinct connected components, which can be implemented via the Laplacian rank constraint [4,5]. According to Theorem 1, the rank constraint can be denoted as $\text{rank}(L_A) = n - c$, where L_A is the Laplacian matrix, $L_A = D_A - (A + A^T)/2$, D_A is the diagonal degree matrix, and its ith diagonal element is defined as $\sum_j (a_{ij} + a_{ji})/2$. Thus, to obtain a consensus graph that has c connected components, problem (11.6) is transformed into the following [3]:

$$\min_A \sum_{v=1}^{V} ||A - Z^{(v)}||_F^2 \tag{11.9}$$
$$\text{s.t. } a_i \geq 0, \qquad a_i^T 1 = 1, \ \text{rank}(L_A) = n - c.$$

According to KyFan's theorem in [6], we have

$$\sum_{i=1}^{c} \sigma_i(L_A) = \min_{F^T F = I} \text{tr}(F^T L_A F), \tag{11.10}$$

where $F \in \mathbb{R}^{N \times k}$ is the spectral embedding matrix corresponding to the consensus graph A, and $F^T F = I$ is utilized to avoid trivial solutions. Let $\sigma_i(L_A) \geq 0$ be the ith smallest eigenvalue of L_A, and if $\sum_{i=1}^{c} \sigma_i(L_A) = 0$, $\text{rank}(L_A) = n - c$ will be satisfied. Thus, the Laplacian rank constraint can be transformed into $\text{tr}(F^T L_A F)$, and model (11.9) is represented as follows:

$$\min_A \sum_{v=1}^{V} \theta^{(v)} ||A - Z^{(v)}||_F^2 + 2\gamma \, \text{tr}(F^T L_A F), \tag{11.11}$$
$$\text{s.t. } a_i \geq 0, \ a_i^T 1 = 1, \ F^T F = I,$$

where γ is a trade-off parameter.

Finally, considering the above aspects, the proposed model is defined as follows:

$$\min_{Z^{(v)}, P^{(v)}, H^{(v)}, F, A, \theta^{(v)}} ||\mathscr{Z}||_{\omega, \circledast} + \alpha \sum_{v=1}^{V} ||X^{(v)} - P^{(v)} H^{(v)}||_F^2$$
$$+ \beta \sum_{v=1}^{V} ||H^{(v)} - H^{(v)} Z^{(v)}||_F^2 + 2\gamma \, \text{tr}(F^T L_A F) + \sum_{v=1}^{V} \theta^{(v)} ||Z^{(v)} - A||_F^2, \tag{11.12}$$
$$\text{s.t. } \mathscr{Z} = \Phi(Z^{(1)}, Z^{(2)}, \dots, Z^{(V)}), \ a_i \geq 0, \ a_i^T 1 = 1, \ F^T F = I, \ P^{(v)^T} P^{(v)} = I,$$

where $\theta^{(v)} = 1/(2||Z^{(v)} - A||_F)$ is an adaptive weight parameter, and α, β, and γ are trade-off parameters.

From model (11.12), first, $||X^{(v)} - P^{(v)} H^{(v)}||_F^2$ maps the original high-dimensional data $X^{(v)}$ to a low-dimensional representation $H^{(v)}$ using the projection matrix $P^{(v)}$, which preserves the essential features of the original data. Then, through

$||H^{(v)} - H^{(v)}Z^{(v)}||_F^2$, the low-dimensional matrix $H^{(v)}$ is used for self-expression operation to generate the representation matrix $Z^{(v)}$. To capture high-order connections of multiple views, $\mathcal{Z} = \Phi(Z^{(1)}, Z^{(2)}, \ldots, Z^{(V)})$ stacks all representation matrices $Z^{(v)}$ into the tensor space to form the representation tensor $\mathcal{Z}$. $||\mathcal{Z}||_{\omega,\circledast}$ represents the weighted tensor nuclear norm imposed on representation tensor $\mathcal{Z}$, which can consider the prior information of singular values and reduce redundant information. $\theta^{(v)}||Z^{(v)} - A||_F^2$ learns a consensus graph A for representation matrix $Z^{(V)}$ adaptively based on its importance in graph learning. $\mathrm{tr}(F^T L_A F)$ results in the learned consensus graph A with c connected principal components. Finally, clustering labels are obtained using the graphconncomp function to A in MATLAB®.

11.2 Optimization of model

Model (11.12) is an optimization problem with multiple variables, and an algorithm based on ADMM [7] is designed to solve it. We introduce the auxiliary variable $\mathcal{G}$, and let $\mathcal{Z} = \mathcal{G}$. The augmented Lagrangian function of model (11.12) can be represented as follows:

$$\min_{Z^{(v)}, P^{(v)}, H^{(v)}, F, A, \theta^{(v)}} ||\mathcal{G}||_{\omega,\circledast} + \alpha \sum_{v=1}^{V} ||X^{(v)} - P^{(v)}H^{(v)}||_F^2$$
$$+ \beta \sum_{v=1}^{V} ||H^{(v)} - H^{(v)}Z^{(v)}||_F^2 + 2\gamma \mathrm{tr}(F^T L_A F) \qquad (11.13)$$
$$+ \sum_{v=1}^{V} \theta^{(v)} ||Z^{(v)} - A||_F^2 + \Psi(\mathcal{W}, \mathcal{Z} - \mathcal{G}),$$
$$\text{s.t. } a_i \geq 0, \ a_i^T 1 = 1, \ F^T F = I, \ P^{(v)^T} P^{(v)} = I,$$

where

$$\Psi(\mathcal{W}, \mathcal{Z} - \mathcal{G}) = \langle \mathcal{W}, \mathcal{Z} - \mathcal{G} \rangle + \frac{\rho}{2} ||\mathcal{Z} - \mathcal{G}||_F^2, \qquad (11.14)$$

Update F: With all other variables fixed, the solution of the subproblem for F can be derived from problem (11.13) as follows:

$$\min_{F^T F = I} \mathrm{tr}(F^T L_A F). \qquad (11.15)$$

Problem (11.15) can be solved by calculating the c smallest eigenvalues of L_A.

Update A: With all other variables fixed, the solution of the subproblem for A can be derived from problem (11.13) as follows:

$$\min_A 2\gamma \, \mathrm{tr}(F^T L_A F) + \sum_{v=1}^{V} \theta^{(v)} ||A - Z^{(v)}||_F^2, \qquad (11.16)$$
$$\text{s.t. } a_{i,j} \geq 0, \ a_i 1 = 1, \ F^T F = I.$$

Problem (11.16) can be transformed into the following:

$$\min_A \gamma \sum_{i,j=1}^{n} ||f_i - f_j||_2^2 a_{ij} + \sum_{v=1}^{V} \theta^{(v)} \sum_{i,j=1}^{n} (a_{ij} - z_{i,j}^{(v)})^2, \qquad (11.17)$$
$$\text{s.t. } a_{i,j} \geq 0, \ a_i 1 = 1, \ F^T F = I.$$

Let $e_{ij} = ||f_i - f_j||_2^2$, and e_i be a vector, whose jth element is denoted as e_{ij}. Therefore, problem (11.17) is equivalent to the following form:

$$\min_{a_i \geq 0, a_i 1 = 1} ||a_i - (\textstyle\sum_{v=1}^{V} \theta^{(v)} z_i^{(v)} - \gamma e_i/2)/\textstyle\sum_{v=1}^{V} \theta^{(v)}||_2^2. \tag{11.18}$$

Problem (11.18) can be solved by an efficient iterative algorithm [8]. To speed up the computation, γ is initialized as a constant, and during each iteration, when the number of connected components is greater than or less than c, we divide or multiply γ by 2. Therefore, γ is a self-tuned parameter.

Update $Z^{(v)}$: With all other variables fixed, the solution of the subproblem for $Z^{(v)}$ can be derived from problem (11.13) as follows:

$$
\begin{aligned}
Z^{(v)*} &= \operatorname*{argmin}_{Z^{(v)}} \textstyle\sum_{v=1}^{V} \beta ||H^{(v)} - H^{(v)} Z^{(v)}||_F^2 \\
&\quad + \textstyle\sum_{v=1}^{V} \theta^{(v)} ||A - Z^{(v)}||_F^2 + \Psi(\mathcal{W}, \mathcal{Z} - \mathcal{G}), \\
&= \operatorname*{argmin}_{Z^{(v)}} \textstyle\sum_{v=1}^{V} \beta ||H^{(v)} - H^{(v)} Z^{(v)}||_F^2 \\
&\quad + \textstyle\sum_{v=1}^{V} \theta^{(v)} ||A - Z^{(v)}||_F^2 + \langle \mathcal{W}, \mathcal{Z} - \mathcal{G} \rangle + \frac{\rho}{2} ||\mathcal{Z} - \mathcal{G}||_F^2.
\end{aligned}
\tag{11.19}
$$

Since all $Z^{(v)}$ are stacked into a tensor to form $\mathcal{Z}$, for each $Z^{(v)}$, we have

$$
\begin{aligned}
Z^{(v)*} &= \operatorname*{argmin}_{Z^{(v)}} \theta^{(v)} ||A - Z^{(v)}||_F^2 + \beta ||H^{(v)} - H^{(v)} Z^{(v)}||_F^2 \\
&\quad + \frac{\rho}{2} ||Z^{(v)} - G^{(v)} + W^{(v)}/\rho||_F^2.
\end{aligned}
\tag{11.20}
$$

Taking the derivative with respect to $Z^{(v)}$ and setting it to zero, $Z^{(v)*}$ is obtained as follows:

$$Z^{(v)*} = B^{(v)^{-1}} C^{(v)}, \tag{11.21}$$

where $B^{(v)} = 2\beta H^{(v)^T} H^{(v)} + 2\theta^{(v)} I + \rho I$, $C^{(v)} = 2\beta H^{(v)^T} H^{(v)} + 2\theta^{(v)} A + \rho(G^{(v)} - W^{(v)}/\rho)$.

Theorem 2. *[9]. Given $M \in \mathbb{R}^{n_1 \times n_2}$ and $l = \min(n_1, n_2)$, for the following weighted nuclear norm minimization problem:*

$$\min_X \tau ||X||_{\omega, \circledast} + \frac{1}{2} ||X - M||_F^2, \tag{11.22}$$

which has the following optimization solution:

$$X^* = \Gamma_{\tau * \omega}(M) = U_M P_{\tau * \omega}(M) V_M^T, \tag{11.23}$$

where $M = U_M * S_M * V_M^T$ is the SVD of M, $P_{\tau * \omega}(M) = \operatorname{diag}(\zeta_1, \zeta_2, \ldots, \zeta_l)$, and $\zeta_i = \operatorname{sign}(\sigma_i(M)) \max(\sigma_i(M) - \tau * \omega_i, 0)$.

Theorem 3. *[2]. For a tensor $\mathcal{M} \in \mathbb{R}^{n_1 \times n_2 \times n_3}$ and $l = \min(n_1, n_2)$, let $\mathcal{M} = \mathcal{U} * \mathcal{S} * \mathcal{V}^T$. For the following weighted tensor nuclear norm minimization problem:*

$$\min_{\mathcal{X}} \tau ||\mathcal{X}||_{\omega, \circledast} + \frac{1}{2} ||\mathcal{X} - \mathcal{M}||_F^2, \tag{11.24}$$

the solution of problem (11.24) is given by

$$\mathscr{X}^* = \Gamma_{\tau * \omega}(\mathscr{M}) = \mathscr{U} * \text{ifft}(P_{\tau * \omega}(\bar{\mathscr{M}})) * \mathscr{V}^T, \tag{11.25}$$

where $\mathscr{U} = \text{ifft}(\bar{\mathscr{U}}, [\,], 3)$, $\overline{U^{(i)}}$ *is the ith frontal slice of* $\bar{\mathscr{U}}$, $\mathscr{V} = \text{ifft}(\bar{\mathscr{V}}, [\,], 3)$, *and* $V^{(i)}$ *is the ith frontal slice of* $\bar{\mathscr{V}}$. *According to Theorem 2, the ith frontal slice of* $P_{\tau * \omega}(\bar{\mathscr{M}})$ *is*

$$P_{\tau * \omega}(\bar{M}^{(i)}) = \text{diag}(\zeta_1, \zeta_2, \ldots, \zeta_l), \tag{11.26}$$

where $\zeta_i = \text{sign}(\sigma_i(\bar{M}^{(i)})) \max(\sigma_i(\bar{M}^{(i)}) - \tau * \omega_i, 0)$.

Update $\mathscr{G}$: With all other variables fixed, the solution of the subproblem for $\mathscr{G}$ can be derived from problem (11.13) as follows:

$$\begin{aligned} \mathscr{G}^* &= \underset{\mathscr{G}}{\text{argmin }} \alpha||\mathscr{G}||_{\omega,\circledast} + \Psi(\mathscr{W}, \mathscr{Z} - \mathscr{G}) \\ &= \underset{\mathscr{G}}{\text{argmin }} \alpha||\mathscr{G}||_{\omega,\circledast} + \rho/2||\mathscr{G} - (\mathscr{Z} + \mathscr{W}/\rho)||_F^2. \end{aligned} \tag{11.27}$$

According to Theorem 3, the solution of problem (11.27) can be obtained as follows:

$$\mathscr{G}^* = \Gamma_{\tau * \omega}(\mathscr{Z} + \mathscr{W}/\rho). \tag{11.28}$$

Theorem 4. *[10]. For the following optimization problem:*

$$\begin{aligned} &\min_X ||M - QX||_F^2, \\ &\text{s.t. } XX^T = X^TX = I, \end{aligned} \tag{11.29}$$

the solution of problem (11.29) is given by

$$X = UV^T, \tag{11.30}$$

where U and V are the left and right singular values of SVD of Q^TM, *respectively.*

Update $P^{(v)}$: With all other variables fixed, the solution of the subproblem for $P^{(v)}$ can be derived from problem (11.13) as follows:

$$\begin{aligned} P^{(v)*} &= \underset{P^{(v)}}{\text{argmin }} ||X^{(v)} - P^{(v)}H^{(v)}||_F^2 \\ &= \underset{P^{(v)}}{\text{argmin }} ||X^{(v)^T} - H^{(v)^T}P^{(v)^T}||_F^2. \end{aligned} \tag{11.31}$$

According to Theorem 4, the solution of problem (11.31) is given by

$$P^{(v)*} = U^{(v)}V^{(v)^T}, \tag{11.32}$$

where $U^{(v)}$ and $V^{(v)^T}$ are the left and right singular values of the SVD of $X^{(v)}H^{(v)^T}$, respectively.

Update $H^{(v)}$: With all other variables fixed, the solution of the subproblem for $H^{(v)}$ can be derived from problem (11.13) as follows:

$$\min_{H^{(v)}} \alpha||X^{(v)} - P^{(v)}H^{(v)}||_F^2 + \beta||H^{(v)} - H^{(v)}Z^{(v)}||_F^2. \tag{11.33}$$

Taking the derivative with respect to $H^{(v)}$ and setting it to zero, we can obtain the following:

$$M^{(v)}H^{(v)} + H^{(v)}Q^{(v)} = K^{(v)}, \tag{11.34}$$

where $M^{(v)} = \alpha P^{(v)^T}P^{(v)}$, $Q^{(v)} = \beta(I + ZZ^{(v)^T} - Z^{(v)} - Z^{(v)^T})$, $K^{(v)} = \alpha P^{(v)^T}X^{(v)}$, (11.34) is a Sylvester equation, which can be efficiently solved via the lyap function in MATLAB.

Adaptive weight $\theta^{(v)}$ can be updated as follows:

$$\theta^{(v)^*} = \frac{1}{2||Z^{(v)} - A||_F}. \tag{11.35}$$

The Lagrange multiplier can be updated as follows:

$$\mathscr{W}^* = \mathscr{W} + \rho(\mathscr{Z} - \mathscr{G}). \tag{11.36}$$

Penalty parameter ρ can be updated as follows:

$$\rho^* = \min(\eta\rho, \rho_{max}), \tag{11.37}$$

where ρ_{max} is the maximum value of the penalty parameter, and η is a parameter designed to speed up convergence.

The convergence condition of the model is set as follows:

$$||Z^{(v)} - G^{(v)}||_\infty < \varepsilon, \tag{11.38}$$

where ε denotes the convergence threshold. The solution procedure of the proposed model is summarized in Algorithm 1.

We also provide a schematic representation of the distributed ADMM process in Figure 11.1. As shown in the figure, this algorithm framework contains two types of nodes. The master node is responsible for maintaining global variables, such as the global Lagrange multiplier $\mathscr{W}$, penalty parameter ρ, and other shared constants, and it also receives the results of sub-variables from the slave nodes. The slave nodes primarily handle the updating of sub-variables and upload the updated results to the master node. First, the master node initializes global variables and sub-variables. When the model updates $P^{(v)}$, the slave node-5 downloads the required variables $H^{(v)}$ and constant $X^{(v)}$ from the master node. It then updates $P^{(v)}$ by solving (11.32), and the information of $P^{(v)}$ is uploaded to the master node. Other slave nodes perform operations similar to the slave node-5 to achieve the updating of sub-variables. ρ and $\mathscr{W}$ are updated at the master node. When all variables have been updated, check whether the convergence condition is satisfied. If the convergence condition is met, stop the iteration and output A; otherwise, continue updating the variables. Therefore, ADMM efficiently solves the subproblems distributed across different nodes, achieving the ultimate solution for the proposed model.

11.3 Experiments process

11.3.1 Multi-view datasets

The datasets used for experiments are as follows:

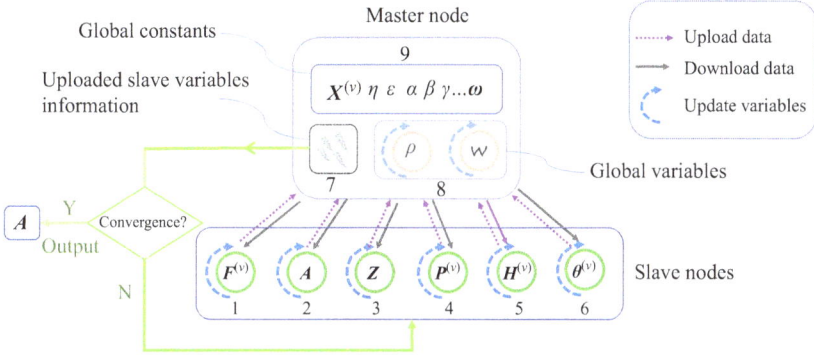

Figure 11.1 Illustration of the optimization process with the distributed ADMM

Algorithm1: AMSLDO for multi-view clustering

Input: Multi-view data: $\{X^{(1)}, \ldots, X^{(V)}\}$, number of clusters c, trade-off parameters α, and β, weight vector w.
Initialize: $\theta^{(v)} = 1/V$, $\rho = 0.1$, number of neighbors $g = 10$, $\rho_{max} = 10^{10}$, $\eta = 2$, $\gamma = 0.1$, $k = 80$, $Iter_{max} = 50$, $\varepsilon = 10^{-7}$.
while not convergence **do**
    1. Update F by Eq. (11.15);
    2. Update A by Eq. (11.18);
    3. Update Z by Eq. (11.21);
    4. Update $\mathscr{G}$ by Eq. (11.28);
    5. Update $P^{(v)}$ by Eq. (11.32);
    6. Update $H^{(v)}$ by Eq. (11.34);
    7. Update $\theta^{(v)}$ by Eq. (11.35);
    8. Update Lagrange multipliers by Eq. (11.36);
    9. Update penalty parameters by Eq. (11.37);
    10. Check the convergence condition by Eq. (11.38).
end
Output consensus matrix A with exact c connected components.

BBC4view* is composed of 685 documents retrieved from the BBC News website, representing stories across five thematic areas during the period of 2004–2005, including business, entertainment, politics, sports, and technology. Each document is divided into four segments by segmenting the content into paragraphs.

BBCSport* comprises 544 documents sourced from the BBC Sport website. These documents correspond to sports news articles from five thematic areas during the 2004–2005 period, including athletics, cricket, football, rugby, and tennis. The

---

*http://mlg.ucd.ie/datasets/.

dataset is described using the term frequency-inverse document frequency (TF-IDF) to provide two views.

Yale[†] is a face image dataset, where each individual is represented by 11 images, each capturing a distinct facial expression or configuration: center-light, left-light, right-light, without glasses, with glasses, happy, normal, sad, and so on. Each image is described by three diverse attributes: 4096d Intensity, 3304d Local Binary Pattern (LBP), and 6750d Gabor.

ORL[‡] is a face image dataset, containing 10 images for each of the 40 unique subjects. For certain individuals, the images are taken on different occasions, introducing variations in lighting, facial expressions (open/closed eyes and smiling/not smiling), and facial details (with/without glasses). All the photographs are taken against a consistent dark background, with subjects maintaining an upright, frontal position, allowing for some permissible side movement. Each image is characterized by three heterogeneous features: 4096d Intensity, 3304d LBP, and 6750d Gabor.

MSRCV1[§] dataset consists of 240 object images distributed across eight classes. For our study, we select seven commonly used classes, including trees, buildings, airplanes, cows, faces, cars, and bicycles. Each class comprises 30 images, and each image is characterized by six heterogeneous features: 1302d CENTRIST feature, 48d Color Moment (CM), 512d GIST, 100d Histogram of Oriented Gradients (HOG), 256d LBP, and 210d Scale-Invariant Feature Transform (SIFT).

Cornell[|] dataset comprises 195 webpages collected from Cornell University. Each webpage is represented by a citation view consisting of 1703 words, along with a content view that includes citation links to 195 other pages.

The dataset employed in our study comprises diverse data types, encompassing text, images, and others. Therefore, the inclusion of such diverse datasets contributes significantly to demonstrating the robustness of our model in the realm of clustering. The summary of these datasets is reported in Table 11.1.

11.3.2   Compared methods

LRR[¶] [11] is a sing-view clustering method that segments subspace by low-rank representation. We choose the view with the best results for the experiment.

SSC[**] [12] is a single-view clustering method that finds a sparse representation of each point in the dictionary and uses the sparse coefficients to construct a similarity graph. Similarly, we choose the view with the best results for the experiment.

DiMSC[††] [13] utilizes the Hilbert Schmidt Independence Criterion (HSIC) as a diversity metric to explore compensatory information between multiple views.

[†] https://cvc.yale.edu/projects/yalefaces/yalefaces.html.
[‡] https://www.cl.cam.ac.uk/research/dtg/attarchive/facedatabase.html.
[§] http://research.microsoft.com/en-us/projects/objectclassrecognition/.
[|] https://lig-membres.imag.fr/grimal/data.html.
[¶] https://sites.google.com/site/guangcanliu/.
[**] http://www.ccis.neu.edu/home/eelhami/codes.htm.
[††] http://cic.tju.edu.cn/faculty/zhangchangqing/code.html.

Table 11.1 *Summary of different datasets*

	BBC4view	Yale	ORL	BBCSport	MSRCV1	Cornell
Content	News stories	Face	Face	News stories	Scene	Webpages
Clusters	5	15	40	5	7	5
Samples	685	165	400	544	210	195
View1	Segment1(4659d)	Intensity(4096d)	Intensity(4096d)	View1(3183d)	CENTRIST(1302d)	Cite(195d)
View2	Segment2(4633d)	LBP(3304d)	LBP(3304d)	View2(3203d)	CM(48d)	Content(1703d)
View3	Segment3(4665d)	Gabor(6750d)	Gabor(6750d)	-	GIST(512d)	-
View4	Segment4(4684d)	-	-	-	HOG(100d)	-
View5	-	-	-	-	LBP(256d)	-
View6	-	-	-	-	SIFT(210d)	-

GMC[‡‡] [14] is a graph-based multi-view clustering method that learns similarity graphs from multiple views and a consistent fusion graph in an adaptive manner.

CSMSC[§§] [15] considers both consistency and diversity of multiple views.

MSC-IAS[||] [16] integrates encoded complementary information to learn the intact space, and the similarity matrices are constructed with maximum correlation to their potential intact points.

LMSC[¶] [17] learns the latent representation from multi-view to explore the shared structure of multiple views.

LT-MSC[***] [1] combines the tensor with low-rank constraint to unveil connections between different views.

WTNNM[†††] [2] considers the prior information using weighted tenor nuclear norm minimization.

CGL[‡‡‡] [18] constructs similarity matrices from the embedding space rather than the original space and stacks the multi-view gram matrices into a third-order tensor and finally a weighted tensor nuclear norm to capture globally consistent information across multiple views.

ETLMSC[§§§] [19] is a spectral clustering method based on Markov chains and incorporates an essential tensor learning approach to explore high-order correlations among multi-view representations. These comparison methods are implemented via source codes provided by the authors.

11.3.3   Evaluation metrics

To evaluation the clustering performance of different models on datasets, seven evaluation metrics are employed for clustering experiments: Accuracy (ACC), Normalized Mutual Information (NMI), Purity, F-score, Precision, Recall, and Adjusted Rank Index (ARI). Larger values indicate better results, and bold values represent the best results. For a dataset with N samples, the formulas of these seven metrics are given as follows:

Let t_i and p_i denote the true labels and prediction labels corresponding to ith sample, respectively. ACC is defined as follows:

$$\text{ACC} = \frac{\sum_{i=1}^{N} \Theta(t_i, \text{map}(p_i))}{N}, \tag{11.39}$$

where $\text{map}(\cdot)$ represents the optimal permutation mapping function that transforms each predicted partition into the target partition. $\Theta(\cdot, \cdot)$ is a discriminant function, which is defined as follows:

$$\Theta(a, b) = \begin{cases} 1, & \text{if } a = b; \\ 0, & \text{otherwise.} \end{cases} \tag{11.40}$$

[‡‡] https://github.com/cshaowang/gmc.
[§§] https://github.com/XIAOCHUN-CAS/Consistent-and-Specific-Multi-View-Subspace-Clustering.
[||] http://www.cbsr.ia.ac.cn/users/xiaobowang.
[¶] http://cic.tju.edu.cn/faculty/zhangchangqing/code.html.
[***] http://cic.tju.edu.cn/faculty/zhangchangqing/code.html.
[†††] https://github.com/xdweixia/AAAI2020_WTNNM.
[‡‡‡] https://github.com/guanyuezhen/CGL.
[§§§] https://github.com/sikid/Code-for-ETLMSC.

Let ν and $\hbar$ be the prediction partition of K clusters and the target partition of L classes, respectively. NMI is defined as follows:

$$\text{NMI}(\nu, \hbar) = \frac{2\sum_{j=1}^{K}\sum_{l=1}^{L}\frac{n_j^l}{N}\log\frac{n_j^l N}{\sum_{i=1}^{K}n_i^l\sum_{i=1}^{L}n_j^i}}{\text{H}(\nu) + \text{H}(\hbar)}, \tag{11.41}$$

where $\text{H}(\cdot)$ is Shannon entropy of a partition, and n_j^i represents the number of sample in cluster j and class i.

Let TP represent the count of correctly labeled positive cluster samples, and FP represent the count of erroneously labeled positive cluster samples. Precision is defined as follows:

$$\text{Precision} = \frac{\text{TP}}{\text{TP} + \text{FP}}. \tag{11.42}$$

If FN represents the count of entries incorrectly labeled as negative cluster, Recall is defined as follows:

$$\text{Recall} = \frac{\text{TP}}{\text{FP} + \text{FN}}. \tag{11.43}$$

Then, F-score is defined as follows:

$$\text{F-score} = 2\frac{\text{Precision} \times \text{Recall}}{\text{Precision} + \text{Recall}}. \tag{11.44}$$

Purity is defined as follows:

$$\text{Purity} = \frac{1}{N}\sum_{i=1}^{K}\max_{j}|D_i \cap G_j|, \tag{11.45}$$

where K is the number of clusters, D_i represents the set of samples corresponding to the ith predicted category, and G_i denotes the set of samples belonging to the jth category in the ground truth labels.

ARI is a measure of similarity between two clusters, which is defined as follows:

$$\text{ARI} = \frac{B - \frac{Q \cdot S}{n(n-1)/2}}{(Q + S)/2 - \frac{Q \cdot S}{n(n-1)/2}}, \tag{11.46}$$

where $B = \sum_{i,j}T_{i,j}(T_{i,j} - 1)/2$, $Q = \sum_{i}T_i(T_i - 1)/2$, and $S = \sum_{j}T_j(T_j - 1)/2$. $T_{i,j}$ represents the number of samples that should be assigned to the ith cluster but are instead assigned to the jth cluster. T_i and T_j denote the number of samples belonging to the ith and jth clusters, respectively.

11.3.4   *Experimental results*

11.3.4.1   Clustering performance comparison

To obtain the fair results, all experiments are repeated ten times, and the average value and standard deviation are recorded. The experimental results of different methods on six datasets and the settings of multiple parameters for the proposed method are displayed in Tables 11.2 and 11.3. Note that CGL is unable to handle the Cornell

Table 11.2 The experimental results of different methods on the BBC4view, Yale, and ORL datasets (average value ± standard deviation)

Datasets	Methods	ACC	NMI	Purity	F-score	Precision	Recall	ARI
BBC4view α = 1, β = 0.5 ω = [40, 20, 100, 10]	LRR	0.735 ± 0.001	0.491 ± 0.001	0.735 ± 0.001	0.574 ± 0.001	0.583 ± 0.001	0.566 ± 0.001	0.446 ± 0.002
	SSC	0.324 ± 0.000	0.011 ± 0.000	0.333 ± 0.000	0.377 ± 0.000	0.234 ± 0.000	0.973 ± 0.000	−0.002 ± 0.000
	DiMSC	0.832 ± 0.000	0.651 ± 0.000	0.832 ± 0.000	0.737 ± 0.000	0.755 ± 0.000	0.720 ± 0.000	0.659 ± 0.000
	GMC	0.693 ± 0.000	0.485 ± 0.000	0.693 ± 0.000	0.633 ± 0.000	0.501 ± 0.000	0.860 ± 0.000	0.479 ± 0.000
	CSMSC	0.810 ± 0.000	0.616 ± 0.001	0.810 ± 0.000	0.727 ± 0.000	0.740 ± 0.001	0.714 ± 0.001	0.645 ± 0.001
	MSC-IAS	0.387 ± 0.052	0.136 ± 0.070	0.457 ± 0.066	0.348 ± 0.023	0.299 ± 0.052	0.437 ± 0.053	0.094 ± 0.068
	LMSC	0.881 ± 0.008	0.690 ± 0.015	0.881 ± 0.008	0.806 ± 0.011	0.807 ± 0.013	0.805 ± 0.012	0.746 ± 0.015
	LT-MSC	0.579 ± 0.001	0.425 ± 0.006	0.633 ± 0.003	0.548 ± 0.003	0.524 ± 0.002	0.574 ± 0.004	0.401 ± 0.003
	WTNNM	0.946 ± 0.000	0.878 ± 0.000	0.946 ± 0.000	0.909 ± 0.000	0.943 ± 0.000	0.878 ± 0.000	0.883 ± 0.000
	CGL	0.861 ± 0.000	0.690 ± 0.000	0.861 ± 0.000	0.775 ± 0.000	0.815 ± 0.000	0.739 ± 0.000	0.711 ± 0.000
	ETLMSC	0.955 ± 0.000	0.892 ± 0.000	0.955 ± 0.000	0.921 ± 0.000	0.952 ± 0.000	0.891 ± 0.000	0.897 ± 0.000
	Ours	**0.987 ± 0.000**	**0.960 ± 0.001**	**0.987 ± 0.000**	**0.978 ± 0.001**	**0.988 ± 0.000**	**0.969 ± 0.001**	**0.971 ± 0.001**
Yale α = 5, β = 5 ω = [20, 30, 50]	LRR	0.571 ± 0.019	0.594 ± 0.014	0.577 ± 0.016	0.412 ± 0.021	0.402 ± 0.021	0.423 ± 0.020	0.373 ± 0.022
	SSC	0.692 ± 0.002	0.712 ± 0.004	0.692 ± 0.002	0.523 ± 0.008	0.487 ± 0.009	0.566 ± 0.006	0.490 ± 0.008
	DiMSC	0.647 ± 0.024	0.678 ± 0.019	0.647 ± 0.024	0.520 ± 0.024	0.506 ± 0.021	0.536 ± 0.029	0.488 ± 0.026
	GMC	0.655 ± 0.000	0.674 ± 0.000	0.661 ± 0.000	0.480 ± 0.000	0.419 ± 0.000	0.562 ± 0.000	0.441 ± 0.000
	CSMSC	0.640 ± 0.018	0.683 ± 0.008	0.640 ± 0.018	0.519 ± 0.011	0.488 ± 0.014	0.553 ± 0.011	0.485 ± 0.012
	MSC-IAS	0.833 ± 0.035	0.838 ± 0.022	0.836 ± 0.032	0.721 ± 0.033	0.696 ± 0.037	0.748 ± 0.031	0.702 ± 0.035
	LMSC	0.664 ± 0.013	0.688 ± 0.021	0.667 ± 0.012	0.495 ± 0.029	0.454 ± 0.030	0.545 ± 0.027	0.459 ± 0.031
	LT-MSC	0.734 ± 0.003	0.757 ± 0.005	0.734 ± 0.003	0.615 ± 0.008	0.592 ± 0.009	0.640 ± 0.007	0.589 ± 0.008
	WTNNM	0.928 ± 0.038	0.946 ± 0.025	0.930 ± 0.037	0.904 ± 0.044	**0.885 ± 0.055**	0.925 ± 0.036	0.898 ± 0.047
	CGL	0.758 ± 0.000	0.772 ± 0.000	0.758 ± 0.000	0.654 ± 0.000	0.645 ± 0.000	0.662 ± 0.000	0.631 ± 0.000
	ETLMSC	0.673 ± 0.000	0.702 ± 0.000	0.685 ± 0.000	0.536 ± 0.000	0.521 ± 0.000	0.552 ± 0.000	0.505 ± 0.000
	Ours	**0.952 ± 0.038**	**0.953 ± 0.032**	**0.953 ± 0.036**	**0.911 ± 0.064**	0.884 ± 0.092	**0.943 ± 0.035**	**0.905 ± 0.069**
ORL α = 1, β = 1 ω = [5, 10, 50]	LRR	0.640 ± 0.020	0.791 ± 0.009	0.667 ± 0.017	0.521 ± 0.019	0.496 ± 0.019	0.549 ± 0.021	0.509 ± 0.020
	SSC	0.742 ± 0.015	0.876 ± 0.006	0.785 ± 0.009	0.667 ± 0.017	0.610 ± 0.025	0.738 ± 0.016	0.659 ± 0.017
	DiMSC	0.813 ± 0.018	0.914 ± 0.009	0.840 ± 0.017	0.766 ± 0.022	0.722 ± 0.029	0.816 ± 0.021	0.760 ± 0.023
	GMC	0.633 ± 0.000	0.804 ± 0.000	0.715 ± 0.000	0.360 ± 0.000	0.232 ± 0.000	0.801 ± 0.000	0.337 ± 0.000
	CSMSC	0.771 ± 0.026	0.890 ± 0.013	0.806 ± 0.019	0.707 ± 0.032	0.652 ± 0.036	0.771 ± 0.026	0.699 ± 0.032
	MSC-IAS	0.867 ± 0.008	0.929 ± 0.006	0.885 ± 0.010	0.819 ± 0.015	0.791 ± 0.020	0.849 ± 0.012	0.815 ± 0.015
	LMSC	0.797 ± 0.039	0.905 ± 0.023	0.830 ± 0.037	0.741 ± 0.052	0.688 ± 0.054	0.803 ± 0.051	0.735 ± 0.054
	LT-MSC	0.816 ± 0.012	0.912 ± 0.007	0.846 ± 0.011	0.762 ± 0.018	0.717 ± 0.024	0.813 ± 0.015	0.756 ± 0.019
	WTNNM	0.974 ± 0.013	0.992 ± 0.004	0.980 ± 0.010	0.974 ± 0.013	0.957 ± 0.021	0.991 ± 0.005	0.973 ± 0.013
	CGL	0.866 ± 0.009	0.926 ± 0.003	0.879 ± 0.005	0.816 ± 0.008	0.799 ± 0.012	0.835 ± 0.006	0.812 ± 0.009
	ETLMSC	0.923 ± 0.000	0.979 ± 0.000	0.948 ± 0.000	0.928 ± 0.000	0.892 ± 0.000	0.967 ± 0.000	0.927 ± 0.000
	Ours	**0.991 ± 0.014**	**0.997 ± 0.003**	**0.994 ± 0.009**	**0.990 ± 0.012**	**0.986 ± 0.020**	**0.994 ± 0.005**	**0.990 ± 0.013**

Table 11.3 The experimental results of different methods on the BBCSport, MSRCV1, and Cornell datasets (average value ± standard deviation)

Datasets	Methods	ACC	NMI	Purity	F-score	Precision	Recall	ARI
BBCSport $\alpha = 1, \beta = 0.5$ $\omega = [8, 50]$	LRR	0.626 ± 0.001	0.419 ± 0.001	0.691 ± 0.000	0.502 ± 0.001	0.535 ± 0.001	0.472 ± 0.001	0.358 ± 0.001
	SSC	0.369 ± 0.002	0.018 ± 0.000	0.369 ± 0.001	0.387 ± 0.001	0.241 ± 0.000	0.980 ± 0.002	0.006 ± 0.001
	DiMSC	0.679 ± 0.005	0.464 ± 0.002	0.720 ± 0.005	0.568 ± 0.003	0.497 ± 0.008	0.664 ± 0.011	0.406 ± 0.005
	GMC	0.739 ± 0.000	0.705 ± 0.000	0.763 ± 0.000	0.721 ± 0.000	0.573 ± 0.000	0.971 ± 0.000	0.601 ± 0.000
	CSMSC	0.947 ± 0.000	0.841 ± 0.000	0.947 ± 0.000	0.894 ± 0.000	0.886 ± 0.000	0.902 ± 0.000	0.860 ± 0.000
	MSC-IAS	0.588 ± 0.084	0.350 ± 0.061	0.638 ± 0.063	0.473 ± 0.057	0.407 ± 0.039	0.573 ± 0.102	0.272 ± 0.069
	LMSC	0.943 ± 0.009	0.843 ± 0.020	0.943 ± 0.009	0.909 ± 0.012	0.915 ± 0.010	0.903 ± 0.017	0.881 ± 0.016
	LT-MSC	0.370 ± 0.005	0.028 ± 0.005	0.378 ± 0.005	0.383 ± 0.000	0.240 ± 0.000	0.950 ± 0.010	0.003 ± 0.001
	WTNNM	0.983 ± 0.000	0.941 ± 0.000	0.983 ± 0.000	0.965 ± 0.000	0.966 ± 0.000	0.963 ± 0.000	0.953 ± 0.000
	CGL	0.759 ± 0.000	0.734 ± 0.000	0.836 ± 0.000	0.755 ± 0.000	0.716 ± 0.000	0.798 ± 0.000	0.673 ± 0.000
	ETLMSC	0.989 ± 0.000	0.967 ± 0.000	0.989 ± 0.000	0.985 ± 0.000	0.989 ± 0.000	0.981 ± 0.000	0.980 ± 0.000
	Ours	**1.000 ± 0.000**	**1.000 ± 0.000**	**1.000 ± 0.000**	**1.000 ± 0.000**	**1.000 ± 0.000**	**1.000 ± 0.000**	**1.000 ± 0.000**
MSRCV1 $\alpha = 5, \beta = 20$ $\omega = [10, 2, 30, 10, 5, 100]$	LRR	0.486 ± 0.021	0.350 ± 0.015	0.524 ± 0.011	0.352 ± 0.011	0.348 ± 0.011	0.357 ± 0.010	0.246 ± 0.013
	SSC	0.776 ± 0.009	0.634 ± 0.011	0.776 ± 0.009	0.633 ± 0.012	0.626 ± 0.012	0.639 ± 0.012	0.573 ± 0.014
	DiMSC	0.699 ± 0.024	0.599 ± 0.024	0.712 ± 0.021	0.587 ± 0.021	0.576 ± 0.022	0.598 ± 0.020	0.519 ± 0.024
	GMC	0.895 ± 0.000	0.816 ± 0.000	0.895 ± 0.000	0.800 ± 0.000	0.786 ± 0.000	0.814 ± 0.000	0.767 ± 0.000
	CSMSC	0.759 ± 0.020	0.699 ± 0.010	0.802 ± 0.006	0.688 ± 0.011	0.668 ± 0.013	0.708 ± 0.009	0.636 ± 0.013
	MSC-IAS	0.747 ± 0.023	0.695 ± 0.017	0.749 ± 0.021	0.645 ± 0.021	0.618 ± 0.025	0.675 ± 0.019	0.585 ± 0.025
	LMSC	0.683 ± 0.064	0.594 ± 0.054	0.706 ± 0.055	0.576 ± 0.058	0.558 ± 0.062	0.596 ± 0.055	0.505 ± 0.069
	LT-MSC	0.843 ± 0.000	0.753 ± 0.001	0.843 ± 0.000	0.737 ± 0.001	0.726 ± 0.002	0.748 ± 0.000	0.694 ± 0.001
	WTNNM	0.990 ± 0.000	0.978 ± 0.000	0.990 ± 0.000	0.981 ± 0.000	0.980 ± 0.000	0.981 ± 0.000	0.978 ± 0.000
	CGL	0.919 ± 0.000	0.834 ± 0.000	0.919 ± 0.000	0.843 ± 0.000	0.836 ± 0.000	0.850 ± 0.000	0.817 ± 0.000
	ETLMSC	0.800 ± 0.000	0.724 ± 0.000	0.814 ± 0.000	0.717 ± 0.000	0.702 ± 0.000	0.732 ± 0.000	0.670 ± 0.000
	Ours	**1.000 ± 0.000**	**1.000 ± 0.000**	**1.000 ± 0.000**	**1.000 ± 0.000**	**1.000 ± 0.000**	**1.000 ± 0.000**	**1.000 ± 0.000**
Cornell $\alpha = 0.5, \beta = 8$ $\omega = [20, 10]$	LRR	0.503 ± 0.004	0.327 ± 0.005	0.656 ± 0.002	0.442 ± 0.002	0.469 ± 0.003	0.418 ± 0.002	0.252 ± 0.003
	SSC	0.446 ± 0.000	0.039 ± 0.000	0.451 ± 0.000	0.427 ± 0.000	0.275 ± 0.000	**0.958 ± 0.000**	0.014 ± 0.000
	DiMSC	0.422 ± 0.002	0.036 ± 0.003	0.447 ± 0.002	0.397 ± 0.000	0.296 ± 0.000	0.602 ± 0.000	0.055 ± 0.000
	GMC	0.462 ± 0.000	0.093 ± 0.000	0.492 ± 0.000	0.414 ± 0.000	0.285 ± 0.000	0.754 ± 0.000	0.037 ± 0.000
	CSMSC	0.505 ± 0.003	0.309 ± 0.001	0.579 ± 0.000	0.423 ± 0.000	0.428 ± 0.002	0.418 ± 0.001	0.213 ± 0.001
	MSC-IAS	0.451 ± 0.032	0.186 ± 0.018	0.523 ± 0.024	0.349 ± 0.019	0.380 ± 0.020	0.325 ± 0.033	0.134 ± 0.021
	LMSC	0.421 ± 0.045	0.212 ± 0.036	0.535 ± 0.024	0.354 ± 0.027	0.349 ± 0.034	0.362 ± 0.032	0.109 ± 0.045
	LT-MSC	0.403 ± 0.012	0.206 ± 0.013	0.532 ± 0.010	0.337 ± 0.008	0.377 ± 0.012	0.305 ± 0.006	0.127 ± 0.013
	WTNNM	0.444 ± 0.003	0.035 ± 0.004	0.450 ± 0.003	0.427 ± 0.001	0.276 ± 0.001	0.946 ± 0.004	0.016 ± 0.002
	CGL	–	–	–	–	–	–	–
	ETLMSC	0.431 ± 0.000	0.173 ± 0.000	0.503 ± 0.000	0.328 ± 0.000	0.378 ± 0.000	0.290 ± 0.000	0.122 ± 0.000
	Ours	**0.711 ± 0.017**	**0.401 ± 0.022**	**0.714 ± 0.014**	**0.611 ± 0.015**	**0.480 ± 0.021**	0.842 ± 0.024	**0.406 ± 0.030**

dataset, possibly because the dataset is very sparse (containing only a small number of nonzero elements).

It can be observed that clustering performance of the proposed model on the BBC4view, ORL, BBCSport, and MSRCV1 datasets outperforms all other models in terms of all metrics. On the Yale dataset, the proposed model performs better than the other models in terms of all metrics except Precision. On the Cornell dataset, the proposed model outperforms the other models in all metrics expect Recall.

Compared with single-view methods: Since both LRR and SSC are single-view clustering methods, they are unable to achieve great clustering results on most datasets. Compared with these single-view clustering methods, our model exhibits notable clustering performance. For instance, on the ORL dataset, our model achieves improvements of 24.9%, 12.1%, 20.9%, 32.3%, 37.6%, 25.6%, and 33.1% compared with SSC in terms of ACC, NMI, Purity, F-score, Precision, Recall, and ARI, respectively.

Compared with multi-view methods: Multi-view clustering methods are capable of extracting more information from multi-view data and achieve superior clustering performance on the most datasets. Compared with multi-view clustering methods (DiMSC, GMC, CSMSC, MSC-IAS, and LMSC), the proposed model also demonstrates a significant advantage in clustering performance. On the BBC4view dataset, the proposed model obviously surpasses the best multi-view based model namely LMSC, achieving improvements of 10.6%, 27.0%, 10.6%, 17.2%, 18.1%, 16.4%, and 22.5% in terms of the corresponding metrics, respectively.

Compared with tensor-based methods: The proposed model represents the multi-view representation matrices as a tensor, compared with the other tensor-based clustering methods (LT-MSC, WTNNM, CGL, and ETLMSC), and it also shows advantages in clustering performance. LT-MSC, CGL, and ETLMSC adopt the tensor nuclear norm to constrain the representation tensor, which does not consider the weights of singular values. By contrast, the weighted tensor nuclear norm is utilized in WTNNM to emphasize the prior information of singular values. Thus, WTNNM achieves better clustering results compared with the other tensor-based clustering methods (LT-MSC, CGL, ETLMSC). Compared with WTNNM, the proposed model projects original data into a low-dimensional space to preserve the critical information, adaptively assigns weights to graph learning based on the contribution of view, and the Laplacian rank constraint helps the model achieve clustering that has the desired number of clusters. Therefore, we have compelling reasons to assert that our model exhibits superior performance in clustering compared to WTNNM. For instance, on the BBCSport dataset, the proposed model outperforms WTNNM by approximately 1.7%, 5.9%, 1.7%, 3.5%, 3.4%, 3.7%, and 4.7% in terms of corresponding metrics. Furthermore, the proposed model obtain clustering results that match the ground-truth labels perfectly on the BBCSport and MSRCV1 datasets. Overall, the proposed model demonstrates excellent clustering performance on six datasets compared with other models.

11.3.4.2   Visualization of clustering

We visualize the clustering results generated by different methods on the BBCSport dataset using t-Distributed Stochastic Neighbor Embedding (t-SNE) [20], and the results are presented in Figure 11.3. It can be visually observed that confusing cluster-ing results were obtained on LRR, SSC, and MSC-IAS models. In contrast, a clear and distinct clustering distribution is obtained by the proposed model, and the distance between clusters is significant.

11.3.4.3   Visualization of affinity matrix

To intuitively showcase the property of the proposed model, we visualize the affinity matrices learned by different models on the Yale dataset. As shown in Figure 11.2, the target matrices generated by SSC, DiMSC, and MSC-IAS are significantly corrupted. In particular, DiMSC cannot detect the obvious block diagonal structure of the target matrix. In contrast, a much more clear graph with a distinct diagonal structure is obtained by the proposed model.

11.3.5   Ablation study

Here, nine special cases of the proposed model are evaluated to prove that the added regularization terms are significantly meaningful for improving clustering performance. First, we define two types of affinity matrices as follows:

$$C_1 = \frac{1}{V}\sum_{v=1}^{V}(|Z^{(v)}| + |Z^{(v)^T}|), \tag{11.47}$$

$$C_2 = (|A| + |A^T|)/2. \tag{11.48}$$

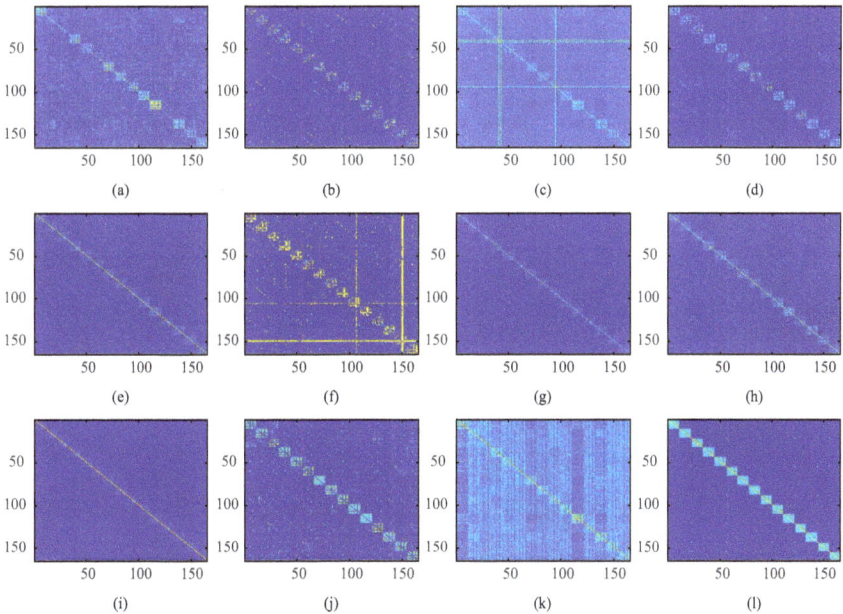

Figure 11.2   *Visualization of affinity matrices of different models on the Yale dataset. (a) LRR, (b) SSC, (c) DiMSC, (d) GMC, (e) CSMSC, (f) MSC-IAS, (g) LMSC, (h) LT-MSC, (i) WTNNM, (j) CGL, (k) ETLMSC and (l) Ours.*

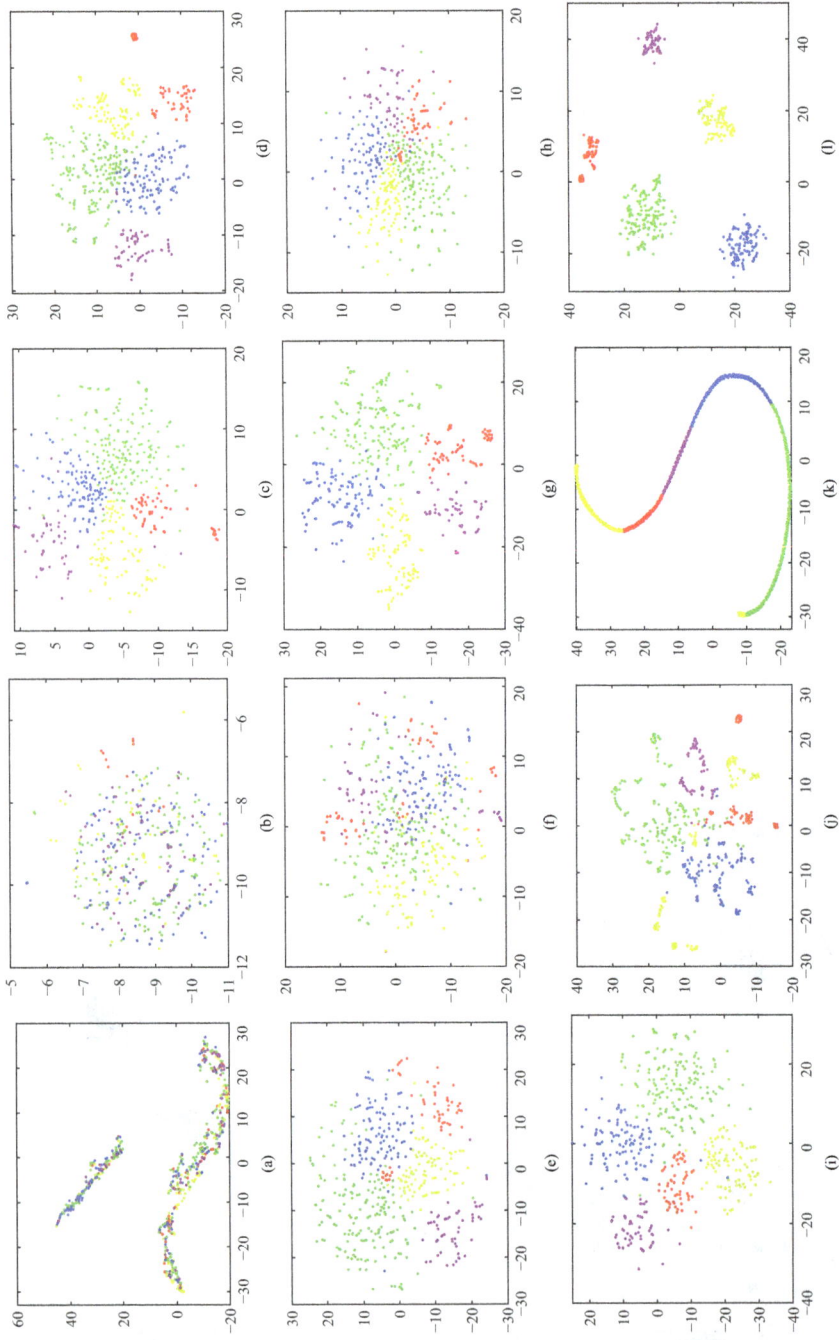

Figure 11.3 Visualization of clustering of different models on the BBCSport dataset, where data points belonging to the same cluster have the same color: (a) LRR, (b) SSC, (c) DiMSC, (d) GMC, (e) CSMSC, (f) MSC-IAS, (g) LMSC, (h) LT-MSC, (i) WTNNM, (j) CGL, (k) ETLMSC and (l) Ours.

where C_1 and C_2 represent the multi-view affinity matrix and the consensus affinity graph matrix, respectively.

11.3.5.1 Consensus graph learning

To analyze the effects of consensus graph learning for clustering, we set $\theta^{(v)} = 0$. The clustering results are obtained by applying spectral clustering to C_1, and we denote this degraded model as AMSLDO-t1.

11.3.5.2 Adaptive weight of graph learning

To analyze the effects of the adaptive weight of graph learning for clustering, we fix $\theta^{(v)} = 1/V$, which implies that all views contribute equally to graph learning, we denote this degraded model as AMSLDO-t2.

11.3.5.3 Laplacian rank constraint

To analyze the effects of the Laplacian rank constraint for clustering, we set $\gamma = 0$. The clustering results are then obtained by applying spectral clustering to C_2, and we denote this degraded model as AMSLDO-t3.

11.3.5.4 Prior information of singular values

To analyze the effects of the weight of singular values for clustering, we fix $\omega = [1, 1, \ldots, 1]$ (each element of the vector is 1), which implies that all singular values have the same weight, and we denote this degraded model as AMSLDO-t4.

11.3.5.5 Other degraded models

Furthermore, the above four ablation conditions are combined in different ways to observe the experimental results. Specifically, we fix $\theta^{(v)} = 1/V$ and $\gamma = 0$. The clustering result is obtained by applying spectral clustering to C_2, and this degraded model is denoted as AMSLDO-t5. We set $\theta^{(v)} = 0$ and fix $\omega = [1, 1, \ldots, 1]$. The clustering results are obtained by applying spectral clustering to C_1, and this degraded model is denoted as AMSLDO-t6. We fix $\theta^{(v)} = 1/V$ and $\omega = [1, 1, \ldots, 1]$, and this degraded model is denoted as AMSLDO-t7. We fix $\omega = [1, 1, \ldots, 1]$ and $\gamma = 0$. The clustering results are obtained by applying spectral clustering to C_2, and this degraded model is denoted as AMSLDO-t8. We fix $\theta^{(v)} = 1/V$, $\omega = [1, 1, \ldots, 1]$, and $\gamma = 0$. The clustering results are obtained by applying spectral clustering to C_2, and this degraded model is denoted as AMSLDO-t9. All degraded models are summarized in Table 11.4.

11.3.5.6 Analysis of ablation experiment results

Ablation experimental results on six datasets are reported in Table 11.5. From the comparison results, it can be observed that AMSLDO-t7 obtains the worst clustering performance than other special cases in terms of ACC and NMI, which indicates that prior information about singular values and adaptive weights in the proposed model plays a crucial role in boosting clustering performance. It is worth noting that, on the BBCSport dataset, the degraded model AMSLDO-t3 does not show significant differences compared to our model, which means that this degraded model is

Table 11.4   *The setting of all degraded models*

	$\theta^{(v)}=0$	$\theta^{(v)}=1/V$	$\gamma=0$	$\omega=[1,\ldots,1]$
AMSLDO				
AMSLDO-t1	✓			
AMSLDO-t2		✓		
AMSLDO-t3			✓	
AMSLDO-t4				✓
AMSLDO-t5		✓	✓	
AMSLDO-t6	✓			✓
AMSLDO-t7		✓		✓
AMSLDO-t8			✓	✓
AMSLDO-t9		✓	✓	✓

Table 11.5   *Ablation experimental results (ACC/NMI) on six datasets*

	BBC4view	Yale	ORL	BBCSport	MSRCV1	Cornell
AMSLDO-t1	0.952/0.887	0.881/0.904	0.974/0.992	0.998/0.991	0.960/0.916	0.310/0.079
AMSLDO-t2	0.986/0.958	0.872/0.892	0.957/0.981	0.948/0.942	0.922/0.940	0.682/0.369
AMSLDO-t3	0.946/0.880	0.879/0.902	0.919/0.879	**1.000/1.000**	0.990/0.977	0.540/0.399
AMSLDO-t4	0.450/0.197	0.641/0.659	0.683/0.817	0.726/0.669	0.705/0.679	0.533/0.275
AMSLDO-t5	0.946/0.880	0.880/0.903	0.980/0.994	0.999/0.998	0.988/0.972	0.549/0.377
AMSLDO-t6	0.898/0.743	0.740/0.769	0.975/0.993	0.890/0.803	0.986/0.969	0.396/0.192
AMSLDO-t7	0.450/0.197	0.636/0.659	0.685/0.800	0.726/0.669	0.705/0.679	0.402/0.132
AMSLDO-t8	0.929/0.803	0.699/0.724	0.861/0.938	0.982/0.936	0.965/0.928	0.493/0.303
AMSLDO-t9	0.927/0.797	0.695/0.730	0.880/0.947	0.981/0.931	0.911/0.885	0.495/0.278
AMSLDO	**0.987/0.960**	**0.952/0.953**	**0.991/0.997**	**1.000/1.000**	**1.000/1.000**	**0.711/0.401**

able to cluster the data quite ideally without the need for the Laplacian rank constraint on the BBCSport dataset. Furthermore, compared to our model, the clustering results of other degraded models also exhibit varying degrees of disadvantage, which means that consensus graph learning, adaptive weight of graph learning, Laplacian rank constraint, and prior information about singular values in the proposed model are important for enhancing clustering performance. Therefore, the proposed model can achieve the best clustering performance only when these four conditions are considered simultaneously.

11.3.6   *Parameters analysis*

We study the sensitivity of the proposed model with respect to different parameter settings. Since $\theta^{(v)}$ and γ are automatically determined, only the trade-off parameters (α and β) and weight vector ω need to be adjusted to observe the clustering results.

11.3.6.1 Trade-off parameters analysis

α and β reflect the influences of dimensionality reduction and self-representation operation, respectively. These two trade-off parameters are tuned in the range [0.5 1 5 10 15 20]. We plot the clustering results in terms of ACC under different parameter settings on six datasets, as shown in Figure 11.5. It is noticeable that the clustering performance remains stable across a wide range of parameter values on the ORL, MSRCV1, and Cornell datasets, which highlights the robustness of the proposed model. However, on the BBC4view, BBCSport, and Yale datasets, clustering performance is sensitive to β. Since β represents the effect of self-expression operation, varying β will greatly affect the generation of the representation matrix $Z^{(v)}$. Meanwhile, the BBC4view and BBCSport datasets are textual datasets sourced from the BBC website, and Yale is a face dataset containing facial images under various conditions, with a potentially uneven internal distribution. Therefore, when these datasets are clustered, the clustering results might be sensitive to the parameter β. Adjusting or optimizing the parameter β may be necessary for obtaining more accurate clustering results, especially when dealing with datasets that exhibit uneven internal distribution.

11.3.6.2 Weight vector analysis

To validate the impact of prior information about singular values on clustering results, different values of ω are selected for clustering. Figure 11.4 displays the clustering performance of different weight vectors on Yale and ORL datasets. Obviously, the proposed model achieves the best results on the Yale dataset with $\omega = [20, 30, 50]$ and the ORL dataset with $\omega = [5, 10, 50]$. It can be observed from the figure that the weight vector has a significant impact on the clustering results, which highlights the importance of prior information about singular values for multi-view clustering.

11.3.7 Convergence analysis

We plot error curves of the proposed model on six datasets, as shown in Figure 11.6. It is evident that the error of updating variables drops to a stable level after a certain

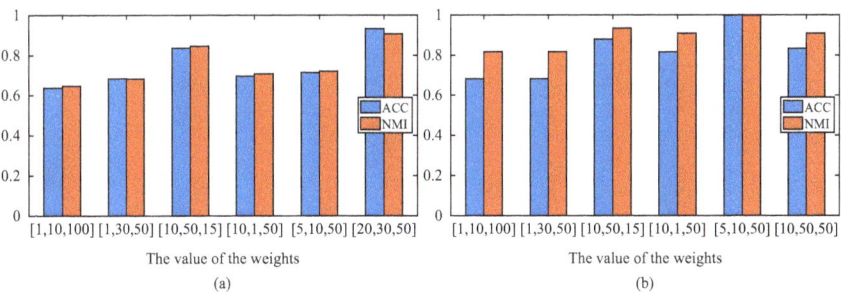

Figure 11.4   Performances of different ω on the Yale and ORL datasets. (a) Yale and (b) ORL.

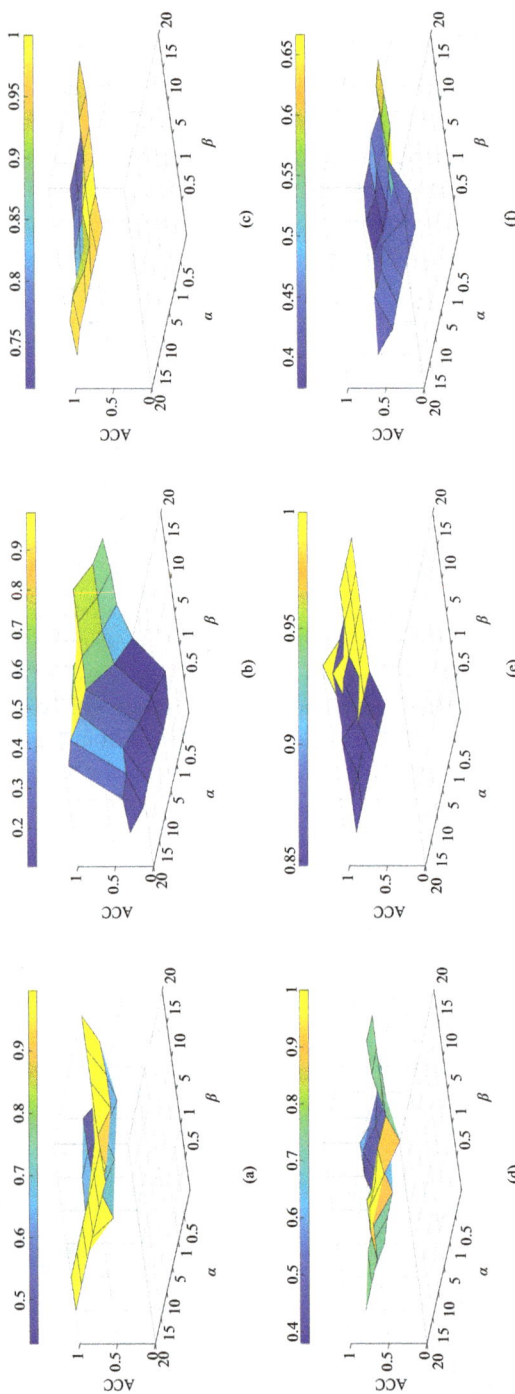

Figure 11.5 Sensitivity of the proposed model on the six datasets. (a) BBC4view, (b) Yale, (c) ORL, (d) BBCSport, (e) MSRCV1 and (f) Cornell.

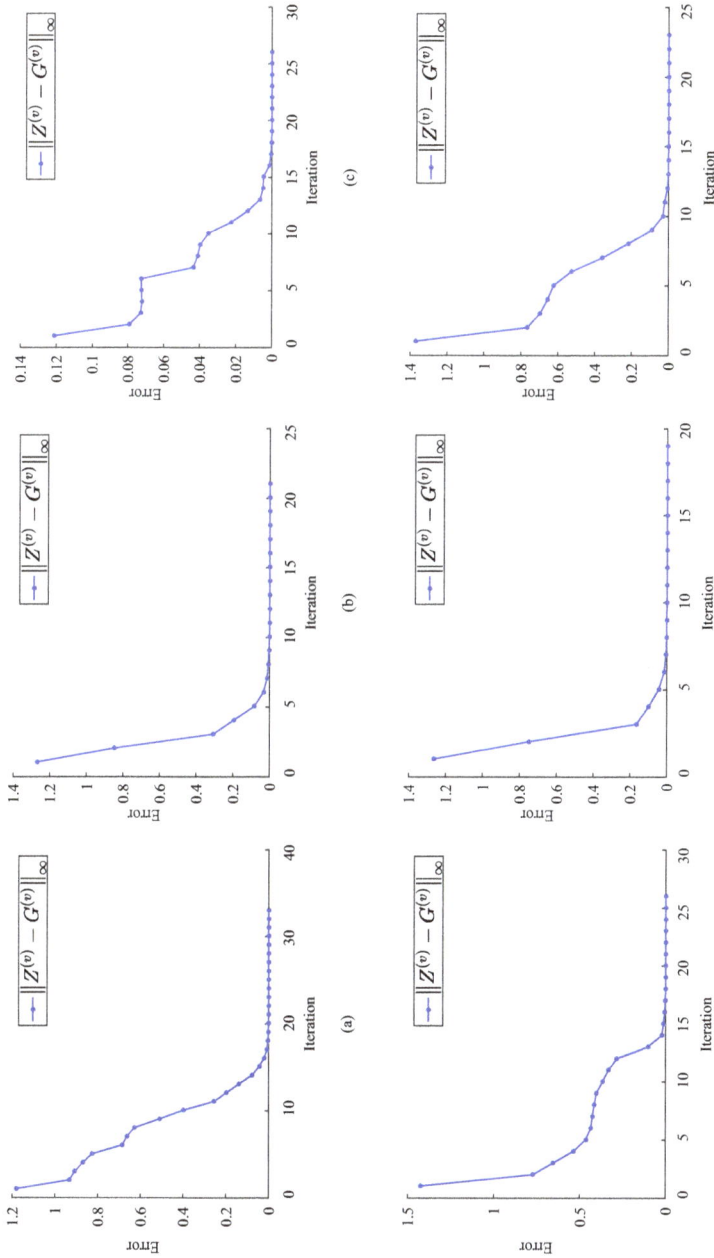

Figure 11.6   Convergence curves of the proposed model on six datasets. (a) BBC4view, (b) Yale, (c) ORL, (d) BBCSport, (e) MSRCV1 and (f) Cornell.

number of iterations, which indicates that our model exhibits excellent convergence properties.

11.3.8   Complexity and runtime

A brief analysis of the main computational complexity is provided in this part. (1) F subproblem: To solve problem (11.15), it is necessary to calculate the c smallest eigenvalues of the Laplacian matrix L_A, with a computational cost of $O(cN^2)$. (2) A subproblem: $O(VN)$ is needed to solve problem (11.18). (3) $Z^{(v)}$ subproblem: The primary computational burden of (11.21) is matrix inversion, with a complexity of $O(VN^3)$. (4) $\mathcal{G}$ subproblem: The solution of (11.28) involves weighted tensor nuclear norm minimization, which leads a complexity of $O(VN^2 \log(N))$. (5) $P^{(v)}$ subproblem: The main complexity lies in performing SVD of matrix $X^{(v)} H^{(v)^T}$, with a complexity of $O(\min(Vk^2, Vd^2))$. (6) $H^{(v)}$ subproblem: The solution of (11.34) involves the Sylvester equation solution, with a computational complexity of $O(VN^3)$. If $k \ll d$, and the number of iterations is t, the overall complexity is $O(t(V(N^3 + N^2 \log(N) + k^2) + cN^2))$. We also present the computational complexities of different models in Table 11.6. As shown in table, most models have a computational cost of $O(N^3)$, and the computational complexity of the proposed model is at a moderate level.

All experiments are performed on MATLAB 2021b installed on MacOS with an M1 processor. The runtime of different clustering methods on six datasets is recorded and shown in Figure 11.7. The figure shows that the proposed model has intermediate running times on most datasets compared to other methods. The main reason is that the Sylvester equation needs to be solved when updating $H^{(v)}$, which leads to a complexity of $O(VN^3)$. Compared with other methods, although the

Table 11.6   *Complexities of different models. For the exact definitions of these notations, refer the respective literature sources*

Models	Complexity
LRR	$O(d^2 N + t(dNr + Nr^2 + r^3))$ [11]
SSC	$O(Nd + sN^2)$ [21]
DiMSC	$O(tVN^3)$ [13]
GMC	$O(tVN^2)$ [14]
CSMSC	$O(tVN(N^2 + d))$ [15]
MSC-IAS	$O(tN^2)$ [16]
LMSC	$O(t(V^3 d^3 + N^3))$ [17]
LT-MSC	$O(tVN^3)$ [19]
WTNNM	$O(N^3 + tVN^2 \log(N))$ [2]
CGL	$O(tVN^2(c + \log(N)))$ [18]
ETLMSC	$O(N^3 + kVN^2(V + \log(N)))$ [19]
Ours	$O(t(V(N^3 + N^2 \log(N) + k^2) + cN^2))$

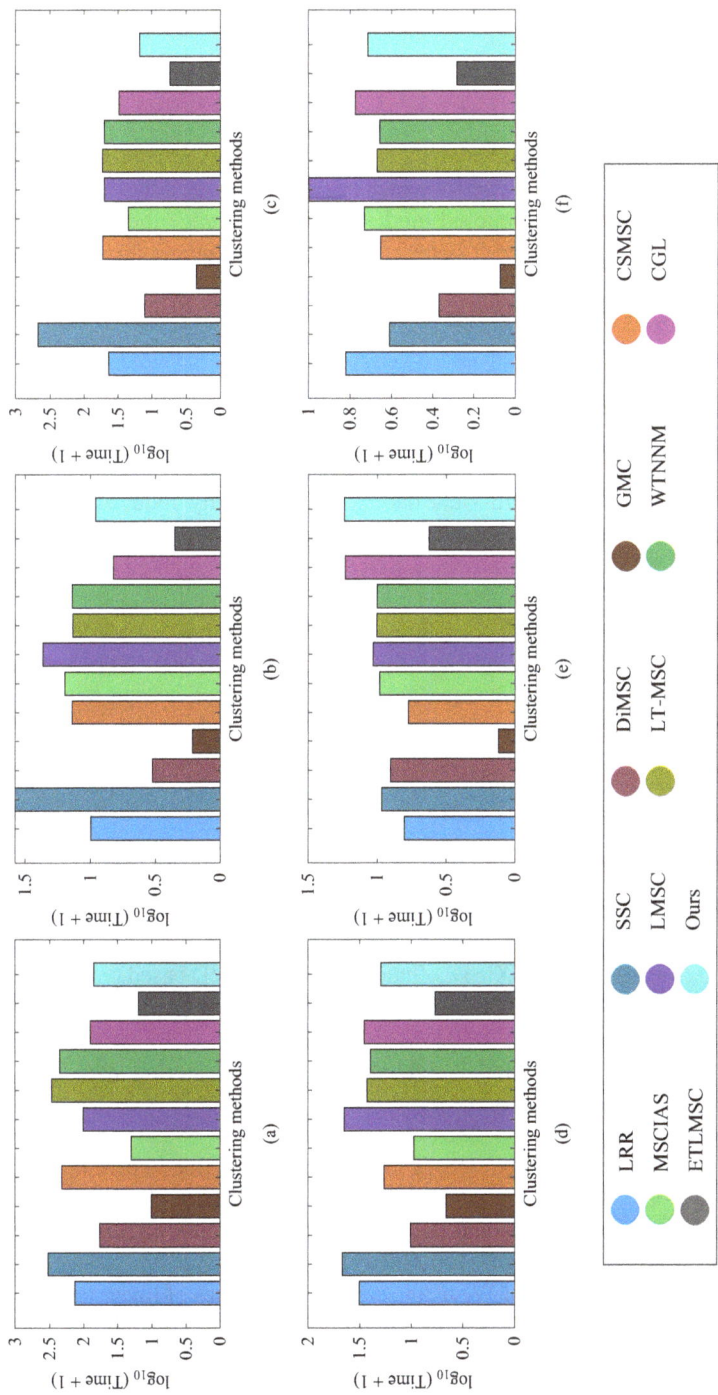

Figure 11.7   Running time (in seconds) on six datasets. (a) BBC4view, (b) Yale, (c) ORL, (d) BBCSport, (e) MSRCV1 and (f) Cornell.

proposed model shows no obvious advantage in runtime, it achieves excellent clustering performance.

11.3.9   Practical implications and potential applications

Based on extensive experimental results, it can be observed that the proposed model demonstrates excellent clustering performance on text and image datasets. Therefore, in practical applications, the proposed model can fully leverage the advantages of multi-view and tensor techniques for clustering in both image and text domains. In the future, employing the proposed model to multi-omics data for identifying disease subtypes could be an intriguing avenue for exploration.

11.4   Chapter summary

In this chapter, we develop a novel multi-view clustering model, AMSLDO. Within this model, the distributed multi-view data is dimensionally reduced to achieve subspace representation in a low-dimensional space. Furthermore, the multiple representation matrices are stacked into the tensor space with a weighted tensor nuclear norm, which efficiently exploit high-order collections among multiple views and keep a property of low-rank. Meanwhile, adaptive graph learning with a Laplacian rank constraint is utilized to acquire a consensus graph with c connected components (c is the number of clusters). Extensive experiments on six different datasets demonstrate the superiority of the model compared to some state-of-the-art models.

References

[1]   Zhang C., Fu H., Liu S., Liu G., Cao X.: "Low-rank tensor constrained multiview subspace clustering." in *Proceedings of the IEEE International Conference on Computer Vision*; 2015. pp. 1582–90.

[2]   Gao Q., Xia W., Wan Z., Xie D., Zhang P.: "Tensor-SVD based graph learning for multi-view subspace clustering." in *Proceedings of the AAAI Conference on Artificial Intelligence*; 2020. Vol. 34. pp. 3930–7.

[3]   Nie F., Li J., Li X.: "Self-Weighted Multiview Clustering with Multiple Graphs." in *Proceedings of the 26th International Joint Conference on Artificial Intelligence*; 2017. pp. 2564–70.

[4]   Chung F. R.: *Spectral graph theory*. Washington, DC: American Mathematical Society; 1997. Vol. 92.

[5]   Mohar B., Alavi Y., Chartrand G., *et al.* "The Laplacian spectrum of graphs." *Graph Theory Combinatorics Appl.* 1991;2(871-898):12.

[6]   Fan K.: "On a theorem of Weyl concerning eigenvalues of linear transformations I." *Proc. Natl. Acad. Sci.* 1949;35(11):652–5.

[7]   Boyd S., Parikh N., Chu E., Peleato B., Eckstein J.: "Distributed optimization and statistical learning via the alternating direction method of multipliers." *Found. Trends Mach. Learn.* 2011;3(1):1–122.

[8]   Duchi J., Shalev-Shwartz S., Singer Y., Chandra T.: "Efficient projections onto the l 1-ball for learning in high dimensions." in *Proceedings of the 25th International Conference on Machine Learning*; 2008. pp. 272–9.

[9]   Chen K., Dong H., Chan K. S.: "Reduced rank regression via adaptive nuclear norm penalization." *Biometrika*. 2013;100(4):901–20.

[10]   Huang J., Nie F., Huang H.: "Spectral rotation versus k-means in spectral clustering." in *Proceedings of the AAAI Conference on Artificial Intelligence;* 2013. Vol. 27. pp. 431–7.

[11]   Liu G., Lin Z., Yan S., Sun J., Yu Y., Ma Y.: "Robust recovery of subspace structures by low-rank representation." *IEEE Trans. Pattern Anal. Mach. Intell.* 2012;35(1):171–84.

[12]   Elhamifar E., Vidal R.: "Sparse subspace clustering: algorithm, theory, and applications." *IEEE Trans. Pattern Anal. Mach. Intell.* 2013;35(11):2765–81.

[13]   Cao X., Zhang C., Fu H., Liu S., Zhang H.: "Diversity-induced multi-view subspace clustering." in *2015 IEEE Conference on Computer Vision and Pattern Recognition* (CVPR); 2015. pp. 586–94.

[14]   Wang H., Yang Y., Liu B.: "GMC: Graph-based multi-view clustering." *IEEE Trans. Knowl. Data Eng.* 2019;32(6):1116–29.

[15]   Luo S., Zhang C., Zhang W., Cao X.: "Consistent and specific multi-view subspace clustering." in *Proceedings of the AAAI Conference on Artificial Intelligence*; 2018. Vol. 32.

[16]   Wang X., Lei Z., Guo X., Zhang C., Shi H., Li S. Z.: "Multi-view subspace clustering with intactness-aware similarity." *Pattern Recogn.* 2019;88:50–63.

[17]   Zhang C., Hu Q., Fu H., Zhu P., Cao X.: "Latent Multi-view Subspace Clustering." in *2017 IEEE Conference on Computer Vision and Pattern Recognition* (CVPR); 2017. pp. 4333–41.

[18]   Li Z., Tang C., Liu X., Zheng X., Zhang W., Zhu E.: "Consensus graph learning for multi-view clustering." *IEEE Trans. Multimedia.* 2021;24:2461–72.

[19]   Wu J., Lin Z., Zha H.: "Essential tensor learning for multi-view spectral clustering." *IEEE Trans. Image Process.* 2019;28(12):5910–22.

[20]   Van der Maaten L., Hinton G.: "Visualizing data using t-SNE." *J. Mach. Learn. Res.* 2008;9:2579–605.

[21]   Liu W., Liu L., Zhang Y., Feng L.: "Enhanced tensor multi-view clustering via dual constraints." *Eng. Appl. Artif. Intell.* 2023;123:106209.

Chapter 12

Tensor factorization with sparse and graph regularization for fake news detection on social networks

Social media has a significant influence, which greatly facilitates people to stay up-to-date with information. Unfortunately, a great deal of fake news on social media misleads people and causes a lot of losses. Therefore, fake news detection is necessary to address this issue. Recently, social content category-based methods have become a crucial component of fake news detection. Unlike a news context-based category, which focuses on word embedding, it tends to explore the potential relationships and structures between users and news. In this paper, a third-order tensor, which obtains massive information and connections, is constructed by the social links and engagements of social networks. Then, a sparse and graph regularized CANDE-COMP/PARAFAC (SGCP) tensor decomposition learning method is proposed for fake news detection on social networks. In SGCP, a news factor matrix is constructed by CP decomposition of the tensor, which reflects the complex connections among users and news. Furthermore, SGCP retains the sparsity of the news factor matrix and preserves the manifold structures from the original space. Additionally, an efficient optimization algorithm, which is proven to be monotonically nonincreasing, is proposed to solve SGCP. Finally, abundant experiments are conducted on real-world datasets and demonstrate the effectiveness of the proposed SGCP.

12.1 Methodology

12.1.1 Sparse and graph regularized CP decomposition learning model

In previous works, the social relationships between users and the interaction between users and news were concluded as two separate relationship matrices. In reality, integrating all of these relationships into a tensor is beneficial in preserving the latent structures and inherent properties. Therefore, the complex relationships among news and users should be unified into an architecture instead of two matrices. Using a tensor $\mathcal{X}$ can express the connection of users and news in their entirety:

$$\mathcal{X}_{ijk} = \begin{cases} 1, \text{user } k \text{ posts new } i, \text{ and user } j \text{ follows user } k, \\ 0, \text{otherwise.} \end{cases} \tag{12.1}$$

where $\mathcal{X} \in \mathbb{R}^{n \times u \times u}$, n is the number of the news, and u is the number of the users.

The tensor $\mathcal{X}$ reflects the complex relationship between news and users. However, it is difficult to classify directly. CP decomposition is an algorithm that reduces the dimension of the data while preserving the original structure. By adopting CP decomposition, the news factor matrix is constructed, which indicates the latent relationships between news and users

$$\min_{A,B,C} \frac{1}{2} \|\mathcal{X} - [[A, B, C]]\|_F^2$$

$$\text{s.t.} \quad A, B, C \geq 0,$$

(12.2)

where $A \in \mathbb{R}^{n \times r}$ denotes the news factor matrix, $B \in \mathbb{R}^{u \times r}$ and $C \in \mathbb{R}^{u \times r}$ denote the users factor matrices, and r is the rank of the CP decomposition.

After getting the news factor matrix A, it is used to train the classifier and obtain the final classification results. Therefore, the structure and properties of matrix A are crucial for achieving superior results. If A is more sparse, its features will be clearer, so sparsity plays an important role in classification. The l_1 norm is added to the function, resulting in

$$\min_{A,B,C} \frac{1}{2} \|\mathcal{X} - [[A, B, C]]\|_F^2 + \lambda_1 \|A\|_1$$

$$\text{s.t.} \quad A, B, C \geq 0,$$

(12.3)

If two data points a_i and a_j have a manifold structure in the original space, their manifold structure in the subspace is similar to the manifold structure in the original space [1]. Moreover, if the Euclidean distance is taken to represent the relationship between views, then the graph regularization [2,3] is expressed as

$$\frac{1}{2} \sum_{i=1}^{n} \sum_{j=1}^{n} w_{ij} \|a_i - a_j\|_2^2 = \text{Tr}(A^T L A)$$

(12.4)

where $L \in \mathbb{R}^{n \times n}$ is the graph Laplacian matrix, $W \in \mathbb{R}^{n \times n}$ is the similarity matrix, $D_{ii} = \sum_j W_{ij}$ is the degree matrix, and $L = D - W$.

Considering all the above components, the final objective function of SGCP is described as

$$\min_{A,B,C} \frac{1}{2} \|\mathcal{X} - [[A, B, C]]\|_F^2 + \lambda_1 \|A\|_1 + \frac{\lambda_2}{2} \text{Tr}(A^T L A),$$

$$\text{s.t.} \, A, B, C \geq 0,$$

(12.5)

where the first term denotes the CP decomposition, the second term enforces the sparsity of the news factor matrix A, and the third term retains the manifold structures from the original data space. Thus, a principled model for fake news detection is constructed by the tensor factorization-based framework. The proposed framework is shown in Figure 12.1.

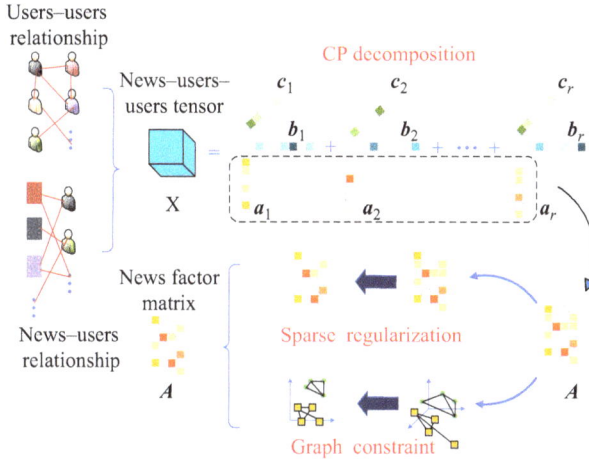

Figure 12.1   *The flowchart of the proposed SGCP. First, construct the news–users–users relationship tensor $\mathcal{X} \in \mathbf{R}^{n \times u \times u}$ using the users–users relationship and news–news relationship, where n is the number of news, and u is the number of users. Then, obtain the news factor matrix $A \in \mathbf{R}^{n \times r}$ by CP decomposition, where r is the CP rank. Moreover, the sparse regularization and the graph constraint are added to A to achieve sparsity and retain the structures from the original space, respectively. Finally, learn the news factor matrix A to obtain the final classification results.*

12.1.2   Optimization

The augmented Lagrangian function of the objective function (12.5) is formulated as:

$$
\begin{aligned}
\mathcal{L}(A, B, C) = \frac{1}{2}\|\mathcal{X} - [[A, B, C]]\|_F^2 + \lambda_1\|A\|_1 \\
+ \frac{\lambda_2}{2}\operatorname{Tr}(A^T L A) + \operatorname{Tr}(\Omega A^T) + \operatorname{Tr}(\Phi B^T) + \operatorname{Tr}(\Pi C^T)
\end{aligned}
\tag{12.6}
$$

where Ω, Φ, and Π are the Lagrangian multipliers.

Then, each variable is updated while keeping other variables fixed at their latest values.

Update A. With the values of B and C fixed, A is updated as follows

$$
\mathcal{L}(A) = \frac{1}{2}\|X_{(1)} - A(C \odot B)^T\|_F^2 + \lambda_1\|A\|_1 + \frac{\lambda_2}{2}\operatorname{Tr}(A^T L A) + \operatorname{Tr}(\Omega A^T)
\tag{12.7}
$$

The partial derivative of $\mathcal{L}(A)$ is

$$
\begin{aligned}
\frac{\partial \mathcal{L}(A)}{\partial A} &= A(C \odot B)^T(C \odot B) - X_{(1)}(C \odot B) + \lambda_1 + \lambda_2 L A + \Omega \\
&= A(C \odot B)^T(C \odot B) - X_{(1)}(C \odot B) + \lambda_1 + \lambda_2(D - W)A + \Omega
\end{aligned}
\tag{12.8}
$$

The complementary relaxation on Karush–Kuhn–Tucker (KKT) conditions [4] for $\mathscr{L}(A)$ is

$$\begin{cases} \omega_{ij}a_{ij} = 0, \\ \omega_{ij} \geq 0, \\ a_{ij} \geq 0, \end{cases} \tag{12.9}$$

By setting $\frac{\partial \mathscr{L}(A)}{\partial A} = 0$, we have

$$[A(C \odot B)^T(C \odot B) - X_{(1)}(C \odot B) + \lambda_1 + \lambda_2(D - W)A + \Omega]_{ij}a_{ij} = 0 \tag{12.10}$$

By rearranging (12.10), we get

$$[A(C \odot B)^T(C \odot B) + \lambda_1 + \lambda_2 DA]_{ij}a_{ij} + \omega_{ij}a_{ij}$$
$$= [X_{(1)}(C \odot B) + \lambda_2 WA]_{ij}a_{ij} \tag{12.11}$$

By considering the KKT conditions in (12.9), the updating rule of the element a_{ij} can be formulated as

$$a_{ij} = a_{ij} \times \frac{[X_{(1)}(C \odot B) + \lambda_2 WA]_{ij}}{[A(C \odot B)^T(C \odot B) + \lambda_1 + \lambda_2 DA]_{ij}} \tag{12.12}$$

Then, the updating rule of A is

$$A \leftarrow A \circledast \frac{X_{(1)}(C \odot B) + \lambda_2 WA}{A(C \odot B)^T(C \odot B) + \lambda_1 + \lambda_2 DA} \tag{12.13}$$

where $\circledast$ denotes the Hardmard product.

Update B. With the value of A and C fixed, B is updated as follows

$$\mathscr{L}(B) = \frac{1}{2}\|X_{(2)} - B(C \odot A)^T\|_F^2 + \mathrm{Tr}(\Phi B^T) \tag{12.14}$$

The partial derivative of $\mathscr{L}(B)$ is

$$\frac{\partial \mathscr{L}(B)}{\partial B} = B(C \odot A)^T(C \odot A) - X_{(2)}(C \odot A) + \Phi, \tag{12.15}$$

The complementary relaxation on KKT conditions for $\mathscr{L}(B)$ is

$$\begin{cases} \phi_{ij}b_{ij} = 0, \\ \phi_{ij} \geq 0, \\ b_{ij} \geq 0, \end{cases} \tag{12.16}$$

Using (12.15) and (12.16), the updating rule of B is

$$B \leftarrow B \circledast \frac{X_{(2)}(C \odot A)}{B(C \odot A)^T(C \odot A)} \tag{12.17}$$

Update C. Similarly, with updating B, C is updated as follows:

$$\mathscr{L}(C) = \frac{1}{2}\|X_{(3)} - C(B \odot A)^T\|_F^2 + \mathrm{Tr}(\Pi C^T) \tag{12.18}$$

The partial derivative of $\mathscr{L}(C)$ is

$$\frac{\partial \mathscr{L}(C)}{\partial C} = C(B \odot A)^T(B \odot A) - X_{(3)}(B \odot A) + \Pi, \tag{12.19}$$

The complementary relaxation on KKT conditions for $\mathscr{L}(C)$ is

$$\begin{cases} \pi_{ij}c_{ij} = 0, \\ \pi_{ij} \geq 0, \\ c_{ij} \geq 0, \end{cases} \tag{12.20}$$

Finally, we can update C by

$$C \leftarrow C \circledast \frac{X_{(3)}(B \odot A)}{C(B \odot A)^T(B \odot A)} \tag{12.21}$$

The convergence condition is set as follows:

$$\frac{|\mathrm{obj}_{(k-1)} - \mathrm{obj}_{(k)}|}{|\mathrm{obj}_{(k)}|} < \mathrm{tol} \tag{12.22}$$

where $\mathrm{obj}_{(k)}$ denotes the value of the objective function at the kth iteration, and tol is a small positive parameter. A summary of SGCP is shown in Algorithm 1.

Algorithm 1 SGCP for fake news detection on social networks

Input: The relationship data $\mathscr{X}$, parameters λ_1 and λ_2, CP rank r;
  1: **Initialize:** Get random initial values between 0 and 1 of A_0, B_0 and C_0, set the toleration parameter $tol = 10^{-5}$ and the iterative number $k = 1$;
  2: **While** not converged **do**
  3: Update A by Eq. (12.13);
  4: Update B by Eq. (12.17);
  5: Update C by Eq. (12.21);
  6: Check the convergence condition in Eq. (12.22);
  7: $k = k + 1$;
  8: **end while**
  9: Classify the news factor matrix A with a classifier to get the final results;
Output: The results of fake news detection.

12.1.3 Convergence analysis

The updating rules of B and C are similar to those of classic non-negative matrix factorization [5], so the objective functions for updating B and C are guaranteed to be convergent. Therefore, only the convergence on updating A needs to be analyzed. An auxiliary function construction method [2,6] is adopted to solve this problem.

Definition 1. $\Psi(a, a')$ *is an auxiliary function of $F(a)$ if the following conditions are satisfied:*

$$\Psi(a, a') \geq F(a), \quad \Psi(a, a) = F(a) \tag{12.23}$$

The property of the auxiliary function is explored in the following lemmas.

Lemma 1. *If Ψ is an auxiliary function of F, then F is nonincreasing under the following updating rule:*

$$a^{(k+1)} = \arg\min_a \Psi(a, a^{(k)}) \tag{12.24}$$

Proof.   The following inequality needs to be proven:

$$F(a^{(k+1)}) \leq \Psi(a^{(k+1)}, a^{(k)}) \leq \Psi(a^{(k)}, a^{(k)}) = F(a^{(k)}) \tag{12.25}$$

Since the updating rule for A is element-wise due to the Hadamard product, we only need to demonstrate that F_{ij}, which denotes the part of $\mathcal{L}(A)$ that is only relevant to a_{ij} is nonincreasing. It is easy to obtain that

$$F'_{ij} = (\frac{\partial \mathcal{L}(A)}{\partial A})_{ij} = [A(C \odot B)^T(C \odot B) - X_{(1)}(C \odot B) + \lambda_1 + \lambda_2 LA]_{ij} \tag{12.26}$$

$$F''_{ij} = [(C \odot B)^T(C \odot B) + \lambda_2 L]_{ij} \tag{12.27}$$

$\square$

Lemma 2. *The auxiliary function for F_{ij} satisfy inequality (12.25)*

$$\Psi_{ij}(a) = F_{ij}(a_{ij}^{(k)}) + F'_{ij}(a_{ij}^{(k)})(a - a_{ij}^{(k)})$$
$$+ [(A(C \odot B)^T(C \odot B))_{ij} + \lambda_2(DA)_{ij}](a - a_{ij}^{(k)})/(2a_{ij}^{(k)}) \tag{12.28}$$

Proof.   Since $\Psi(a, a) \geq F_{ij}(a)$ obviously holds, only $\Psi(a, a_{ij}^{(k)}) \geq F_{ij}(a)$ needs to be demonstrated. Then, the Taylor expansion of $F_{ij}(a)$ is given by

$$F_{ij}(a) = F_{ij}(a_{ij}^{(k)}) + F'_{ij}(a_{ij}^{(k)})(a - a_{ij}^{(k)})$$
$$+ [((C \odot B)^T(C \odot B))_{ii} + \lambda_2 L_{jj})](a - a_{ij}^{(k)})/2 \tag{12.29}$$

The inequality (12.25) holds if the following inequality is satisfied:

$$\frac{[A(C \odot B)^T(C \odot B)]_{ij} + \lambda_2(DA)_{ij}}{a_{ij}^{(k)}} \geq [(C \odot B)^T(C \odot B)]_{ii} + \lambda_2 L_{jj} \tag{12.30}$$

We can obtain

$$(A(C \odot B)^T(C \odot B))_{ij} = \sum_{l=1}^{r} a_{il}^{(k)}((C \odot B)^T(C \odot B))_{lj}$$
$$\geq a_{il}^{(k)}((C \odot B)^T(C \odot B))_{jj} \tag{12.31}$$

and

$$\lambda_2(DA)_{ij} = \lambda_2 \sum_{m=1}^{n} D_{im}a_{mj}^{(k)} \geq \lambda_2 D_{ii}a_{ij}^{(k)} \geq \lambda_2(D - W)_{ii}a_{ij}^{(k)} = \lambda_2 L_{ii}a_{ij}^{(k)} \tag{12.32}$$

Thus, the inequality (12.30) holds. As $\Psi(a, a_{ij}^{(k)}) \geq F_{ij}(a)$, the inequality (12.25) holds. Therefore, the objective function (12.5) is nonincreasing under the updating rule in (12.13), (12.17), and (12.21). $\square$

12.1.4   Complexity analysis

In fake news detection, the number of users, u, is usually much greater than the number of news, n, and the rank of the CP decomposition, r. Thus, the complexity cost of updating A is mainly in calculating $X_{(1)}(C \odot B)$ and $A(C \odot B)^T(C \odot B)$. Calculating $C \odot B$ costs $\mathcal{O}(u^2 r)$, so calculating $X_{(1)}(C \odot B)$ costs $\mathcal{O}(nu^2 r + u^2 r)$. If $(C \odot B)^T(C \odot B)$ is computed first, updating $A(C \odot B)^T(C \odot B)$ costs $\mathcal{O}(u^2 r + u^2 r^2 + nr^2)$. Consequently, updating A costs $\mathcal{O}(nu^2 r + u^2 r^2 + nr^2)$. Similarly, updating B or C costs $\mathcal{O}(u^2 nr + unr^2 + nr^2)$. To summarize, the total complexity of the algorithm is $\mathcal{O}(u^2 nr + unr^2 + nr^2 + u^2 r^2)$.

12.2   Experiments

12.2.1   Datasets

In the experiments, a real-world fake news detection benchmark dataset named FakeNewsNet* is adopted. It contains two datasets: BuzzFeed and PolitiFact. Both datasets include news text with labels, engagement content, and social content. The news text includes id, title, text content, URL, and authors of the news. The engagement content includes the interactive behavior between users and news, and the social content reflects the social links among users on social media.

Due to the SGCP being based on a social network, it is not necessary to regard all users as the research object. This is conducive to improving the running speed and reducing the sparsity by removing some redundant information appropriately. For example, the relationship tensor $\mathscr{X}$ constructed by news–users connections on BuzzFeed has a size of $182 \times 15257 \times 15257$. In MATLAB®, it would cost around 200 GB in random access memory (RAM). Currently, the RAM of mainstream personal computers is 16 GB or 32 GB and 128 GB or 256 GB for server computers. Therefore, it is necessary to reduce the data size appropriately. We exclude users with less than three engagements with news and construct the BuzzFeed-New and PolitiFact-New datasets. In Table 12.1, the information of BuzzFeed, PolitiFact, and the versions after data reduction are shown.

Table 12.1   Information of the datasets

Dataset	News	Users	Engagements	Social links
BuzzFeed	182	15257	22779	637450
PolitiFact	240	23865	32791	574744
BuzzFeed-New	182	1417	7354	6050
PolitiFact-New	240	1703	8138	3159

*https://github.com/KaiDMML/FakeNewsNet

12.2.2   Experimental settings

Four popular evaluation metrics are adopted to evaluate classifiers: Accuracy (ACC), F-score, Precision, and Recall. All results are measured 10 times, and the average and standard deviation values are taken. All experiments are implemented in MATLAB 2020a on a server computer with 256G RAM and 3.00 GHz CPU.

The news factor matrix A is obtained by SGCP in Algorithm 1. The final classification results are then tested by different learning algorithms on A. These algorithms include K-Nearest Neighbors (KNN), Linear Discriminant Analysis (LDA), Decision Tree (DTree), Support Vector Machines (SVM), and Random Forest (RF). All of them are adopted from the toolbox in MATLAB. The default parameter setting is adopted in all algorithms to make a fair comparison. Besides, the cross-validation strategy is adopted in the experiments. On BuzzFeed-New, seven-fold cross-validation is performed, and on PolitiFact-New, a five-fold cross-validation is performed.

12.2.3   Performance comparison

Three parameters are used in the experiments: λ_1, λ_2, and r. The classification results for fake news detection are shown in Table 12.2. On BuzzFeed-New, $SGCP + SVM$ performs best and is slightly better than $SGCP + RF$. Compared with $SGCP + LDA$, $SGCP + SVM$ shows improvements of approximately 20%, 8%, 10%, and 6% in ACC, F-score, Precision, and Recall, respectively. On PolitiFact-New, $SGCP + RF$ performs best, with an improvement of approximately 5% compared with $SGCP + DTree$ or $SGCP + SVM$ and 15% compared with $SGCP + KNN$ or $SGCP + LDA$. Due to the complex and nonlinear potential relationships between news and users, LDA performs the worst in the two datasets. SVM and RF perform the best due to their excellent generalization ability.

12.2.4   Influence of the number of core users

In the experiments, the redundant users on datasets are removed, and users with more than three engagements with news are reserved. These reserved users are significant

Table 12.2   *Classification results for fake news detection (mean ± standard deviation)*

Datasets	Methods	ACC	F-score	Precision	Recall
BuzzFeed-New	SGCP + KNN	0.7914 ± 0.0281	0.6738 ± 0.0138	0.6644 ± 0.0158	0.6838 ± 0.0121
	SGCP + LDA	0.6137 ± 0.0218	0.6137 ± 0.0218	0.5897 ± 0.0197	0.6416 ± 0.0313
	SGCP + DTree	0.7578 ± 0.0171	0.6422 ± 0.0161	0.6259 ± 0.0174	0.6060 ± 0.0208
	SGCP + SVM	**0.8138 ± 0.0301**	**0.6999 ± 0.0343**	**0.6909 ± 0.0405**	**0.7095 ± 0.0280**
	SGCP + RF	0.8077 ± 0.0116	0.6819 ± 0.0135	0.6762 ± 0.0132	0.6878 ± 0.0141
PolitiFact-New	SGCP+KNN	0.7079 ± 0.0195	0.6037 ± 0.0142	0.5783 ± 0.0181	0.6328 ± 0.0174
	SGCP+LDA	0.7236 ± 0.0245	0.6043 ± 0.0212	0.5985 ± 0.0210	0.6103 ± 0.0218
	SGCP+DTree	0.8078 ± 0.0185	0.6945 ± 0.0223	0.6805 ± 0.0220	0.7112 ± 0.0233
	SGCP+SVM	0.8102 ± 0.0080	0.7041 ± 0.0083	0.6789 ± 0.0105	0.7327 ± 0.0070
	SGCP+RF	**0.8421 ± 0.0092**	**0.7373 ± 0.0124**	**0.7259 ± 0.0134**	**0.7493 ± 0.0122**

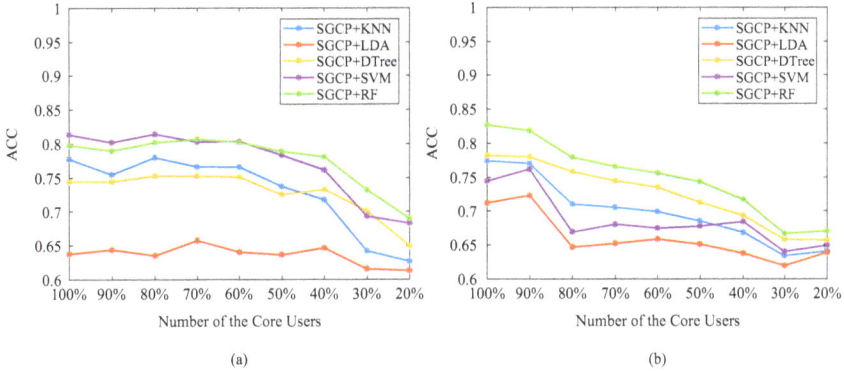

Figure 12.2   The relationships between the number of the core users and ACC. (a) BuzzFeed-New and (b) PolitiFact-New

to express the latent social links and are therefore called core users. Figure 12.2 shows the relationships between the number of users and the ACC value of the classification on BuzzFeed-New and PolitiFact-New. In Figure 12.2, ACC declines slowly when the number of the core users decreases little. When 50% of users are removed, the ACC value starts to decline rapidly. It can be concluded that the number of core users has robustness for classification, and reducing a small number of core users does not affect the experimental results. However, if a large number of samples are lost, it will reduce the performance of the detection.

12.2.5   Parameter analysis

There are three parameters: λ_1, λ_2, and r, in SGCP. λ_1 controls the sparsity of the news factor matrix A, λ_2 is used to maintain the manifold structures from the original space, and r is the CP rank. As solving the real CP rank is an NP-hard problem, r can only be used as a tuning parameter. The grid search method is adopted for tuning the parameters, and r is selected from [2, 5, 10, 20, 50, 100], λ_1 is chosen from [0.001, 0.01, 0.1, 0.5, 1, 2, 5, 10, 100], and λ_2 is chosen from [0.001, 0.01, 0.05, 0.1, 0.2, 0.5, 1, 10, 100].

In Figure 12.3, the values of ACC and F-score with different parameter settings of λ_1 and λ_2 by taking SGCP + SVM are shown. In the experiments on BuzzFeed-New and PolitiFact-New, r is set to 20 and 100, respectively. As shown in Figure 12.3, on both BuzzFeed-New and PolitiFact-New datasets, the ACC and F-score are relatively insensitive over a wide range when selecting parameters λ_1 and λ_2.

In Figure 12.4, the relationship between CP rank r and the evaluation metrics of SGCP + SVM on the BuzzFeed-New and PolitiFact-New datasets is shown. On BuzzFeed-New, the best results appear with $r = 20$. On PolitiFact-New, the value of the results increases with the increase of the value of r; however, the growth of the evaluation values tends to be flat when r is greater than 20. Furthermore, the value of r has a significant impact on the consumption of time in SGCP. The relationships between CP rank r and the runtime of SGCP on BuzzFeed-New and PolitiFact-New

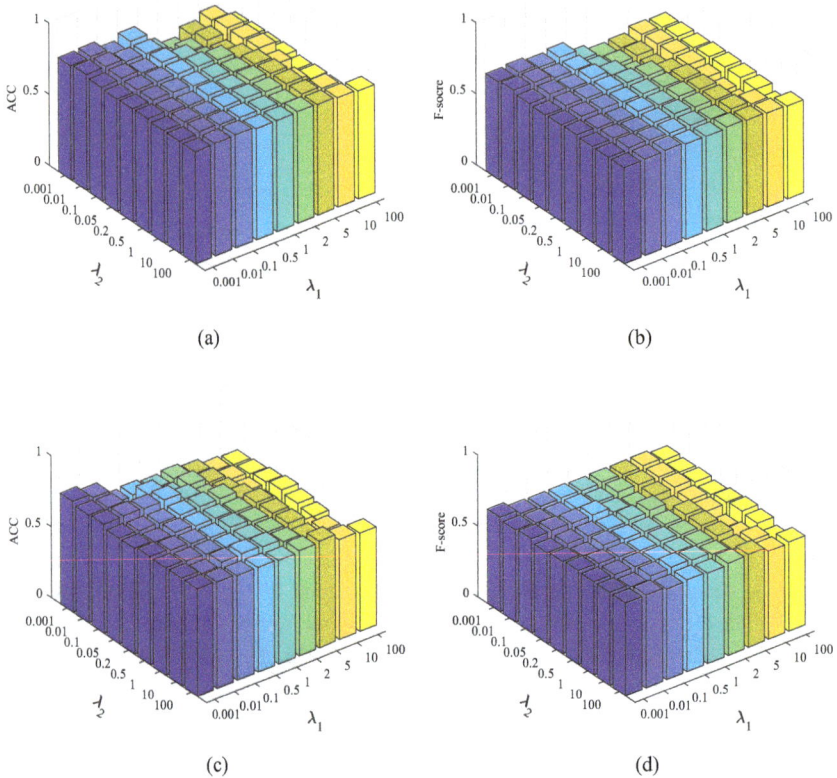

(a)

(b)

(c)

(d)

Figure 12.3   ACC and F-score values on real-world datasets with different parameter settings λ_1 and λ_2. (a) ACC on BuzzFeed-New, (b) F-score on BuzzFeed-New, (c) ACC on PolitiFact-New and (d) F-score on PolitiFact-New.

datasets are shown in Table 12.3; all values of runtime are measured in seconds. It can be concluded that the cost of time increases with the increase of CP rank r; for example, the time consumption of taking $r = 100$ is about three times that of taking $r = 20$. To summarize, the recommended value of r is 20.

12.2.6   Ablation analysis

In this section, the effectiveness of the graph regularization term and sparse constraint term in the proposed SGCP is demonstrated. To verify the effectiveness of the sparse constraint term, the parameter λ_1 is set to 0 in the case of the ablation study, and this ablation method is named graph regularized CP decomposition (GCP). To verify the effectiveness of the graph regularization, the parameter λ_2 is set to 0 in the case of the ablation study, and this ablation method is named sparse regularized CP decomposition (SCP).

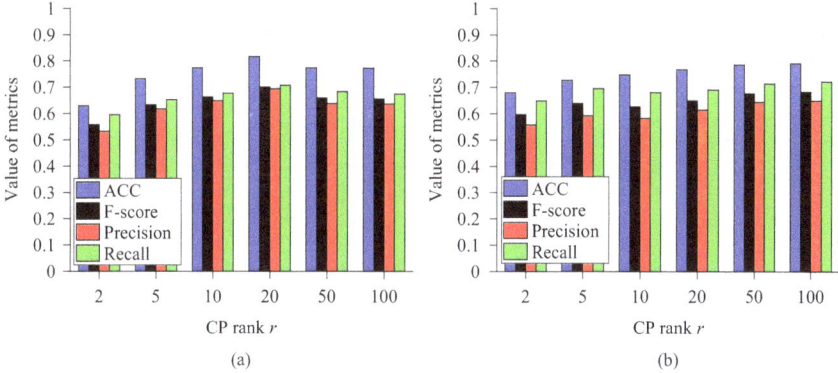

Figure 12.4   Relationship between evaluation metrics and CP rank r on. (a) BuzzFeed-New and (b) PolitiFact-New

Table 12.3   Comparison of runtime (s) of SGCP with different CP rank r

CP rank r	2	5	10	20	50	100
BuzzFeed-New	7.45	14.88	18.77	29.05	58.73	96.06
PolitiFact-New	10.64	14.65	36.71	41.56	67.98	105.63

Table 12.4   Comparison of SGCP + SVM and the ablation methods on classification results for fake news detection (mean ± standard deviation)

Datasets	Methods	ACC	F-score	Precision	Recall
BuzzFeed-New	SGCP + SVM	**0.8138 ± 0.0301**	**0.6999 ± 0.0343**	**0.6909 ± 0.0405**	**0.7095 ± 0.0280**
	SCP + SVM	0.8089 ± 0.0204	0.6933 ± 0.0178	0.6842 ± 0.0294	0.7033 ± 0.0117
	GCP +SVM	0.8019 ± 0.0347	0.6854 ± 0.0410	0.6767 ± 0.0441	0.6944 ± 0.0380
PolitiFact-New	SGCP + SVM	**0.8102 ± 0.0080**	**0.7041 ± 0.0083**	**0.6789 ± 0.0105**	**0.7327 ± 0.0070**
	SCP + SVM	0.7643 ± 0.0139	0.6567 ± 0.0160	0.6292 ± 0.0146	0.6879 ± 0.0283
	GCP + SVM	0.7629 ± 0.0315	0.6462 ± 0.0300	0.6340 ± 0.0322	0.6594 ± 0.0283

The comparison of *SGCP + SVM, SCP + SVM,* and *GCP + SVM* on BuzzFeed-New and PolitiFact-New is shown in Table 12.4. It is obvious that both graph regularization and sparse constraint have a significant impact on PolitiFact-New. Moreover, they also enhance the performance of classification on BuzzFeed-New. In conclusion, both regularization terms significantly improve the performance of the algorithm.

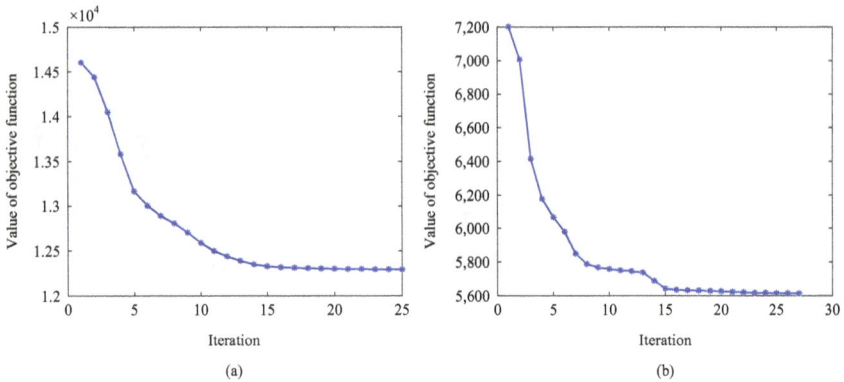

*Figure 12.5   Convergence results of SGCP on. (a) BuzzFeed-New and
(b) PolitiFact-New*

12.2.7   Convergence results

In Figure 12.5, the relationship between the value of the objective function and the iteration on BuzzFeed-New and PolitiFact-New is shown. It can be observed that the values of the objective function decrease as the number of iterations increases. Therefore, the proof of the convergence in Section 12.1.3 is verified by the experimental convergent results.

12.3   Chapter summary

By taking into account the inherent connection between news and users, a third-order tensor is constructed, which reflects the complex relationships among them. To reduce the dimensions of data and uncover the potential structure, an SGCP learning method is proposed. Through the sparse and graph regularization, the news factor matrix can retain the structure from the original data space. Additionally, extensive experiments on real-world datasets highlight the superiority of the proposed SGCP.

References

[1]   Belkin M., Niyogi P.: "Laplacian eigenmaps and spectral techniques for embedding and clustering." *Advances in Neural Information Processing Systems*. 2001. p. 14

[2]   Cai D., He X., Han J., Huang T.S.: "Graph regularized nonnegative matrix factorization for data representation." *IEEE Trans. Pattern Anal. Mach. Intell.* 2010;33(8):1548–60

[3]   Wang S., Zhang H., Chen Z.: "Adaptive cooperative tracking and parameter estimation of an uncertain leader over general directed graphs." *IEEE Trans. Autom. Control.* 2023;68(7):3888–901

[4]   Boyd S., Boyd S. P., Vandenberghe L.: "Convex Optimization." Cambridge: Cambridge University Press; 2004

[5]   Seung D., Lee L.: "Algorithms for non-negative matrix factorization." *Adv. Neural Inf. Process. Syst.* 2001;13:56–62

[6]   Chen K., Che H., Li X., Leung M.F.: "Graph non-negative matrix factorization with alternative smoothed L 0 regularizations." *Neural Comput. Appl.* 2023;35(14):9995–10009

Chapter 13
Matrix factorization for community detection

Multi-layer network community detection plays an important role in data mining. It can discover the latent representations of network structures for effectively completing downstream tasks. However, existing community detection methods rarely consider the relationships between multi-layer networks. Additionally, the noise contained in the networks always leads to the degradation of detection performance. To address the above issues, this chapter proposes an orthogonal symmetric non-negative matrix factorization with low-rank tensor representation (OSNMFTR) for multi-layer network community detection. Specifically, the proposed approach obtains the latent representation of each network via orthogonal symmetric non-negative matrix factorization (SNMF), then a clean self-representation tensor is obtained based on subspace learning. Finally, to discover the high-order relationships among each network, a weighted tensor nuclear norm is utilized to constrain the tensor to make it low-rank. An algorithm based on the Alternating Direction Method of Multipliers (ADMM) is designed to solve the OSNMFTR model. Abundant experiments on nine datasets show the superior performance of the proposed approach.

13.1   Model formulation

In this section, an OSNMFTR for a multi-layer network community detection model is proposed. After that, the updating rules for the proposed model are created. The time complexity is also analyzed.

Given a community network node matrix of lth layer $X^{(l)} \in \mathbb{R}^{m \times n}$, where n is the number of nodes and m is the number of features of nodes. It may contain noise. To prevent potential noise from affecting the detection results, subspace learning is considered to separate it into a clean representation matrix and a noise matrix. Then, the $l_{2,1}$ norm is used to eliminate noise, and the tensor nuclear norm is used to constrain the low-rank property of the self-representation tensor. The model can then be represented by the following optimization problem:

$$
\min_{\mathscr{Z}, E^{(l)}} \|\mathscr{Z}\|_{\circledast, w} + \lambda \sum_{l=1}^{L} \|E^{(l)}\|_{2,1}
$$
$$
\text{s.t. } X^{(l)} = X^{(l)} Z^{(l)} + E^{(l)}
$$

(13.1)

where the tensor $\mathscr{Z}$ is formed by stacking the similarity matrices of each layer after denoising, $\mathscr{Z} = \Phi(Z^{(1)}, Z^{(2)}, \ldots, Z^{(L)})$. $E^{(l)}$ can be regarded as the noise matrix of each layer. As small singular values are often discarded and some big singular values are typically retained in tensor nuclear norm minimization, a weighted tensor nuclear norm is used to solve the problem by decreasing singular values with varying parameters. Using tensor representation and minimization of weighted tensor nuclear norm, we can effectively capture the prior information of higher-order relationships and singular values among nodes in multi-layer network communities. At the same time, the similarity matrix of the community member matrix constrained by the weighted tensor nuclear norm can be denoised by the $l_{2,1}$ norm to obtain a more pure multi-layer network community similarity matrix.

An orthogonal non-negative matrix tri-factorization (ONMTF) model can be used to decompose the adjacency matrix of each layer for multi-layer network community detection [1]. Let $A^{(l)} \in \mathbb{R}^{n \times n}$ represent the adjacent matrix of the lth layer in multi-layer networks, the optimization problem can be expressed as follows:

$$\underset{H \geq 0, H_l \geq 0, S_l \geq 0, G_l \geq 0}{\mathrm{argmin}} \sum_{l=1}^{2} \left\| A_l - H S_l H^T - H_l G_l H_l^T \right\|_F^2 \tag{13.2}$$
$$\text{s.t.} \quad H^T H = I, H_1^T H_1 = I, H_2^T H_2 = I, l \in \{1,2\},$$

where H represents the common communities among all layers, and $H^{(l)}$ corresponds to the private communities for each layer. Unlike other methods, the model takes into account the common and private communities in each layer of the multiplex network.

However, the representation matrix obtained through direct subspace decomposition of the data matrix usually loses important information and increases its sensitivity to noise, thus affecting the community detection results. When both the common and private communities of a multi-layer network are considered at the same time, the final detection results may interfere with each other. For example, nodes that belong to a private community may be partitioned into a common community. Additionally, the non-negative matrix factorization (NMF) method is also difficult to achieve good results in dealing with nonlinear data.

Considering that the communities formed by the network nodes at each layer often exhibit consistency, the SNMF model is first used to decompose the adjacency matrix of each layer. Subsequently, further decomposition and denoising are performed on the low-dimensional representation matrix. The similarity matrices of each layer are stacked into a tensor form, and the weighted tensor nuclear norm is cleverly utilized in this process. Then, the community detection can be represented by the following optimization problem:

$$\underset{Z^{(l)}, A^{(l)}, E^{(l)}, H^{(l)}}{\min} \sum_{l=1}^{L} \left\| A^{(l)} - H^{(l)} H^{(l)^T} \right\|_F^2 + \lambda \| \mathscr{Z} \|_{\circledast, w} + \beta \sum_{l=1}^{L} \left\| E^{(l)} \right\|_{2,1} \tag{13.3}$$
$$\text{s.t. } H^{(l)} = H^{(l)} Z^{(l)} + E^{(l)}, \mathscr{Z} = \Phi(Z^{(1)}, Z^{(2)}, \ldots, Z^{(L)}), H^{(l)} H^{(l)^T} = I.$$

For each layer of the network's consensus community, there is still some noise that leads to errors in the final detection results, so the optimal graph is taken into account in the graph design of the proposed model. By intersecting the similarity matrices constructed for each layer, it further constrains the consistency information within each layer of the network. Considering the factors mentioned above, the proposed model can be ultimately formulated as follows:

$$\min_{Z^{(l)},A^{(l)},E^{(l)},H^{(l)}} \sum_{l=1}^{L} \left\| A^{(l)} - H^{(l)}H^{(l)^T} \right\|_F^2 + \lambda \left\| \mathscr{Z} \right\|_{\circledast,w}$$

$$+ \beta \sum_{l=1}^{L} \left\| E^{(l)} \right\|_{2,1} + \alpha \sum_{l=1}^{L} Tr(H^{(l)^T}L^*H^{(l)}) \tag{13.4}$$

$$s.t.\ H^{(l)} = H^{(l)}Z^{(l)} + E^{(l)},\ \mathscr{Z} = \Phi(Z^{(1)},Z^{(2)},\ldots,Z^{(L)}),\ H^{(l)}H^{(l)^T} = I,$$

where function Φ constructs the tensor $\mathscr{Z}$ by combining the de-noised similar matrices $\{Z^{(l)}\}_{l=1}^{L}$ into a third-order tensor of size $n \times n \times L$, then rotating it as $n \times L \times n$. $A^{(l)} \in \mathbb{R}^{n \times n}$ is the adjacency matrix of each layer constructed from the data matrix $X^{(l)} \in \mathbb{R}^{n \times n}$. $H^{(l)} \in \mathbb{R}^{n \times k}$ is obtained by SNMF. It is applied to the optimal graph constraint to retain its geometric consistency. By intersecting the weight matrix of each layer, the consensus Laplacian matrix is obtained by $L^* = \overline{W}^* - W^*$. Finally, $H^{(l)}$ is decomposed again, and the noise is diluted with the $l_{2,1}$ norm. The final consensus community of each layer is found by analyzing the similarity matrix $Z^{(l)} \in \mathbb{R}^{n \times n}$. The flowchart of the proposed model is exhibited in Figure 13.1.

13.2   Optimization of model

Since problem (13.15) is a multivariable problem, the ADMM algorithm is employed to solve the optimization problem of problem (13.15). ADMM is especially suited for addressing large-scale and distributed optimization challenges. Through its application, complex original problems are decomposed into simpler subproblems that can be tackled more efficiently either in parallel or sequentially. Such decomposition is particularly beneficial for problems characterized by separable structures, wherein the objective function naturally divides into distinct components associated with separate variables. The auxiliary variable $\mathscr{G}$ is introduced, and let $\mathscr{Z} = \mathscr{G}$. Therefore, the augmented Lagrangian function for problem (13.15) is formulated as follows:

$$\mathscr{L}\left(Z^{(l)},E^{(l)},H^{(l)},\mathscr{G},Y^{(l)},\mathscr{W},\mu,\rho\right)$$

$$= \lambda\|\mathscr{G}\|_{\omega,\circledast} + \beta\sum_{v=l}^{L}\left\|E^{(l)}\right\|_{2,1} + \alpha\sum_{l=1}^{L}\text{tr}\left(H^{(l)^T}L^*H^{(l)}\right)$$

$$+ \sum_{l=1}^{L}\Psi\left(Y^{(l)},H^{(l)} - H^{(l)}Z^{(l)} - E^{(l)}\right) \tag{13.5}$$

$$+ \sum_{l=1}^{L}\left\|A^{(l)} - H^{(l)}H^{(l)^T}\right\|_F^2 + \Psi\left(\mathscr{W},\mathscr{Z} - \mathscr{G}\right),$$

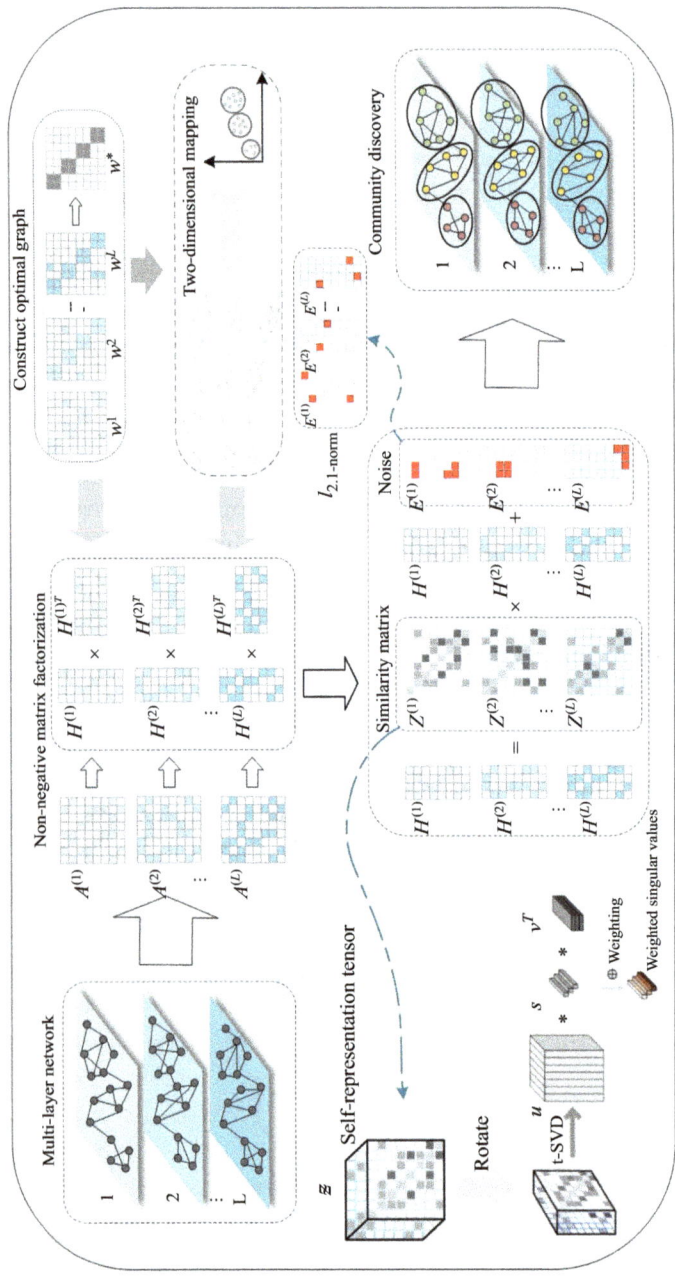

Figure 13.1 *The flowchart of the model. First, extract the adjacency matrix* $A^{(l)}$ *from the multi-layer network. Then, OSNMFTR decomposes the adjacency matrix* $A^{(l)}$ *into a low-dimensional coefficient matrix* $H^{(l)}$ *via orthogonal symmetric non-negative matrix factorization. The optimal graph is used on* $H^{(l)}$ *to preserve the local geometric structure. It greatly reduces false neighbor assignments. Then, the* $H^{(l)}$ *matrix for each layer is stacked into a tensor. Additionally, clean self-representation matrix* $Z^{(l)}$ *is separated from* $H^{(l)}$ *by utilizing a linear constraint.* $Z^{(l)}$ *is stacked into a self-representation tensor, and a weighted tensor nuclear norm is used to preserve the low-rank property. Finally, a consensus* Z^* *is obtained by averaging the* $Z^{(l)}$ *of each layer to complete the community detection.*

where

$$\Psi\left(Y^{(l)}, H^{(l)} - H^{(l)}Z^{(l)} - E^{(l)}\right)$$

$$= \langle Y^{(l)}, H^{(l)} - H^{(l)}Z^{(l)} - E^{(l)}\rangle + \frac{\mu}{2}\left\|H^{(l)} - H^{(l)}Z^{(l)} - E^{(l)}\right\|_F^2, \quad (13.6)$$

$$\Psi\left(\mathscr{W}, \mathscr{L} - \mathscr{G}\right) = \langle\mathscr{W}, \mathscr{L} - \mathscr{G}\rangle + \frac{\rho}{2}\|\mathscr{L} - \mathscr{G}\|_F^2,$$

where $Y^{(l)}$ and $\mathscr{W}$ are Lagrange multipliers, μ and ρ are penalty parameters, $\langle\cdot, \cdot\rangle$ is the inner product of matrices.

13.2.1 $E^{(l)}$ subproblem

If other variables are fixed, for each layer, $E^{(l)}$ subproblem can be written as follows:

$$\min_{E^{(l)}} \frac{\beta}{\mu}\left\|E^{(l)}\right\|_{2,1} + \frac{1}{2}\left\|E^{(l)} - X^{(l)}\right\|_F^2, \quad (13.7)$$

where $X^{(l)} = H^{(l)} - H^{(l)}Z^{(l)} + Y^{(l)}/\mu$.

Lemma 1. *[2]. Given the matrix Q, for the optimization problem:*

$$\min_E \lambda \|E\|_{2,1} + \frac{1}{2}\|E - Q\|_F^2, \quad (13.8)$$

E^* *is the optimal solution, and the ith column of E^* is*

$$[E^*]_{:,i} = \begin{cases} \frac{\|Q_{:,i}\|_2 - \lambda}{\|Q_{:,i}\|_2}Q_{:,i}, & \text{if } \|Q_{:,i}\|_2 > \lambda; \\ 0, & \text{otherwise.} \end{cases} \quad (13.9)$$

according to Lemma 1, the *i*th column of $E^{(l)*}$ is

$$\left[E^{(l)*}\right]_{:,i} = \begin{cases} \frac{\|X_{:,i}^{(l)}\|_2 - \frac{\beta}{\mu}}{\|X_{:,i}^{(l)}\|_2}X_{:,i}^{(l)}, & \text{if } \|X_{:,i}^{(l)}\|_2 > \frac{\beta}{\mu}; \\ 0, & \text{otherwise.} \end{cases} \quad (13.10)$$

13.2.2 $H^{(l)}$ subproblem

If other variables are fixed, $H^{(l)}$ can be updated by solving the following subproblem:

$$\min_{H^{(l)}} \sum_{l=1}^{L}\left\|A^{(l)} - H^{(l)}H^{(l)^T}\right\|_F^2 + \alpha\sum_{l=1}^{L}\mathrm{tr}(H^{(l)^T}L^*H^{(l)})$$

$$+ \sum_{l=1}^{L}\Psi\left(Y^{(l)}, H^{(l)} - H^{(l)}Z^{(l)} - E^{(l)}\right), \quad (13.11)$$

Thus, the above problems can be further expressed as

$$\min_{H^{(l)}} \sum_{l=1}^{L} \left\| A^{(l)} - H^{(l)} H^{(l)^T} \right\|_F^2 + \alpha \sum_{l=1}^{L} \text{tr}(H^{(l)^T} L^* H^{(l)}) \tag{13.12}$$

$$+ \sum_{l=1}^{L} \frac{\mu}{2} \left\| H^{(l)} - H^{(l)} Z^{(l)} - E^{(l)} + \frac{Y^{(l)}}{\mu} \right\|_F^2,$$

$$\frac{\partial \mathscr{L}(H^{(l)})}{\partial H^{(l)}} = 2H^{(l)} - 2B_1 H^{(l)} + 2\alpha L^* H^{(l)} + \mu B_2 H^{(l)} \tag{13.13}$$

$$+ \mu H^{(l)} Z^{(l)} Z^{(l)^T} - (\mu B_3 - \mu B_3 Z^{(l)}) = 0,$$

where $B_1 = A^{(l)} + A^{(l)^T}$, $B_2 = I - Z^{(l)} - Z^{(l)^T}$, and $B_3 = E^{(l)} - Y^{(l)}/\mu$. Finally, the updating rule for $H^{(l)}$ is given as follows:

$$H^{(l)} = (2I - 2B_1 + 2\alpha L^* + \mu B_2 + \mu Z^{(l)} Z^{(l)^T})^{-1} (\mu B_3 - \mu B_3 Z^{(l)}), \tag{13.14}$$

13.2.3 $Z^{(l)}$ *subproblem*

If other variables are fixed, the subproblem of $Z^{(l)}$ based on (13.16) is written as follows:

$$\min_{H^{(l)}} \sum_{l=1}^{L} \frac{\mu}{2} \left\| H^{(l)} - H^{(l)} Z^{(l)} - E^{(l)} + Y^{(l)}/\mu \right\|_F^2 \tag{13.15}$$

$$+ \frac{\rho}{2} \| \mathscr{Z} - \mathscr{G} + \mathscr{W}/\rho \|_F^2,$$

By taking the derivative of $Z^{(l)}$ and setting it to zero, the optimal solution can be obtained as follows:

$$Z^{(l)} = B^{-1} C^{(l)}, \tag{13.16}$$

where $B = \rho I + \mu I$, $C^{(l)} = \rho G^{(l)} + \mu I + H^{(l)^T} Y^{(l)} - \mu H^{(l)^T} E^{(l)} - W^{(l)}$.

13.2.4 $\mathscr{G}$ *subproblem*

If other variables are fixed, the subproblem of $\mathscr{G}$ based on (13.16) is written as follows:

$$\min_{\mathscr{G}} \lambda \| \mathscr{G} \|_{\omega,\circledast} + \frac{\rho}{2} \| \mathscr{G} - (\mathscr{Z} + \mathscr{W}/\rho) \|_F^2. \tag{13.17}$$

Theorem 1 [3]. For a given third-order tensor $\mathscr{Q} \in \mathbb{R}^{n_1 \times n_2 \times n_3}$, $l = \min(n_1, n_2)$, let $\mathscr{Q} = \mathscr{U} \times \mathscr{S} * \mathscr{V}^T$. The following is the definition of the weighted tensor nuclear norm minimization problem:

$$\min_{\mathscr{X}} \tau \| \mathscr{X} \|_{\omega,\circledast} + \frac{1}{2} \| \mathscr{X} - \mathscr{Q} \|_F^2, \tag{13.18}$$

the solution of problem (13.18) is

$$\mathscr{X}^* = \Gamma_{\tau * \omega}(\mathscr{Q}) = \mathscr{U} * \text{ifft}\left(P_{\tau * \omega}(\bar{\mathscr{Q}})\right) * \mathscr{V}^T, \tag{13.19}$$

where $\mathscr{U} = \text{ifft}(\overline{\mathscr{U}}, [], 3)$, $\mathscr{V} = \text{ifft}(\overline{\mathscr{V}}, [], 3)$, $\text{ifft}(\overline{\mathscr{V}}, [], 3)$ is inverse FFT of $\overline{\mathscr{U}}$ along the third dimension. The ith frontal slice of $P_{\tau * \omega}$ is

$$P_{\tau * \omega}\left(\bar{Q}^{(i)}\right) = \text{diag}\left(\zeta_1, \zeta_2, \ldots, \zeta_l\right), \tag{13.20}$$

according to Theorem 1, the solution of problem (13.17) can be obtained by

$$\mathscr{G}^* = \Gamma_{\frac{\alpha}{\rho} * \omega}\left(\mathscr{L} + \mathscr{W}/\rho\right), \tag{13.21}$$

Lagrange multipliers can be updated by the following:

$$Y^{(l)^*} = Y^{(l)} + \left(H^{(l)} - H^{(l)}Z^{(l)} - E^{(l)}\right), \tag{13.22}$$

$$\mathscr{W}^* = \mathscr{W} + \rho\left(\mathscr{L} - \mathscr{G}\right), \tag{13.23}$$

Penalty parameters μ and ρ can be updated by the following:

$$\mu^* = \min(\eta_1 \mu, \mu_{\max}), \tag{13.24}$$

$$\rho^* = \min\left(\eta_2 \rho, \rho_{\max}\right), \tag{13.25}$$

where η_1 and η_2 are parameters intended to accelerate convergence, and $\mu_{\max}$ and $\rho_{\max}$ are the maximum values of the penalty parameters.

The convergence condition is set as follows:

$$\left\|H^{(l)} - H^{(l)}Z^{(l)} - E^{(l)}\right\|_{\infty} < \varepsilon, \tag{13.26}$$

where ε is the convergence threshold, the solution procedure of the problem (13.16) is outlined in Algorithm 1.

13.2.5   Complexity analysis

The complexity of the proposed model mainly consists of four parts, which are (13.26), (13.11), (13.14), and (13.21). For updating $E^{(l)}$, it takes $O(Ldn^2)$. For updating $H^{(l)}$, the complexity of $Z^{(l)} \times Z^{(l)^T}$ is $O(n^2 k)$, it takes $O(n^3)$. The complexity of $E^{(l)} \times Z^{(l)}$ is $O(n^2 k)$. The total computational complex of updating $H^{(l)}$ is $O(n^5 k)$. For updating $Z^{(l)}$, it takes $O(Ln^3)$. In (13.21), updating $\mathscr{G}$ needs to execute FFT, inverse FFT, and SVD, which takes $O(n^2 L \log(n))$. Overall, the computational complexity of the optimization algorithm is $O(t(Ldn^2 + n^5 k + Ln^3 + n^2 L \log(n)))$, where t is the number of iterations.

13.3   Experiments

13.3.1   Datasets

MSRCV1:[*] The MSRCV1 dataset contains eight classes and 240 photos. Seven classes – trees, buildings, aircraft, cows, faces, vehicles, and bicycles – are selected, with 30 photos per class. Each image has six features.

---

[*] http: /research.microsoft.com/en-us/projects/objectclassrecognition/.

Algorithm 1: Algorithm for solving OSNMFTR

Input: Adjacency matrix: $\{A^{(1)}, \ldots, A^{(l)}\}$, trade-off parameters α, β, λ, weight vector ω and the number of communities k.
Initialize: $\rho = \mu = 10^{-4}$, $\eta_1 = \eta_2 = 2$, $\rho_{max} = \mu_{max} = 10^{11}$
Construct coefficient matrix $H^{(l)}$ and consensus similarity matrix Z^* randomly.
$Iter_{max} = 1000$, $\varepsilon = 10^{-6}$.
1. Construct similarity matrix W^* and degree matrix $\overline{W}^*$.
2. Calculate Laplacian matrix L^*.
3. While not converge do
4.   For $l = 1$ to L
5.   Update $E^{(l)}$ by Eq. (22);
6.   Update $H^{(l)}$ by Eq. (26);
7.   Update $Z^{(l)}$ by Eq. (28);
8.   Update $\mathscr{G}$ by Eq. (33);
9.   Update Lagrange multipliers by Eq. (34) and Eq. (35);
10.   end for
11.   Update penalty parameters by Eq. (36) and Eq. (37);
12.   Check the convergence condition by Eq. (38);
13. end while
Output the consensus similarity $Z^* = |\sum_{l=1}^{L} Z^{(l)}|/L$.
Using Z^* as the input for spectral clustering to perform community detection.

YaleA-3view:[†] The YaleA-3view dataset, used for face recognition, includes images of 30 subjects in various poses, expressions, and lighting conditions, captured from multiple angles.

BBC-4view:[‡] The BBC-4view dataset is an image and video collection primarily used for computer vision research. It supports tasks such as object identification, categorization, and activity recognition, featuring a variety of settings, objects, and actions.

ORL:[§] The 400 face photos in the dataset are obtained from 40 different participants with 10 images per person. Each image is grayscale with a resolution of 92×112 pixels.

WikipediaArticles: The dataset comprises 100 000 Wikipedia articles covering diverse subjects, with metadata such as categories, publication dates, and languages. It provides varied textual content suitable for information retrieval, summarization, and classification in natural language processing (NLP).

Cornell: The Cornell dataset includes multi-angle images of everyday objects, such as books, cups, and scissors, captured as both RGB color images and depth data. Each object is well-annotated with bounding boxes, grasp locations, and orientations, making it ideal for training robotic manipulation algorithms.

Texas: The Texas dataset includes demographics, health statistics, education levels, and economic information, supporting a wide range of statistical analyses and providing insights into population dynamics and resource management in Texas.

[†] https://cvc.yale.edu/projects/yalefaces/yalefaces.html.
[‡] http://mlg.ucd.ie/datasets/.
[§] https://www.cl.cam.ac.uk/research/dtg/attarchive/facedatabase.html.

Table 13.1   Summary of different datasets

Dataset	Communities	Samples	Layers
YaleA-3view	15	165	3
BBC-4views	5	685	4
Citeseer	6	3312	2
Cornell	5	195	2
MSRCV1	7	210	6
ORL	40	400	3
WikipediaArticles	10	693	2
Texas	5	187	2
Washington	5	230	2

Washington:[|] The Washington dataset is gathered from an academic institution. It is separated into five groups and offers two informational views: link view and content view.

Citeseer[¶]: The dataset contains a total of 3,312 documents categorized into six classes. It provides two views: one representing paper reference information and the other representing content information.

13.3.2   Compared methods

LRR[**] [4]: LRR aims to create a linear combination of low-rank matrices to represent high-dimensional raw data. Table 13.1 summarizes the detailed contents of these datasets.

NMF [5]: NMF decomposes the adjacency matrix of a network into two lower-dimensional non-negative matrices. This decomposition helps to reveal the latent community structure by associating each node with one or more communities based on their connection patterns.

GNMF:[††] [6] The GNMF method improves upon the classic NMF algorithm by including a graph regularization term through the creation of an affinity graph that encodes geometric data. It gets beyond the NMF algorithm's drawback of failing to take into account the intrinsic geometric structure between nodes, better capturing the local structural aspects of the data.

RMKMC[‡‡] [7]: RMKMC is used in community detection to harness multiple types of data within a network to uncover communities. This method enhances the robustness of community detection by aligning disparate data into a coherent community structure, despite potential noise and inconsistencies in individual layers.

AMvDMD[§§] [8]: AMvDMD combines the ideas of DMD (dynamic mode decomposition) with multi-view learning to divide the dataset into several modes.

[|] https://lig-membres.imag.fr/grimal/data.html.
[¶] https://lig-membres.imag.fr/grimal/data.html.
[**] https://sites.google.com/site/guangcanliu/.
[††] http://www.cad.zju.edu.cn/home/dengcai/Data/GNMF.html.
[‡‡] https://sites.google.com/site/fiipingnie/publications.
[§§] https://github.com/huangsd/DeepMVC.

It records the dynamic evolution of the data and communicates information between each mode to boost the detection results.

MulitiNMF[||] [9]: MultiNMF incorporates regularization for graphs. During the decomposition process, information is shared throughout the matrices to enhance the ability to extract latent characteristics and data structure from the adjacency matrix of a multi-layer network.

DiNMF [10]: DiNMF applies a diversity learning constraint to capture the different information among all coefficient matrices. The diversity learning constraint aims to ensure that the related coefficient vectors from various perspectives are as orthogonal as feasible.

MvDGNMF [11]: MvDGNMF factorizes matrices from each layer and aligns them through regularization. This approach ensures robust and cohesive data representation across different sources.

MCPL[¶¶] [12]: MCPL is able to learn the consensus proximity matrix by applying a rank restriction to the Laplacian matrix and integrating data from all viewpoints in a self-weighted way.

RMvHGDNMF [3]: RMvHGDNMF creates a hyper-graph regularization to help identify the higher-order relationships between the data instances. Additionally, consistency information in multi-view data is mined using a pair-wise consistency learning term.

RMvDNMF-FG [13]: RMvDNMF-FG designs a noise insensitive logarithmic loss function to measure the factorization error. The algorithm simultaneously utilizes factorization error and the minimization of the inner product of basis vectors to achieve feature diversity.

13.3.3 Evaluation metrics

Six assessment metrics – Accuracy (ACC), Normalized Mutual Information (NMI) [14], Purity [15], F-score, Precision, and Adjusted Rank Index (ARI) – are used to assess the performance of different models and capture detection results. The definitions of these metrics are provided in [16]. Higher values of the metrics indicate better performance of the algorithms.

13.3.4 Detection results

Tables 13.2 and 13.3 provide all the experimental findings for the 12 comparison techniques used in the nine datasets. The bold results for each parameter indicate the best outcomes.

From Tables 13.2 and 13.3 it can be observed that the suggested model outperforms the other six datasets, with the exception of the YaleA-3view, Texas, and Washington datasets. Among them, on BBC-4view, WikipediaArticles, MSRCV1, Cornell, and Citeseer datasets, OSNMFTR shows significant improvements across all

---

[||] http://jialu.info/.
[¶¶] https://github.com/AllminerLab/Code-for-MCPL-master.

Dataset	Methods	ACC	NMI	Purity	F-score	Precision	ARI
YaleA-3view	LRR	0.530 ± 0.014	0.580 ± 0.008	0.555 ± 0.015	0.369 ± 0.015	0.356 ± 0.014	0.326 ± 0.016
	GNMF	0.383 ± 0.015	0.475 ± 0.010	0.425 ± 0.013	0.250 ± 0.031	0.275 ± 0.036	0.197 ± 0.033
	RMKMC	0.561 ± 0.034	0.616 ± 0.024	0.656 ± 0.027	0.416 ± 0.032	0.469 ± 0.033	0.373 ± 0.035
	MultiNMF	0.304 ± 0.008	0.404 ± 0.005	0.344 ± 0.007	0.202 ± 0.005	0.148 ± 0.004	0.129 ± 0.006
	AMvDMD	0.556 ± 0.066	0.625 ± 0.041	0.581 ± 0.059	0.432 ± 0.045	0.354 ± 0.048	0.386 ± 0.050
	DiNMF	0.442 ± 0.028	0.498 ± 0.028	0.468 ± 0.030	0.270 ± 0.030	0.250 ± 0.029	0.219 ± 0.032
	NMF	0.413 ± 0.032	0.453 ± 0.028	0.485 ± 0.031	0.253 ± 0.028	0.282 ± 0.028	0.199 ± 0.031
	MvDGNMF	0.413 ± 0.045	0.473 ± 0.025	0.447 ± 0.037	0.255 ± 0.029	0.230 ± 0.027	0.187 ± 0.025
	RMvDNMF-FG	0.587 ± 0.017	0.643 ± 0.004	0.612 ± 0.008	0.451 ± 0.005	0.418 ± 0.010	0.413 ± 0.006
	MCPL	0.800 ± 0.000	**0.873 ± 0.000**	0.806 ± 0.000	**0.768 ± 0.000**	**0.699 ± 0.000**	**0.751 ± 0.000**
	RMvHGDNMF	0.592 ± 0.030	0.642 ± 0.018	0.612 ± 0.026	0.340 ± 0.023	0.346 ± 0.029	0.410 ± 0.029
	OURS	**0.804 ± 0.043**	0.839 ± 0.017	**0.807 ± 0.037**	0.688 ± 0.042	0.682 ± 0.043	0.668 ± 0.045
BBC-4view	LRR	0.425 ± 0.000	0.182 ± 0.000	0.439 ± 0.000	0.331 ± 0.000	0.322 ± 0.000	0.118 ± 0.000
	GNMF	0.595 ± 0.092	0.396 ± 0.055	0.644 ± 0.062	0.507 ± 0.068	0.534 ± 0.078	0.345 ± 0.096
	RMKMC	0.567 ± 0.091	0.432 ± 0.065	0.627 ± 0.071	0.488 ± 0.077	0.466 ± 0.070	0.322 ± 0.100
	MultiNMF	0.437 ± 0.001	0.306 ± 0.001	0.488 ± 0.000	0.349 ± 0.000	0.303 ± 0.001	0.109 ± 0.001
	AMvDMD	0.511 ± 0.109	0.307 ± 0.140	0.548 ± 0.0114	0.482 ± 0.106	0.391 ± 0.116	0.256 ± 0.185
	DiNMF	0.525 ± 0.060	0.331 ± 0.045	0.559 ± 0.040	0.423 ± 0.040	0.375 ± 0.051	0.213 ± 0.067
	NMF	0.331 ± 0.000	0.006 ± 0.000	0.000 ± 0.000	0.379 ± 0.000	0.000 ± 0.000	0.001 ± 0.000
	MvDGNMF	0.541 ± 0.060	0.380 ± 0.068	0.612 ± 0.060	0.463 ± 0.050	0.424 ± 0.057	0.277 ± 0.074
	RMvDNMF-FG	0.713 ± 0.082	0.507 ± 0.081	0.713 ± 0.082	0.627 ± 0.055	0.554 ± 0.087	0.490 ± 0.088
	MCPL	0.531 ± 0.048	0.305 ± 0.060	0.531 ± 0.048	0.471 ± 0.048	0.334 ± 0.059	0.203 ± 0.092
	RMvHGDNMF	0.674 ± 0.080	0.498 ± 0.050	0.686 ± 0.065	0.577 ± 0.071	0.563 ± 0.071	0.444 ± 0.091
	OURS	**0.811 ± 0.024**	**0.715 ± 0.021**	**0.811 ± 0.024**	**0.703 ± 0.021**	**0.766 ± 0.023**	**0.622 ± 0.018**
ORL	LRR	0.630 ± 0.011	0.785 ± 0.011	0.660 ± 0.010	0.509 ± 0.015	0.483 ± 0.017	0.497 ± 0.016
	GNMF	0.601 ± 0.034	0.757 ± 0.015	0.715 ± 0.017	0.477 ± 0.038	0.600 ± 0.017	0.462 ± 0.040
	RMKMC	0.035 ± 0.000	0.121 ± 0.000	0.110 ± 0.000	0.049 ± 0.000	0.020 ± 0.000	0.005 ± 0.000
	MultiNMF	0.559 ± 0.029	0.715 ± 0.024	0.610 ± 0.028	0.312 ± 0.046	0.216 ± 0.044	0.289 ± 0.049
	AMvDMD	0.556 ± 0.026	0.729 ± 0.014	0.603 ± 0.019	0.386 ± 0.032	0.289 ± 0.032	0.367 ± 0.033
	DiNMF	0.557 ± 0.021	0.753 ± 0.013	0.609 ± 0.020	0.430 ± 0.024	0.370 ± 0.025	0.415 ± 0.025
	NMF	0.623 ± 0.017	0.773 ± 0.013	0.715 ± 0.011	0.448 ± 0.038	0.602 ± 0.015	0.432 ± 0.040
	MvDGNMF	0.693 ± 0.048	0.836 ± 0.032	0.746 ± 0.041	0.558 ± 0.080	0.463 ± 0.097	0.545 ± 0.083
	RMvDNMF-FG	0.711 ± 0.025	0.859 ± 0.010	0.752 ± 0.017	0.636 ± 0.023	0.561 ± 0.030	0.626 ± 0.024
	MCPL	0.389 ± 0.008	0.557 ± 0.014	0.438 ± 0.012	0.159 ± 0.011	0.094 ± 0.008	0.126 ± 0.012
	RMvHGDNMF	0.621 ± 0.032	0.801 ± 0.023	0.677 ± 0.028	0.520 ± 0.041	0.447 ± 0.047	0.507 ± 0.043
	OURS	**0.739 ± 0.037**	**0.868 ± 0.012**	**0.765 ± 0.030**	**0.644 ± 0.035**	**0.631 ± 0.036**	**0.636 ± 0.036**

continued

Table 13.2 Continued

Dataset	Methods	ACC	NMI	Purity	F-score	Precision	ARI
WikipediaArticles	LRR	0.193 ± 0.000	0.052 ± 0.000	0.212 ± 0.000	0.121 ± 0.000	0.123 ± 0.000	0.015 ± 0.000
	GNMF	0.178 ± 0.005	0.058 ± 0.003	0.230 ± 0.021	0.125 ± 0.003	0.128 ± 0.008	0.015 ± 0.002
	RMKMC	0.331 ± 0.033	0.238 ± 0.037	0.359 ± 0.045	0.229 ± 0.029	0.223 ± 0.030	0.137 ± 0.032
	MultiNMF	0.419 ± 0.017	0.304 ± 0.010	0.459 ± 0.011	0.272 ± 0.012	0.233 ± 0.017	0.165 ± 0.017
	AMvDMD	0.339 ± 0.051	0.264 ± 0.057	0.383 ± 0.053	0.234 ± 0.025	0.151 ± 0.022	0.076 ± 0.037
	DiNMF	0.429 ± 0.018	0.282 ± 0.011	0.471 ± 0.013	0.288 ± 0.011	0.298 ± 0.012	0.204 ± 0.012
	NMF	0.156 ± 0.000	0.012 ± 0.000	0.630 ± 0.000	0.196 ± 0.000	0.483 ± 0.000	0.109 ± 0.000
	MvDGNMF	0.413 ± 0.019	0.265 ± 0.010	0.456 ± 0.013	0.277 ± 0.012	0.282 ± 0.013	0.190 ± 0.014
	RMvDNMF-FG	0.264 ± 0.024	0.147 ± 0.032	0.297 ± 0.029	0.178 ± 0.015	0.164 ± 0.014	0.067 ± 0.017
	MCPL	0.536 ± 0.025	0.500 ± 0.021	0.584 ± 0.026	0.447 ± 0.030	0.384 ± 0.056	0.365 ± 0.041
	RMvHGDNMF	0.496 ± 0.028	0.439 ± 0.034	0.544 ± 0.019	0.387 ± 0.033	0.379 ± 0.035	0.310 ± 0.037
	OURS	**0.708 ± 0.011**	**0.756 ± 0.005**	**0.717 ± 0.017**	**0.616 ± 0.010**	**0.648 ± 0.011**	**0.571 ± 0.012**
MSRCV1	LRR	0.484 ± 0.028	0.348 ± 0.016	0.523 ± 0.019	0.353 ± 0.018	0.348 ± 0.018	0.247 ± 0.021
	GNMF	0.719 ± 0.055	0.619 ± 0.019	0.735 ± 0.030	0.511 ± 0.017	0.653 ± 0.022	0.411 ± 0.023
	RMKMC	0.660 ± 0.089	0.571 ± 0.050	0.722 ± 0.051	0.552 ± 0.060	0.589 ± 0.055	0.474 ± 0.072
	MultiNMF	0.514 ± 0.040	0.372 ± 0.023	0.529 ± 0.029	0.314 ± 0.013	0.232 ± 0.012	0.156 ± 0.018
	AMvDMD	0.457 ± 0.000	0.366 ± 0.000	0.471 ± 0.000	0.355 ± 0.000	0.274 ± 0.000	0.214 ± 0.000
	DiNMF	0.148 ± 0.000	0.030 ± 0.000	0.171 ± 0.000	0.243 ± 0.000	0.139 ± 0.000	0.001 ± 0.000
	NMF	0.678 ± 0.055	0.605 ± 0.018	0.755 ± 0.012	0.513 ± 0.018	0.663 ± 0.023	0.414 ± 0.026
	MvDGNMF	0.147 ± 0.000	0.029 ± 0.000	0.171 ± 0.000	0.243 ± 0.000	0.139 ± 0.000	0.001 ± 0.000
	RMvDNMF-FG	0.259 ± 0.022	0.099 ± 0.030	0.275 ± 0.028	0.197 ± 0.023	0.160 ± 0.014	0.032 ± 0.022
	MCPL	0.748 ± 0.002	0.749 ± 0.001	0.815 ± 0.002	0.711 ± 0.000	0.665 ± 0.011	0.661 ± 0.001
	RMvHGDNMF	0.164 ± 0.051	0.056 ± 0.008	0.187 ± 0.047	0.251 ± 0.025	0.146 ± 0.021	0.015 ± 0.003
	OURS	**0.954 ± 0.010**	**0.915 ± 0.014**	**0.954 ± 0.010**	**0.912 ± 0.017**	**0.911 ± 0.018**	**0.898 ± 0.020**
Texas	LRR	0.323 ± 0.004	0.046 ± 0.001	0.551 ± 0.000	0.282 ± 0.001	0.399 ± 0.001	0.028 ± 0.001
	GNMF	0.549 ± 0.005	0.168 ± 0.011	0.507 ± 0.015	0.380 ± 0.011	0.337 ± 0.013	0.084 ± 0.012
	RMKMC	0.475 ± 0.076	0.165 ± 0.049	0.489 ± 0.071	0.409 ± 0.060	0.334 ± 0.067	0.177 ± 0.065
	MultiNMF	0.371 ± 0.020	0.141 ± 0.010	0.625 ± 0.011	0.334 ± 0.018	0.401 ± 0.010	0.037 ± 0.010
	AMvDMD	0.352 ± 0.045	0.134 ± 0.038	0.610 ± 0.050	0.329 ± 0.037	0.424 ± 0.054	0.057 ± 0.056
	DiNMF	0.452 ± 0.048	0.172 ± 0.026	0.621 ± 0.026	0.402 ± 0.048	0.457 ± 0.032	0.116 ± 0.054
	NMF	0.446 ± 0.047	0.163 ± 0.008	0.500 ± 0.040	0.390 ± 0.038	0.344 ± 0.047	0.107 ± 0.042
	MvDGNMF	**0.599 ± 0.058**	0.222 ± 0.037	0.648 ± 0.035	0.535 ± 0.059	0.503 ± 0.025	0.234 ± 0.050
	RMvDNMF-FG	0.427 ± 0.037	0.206 ± 0.012	0.657 ± 0.000	0.358 ± 0.013	0.500 ± 0.024	0.127 ± 0.021
	MCPL	0.582 ± 0.000	0.222 ± 0.000	0.668 ± 0.000	0.528 ± 0.000	0.478 ± 0.000	0.203 ± 0.000
	RMvHGDNMF	0.504 ± 0.044	0.238 ± 0.014	0.684 ± 0.010	0.417 ± 0.033	0.548 ± 0.026	0.190 ± 0.035
	OURS	0.571 ± 0.020	**0.549 ± 0.007**	**0.878 ± 0.005**	**0.558 ± 0.007**	**0.806 ± 0.010**	**0.406 ± 0.009**

Table 13.3   Six evaluation metrics of algorithms on Cornell, Citeseer, and Washington datasets

Dataset	Methods	ACC	NMI	Purity	F-score	Precision	ARI
Cornell	LRR	0.355 ± 0.002	0.122 ± 0.003	0.497 ± 0.002	0.310 ± 0.002	0.356 ± 0.003	0.098 ± 0.003
	GNMF	0.509 ± 0.023	0.380 ± 0.013	0.583 ± 0.026	0.446 ± 0.009	0.400 ± 0.006	0.272 ± 0.016
	RMKMC	0.356 ± 0.017	0.126 ± 0.020	0.478 ± 0.020	0.295 ± 0.014	0.317 ± 0.016	0.058 ± 0.017
	MultiNMF	0.405 ± 0.031	0.109 ± 0.008	0.451 ± 0.008	0.358 ± 0.021	0.291 ± 0.020	0.039 ± 0.038
	AMvDMD	0.360 ± 0.022	0.098 ± 0.031	0.449 ± 0.023	0.328 ± 0.016	0.280 ± 0.011	0.016 ± 0.018
	DiNMF	0.439 ± 0.097	0.200 ± 0.088	0.533 ± 0.079	0.372 ± 0.087	0.377 ± 0.089	0.143 ± 0.120
	NMF	0.425 ± 0.000	0.019 ± 0.000	0.000 ± 0.000	0.419 ± 0.000	0.000 ± 0.000	0.000 ± 0.000
	MvDGNMF	0.437 ± 0.030	0.070 ± 0.028	0.458 ± 0.012	0.406 ± 0.032	0.296 ± 0.022	0.053 ± 0.040
	RMvDNMF-FG	0.351 ± 0.032	0.173 ± 0.050	0.507 ± 0.050	0.320 ± 0.000	0.316 ± 0.007	0.064 ± 0.008
	MCPL	0.451 ± 0.000	0.229 ± 0.000	0.600 ± 0.000	0.390 ± 0.000	0.344 ± 0.000	0.121 ± 0.000
	RMvHGDNMF	0.407 ± 0.025	0.203 ± 0.030	0.541 ± 0.020	0.340 ± 0.023	0.346 ± 0.019	0.337 ± 0.044
	OURS	**0.602 ± 0.002**	**0.641 ± 0.005**	**0.800 ± 0.004**	**0.614 ± 0.007**	**0.730 ± 0.008**	**0.501 ± 0.009**
Citeseer	LRR	0.306 ± 0.000	0.053 ± 0.000	0.317 ± 0.000	0.234 ± 0.000	0.204 ± 0.000	0.037 ± 0.000
	GNMF	0.292 ± 0.040	0.063 ± 0.031	0.743 ± 0.103	0.299 ± 0.011	0.632 ± 0.118	0.040 ± 0.032
	RMKMC	0.377 ± 0.051	0.140 ± 0.038	0.494 ± 0.063	0.291 ± 0.029	0.360 ± 0.047	0.101 ± 0.036
	MultiNMF	0.272 ± 0.017	0.110 ± 0.018	0.290 ± 0.020	0.297 ± 0.001	0.181 ± 0.002	0.042 ± 0.004
	AMvDMD	0.245 ± 0.004	0.030 ± 0.005	0.247 ± 0.003	0.297 ± 0.001	0.178 ± 0.000	0.000 ± 0.000
	DiNMF	0.368 ± 0.033	0.160 ± 0.021	0.387 ± 0.030	0.309 ± 0.014	0.211 ± 0.015	0.064 ± 0.027
	NMF	0.212 ± 0.000	0.001 ± 0.000	0.000 ± 0.000	0.302 ± 0.000	0.000 ± 0.000	0.178 ± 0.000
	MvDGNMF	0.333 ± 0.018	0.129 ± 0.025	0.352 ± 0.023	0.293 ± 0.008	0.196 ± 0.011	0.035 ± 0.007
	RMvDNMF-FG	0.477 ± 0.054	0.233 ± 0.040	0.503 ± 0.045	0.357 ± 0.042	0.348 ± 0.044	0.212 ± 0.052
	MCPL	0.217 ± 0.000	0.015 ± 0.000	0.223 ± 0.000	0.302 ± 0.000	0.178 ± 0.000	0.000 ± 0.000
	RMvHGDNMF	0.329 ± 0.035	0.107 ± 0.029	0.335 ± 0.035	0.324 ± 0.021	0.213 ± 0.023	0.070 ± 0.042
	OURS	**0.743 ± 0.000**	**0.725 ± 0.000**	**0.758 ± 0.000**	**0.671 ± 0.000**	**0.696 ± 0.000**	**0.648 ± 0.000**
Washington	LRR	0.434 ± 0.007	0.205 ± 0.007	0.647 ± 0.004	0.395 ± 0.006	0.501 ± 0.009	0.192 ± 0.009
	GNMF	0.540 ± 0.041	0.261 ± 0.040	0.592 ± 0.045	0.491 ± 0.041	0.461 ± 0.045	0.275 ± 0.055
	RMKMC	0.574 ± 0.072	0.365 ± 0.053	0.711 ± 0.027	0.541 ± 0.063	0.604 ± 0.046	0.358 ± 0.069
	MultiNMF	**0.641 ± 0.002**	0.221 ± 0.005	0.654 ± 0.002	**0.566 ± 0.002**	0.500 ± 0.003	0.321 ± 0.004
	AMvDMD	0.577 ± 0.046	0.189 ± 0.056	0.633 ± 0.054	0.511 ± 0.026	0.449 ± 0.046	0.224 ± 0.079
	DiNMF	0.531 ± 0.078	0.168 ± 0.078	0.600 ± 0.073	0.487 ± 0.055	0.454 ± 0.075	0.210 ± 0.109
	NMF	0.503 ± 0.017	0.311 ± 0.024	0.532 ± 0.018	0.481 ± 0.022	0.422 ± 0.030	0.285 ± 0.027
	MvDGNMF	0.540 ± 0.073	0.254 ± 0.030	0.674 ± 0.018	0.510 ± 0.060	0.477 ± 0.018	0.259 ± 0.051
	RMvDNMF-FG	0.396 ± 0.034	0.092 ± 0.037	0.534 ± 0.047	0.347 ± 0.027	0.368 ± 0.042	0.061 ± 0.047
	MCPL	0.608 ± 0.000	0.210 ± 0.000	0.639 ± 0.000	0.531 ± 0.000	0.404 ± 0.000	0.192 ± 0.000
	RMvHGDNMF	0.583 ± 0.024	0.321 ± 0.041	0.690 ± 0.015	0.520 ± 0.030	0.551 ± 0.026	0.313 ± 0.040
	OURS	0.587 ± 0.007	**0.565 ± 0.007**	**0.801 ± 0.002**	0.562 ± 0.007	**0.738 ± 0.009**	**0.421 ± 0.009**

metrics. For example, in the "NMI" evaluation index, OSNMFTR achieves improvements of 20.8%, 0.9%, 25.6%, 16.6%, 31.1%, 26.1%, 49.2%, and 20.0% on eight datasets compared to the second-best algorithm. It is worth noting that the "NMI" indicator achieves the closest result to 1 on the MSRCV1 dataset. This shows that the communities found by the OSNMFTR algorithm are closer to real communities than most methods.

Furthermore, OSNMFTR produces the best results in "F-score," "Precision," and "ARI" metrics across all datasets. For the "Purity" metric, the results on YaleA-3view, BBC-4view, MSRCV1, Texas, Cornell, and Washington datasets all exceed 80%. On the MSRCV1 dataset, results of the proposed method exceeds 90% in "ACC," "NMI," "Purity," "F-score," and "Precision" metrics. Notably, an improvement of approximately 50% in "NMI" and "ARI" is observed on the Citeseer dataset.

Table 13.4   *Running time of comparisons between the proposed method and other methods on datasets*

	YaleA	BBC	ORL	MSRCV1	Wikipedia-Articles	Citeseer	Washington	Texas	Cornell
LRR	2.19E+00	1.59E+01	2.26E+01	4.19E+00	2.94E+01	1.07E+03	1.87E+00	1.47E+00	4.37E+00
GNMF	8.32E−01	3.83E−01	3.78E−01	6.20E−02	3.94E−01	6.28E−01	1.58E−01	6.93E−02	1.35E−01
RMKMC	1.16E+03	1.18E+03	1.02E+01	6.30E−01	5.14E−01	9.46E+01	3.32E−01	1.46E+01	2.52E−01
MultiNMF	3.68E+00	1.03E+02	1.67E+01	3.95E+00	1.05E+01	1.84E+02	1.82E+00	1.35E+00	4.25E+00
AMvDMD	5.06E+01	8.00E+01	1.21E+02	1.52E+02	2.24E+00	6.75E+02	2.55E+00	6.73E−01	5.96E+01
DiNMF	1.86E+02	2.30E+02	8.94E+00	3.87E+01	3.99E+00	1.18E+02	7.41E−01	1.17E+02	1.36E+02
NMF	1.05E−01	4.15E−01	5.08E−01	5.95E−02	8.39E−01	5.39E−01	1.82E−01	6.64E−02	1.88E−01
MvDGNMF	7.06E+02	7.28E+02	7.70E+02	8.16E+02	8.34E+02	8.65E+02	8.95E+02	9.08E+02	9.31E+02
RMvDNMF−FG	9.72E+02	1.78E+03	1.45E+03	1.51E+03	1.56E+03	1.61E+03	1.68E+03	1.71E+03	1.73E+03
MCPL	1.50E−01	5.04E−01	3.31E+00	4.22E−01	9.42E+00	1.31E+04	4.24E−01	2.20E−01	2.95E−01
RMvHGDNMF	4.60E+02	4.91E+02	7.24E+02	7.58E+02	7.81E+02	1.04E+03	8.04E+02	8.33E+02	8.47E+02
OURS	9.50E−01	1.46E+01	4.52E+00	1.84E+00	7.37E+00	3.20E+02	3.50E+00	2.27E+00	2.77E+00

However, the proposed model still shows relatively poor performance on certain evaluation metrics across a few datasets. For example, on the YaleA-3view dataset, OSNMFTR achieves the second-best results in "NMI," "Purity," "F-score," "Precision," and "ARI." Among these, "NMI" and "Precision" are only 2% lower than the best results. On the Texas dataset, "ACC" metric is only 2.8% lower than the best result. However, for other five metrics, the proposed model performs the best. In the Washington dataset, "F-score" metric is only 0.4% lower than the best result. Comparing to other models, the suggested OSNMFTR obtains superior overall detection performance.

13.3.5   *P-value test*

P-value experiments are carried out by comparing OSNMFTR against the benchmark techniques across all metrics in ten runs. The findings are shown in tables. The purpose of the experiments is to determine the relevance of the proposed OSNMFTR method in comparison to other benchmark methods. Every dataset has P-values that are noticeably low – significantly below 0.05. By comparing the OSNMFTR model to 12 state-of-the-art approaches, it is evident that the model performs much better in community detection across nine datasets. Tables 13.5–13.13 present the statistical test findings for ARI, NMI, ACC, Purity, F-score, and Precision.

In most datasets, excluding YaleA-3view, Texas, ORL, and Washington, the OSNMFTR algorithm yields P-values below the selected significance level (0.05) when compared to other benchmark algorithms, indicating statistically significant results. On the YaleA-3view dataset, however, the P-values for OSNMFTR versus the MCPL algorithm exceed the significance level for three metrics: ACC, Purity, and Precision. Similarly, a few instances of P-values greater than the significance level are observed on the three additional datasets. Nonetheless, cases where P-values exceed 0.05 remain infrequent.

Table 13.5   P-values of comparisons between the proposed method and other methods on the YaleA-3view dataset

YaleA-3view	ACC	NMI	Purity	F-score	Precision	ARI
LRR	6.18E−12	7.78E−18	1.84E−10	3.31E−11	2.95E−13	2.99E−11
GNMF	1.17E−10	1.23E−20	8.10E−12	4.11E−11	7.72E−12	4.87E−11
RMKMC	4.52E−09	1.66E−10	7.09E−08	6.115E−11	3.12E−09	6.00E−11
MultiNMF	4.53E−08	1.14E−07	3.70E−08	6.35E−08	1.26E−08	6.13E−08
AMvDMD	4.71E−11	2.78E−14	5.13E−11	2.55E−11	7.80E−12	2.57E−11
DiNMF	8.38E−14	7.78E−17	7.20E−14	4.00E−15	4.35E−15	4.20E−15
NMF	8.38E−14	7.78E−17	7.20E−14	4.00E−15	4.35E−15	4.20E−15
MvDGNMF	2.66E−14	3.03E−19	4.88E−15	4.49E−16	4.44E−13	3.67E−16
RMvDNMF−FG	6.63E−10	1.41E−09	4.42E−10	2.83E−11	5.96E−12	2.77E−11
MCPL	**0.776671**	2.6E−04	**0.925716**	3.5E−04	**0.275037**	3.9E−04
RMvHGDNMF	5.52E−10	8.54E−15	2.18E−10	2.88E−11	4.28E−11	2.94E−11

Table 13.6   P-values of comparisons between the proposed method and other methods on the BBC-4view dataset

BBC-4view	ACC	NMI	Purity	F-score	Precision	ARI
LRR	3.15E−19	2.07E−33	4.48E−19	1.04E−19	7.90E−20	8.09E−20
GNMF	5.80E−05	2.23E−08	1.83E−05	1.10E−05	8.51E−06	1.13E−05
RMKMC	1.99E−05	1.74E−06	8.56E−05	3.20E−05	9.78E−06	2.63E−05
MultiNMF	2.60E−33	1.87E−19	5.29E−19	2.77E−21	1.10E−22	1.06E−23
AMvDMD	3.82E−07	7.04E−07	1.49E−06	2.85E−06	2.49E−07	1.27E−05
DiNMF	8.16E−11	3.44E−10	3.70E−09	7.12E−11	1.88E−10	3.35E−10
NMF	9.16E−20	4.18E−20	5.71E−16	8.60E−19	5.43E−17	2.18E−20
MvDGNMF	4.73E−09	1.13E−07	1.64E−07	1.15E−07	8.44E−09	1.96E−07
RMvDNMF−FG	2.40E−10	4.46E−11	1.18E−09	7.25E−12	4.20E−11	5.48E−11
MCPL	1.04E−12	7.35E−14	1.04E−12	6.73E−12	6.37E−15	8.05E−12
RMvHGDNMF	5.86E−04	1.22E−06	2.67E−04	4.98E−04	1.23E−05	2.36E−04

Table 13.7   P-values of comparisons between the proposed method and other methods on the ORL dataset

ORL	ACC	NMI	Purity	F-score	Precision	ARI
LRR	2.15E−08	8.38E−10	2.69E−08	4.10E−09	5.41E−10	3.96E−09
GNMF	4.61E−10	4.61E−16	1.40E−05	6.77E−12	3.92E−04	6.55E−12
RMKMC	1.59E−14	6.97E−19	2.22E−14	9.31E−14	4.15E−14	6.85E−14
MultiNMF	3.46E−11	4.83E−17	4.50E−11	1.74E−14	4.86E−16	1.98E−14
AMvDMD	1.43E−08	1.42E−07	5.04E−09	3.63E−08	2.43E−09	4.23E−08
DiNMF	1.20E−07	1.47E−10	7.70E−07	1.28E-08	4.45E−10	1.23E−08
NMF	4.64E−09	3.97E−09	6.04E−05	6.24E−08	1.20E−03	7.10E−08
MvDGNMF	4.18E−09	6.30E−09	2.20E−08	1.71E−10	4.66E−12	1.63E−10
RMvDNMF−FG	2.10E−02	4.66E−03	**9.52E−02**	1.05E−01	5.55E−06	**9.13E−02**
MCPL	6.01E−12	1.72E−25	9.90E−12	2.38E−13	7.39E−14	1.66E−13
RMvHGDNMF	5.26E−08	5.80E−08	5.96E−07	1.35E−07	1.99E−09	1.31E−07

Table 13.8   P-values of comparisons between the proposed method and other methods on the WikipediaArticles dataset

WikipediaArticles	ACC	NMI	Purity	F-score	Precision	ARI
LRR	3.39E−17	4.73E−21	3.76E−16	1.07E−16	1.00E−16	1.00E−16
GNMF	2.61E−29	3.98E−36	1.09E−17	1.21E−20	1.10E−27	1.08E−18
RMKMC	2.78E−15	3.26E−15	1.00E−15	6.53E−23	3.08E−23	4.33E−23
MultiNMF	1.80E−20	4.17E−20	2.09E−18	1.85E−24	5.18E−24	8.74E−24
AMvDMD	5.68E−09	5.41E−09	1.43E−08	1.29E−11	1.24E−12	1.68E−10
DiNMF	3.23E−19	7.20E−17	7.44E−19	1.42E−22	1.46E−22	1.45E−22
NMF	1.82E−17	2.93E−21	1.72E−17	4.56E−16	1.58E−17	5.11E−16
MvDGNMF	2.48E−19	2.69E−26	2.74E−19	1.44E−21	3.06E−16	3.27E−21
RMvDNMF−FG	8.96E−15	3.29E−13	2.63E−19	1.38E−23	1.13E−24	5.57E−24
MCPL	2.63E−07	2.86E−08	1.38E−05	9.14E−08	2.58E−06	5.83E−07
RMvHGDNMF	2.06E−10	3.23E−10	2.43E−15	6.39E−10	3.10E−10	7.21E−10

Table 13.9   P-values of comparisons between the proposed method and other methods on the MSRCV1 dataset

MSRCV1	ACC	NMI	Purity	F-score	Precision	ARI
LRR	1.62E−17	7.42E−20	6.15E−19	1.02E−18	7.77E−19	9.81E−19
GNMF	5.06E−09	2.04E−15	4.72E−10	9.97E−14	2.10E−10	1.92E−13
RMKMC	2.41E−07	4.85E−14	1.84E−13	3.14E−13	1.28E−13	4.67E−13
MultiNMF	8.39E−13	3.30E−20	1.61E−18	4.22E−21	3.93E−22	2.18E−21
AMvDMD	2.18E−14	3.17E−13	2.84E−14	1.62E−12	4.97E−13	9.82E−13
DiNMF	2.78E−16	4.29E−15	3.64E−16	3.09E−13	8.76E−14	8.51E−14
NMF	1.41E−21	8.24E−21	1.64E−20	2.14E−13	6.38E−13	6.42E−14
MvDGNMF	2.78E−16	4.29E−15	3.64E−16	3.09E−13	8.76E−14	8.51E−14
RMvDNMF−FG	1.16E−23	2.60E−22	2.43E−22	1.94E−21	1.04E−22	3.00E−22
MCPL	2.69E−11	1.33E−08	1.09E−09	1.55E−08	1.54E−10	1.30E−08
RMvHGDNMF	1.08E−19	5.92E−17	4.55E−20	1.61E−20	3.41E−22	2.60E−20

Table 13.10   P-values of comparisons between the proposed method and other methods on the Texas dataset

Texas	ACC	NMI	Purity	F-score	Precision	ARI
LRR	1.21E−11	2.76E−18	1.56E−16	1.05E−15	2.79E−16	3.79E−16
GNMF	1.13E−02	7.78E−10	**6.17E−02**	2.51E−06	**6.95E−02**	3.18E−07
RMKMC	8.17E−03	1.04E−12	3.09E−08	1.86E−04	1.83E−09	5.43E−06
MultiNMF	8.97E−15	4.06E−27	1.97E−24	2.78E−20	9.72E−24	9.23E−25
AMvDMD	2.21E−12	2.28E−23	1.36E−11	1.98E−11	4.38E−21	9.86E−20
DiNMF	2.25E−06	5.90E−13	2.90E−16	3.77E−06	6.50E−17	3.67E−08
NMF	1.82E−06	1.22E−24	2.70E−10	9.23E−07	2.81E−10	1.23E−08
MvDGNMF	**0.205942**	3.01E−12	2.55E−14	**0.372681**	2.77E−19	2.87E−06
RMvDNMF−FG	3.28E−07	1.29E−09	2.77E−11	6.11E−18	7.87E−10	1.07E−09
MCPL	**0.136976**	4.97E−16	5.41E−15	4.09E−07	8.12E−15	2.93E−13
RMvHGDNMF	1.32E−03	7.05E−22	2.10E−20	2.44E−07	8.15E−12	5.41E−09

Table 13.11   P-values of comparisons between the proposed method and other methods on the Cornell dataset

Cornell	ACC	NMI	Purity	F-score	Precision	ARI
LRR	3.33E−23	2.03E−31	8.72E−34	7.80E−28	3.41E−28	4.84E−28
GNMF	1.82E−04	2.24E−12	2.80E−08	2.84E−06	1.61E−06	1.43E−02
RMKMC	1.09E−07	5.28E−13	6.45E−09	4.69E−11	2.34E−10	1.79E−13
MultiNMF	9.48E−10	1.21E−16	4.78E−27	2.25E−13	5.14E−16	6.81E−12
AMvDMD	3.63E−09	9.45E−16	1.71E−11	1.18E−20	1.42E−15	1.05E−12
DiNMF	6.11E−04	7.66E−08	3.56E−06	1.92E−05	5.47E−08	2.02E−06
NMF	5.14E−16	1.30E−18	4.71E−23	2.58E−14	8.60E−19	5.17E−14
MvDGNMF	5.77E−11	9.56E−13	9.71E−11	1.31E−08	4.97E−13	9.76E−10
RMvDNMF−FG	6.47E−05	4.68E−08	7.46E−07	1.94E−07	3.32E−08	1.48E−07
MCPL	2.11E−15	5.12E−17	1.19E−17	7.44E−15	2.53E−16	6.74E−16
RMvHGDNMF	1.29E−09	9.68E−13	1.47E−11	4.46E−12	3.92E−16	8.03E−07

Table 13.12   P-values of comparisons between the proposed method and other methods on the Citeseer dataset

Citeseer	ACC	NMI	Purity	F-score	Precision	ARI
LRR	3.33E−23	2.03E−31	8.72E−34	7.80E−28	3.41E−28	4.84E−28
GNMF	1.82E−04	2.24E−12	2.80E−08	2.84E−06	1.61E−06	1.43E−02
RMKMC	1.09E−07	5.28E−13	6.45E−09	4.69E−11	2.34E−10	1.79E−13
MultiNMF	9.48E−10	1.21E−16	4.78E−27	2.25E−13	5.14E−16	6.81E−12
AMvDMD	3.63E−09	9.45E−16	1.71E−11	1.18E−20	1.42E−15	1.05E−12
DiNMF	6.11E−04	7.66E−08	3.56E−06	1.92E−05	5.47E−08	2.02E−06
NMF	5.14E−16	1.30E−18	4.71E−23	2.58E−14	8.60E−19	5.17E−14
MvDGNMF	5.77E−11	9.56E−13	9.71E−11	1.31E−08	4.97E−13	9.76E−10
RMvDNMF−FG	6.47E−05	4.68E−08	7.46E−07	1.94E−07	3.32E−08	1.48E−07
MCPL	2.11E−15	5.12E−17	1.19E−17	7.44E−15	2.53E−16	6.74E−16
RMvHGDNMF	1.29E−09	9.68E−13	1.47E−11	4.46E−12	3.92E−16	8.03E−07

Table 13.13   P-values of comparisons between the proposed method and other methods on the Washington dataset

Washington	ACC	NMI	Purity	F-score	Precision	ARI
LRR	8.80E−21	2.04E−23	3.48E−23	5.41E−19	8.70E−20	2.61E−19
GNMF	9.42E−03	3.16E−08	1.84E−07	6.06E−04	5.47E−09	1.98E−05
RMKMC	**0.443190**	2.59E−09	1.05E−05	**0.200791**	1.53E−06	5.99E−04
MultiNMF	2.87E−13	4.48E−26	2.65E−20	**0.205229**	8.39E−18	8.96E−14
AMvDMD	**0.631485**	1.30E−13	5.94E−06	2.14E−04	5.80E−13	3.47E−05
DiNMF	**6.97E−02**	8.53E−08	1.67E−05	9.29E−04	9.46E−07	2.70E−04
NMF	1.50E−08	8.58E−17	1.47E−19	4.69E−07	1.51E−16	1.10E−08
MvDGNMF	**9.69E−02**	2.97E−11	1.20E−09	2.97E−02	4.82E−18	3.84E−06
RMvDNMF−FG	2.14E−08	2.23E−18	3.49E−08	2.09E−10	1.65E−15	1.91E−14
MCPL	5.55E−06	3.54E−16	4.80E−15	2.44E−06	1.80E−14	5.61E−13
RMvHGDNMF	**0.762506**	1.45E−08	6.54E−14	9.86E−04	2.09E−13	1.26E−05

These experimental outcomes suggest that the performance of OSNMFTR is indeed enhanced relative to the comparative algorithms.

13.3.6   Parameters analysis

There are three parameters in the model that need to be adjusted: λ, β, and the trade-off parameter α for the constrained optimal graph. Figure 13.2 shows the parameter sensitivity of λ and β across nine datasets. λ is used to balance the tensor nuclear norm, while β is used to balance the $l_{2,1}$ norm of the noise matrix. It can be seen that the performance of community detection is sensitive to λ on most datasets, and λ could have an impact on the low-rank structure of the self-representation tensor. At the same time, for most datasets, community detection tends to be most effective if λ and β are combined in a certain fixed numerical way. For example, on the YaleA-3view dataset, the model performs very well when $\lambda = 0.001$ and $\beta = 0.01$. On the Cornell dataset, ACC metric is highest when $\lambda = 0.1$ and $\beta = 100$. Notably, on the Citeseer dataset, the parameters λ and β have little impact on the results. This may indicate that for datasets with a large number of nodes, adjusting the model's parameters often does not yield better results.

Furthermore, we adjust parameter α across nine datasets and obtain its variation results across six metrics. From Figure 13.3, it can be seen that on the Washington, Cornell, Texas, Citeseer, WikipediaArticles and BBC-4view datasets, the results of community detection are not sensitive to changes in α across the six metrics. At the same time, when the parameters change, the six indicators show an upward or downward trend at the same time.

The influence of the tensor weight vector ω on the model was evaluated across nine datasets. Figure 13.4 demonstrates that, irrespective of variations in ω, the results of the six evaluation metrics remain largely consistent across all datasets. This highlights the robust stability of the OSNMFTR model.

13.3.7   Ablation study

To confirm the effectiveness of each module, two degraded models based on the OSN-MFTR model have been designed. An ablation study involving six metrics across nine datasets has been conducted. The experimental results are shown in Figure 13.5.

13.3.7.1   Effectiveness of the denoising strategy

First, β is set to 0 to examine the impact of noise on the results of community detection, and this degraded model is called OSNMFTR. From Figure 13.5, it can be seen that compared to OSNMFTR, the model before denoising shows a decrease in various metrics across the majority of datasets. On YaleA-3view, BBC4-view, ORL, WikipediaArticles, MSRCV1, Texas, Cornell, and Washington datasets, the "ACC" results decrease by 2.4%, 1.2%, 4.1%, 2.0%, 1.9%, 2.4%, 1.5%, and 2.7%, respectively. Among them, the six metrics on the ORL dataset all decrease by approximately 4%. Additionally, on the YaleA-3view, MSRCV1, Texas, and Washington datasets, all metrics decrease by about 2%.

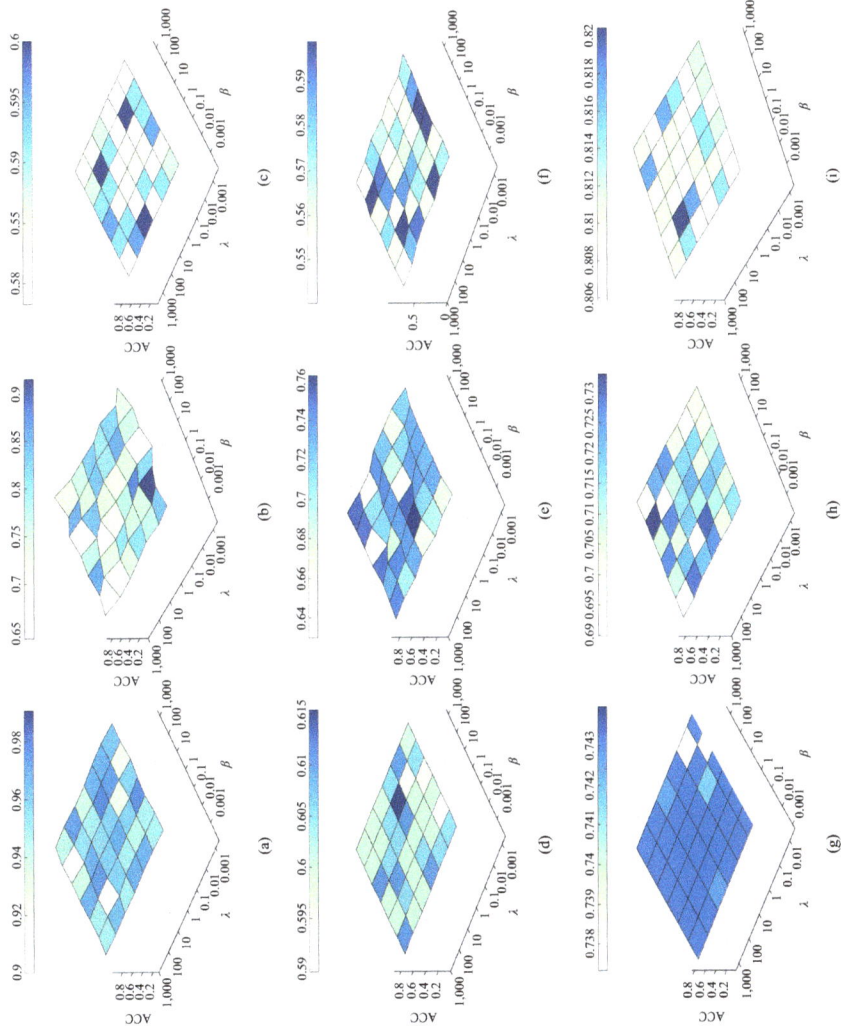

Figure 13.2 The sensitivity analysis on nine datasets. (a) MSRCV1, (b) YaleA-3view, (c) Washington, (d) Cornell, (e) ORL, (f) Texas, (g) Citeseer, (h) WikipediaArticles and (i) BBC-4view.

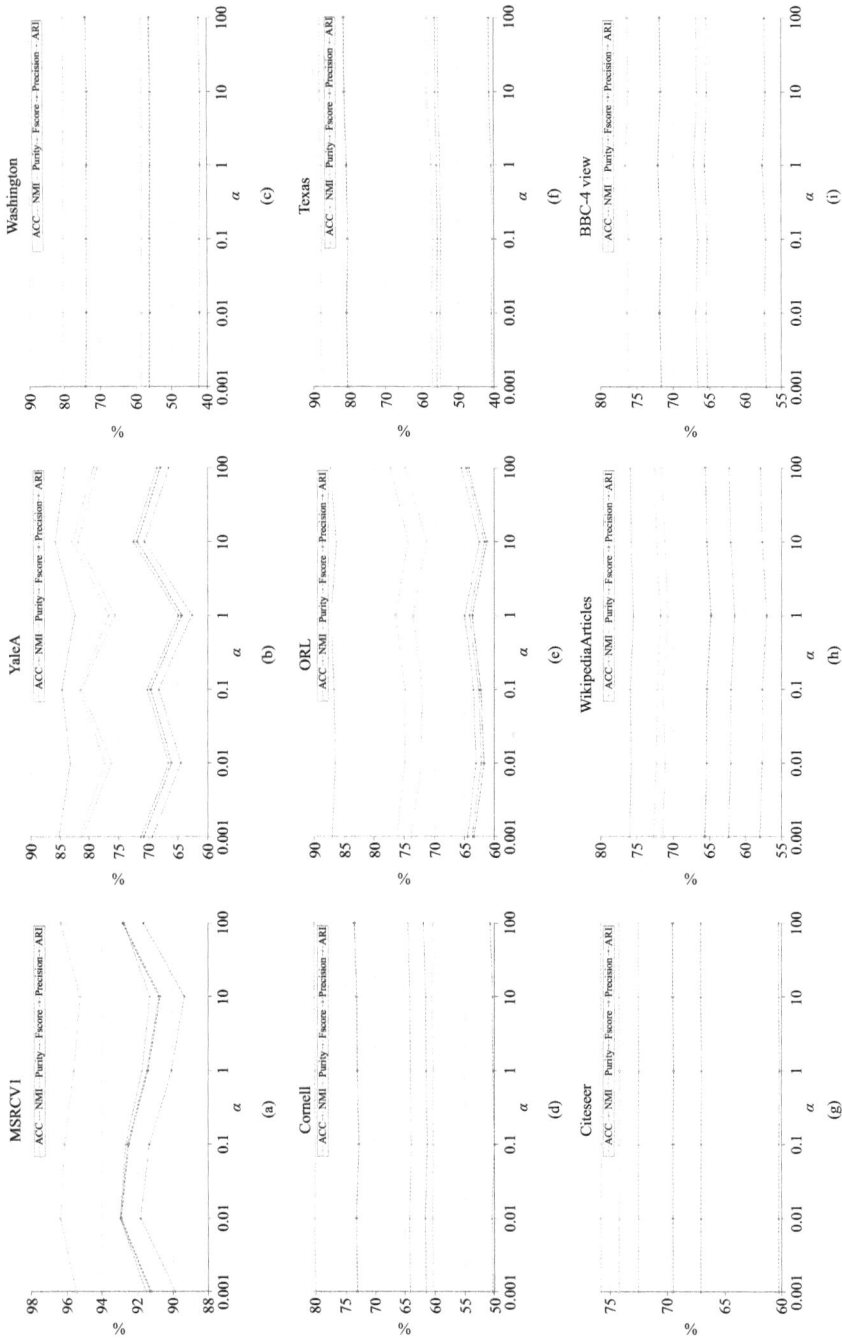

Figure 13.3   The sensitivity analysis for α on nine datasets. (a) MSRCV1, (b) YaleA-3view, (c) Washington, (d) Cornell, (e) ORL, (f) Texas, (g) Citeseer, (h) WikipediaArticles and (i) BBC-4view.

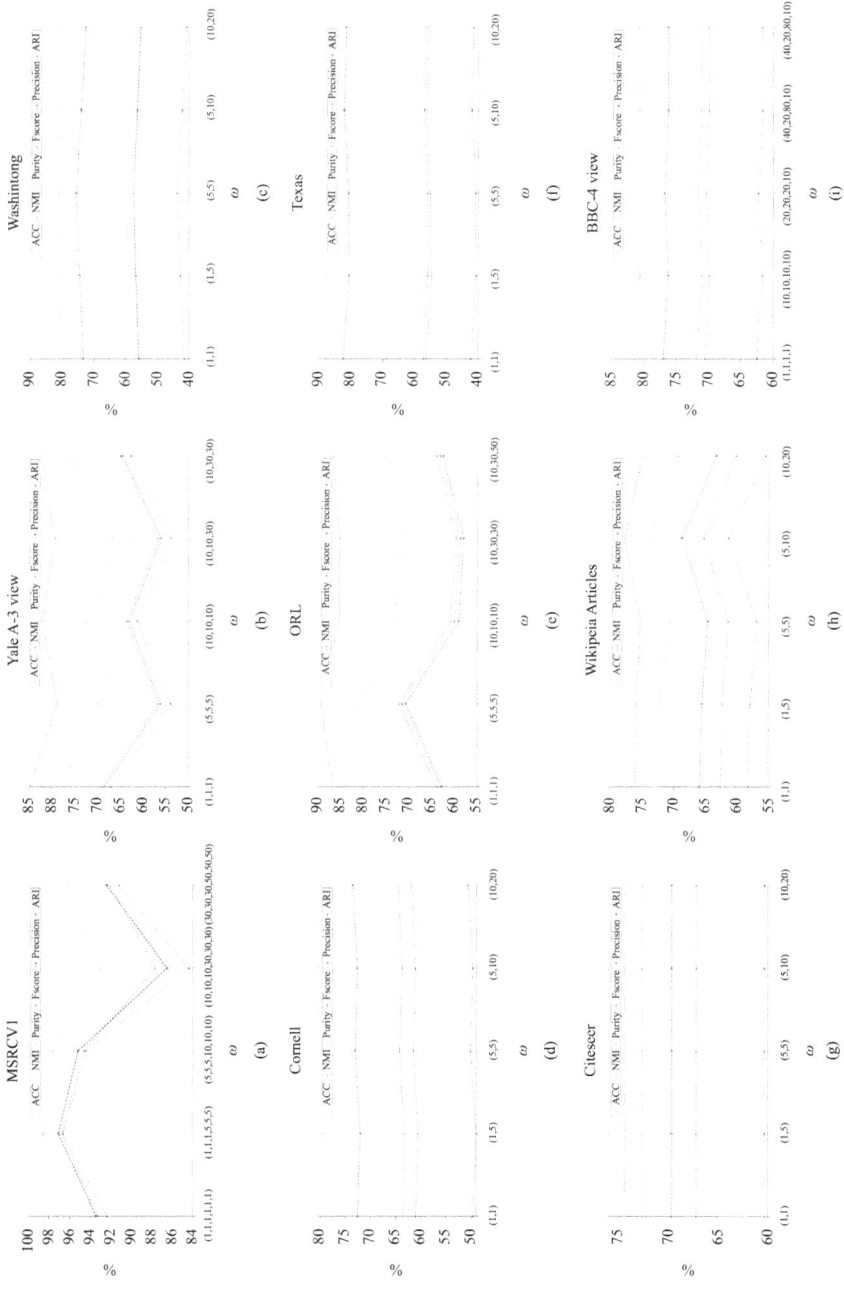

Figure 13.4 The sensitivity analysis for ω on nine datasets. (a) MSRCV1, (b) YaleA-3view, (c) Washington, (d) Cornell, (e) ORL, (f) Texas, (g) Citeseer, (h) WikipediaArticles and (i) BBC4-view.

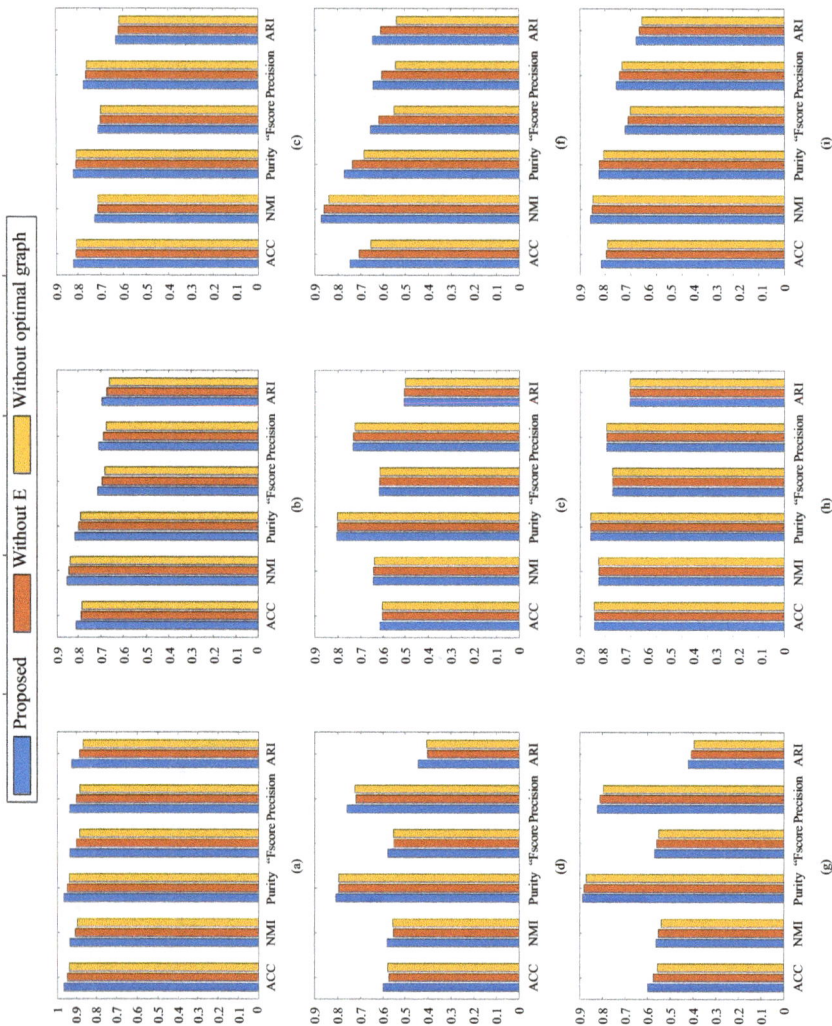

Figure 13.5   Ablative analysis of model performance: comparative study of ACC and other metrics across original and modified models. (a) MSRCV1, (b) YaleA-3view, (c) BBC4-view, (d) Washington, (e) Cornell, (f) ORL, (g) Texas, (h) Citeseer and (i) WikipediaArticles.

13.3.7.2   Effectiveness of optimal graph regularization term

To examine the effect of local geometric structure on community detection results, α is set as 0. In other words, the optimal graph regularization term is removed from model (13.15). This degraded model is referred to as OSNMFTRt2. For example, on YaleA-3view, ORL, WikipediaArticles, MSRCV1, Texas, and Washington datasets, the "ACC" metric decreases by 2.7%, 9.4%, 2.5%, 2.9%, 4.3%, and 2.3%, respectively. It is noteworthy that all the metrics on the ORL dataset decrease by 9%.

In summary, the two degradation models show different degrees of disadvantage compared to the OSNMFTR model on most datasets. This shows that communities can be found more accurately when the relationship between noise and local geometry of different layers on the dataset is taken into account.

13.3.8   *Convergence analysis*

The convergence behavior of Algorithm 1 is confirmed by examining convergence curves on the nine datasets. In Figure 13.6, the convergence findings are shown, in

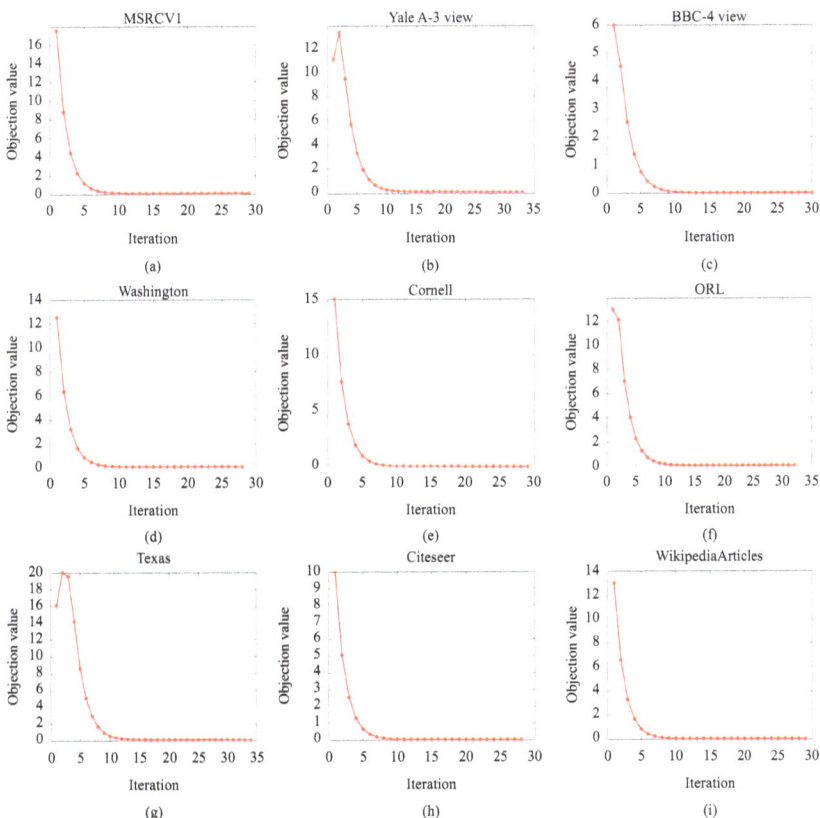

Figure 13.6   Convergent results on nine datasets. (a) MSRCV1, (b) YaleA-3view, (c) BBC4-view, (d) Washington, (e) Cornell, (f) ORL, (g) Texas, (h) Citeseer and (i) WikipediaArticles.

which $\left\| H^{(l)} - H^{(l)}Z^{(l)} - E^{(l)} \right\|_{\infty}$ is recorded. It is evident that after 30 iterations, the variable errors on nine datasets reduce dramatically and stabilize, suggesting that the suggested approach converges enough.

13.4   Chapter summary

To address the challenge of community detection in multi-layer networks, the OSN-MFTR model is proposed. Community detection performance is enhanced through the use of the weighted tensor nuclear norm and optimal graph regularization, which helps to uncover the intrinsic geometric information across networks. Extensive experiments comparing OSNMFTR against 10 state-of-the-art algorithms were carried out on nine real-world datasets. The results indicate that OSNMFTR achieves superior ACC in community detection, thereby better addressing the task of identifying communities within complex networks.

References

[1]   Ortiz-Bouza M., Aviyente S.: "Orthogonal nonnegative matrix tri-factorization for community detection in multiplex networks." in *ICASSP 2022 - 2022 IEEE International Conference on Acoustics, Speech and Signal Processing (ICASSP)*; 2022. pp. 5987–91.

[2]   Liu G., Lin Z., Yan S., Sun J., Yu Y., Ma Y.: "Robust recovery of subspace structures by low-rank representation." *IEEE Trans. Pattern Anal. Mach. Intell.* 2013;35(1):171–84.

[3]   Hangjun C., Li C., Leung M. F., Ouyang D., Dai X., Wen S.: "Robust hypergraph regularized deep non-negative matrix factorization for multi-view clustering." *IEEE Trans. Emerging Topics Comput. Intell.* 2024;09:1817–29.

[4]   Liu G., Lin Z., Yan S., Sun J., Yu Y., Ma Y.: "Robust Recovery of Subspace Structures by Low-Rank Representation." *IEEE Trans. Pattern Anal. Mach. Intell.* 2013;35(1):171–84.

[5]   Lee D., Seung H. S.: "Algorithms for non-negative matrix factorization." *Advances in Neural Information Processing Systems.* 2000;13.

[6]   Cai D., He X., Han J., Huang T. S.: "Graph regularized nonnegative matrix factorization for data representation." *IEEE Trans. Pattern Anal. Mach. Intell.* 2010;33(8):1548–60.

[7]   Cai X., Nie F., Huang H.: "Multi-view k-means clustering on big data." in *Twenty-Third International Joint conference on artificial intelligence*; 2013.

[8]   Huang S., Kang Z., Xu Z.: "Auto-weighted multi-view clustering via deep matrix decomposition." *Pattern Recogn.* 2020;97:107015.

[9]   Liu J., Wang C., Gao J., Han J.: "Multi-view clustering via joint nonnegative matrix factorization." in *Proceedings of the 2013 SIAM International Conference on Data Mining.* Philadelphia: SIAM; 2013. pp. 252–60.

[10] Wang J., Tian F., Yu H., Liu C. H., Zhan K., Wang X.: "Diverse non-negative matrix factorization for multiview data representation." *IEEE Trans. Cybern.* 2017;48(9):2620–32.

[11] Li J., Zhou G., Qiu Y., Wang Y., Zhang Y., Xie S.: "Deep graph regularized non-negative matrix factorization for multi-view clustering." *Neurocomputing.* 2020;390:108–16.

[12] Liu B.Y., Huang L., Wang C.D., Lai J.H., Yu P.S.: "Multi-view consensus proximity learning for clustering." *IEEE Trans. Knowl. Data Eng.* 2022;34(7):3405–17.

[13] Che H., Li C., Pan B., Cao Y.: "Diversity embedding deep optimal graph regularized nonnegative matrix factorization for robust multiview clustering." *IEEE Trans. Comput. Soc. Syst.* 2024; 1–13.

[14] Luo P., Peng J., Guan Z., Fan J.: "Dual regularized multi-view non-negative matrix factorization for clustering." *Neurocomputing.* 2018;294:1–11.

[15] Wang C.D., Lai J.H., Philip S.Y.: "Multi-view clustering based on belief propagation." *IEEE Trans. Knowl. Data Eng.* 2015;28(4):1007–21.

[16] Peng C., Zhang Y., Chen Y., Kang Z., Chen C., Cheng Q.: "Log-based sparse nonnegative matrix factorization for data representation." *Knowl. Based Syst.* 2022;251:109127.

Chapter 14
Conclusion

In multimedia clustering, matrix factorization plays a crucial role. Non-negative matrix factorization (NMF), non-negative matrix tri-factorization (NMTF), and deep matrix factorization (DMF) each have distinct properties and applications in different scenarios. When dealing with high-dimensional problems, tensor decomposition perfectly addresses the limitations of 2D matrix factorization. This book also discusses optimization algorithms used to solve these decomposition models and provides specific practical applications. Additionally, it offers detailed mathematical explanations and in-depth analyses of experimental results for each model proposed later in the book.

14.1   Conclusion of the book

In the previous chapters, we introduced the theoretical knowledge and specific applications of multimedia clustering.

In Chapter 1, we have explored the theoretical foundations and practical applications of matrix factorization, demonstrating its crucial role in data analysis, machine learning, and optimization problems. Matrix factorization serves as a fundamental tool for uncovering latent structures in high-dimensional data, enabling efficient representations and feature extraction. Despite its remarkable success, matrix factorization still faces several challenges. The computational cost of large-scale factorizations, sensitivity to missing or noisy data, and the interpretability of multi-dimensional data representations remain active areas of research [1].

In Chapter 2, tensor decomposition is presented as an extension of matrix factorization to multi-dimensional data, providing a powerful framework for analyzing high-order structures. The two most widely used tensor decomposition methods are CANDECOMP/PARAFAC (CP) decomposition and Tucker decomposition. CP decomposition expresses a tensor as a sum of rank-one tensors, facilitating interpretability and efficient storage. Tucker decomposition, in contrast, generalizes principal component analysis (PCA) to tensors, capturing interactions between different modes through a core tensor and factor matrices. Despite its advantages, tensor decomposition poses several computational challenges, including high storage costs and complex optimization procedures.

In Chapter 3, graph theory-related knowledge is introduced [2]. A graph consists of a set of vertices (nodes) and a set of edges (connections) among them. Graph-based methods are widely used to model relationships in various fields, including social networks, recommendation systems, and scientific computing. A similarity graph is a weighted graph, where edges represent the degree of similarity between nodes. A hyper-graph is a generalization of a graph, where an edge can connect more than two vertices. Unlike traditional graphs, where an edge connects exactly two nodes, hyper-graphs allow for more expressive modeling of group relationships. A fusion graph integrates multiple graphs into a unified representation, allowing information from different sources to be combined effectively. Similarity graphs enhance clustering and representation learning, hyper-graphs capture higher-order interactions, and fusion graphs enable the integration of multi-modal and heterogeneous data.

In Chapter 4, two optimization methods are introduced. Multiplicative update (MU) is usually used to solve non-negative matrix decomposition problems [3,4]. It can achieve simultaneous optimization of the objective function value while ensuring non-negativity until convergence. Alternating direction method of multipliers (ADMM) performs well in solving convex optimization problems. ADMM is usually applied to multi-block problems and optimizes the target model by iteratively updating the variables alternately [5]. ADMM converges well for convex optimization problems and also performs well in many non-convex problems.

Some practical applications of matrix decomposition and tensor decomposition are introduced. In the sparse graph non-negative matrix factorization (SGNMF) model, the l_0 norm is applied to enhance the sparsity of factorized matrices, a new algorithm is designed to solve the problem, and the convergence of the algorithm is proven. In the self-paced non-negative matrix factorization with adaptive neighbors (SPLNMFAN) model, a self-paced regularization is applied, and an adaptive graph is introduced using dynamic neighbor assignment. In Chapter 7, a novel multi-view NMF is proposed, where the hidden representation of different attributes is learned through centric graph regularization and pairwise co-regularization of the coefficient matrix. To obtain effective sparse solutions, the $l_{2,\log}$-(pseudo) norm is introduced. In Chapter 8, the proposed model emphasizes diversity between views and samples, and the $l_{2,1}$ norm is introduced further to improve the robustness of the model. In the robust non-negative matrix tri-factorization with dual hyper-graph regularization (RDHNMTF) model, a dual hyper-graph is established to uncover the higher-order inherent information within the sample space and feature spaces for clustering, and to further reduce the error, the $l_{2,1}$ norm is used. In Chapter 10, the multi-kernel-based multi-view deep non-negative matrix factorization with optimal consensus graph (OGMKMDNMF) is proposed, and this approach utilizes deep non-negative matrix factorization after projecting the data matrix into a high-dimensional kernel space to improve the effect of the cluster. In Chapter 11, a subspace-based matrix factorization model for multi-view image clustering is proposed. In this model, the original data is projected into a robust subspace, and a consensus matrix is learned via an adaptive weight strategy. In Chapter 12, targeting fake news from social media, a sparse and graph regularized CP tensor decomposition method is proposed. In this method, a news factor matrix is constructed by CP decomposition and combines the sparse learning and graph learning to further improve the detection effect. In Chapter 14, some applications of matrix decomposition are introduced in community detection. This chapter introduces an orthogonal symmetric non-negative matrix factorization with low-rank tensor representation (OSNMFTR) for multi-layer network community detection.

14.2   Future work of the matrix factorization in multimedia clustering

Matrix factorization has demonstrated significant promise in multimedia clustering, offering effective low-dimensional representations and improved clustering performance. However, several challenges and opportunities remain for future research:

Scalability and Efficiency: As multimedia datasets grow in size and complexity, enhancing the scalability of matrix factorization techniques is crucial. Future research should focus on developing more efficient algorithms, leveraging distributed and parallel computing frameworks to handle large-scale multimedia data.

Incorporation of Deep Learning: Integrating deep learning models with matrix factorization techniques can further enhance feature learning and representation quality. Hybrid approaches, such as deep matrix factorization or graph neural networks combined with matrix factorization, could improve clustering results by capturing complex data relationships.

Multi-modal Data Integration: Multimedia data often includes various modalities, such as images, text, and audios. Extending matrix factorization methods to effectively fuse and exploit multi-modal information can enhance clustering accuracy and robustness.

Dynamic and Online Learning: Many multimedia applications require real-time clustering, necessitating the development of dynamic and online matrix factorization methods. Incremental learning approaches that adapt to streaming data changes without reprocessing the entire dataset should be explored.

Regularization and Sparsity Constraints: Imposing structured regularization, such as sparsity or manifold constraints, can improve factorization interpretability and robustness. Future work should investigate novel regularization techniques tailored to multimedia clustering tasks.

Robustness to Noise and Missing Data: Multimedia datasets often contain noise and missing values. Developing robust matrix factorization techniques that can handle incomplete and corrupted data will be essential for improving clustering reliability.

Explainability and Interpretability: As matrix factorization-based clustering becomes more widely used, ensuring that results are interpretable and explainable to users is crucial. Future studies should explore methods to enhance the transparency of factorization results.

Applications to Emerging Domains: Expanding the application of matrix factorization in emerging fields such as biomedical imaging, video surveillance, and social media analysis will offer new insights and challenges. Exploring domain-specific adaptations of matrix factorization techniques can lead to more effective clustering solutions.

By addressing these challenges, future research can push the boundaries of matrix factorization in multimedia clustering, making it more effective, scalable, and applicable to a broader range of real-world problems.

In summary, future research should focus on improving the scalability, robustness, and interpretability of matrix factorization techniques while exploring their integration with deep learning and multi-modal data fusion. Advancements in these areas will enhance the applicability of matrix factorization in diverse multimedia clustering tasks, addressing real-world challenges and unlocking new opportunities for intelligent data analysis.

References

[1]   Lee D.D., Seung H.S.: "Learning the parts of objects by non-negative matrix factorization." *Nature.* 1999;401(6755):788–91.

[2]   Chen K., Che H., Li X., Leung M.F., Leung M.F.: "Graph non-negative matrix factorization with alternative smoothed L_0 regularizations." *Neural Comput. Appl.* 2022;35: 9995–10009.

[3]   Luo G., Zhao Z., Liu S., Wu S., Hu A., Zhang N.: "Integrating topology and content equally in non-negative matrix factorization for community detection." *Expert Syst. Appl.* 2024;255:124713.

[4]   Kong Q., Sun J., Xu Z.: "Joint orthogonal symmetric non-negative matrix factorization for community detection in attribute network." *Knowledge-Based Systems.* 2024;283:111192.

[5]   Guo W., Che H., Leung M.F.: "Tensor-based adaptive consensus graph learning for multi-view clustering." *IEEE Transactions on Consumer Electronics*; 2024.

Index